STRUCTURE AND COGNITION IN ART

STRUCTURE AND COGNITION IN ART

EDITED BY DOROTHY K. WASHBURN

CAMBRIDGE UNIVERSITY PRESS
CAMBRIDGE
LONDON NEW YORK NEW ROCHELLE
MELBOURNE SYDNEY

Published by the Press Syndicate of the University of Cambridge
The Pitt Building, Trumpington Street, Cambridge CB2 1RP
32 East 57th Street, New York, NY 10022, USA
296 Beaconsfield Parade, Middle Park, Melbourne 3206, Australia

First published 1983

Printed in Great Britain at the University Press, Cambridge

Library of Congress catalogue card number: 82–14644

British Library Cataloguing in Publication Data

Structure and cognition in art. – (New directions
in archaeology)
1. Art – Addresses, essays, lectures
2. Archaeology – Addresses, essays, lectures
I. Washburn, Dorothy K. II. Series
709 N7443.2

ISBN 0 521 23471 9

WD

To Bill, my husband, and Nancy, my cousin, for giving me the time and space to bridge the continent

CONTENTS

CONTRIBUTORS

Marie Jeanne Adams, Research Associate, Peabody Museum, Harvard University.

Dean E. Arnold, Associate Professor of Anthropology, Wheaton College.

James C. Faris, Professor of Anthropology, University of Connecticut.

F. Allan Hanson, Professor of Anthropology, University of Kansas.

Margaret Ann Hardin, Research Associate, Archaeology Program, Pueblo of Zuni.

Kate P. Kent, Professor of Anthropology, Emeritus, University of Denver.

Donald W. Lathrap, Professor of Anthropology, University of Illinois, Urbana–Champaign.

Dorothy K. Washburn, Associate Curator of Anthropology, California Academy of Sciences.

Chapter 1

Toward a theory of structural style in art

Dorothy K. Washburn

Introduction

This volume presents a set of papers which represent a collective effort to examine the structure of art and its social relationships. The authors focus on the systemic aspects of art and how these relate to and reflect the larger social system. Art forms are seen as belonging to a system just as other behaviours and objects in other aspects of culture are parts of systems. Systems produce consistent patterns of activity and are built of parts that fit together neatly and economically. They are long-lived, to the extent that they may be recognized and observed by investigators. They may encompass great variability, yet it is variation which, I argue, can be accommodated by the basic structural organization of the parts of the system. Thus, while art forms in a given culture may, in one sense, be specifically iconographic or functional or decorative, on a more basic level, they share fundamental similarities which are structural in nature.

The authors in this book seek to delineate the presence, articulation and, where possible, the contextual meaning of the structural systems in various types of art forms. Although each of the authors examines different aspects of this problem, all focus on understanding the nature of consistencies in a given art form – how best to define them, what they might mean, and how they relate to their larger cultural context.

Culture and system are used here as general concepts. As we feel our way in the business of showing how art structures are part of the larger cultural structural system, we speak generally first and, we hope, more specifically later as we refine the concepts. Thus, while we know that there can be many cultures, and thus, undoubtedly, many art structure styles in a society, we speak here in the singular. We want to simply establish the presence of structures in art, and later, building on this basis, to offer studies of the diachronic and synchronic nature of these systems.

I begin not by offering the usual review of style studies to date, for this has been done recently, for example by Silver (1979). Rather, I want to look ahead and offer some ideas about perception, categorization and structure and how these concepts may in some way help us to understand the structural consistencies in art forms.

I rely heavily on the work of Rudolf Arnheim, who has extensively discussed art and perception (1969, 1974). Arnheim shows us how physiology conditions how we see, but culture conditions what we see and how we organize what we see into a given image. It is useful to review in some detail Arnheim's work because his discussion of perception suggests that it is possible to understand that some aspects of the structure underlying art forms may be a result of the perception process, while others are the result of cultural factors.

The structure in perception

Vision is not a mechanical recording of elements but rather the apprehension of significant structural patterns (Rudolf Arnheim 1974: 6).

Perception consists of three stages: (1) filtering and selection of information necessary to focus on the general character of objects – especially their shape and structure; (2) recognition of the shapes in their cultural context and categorization of the shapes into general classes of things; and (3) filling in details of the shapes from prior knowledge and visual experience. Each stage will be further described with emphasis on its relevance to art forms.

First, perception is selective. The eye and mind cannot absorb everything in any given visual field. In order to protect the mind from being swamped with more information than it can handle, the process of perception involves constant filtering and selection.

During this filtering process, the eye most easily recognizes general characteristics, rather than particular details, particularly qualities which differentiate one thing from another. Results from numerous studies indicate that the eye sees shape as the most important of these essential features. Because perception involves organization of the generalized shapes into culturally recognizable forms, the structural features of a given shape which underlie the organization of its parts into a culturally familiar whole are essential not only for its formation, but also for its identification and categorization.

Arnheim uses the example of a person, asked to describe a winding staircase, who responds by tracing a spiral in the air with his finger. By this action, the person is simplifying and abstracting the staircase to its most essential structural feature – a spiral. It is this feature which is most easily recognizable to everyone familiar with spiral staircases and which allows us to interpret the gesture as a spiral staircase.

There is a common misconception that realistic or naturalistic art representations are exact mirror portrayals of a given scene or object. But, since we do not see all the details as in a photographic image, all renderings are actually reworkings of the individual artist's own perceptions of what he sees when looking at a scene. Depending on his cultural biases, some aspects are emphasized while others are minimized or omitted.

In this sense, the basic structure underlying an art form may be seen as a summary of the perceptions the individual artist had about his world through his culturally tinted glasses. His visual faculties perceived general shapes which were interpreted and elaborated into a whole by his cultural preconditioning and memory of things past. For him, it is a meaningful restatement of what he thought he saw. It reflects his world and serves as a guidepost to present and future action.

These differences between what is, what is seen, and what is represented have important bearing on our understanding of art. Preconditioned by previous cultural experiences, the eye selects and processes only that information which is considered important for a given activity. This reduces the visual overload and focuses the thought processes on organizing the information received. It is thus irrelevant whether the image accurately represents the object perceived. Rather, the representation is a summary of certain aspects of a culture's world which everyone in that world recognizes as being fundamental to everyday activity, both sacred and secular. The art form thus projects a statement about the focal points of a culture's world.

Second, perception involves categorization of ever-changing phenomena. In a given cultural environment, visual perception always proceeds from a baseline of known concepts. From these, the individual can elaborate the general shapes perceived. He can also, most importantly, confront and adjust to variation, because his powers of abstraction enable him to generalize and categorize these variations within the basic concepts underlying his culture. Every culture, by virtue of its cognitive integrity, has this baseline of conceptual premises which promote and perpetuate appropriate cultural activity. Further, the relational aspect of perception and categorization causes people to see shapes always in juxtaposition to the things around them and not as isolates. From this comfortable reference point, a given individual can perceive how a myriad of changes and variations relate to the general ordered precepts underlying his culture.

Third, this cultural essence is represented as basic shapes which the memory, with its bank of knowledge derived from prior encounters within that same cultural environment, distills and organizes into images that are recognizable, and meaningful to the observers. The essence of an art form, then, is a visual embodiment of the regularities which represent the culture bearer's generalizations about important parts of his world. The shapes and their organization are thus representative of aspects of the several ordering (rule) systems basic to a given culture which operate to maintain that culture as a cohesive, ongoing whole.

The backlog of cultural tradition and the individual's personal experiences in that cultural milieu enable him to respond to observed images with the 'correct' behaviour in specific situations. Thus, perception does not depend totally on just the information received by the retina at a given time. Rather, the brain receives generalized images and quickly 'fills in' the details from this backlog of prior visual experience.

A good instance of this process is Arnheim's example of the visualization of the head and chest of a person looking over a wall and the mental completion of this partial image with a torso and legs. From prior knowledge we know that human beings have a set array of features. Thus, the mind not only recreates the whole form, in this case the human body, but also recreates it in its proper configuration; i.e., placing the torso and legs in the proper position relative to the observed head, arms and chest. In other words, the human memory bank of prior knowledge and experience can thus organize parts into wholes, and this reorganizational ability of the brain is central to the process of perception. The reliance on a reservoir of cultural experience thus signals how a thing is to be perceived and slotted into the whole system of ongoing activity.

The culture in art structure

> . . . we need to look for systematic relationships among diverse phenomena, not for substantive identities among similar ones (Clifford Geertz 1965: 106).

It is useful to look at efforts by anthropologists who are seeking to define the system underlying other spheres of culture to see if and how aspects of the perception process are incorporated into the classification systems they develop.

Ethnoscientists, for example, focus on discovering classification systems of folk categories which reveal how a given people organizes items in their world. These folk classifications persist because the relationships among the units have meaning for their users. The classes, whether they be kin terms of plant names, are functional because the system of the named classes offers a meaningful way to organize the world. Each category has a function and meaning only because it is a part of a larger system. As each new generation of category users grows up within the culture, its activities basically revolve around the business of learning and using categories which represent how that culture organizes its world. Indeed, these 'categories . . . reflect deeply the culture into which [man] is born' (Bruner *et al.* 1972: 177).

Similarly, symbol systems also derive their meaning from their relationships to the other parts of the system. Mary Douglas reminds us that 'A symbol only has meaning from its relation to other symbols in a pattern. The pattern gives the meaning. Therefore, no one item in the pattern can carry meaning by itself isolated from the rest' (Douglas 1973: 11).

A number of studies have demonstrated how symbols are structured within the ritual system (cf. Reichel-Dolmatoff 1971; Thompson 1945; Vogt 1976); are structured as status indicators (Faris 1972); or how their structure transmits oral histories and traditions (Munn 1973). All these forms of abbreviated representation are 'attempts to provide orientation for an organism which cannot live in a world it is unable to understand' (Geertz 1973: 140–1). In other words, despite their differing levels of abstraction, all types of symbolic representational systems seem to operate to categorize information as an aid to the regulation and direction of appropriate behaviour.

So, folk taxonomies and symbol systems categorize, organize and reveal the structure of specific aspects of a cultural world. They make explicit the organization of the inherent structure behind the series of names or symbols verbalized by the participants and perceived by the observers. They organize the world by relating items in terms of the meaning that the similar and different properties of those items have for each other. Furthermore, because these categories are shared among members of a given culture, they form the basis for communication about the items in question.

Similarly, it should be possible to define art systems by describing the consistencies in their formal organization. However, too often the classifications are too culturally specific to allow cross-cultural comparisons or their units cannot be easily used for diachronic studies of change (cf. Watt's grammar of Nevada cattle brands, 1966, 1967). Furthermore, the structure outlined is often one unconsciously seen and modelled through a Western perspective and value system.

For example, Deregowski (1972: 84) attempted to show how certain African tribes lacked the ability to represent images in central perspective. However, central perspective, introduced in the Renaissance, describes art of the Western world and therefore is not an unbiased reference point for the analysis of art of non-Western representational systems. In fact, central perspective organization of the picture plane is far from being an accurate representation of the real world. Central perspective actually requires 'violent and intricate deformation of the normal shape of things' (Arnheim 1974: 283). In a sense, central perspective makes things look right by representing them wrong.

In much 'primitive' art, two-dimensional images are often simply presented in side or front view outline. It is interesting that studies (Ryan and Schwartz 1956, cited by Haber 1980: 377) have shown that such simple flat outline representations are in fact easier to recognize than detailed three-dimensional realistic representations. Subjects given four different representations of a human hand: a black-on-white photograph, a detailed scientific drawing, an outline sketch, and a cartoon, most quickly recognized the cartoon as a hand. The last image to be recognized was the photograph which provided the most detailed information. Thus it appears that the simplicity in 'primitive' representation actually conveys the necessary information perhaps even more effectively than detailed realistic representations.

Caricature is another way in which images are simplified and key features are emphasized. Consider how quickly and infallibly everyone recognizes cartoons of politicians which emphasize familiar facial expressions or mannerisms. Such caricatures almost invariably distort or alter the actual image, yet they are almost always identifiable. This is because exaggerations of facial features are purposeful distortions of essential, distinctive features that everyone who belongs to that cultural group recognizes. Perhaps for non-literate cultures, such forms of representation are specifically chosen because they focus on critical features as systems of signs which enable all viewers to identify the images as belonging within their own cultural sphere.

Indeed, outline simplification or caricature seems to define certain types of style, just as central perspective defines others. The critical aspects of a thing which are emphasized may be exaggerated, distorted or represented in a way which, while not maintaining photographic reality, serve to capture and communicate the essence of the object or concept. But, however particularistically we describe these styles, they are all ultimately based on specific *structurings* of the essential features, whether they be emphasized, repeated, exaggerated, distorted or realistically represented. It is this structuring that we are seeking to delineate and understand.

The interest in classifications of structure in art forms is actually not unlike extant studies of structure in other aspects of culture. For example, Lomax has developed the methodology of cantometrics to describe features and their organization within song systems. He argues that 'each song performance is a symbolic reenactment of crucial behaviour patterns upon which the continuity of a culture hangs' (1968: 8). Dundes argues that there is patterned structure in folktales (1964) and Hymes (1964: 386) and Bauman (1975: 296) have shown how speech is equally conventionalized and peculiarly organized within communities. Indeed, Hymes points out that the very structured nature of a speech community is a boundary maintaining mechanism. It not only serves to enhance the community's distinctive sense of self, but also operates to exclude those who do not participate in that system (1964: 388).

The very organization inherent in these other verbal and visual representational systems suggests that art styles also can be analysed by structural principles. In fact, there have been an increasing number of studies which have attempted to demonstrate that structural principles, such as symmetry, underlie art forms. As early as 1932 Lila O'Neale discovered that Yurok–Karok basket-weavers followed well-defined rule systems for vessel shape and design proportion. Mills (1959) found that Navajos, and Salvador (1978) found that Kuna have definite ideas about balance, filling of space, and symmetry of design. Indeed, the structures in their designs seemed to reinforce these peoples' conceptual order of their world. Statements by artisans that they plan their design structures in their heads before execution (cf. Wood for the Tzeltal (1975), and Roe for the Shipibo (1980)) strongly suggest that proper organization of the parts of an art form is of fundamental importance to these peoples.

Furthermore, some analysts have sought to show that the structure they find in art is similar to that in the other cultural subsystems. Fernandez enumerates aspects of the dual balance in Fang sculpture which he feels is also reflected in village layout, in procedures for settling disputes and even in establishing genealogies (1966). Cunningham finds the Atoni house structure a symbolic visual of their properties of classification (1973), and Glassie finds that cognitive concepts which Middle Virginians brought from England are expressed in the layout of their houses (1975). Adams' analysis of Sumba ceremonial mantles reveals similarities between the structure of the design and village organization, ceremonial language, and aspects of ritual (1973). Perhaps Munn best summarizes these efforts to show how art structure can be an accurate mirror of cognitive models of the natural world.

> I would stress in particular that a structural analysis of the representational system is essential not only to an interpretation of the dynamics through which the forms are generated, but also to an explanation of the relations between the graphic system and the wider sociocultural order. (Munn 1973: 3)

In essence, art structure refers not only to a set of distinctive features but also to the organization of those features. Further, the structure of these features seems to embody the way a culture perceives, categorizes, and organizes a particular segment of its world. The relating and classifying processes in effect organize, i.e., give structure to the images seen.

We can most easily describe the system in these images by describing the consistencies in their structure. Thus, just as the critical features of perception concern the way the parts seen are organized, similarly the consistencies in art structure may be interpreted as the units carrying cognitive import.

Art structures so described do not communicate particularistic information only because they are part of a larger system. In other words, what is communicated has a formal organization and, as such, is 'larger than life'. It becomes a representation of the whole system of which it is a part. In this sense art is redundant – it communicates and repeats information expressed in other subsystems. As Bateson reminds us, it is the quality of redundancy wherein the same message can be pronounced in a number of different ways which unites each of the subsystems of culture into a functional whole (Bateson 1973).

Ethnographic studies of the structure in art

The papers in this volume focus on defining the structural/conceptual systematics of art. Five are studies of ethnographic situations which use informant testimony, participant observation and document research to define structural grammars of art and how these grammars can be meaningful statements about the place of an art form in a particular cultural situation.

Hardin's study (Ch. 2) of the structure of decoration on Tarascan greenware ollas is a highly formalized dissection of a particular design style. Borrowing her approach from linguistic anthropology, she proposes that: 'A design structure is the cognitive system underlying a particular style.' She takes advantage of her privileged position as an ethnographer to draw on verbalized comments from the potters as well as her own observations to define the series of rules Tarascan potters seem to follow when laying out their designs. Her observations a decade ago (Friedrich 1970) that the configuration is the cognitive unit appear even stronger and more meaningful juxtaposed to the other papers in this volume.

Whereas Hardin explicitly shows us the consistency underlying Tarascan design, Lathrap (Ch. 3) focuses on the variability within a design system, and uses this approach to test the earlier premises of Deetz (1965) and Longacre (1964), who proposed a relationship between residence rules and design variation. Lathrap's work is a superior example because his data base combines the ethnographic present with 4,000 years of prehistory along the Ucayali River in eastern Peru. In this paper, Lathrap's observations about contemporary Shipibo–Conibo pottery-making show how adoptions, yearly family visits, personal experiences of individuals, competition among potters within a tightly knit potting family, and ostracism of a potting family from the rest of the village, can be sources of design variation. What Lathrap has uncovered are individual micro-traditions within a village. On this level, where others predicted homogeneity, he has isolated sources of variability.

We can also see in this same data base an incredible amount of homogeneity that can be labelled, on another stylistic level, as the Shipibo–Conibo style. I have taken the liberty of analysing the data illustrated in this article (according to the method of symmetry analysis outlined in Washburn 1977) and find that, structurally, Shipibo–Conibo designs are consistently organized by two particular design layouts: all interior designs on bowls have finite vertical and horizontal reflection structures (211), and all banded designs on bowl and jar exteriors have one-dimensional vertical reflection structures (1–101). Vertical reflection predominates in all layouts, regardless of family, village, age of potter or particular individual situations. These structures represent the culturally recognized, appropriate, gramatically correct way to arrange design elements on a specific space to be decorated. Here is a culture's stylistic tradition, described by symmetry in an excellently documented ethnographic example.

On this level, within-village variation is obscured. The efforts of two sisters, Ana and Jesusa, to differentiate their output may be observed in differences in elements used, but because they both adhere to a culture-wide layout – 1–101 for bands and 211 for finite designs – their output is structurally identical (Figs. 3.4b–f, 3.5c–f). Likewise, age does not seem to be a factor. The slightly irregular designs (Fig. 3.4a) of the matriarch Asunsiana, or the beginning efforts of seven-year-old Ermelinda (Fig. 3.5j) and ten-year-old Isabella (Fig. 3.5k) are all identically structured. Thus, element details will vary, but the structuring of those elements will be culturally consistent.

This culture-wide structural style does not negate Lathrap's observations or his objections to Deetz's and Longacre's original hypotheses. As Lathrap points out, stylistic variation can be observed on several levels. Cultural groups have unique styles which differentiate them from other cultural groups, and individuals have unique styles which differentiate themselves from other members of their potting family or village. Group styles are *structurally* different one from another, whereas individual styles employ uniquely different *element* combinations. Thus, whereas Lathrap's studies show how the variability of individual styles within a potting community relates to specific experiences and life schedules, it is also true that, on a culture-wide level, there is a structural style which relates to a much broader activity spectrum. Similarities in the outlook and activities of one people results in groupings we can distinguish as separate cultures. Each of these groups communicates to its members, by various media, its uniqueness. A culture's uniquely structured design style is one such way in which this information is communicated.

Arnold (Ch. 5) explicitly relates design layout of four pottery shapes to arrangements of environmental and social space in the contemporary village of Quinua, Peru. As an archaeologist, Arnold is concerned with discovering ways by which we might be able to define past interaction between groups solely through material culture remains. Taking off from Friedrich's (1970) work concerning how similarities and differences in design structure reflect interaction patterns of the potters, Arnold seeks to demonstrate that the structure of decorative space reflects basic structural patterns which organize other kinds of space use within a community. This goes beyond the problem of defining the interaction patterns of the people who made the designs, to address the problem of whether these consistent layouts in design reflect similar structuring in other, non-pottery-related activities.

Hanson (Ch. 6) shows clearly that a focus on meaning, form and content can often be misleading for some art, such as that of the Maori, which is largely purely decorative. This is not to imply, however, that its non-representational quality relieves it of meaningful content, for he shows us a number of homologous relations between art structure and other cultural patterns. For Hanson, 'the meaning of an object is located in the constellations of formal relationships in which it participates'. For the Maori the general pattern of dualism and complementarity is expressed, for example, in wood-carving designs with bilateral symmetry.

Adams (Ch. 4) relates the degree of form dimensionality to access to political authority. Sculpture in the round is found only in the royal sphere, while flat mats and cloths are found in all sectors of the population. In between are three-dimensional objects decorated with motifs found on flat two-dimensional pieces. These were used and worn principally by those competing for a place in the political sphere surrounding the royalty.

Faris' paper (Ch. 7) exemplifies another direction which structural studies may take in an effort to understand how art operates within the cultural constellation. Faris is concerned with three examples of art forms whose culturally accepted, grammatically correct structures are distinctively elaborated. But he is looking beyond the structures to the context in structure. He moves beyond his earlier position

(1972) of defining the organization of art forms and how they relate to the social context to an attempt to specify the ideology behind the art forms. Thus, Nuba body painting, for example, is read as the marking of man's productive specialization. But for some Northwest Coast art, Nuba body art, and Upper Paleolithic parietal and mobile art, excessive elaboration has compromised the functional meaning of the art so that, in fact, the meaning in the form can be read to be secondary to the elaboration of the form itself.

Archaeological studies of the structure in art

Given the current interest in defining interaction spheres in prehistory, this book began as an effort to develop a more systematic way of describing and interpreting patterning among sites in archaeological contexts. It appeared, however, that first we needed a more systematic way to *describe* the patterns observed before we chose statistically sophisticated techniques to *analyse* the patterns. Two criteria seem to be essential to systematic description: (1) the units of analysis must produce an objective description; and (2) the units of analysis must allow comparison between relationships in the system being described and those of other systems in the culture with which they are related.

Just as the relational character of perspective dictates that we see objects only as they relate to others around them, so does the position of art forms in a culture mean that they are not seen and used as isolates by their cultural makers and users, but as parts of a larger cultural system in which they are inextricably related. Thusly, our analytical mode should be one which facilitates discovery of those relationships.

In 1948 Shepard (Shepard 1948) and again in 1977 Zaslow (Zaslow 1977) and I (Washburn 1977) suggested that symmetry is an objective analytical unit which can be used to describe the grammar of art systems. As a mathematical concept symmetry describes the repetitive property of structure; that is, how a given part is moved a given distance along and/or about an axis to superimpose upon itself. This property can be used to describe all repeated patterns, whether on textiles, ceramics, tile, wood or other media. Because both the simplicities and the complexities of most primitive and Western art can be described using these geometric motion classes, symmetry is free of particularistic stylistic criteria such as central perspective.

It was clear, however, once recurrent patternings were discovered in cultural situations, that a greater understanding was needed of the nature of these structural consistencies before we could blithely apply this idea to study past behavioural patternings. Thus, I have gathered a series of papers in the first part of this volume by ethnographers, and archaeologists-temporarily-turned-ethnographers. These have shown how structural consistencies relate to and reflect other aspects of the cultural system. But, to close, I have included two studies which suggest the potential uses of this concept for archaeological material. These papers represent analyses of archaeological situations where structural studies add new dimensions to well-known examples of change and continuity.

Kent (Ch. 8) identifies six distinct regional and temporal styles of weaving in the prehistoric American Southwest and, within these, is able to define two dramatic structural shifts in design which correlate with other artifact and population introductions. From this analysis, she is able to offer an archaeological case where the survival of a design style can be interpreted as a statement of cultural persistence in the face of radical change.

I use symmetry analysis to reanalyse and give new life to old data. Structural shifts in incised designs through 3,000 years of prehistory at Knossos are shown to correlate with the beginnings of outside contacts with other Aegean communities. Such sensitivity of design structure to temporal change can be matched by studies of the sensitivity of structural change through space. Painted ceramics from Early Neolithic sites on mainland Greece show distinct regional clusters that appear closely associated with major geographical barriers. In contrast, incised ceramics from Late Neolithic sites reveal that some centrally placed sites have all the patterns represented, while surrounding sites have only one or two. This is suggested to be an indication of the possible development of marketing centres, an event not surprising in view of the coincident opening of trading contacts throughout the Aegean during this period.

Toward a theory of structural style in art

The papers in this volume are concerned with the structure of art and how it operates as one of the organizational concepts that underlie cultural systems. Art structures describe aspects of the balance, harmony and order within a given culture that makes life comfortable and predictable for its members. Art structures are perceived, although perhaps not explicitly verbalized. For example, Lila O'Neale (1932) found that Northwest Coast California Indian basket-weavers identified baskets as 'good' if they had designs that were pleasing and properly arranged. Analysis revealed that all these 'good' baskets were consistently structured. In contrast, 'bad' baskets were those with designs copied from items external to their culture, and those designs were heterogeneously structured. Only 'good' baskets were worn and used by the Indians; 'bad' baskets were made to sell to tourists. Thus, just as Hodder suggests that aspects of social organization will have spatial expressions (1978: 211), we are suggesting here that social activities and cultural values will have graphic expressions as well.

But it must be emphasized that persons external to a given system may not recognize the structure that is perceived within, since what is an orderly world to those within a system may be perceived as chaotic and disorienting for those external to it. Further, we would not want to conclude, at this writing, that within a given culture the structure of art will necessarily always be the same as the structure of dance, political relations, or any other behavioural system. We have examined some cases where this is so, however, and we are endeavouring to understand what these congruencies may mean. We are presenting our first efforts to examine these structural consistencies so that we may study their relationships to other cultural behaviours.

In sum, we have sought to map the aesthetic component of culture in terms of its structural base. We have all, I think, moved toward more explicit statements about the internal grammar of a culture's art forms, which, in turn, enables us to understand more clearly how art relates to objects, ideas, and activities in other systems of the culture because those aspects can also be understood by the same grammatical principles. We do not pretend completely to understand at this writing why art is so structured, nor exactly how this structure relates to its social context. What we offer here, we hope, are more systematic investigations of art structures and related aspects, and some initial approaches to their contextual relationships within the larger cultural whole.

References

Adams, Marie Jeanne, 1973. Structural aspects of a village art. *American Anthropologist* 75 (1): 265–79.

Arnheim, Rudolf, 1969. *Visual Thinking.* University of California Press, Berkeley.

1974. *Art and Visual Perception.* University of California Press, Berkeley.

Bateson, Gregory, 1973. Style, grace and information in primitive art. In *Primitive Art and Society*, edited by Anthony Forge, pp. 235–55. Oxford University Press, Oxford.

Bauman, Richard, 1975. Verbal art as performance. *American Anthropologist* 77 (2): 290–311.

Bruner, Jerome S., Jacqueline J. Goodnow and George A. Austin, 1972. Categories and cognition. In *Culture and Cognition*, edited by James P. Spradley, pp. 168–90. Chandler, San Francisco.

Cunningham, Clark E., 1973. Order in the Atoni house. In *Right and Left: Essays on Dual Symbolic Classification*, edited by Rodney Needham, pp. 204–38. University of Chicago Press, Chicago.

Deetz, James, 1965. *The Dynamics of Stylistic Change in Arikara Ceramics.* Illinois Studies in Anthropology No. 4, University of Illinois Press, Urbana.

Deregowski, Jan B., 1972. Pictorial perception and culture. In *Scientific American* 227 (5): 82–8.

Douglas, Mary, 1973. *Natural Symbols: Explorations in Cosmology* (2nd revised edn). Vintage Books, New York.

Dundes, Alan, 1964. The morphology of North American Indian folktales. *Folklore Fellows Communication* No. 195, Academia Scientiarum Fennica, Helsinki.

Faris, James C., 1972. *Nuba Personal Art.* University of Toronto Press, Toronto.

Fernandez, James W., 1966. Principles of opposition and vitality in Fang aesthetics. *Journal of Aesthetics and Art Criticism* 25 (1): 53–64.

Friedrich, Margaret Hardin, 1970. Design structure and social interaction: archaeological implications of an ethnographic analysis. *American Antiquity* 35 (3): 332–43.

Geertz, Clifford, 1965. The impact of the concept of culture on the concept of man. In *New Views of the Nature of Man*, edited by John R. Platt, pp. 93–118. University of Chicago Press, Chicago.

1973. *The Interpretation of Cultures.* Basic Books, New York.

Glassie, Henry, 1975. *Folk Housing in Middle Virginia.* University of Tennessee Press, Knoxville.

Haber, Ralph Norman, 1980. How we perceive depth from flat pictures. *American Scientist* 68 (4): 370–80.

Hodder, Ian (ed.), 1978. *The Spatial Organization of Culture.* University of Pittsburgh Press, Pittsburgh.

Hymes, Dell (ed.), 1964. *Language in Culture and Society.* Harper and Row, New York.

Lomax, Alan *et al.*, 1968. *Folk Song Style and Culture.* American Association for the Advancement of Science Publication 88, Washington D.C.

Longacre, William A., 1964. Sociological implications of the ceramic analysis. *Fieldiana: Anthropology* 55: 155–70. Chicago, Field Museum of Natural History.

Mills, George, 1959. *Navaho Art and Culture.* The Taylor Museum of the Colorado Springs Fine Arts Center.

Munn, Nancy D., 1973. *Walbiri Iconography: graphic representation and cultural symbolism in a Central Australian society.* Cornell University Press, Ithaca.

O'Neale, Lila M., 1932. Yurok–Karok basket weavers. *University of California Publications in American Archaeology and Ethnology* 32 (1).

Reichel-Dolmatoff, Gerardo, 1971. *Amazonian Cosmos: the sexual and religious symbolism of the Tukano Indians.* University of Chicago Press, Chicago.

Roe, Peter G., 1980. Art and residence among the Shipibo Indians of Peru: a study in microacculturation. *American Anthropologist* 82 (1): 42–71.

Ryan, T.A. and C. Schwartz, 1956. Speed of perception as a function of mode of presentation. *American Journal of Psychology* 69: 60–9.

Salvador, Mari Lyn, 1978. *Yer Dailege! Kuna women's art.* Maxwell Museum of Anthropology, Albuquerque.

Shepard, Anna O., 1948. The symmetry of abstract design with special reference to ceramic decoration. *Carnegie Institution of Washington Publication* 574: 211–93.

Silver, Harry R., 1979. Ethnoart. *Annual Review of Anthropology* 8: 267–307.

Thompson, Laura, 1945. Logico-aesthetic integration in Hopi culture. *American Anthropologist* 47 (4): 540–53.

Vogt, Evon Z., 1976. *Tortillas for the Gods: a symbolic analysis of Zinacanteco rituals.* Harvard University Press, Cambridge, Mass.

Washburn, Dorothy K., 1977. A symmetry analysis of Upper Gila area ceramic design. *Papers of the Peabody Museum* 68. Harvard University, Cambridge, Mass.

Watt, William C., 1966. *Morphology of the Nevada Cattlebrands and Their Blazons, Part I.* United States Department of Commerce, National Bureau of Standards Report 9050.

1967. Morphology of the Nevada Cattlebrands and Their Blazons, Part II., published as *Structural Properties of the Nevada Cattlebrands. Computer Science Research Review* 2: 21–8, Carnegie-Mellon University, Pittsburgh.

Wood, Denis, 1975. Making seen: the perception and generation of patterns in the clothing of the highlands of Chiapas, Mexico. In *Patterns*, School of Design, North Carolina State University, Raleigh, Student Publication.

Zaslow, Bert, 1977. A guide to analyzing prehistoric ceramic decorations by symmetry and pattern mathematics. In *Pattern Mathematics and Archaeology*, edited by G.A. Clarke. Arizona. State University Anthropological Research Paper 2. Tempe.

Chapter 2

The structure of Tarascan pottery painting

Margaret Ann Hardin

Introduction

This paper presents a method for analysing the cognitive structures reflected in decorative art styles and illustrates it with a study of Tarascan greenware painting.[1] The procedure outlined is designed for ethnographic data; that is, the resulting analysis depends not only upon formal comparisons of representative craft products but also upon the statements of craftsmen. In its approaches toward these two sources of information about the structure of the style, the paper owes a double debt.

The framework used to describe the physical appearance of the style is essentially the same as that used for systematic description of decorative styles within the tradition of American anthropology (Boas 1955: 183–298; Bunzel 1926). More specifically, this paper draws heavily upon the detailed instructions provided by Anna Shepard (1956: 259–305) for the description of decorations on ceramic vessels.

The mode of analysis to be detailed rests upon the methods and assumptions of linguistic anthropology in both its use of verbal data and its overall aims. Although it has long been recognized that these methods are particularly suited to the study of material culture (Sturtevant 1964: 107), this field of interest has received relatively little attention in comparison with others, such as kinship and biological classification. Similarly, while the approach has been used successfully in studies of material culture, including technological aspects of pottery making (Conklin 1953; Arnold 1971; Kaplan 1976), studies of complex systems of decoration are lacking. This paper assumes that a systematically organized body of knowledge must underlie a productive decorative art style, an assumption, incidentally, that it shares with other approaches to the description of art styles that rest more heavily upon linguistic analogy (Muller 1966 and 1979; Faris 1972; DeBoer 1975; Mead *et al.* 1975; Green 1979; Roe 1980). The paper is not, however, committed to applying any specific model of language, but, rather, seeks to follow the sensible although brief injunction of Hymes that models of art styles should account for the units used by the artist, their classification, and the rules for their use.[2]

Framework: definitions and procedures

Two concepts are of central importance to this paper: decorative style and design structure. A decorative style is a system of design used to embellish the surface of an object. Such styles are essentially two-dimensional systems. Their organization is to a great extent independent of the object on which they occur although, obviously, the form of the artifact may place some restrictions on the size and shape of the decorated area. A design structure is the cognitive system underlying a particular style. It provides the artist with a means of organizing the information needed to create objects in that style.

The analysis of a particular system of design structure and resultant decorative style is an attempt to organize systematically the information used by artists in embellishing objects decorated in that style. In the more specific case of decorative art styles, Hymes' basic framework for an account of the underlying cognitive structure can be stated in greater detail. These cognitive systems are best described in terms of four components: (1) a definition of the decorative problem; (2) a basic unit of design; (3) a system for the classification of these units; and (4) a set of rules governing the use of basic units in solving the decorative problem.

The procedures used in the analysis that follows rest upon the assumption that the picture of design structure that is built up should be based upon all available bodies of evidence. Because the account is based upon more than one level of evidence, the relationship of the resulting model to any one level of evidence is defined and limited in certain ways.

First, an account of design structure necessarily rests partly upon the evidence provided by material objects, but its aim is not simply to describe the appearance of the decoration. On the one hand, the account should describe the corpus of decorative style available correctly and adequately. On the other hand, because other data are also being taken into account, the analysis resulting may not be the most elegant description of the designs that is possible. In those cases where available data are largely limited to completed objects, it is possible, as the work of Holm (1965) and Rowe (1962) well demonstrates, to base an analysis that arrives at general principles underlying the style, largely or totally upon the evidence provided by the pieces themselves.

Second, the account of design structure may make use of evidence provided by observations of the ordered steps used to construct decoration. Here it must be cautioned that the processual order in which design structure is realized must be distinguished from design structure itself; that is, the fact that one element is painted after another does not necessarily mean that the second is structurally subordinate to the first. At other times, however, order of execution can provide information about structural relations between the various components of design. Sequences in which decisions about the form of a component of design restrict the possible forms of components executed later represent cases where order reflects structure.

Third, in building up a description of design structure, the analyst should take into account artists' verbalizations about design. The description should summarize the visual evidence without directly contradicting what is said by practitioners of the style. As is the case with San José greenware painting, however, these often-repeated and somewhat standard ways of talking about design may focus narrowly on specific aspects of design. The framework provided by the physical evidence is thus needed both to interpret sets of statements and to relate them to each other. For this reason, the model of design structure need not be limited to the standard statements of painters. Rather, their most important use in analysis is to provide clues to the organization of design structure, which can then be elaborated from further analysis of a corpus of objects decorated in the style.

A model of the design structure associated with a particular decorative style is thus built up from the analysis and comparison of various categories of ethnographic evidence. Procedures for eliciting and analysing data necessarily vary from style to style, as they must be designed to fit both the formal properties of the style and the extent to which, and the ways in which artists customarily talk about their work. While there is no single detailed procedure appropriate for the analysis of all decorative art styles, further guidelines can be provided and illustrated with the analysis of a specific case. Components of design structure associated with decorative style and their relationships to various levels of data provide an outline of general features and alternate structures against which the information available for a particular style can be checked. The analysis of the painting in Tarascan green-glazed pottery from San José serves as an illustration of the complex interplay between categories of evidence and the alternative structural analyses. This is possible because common formal constraints on the organization of such styles limit their variability and thus make it possible to offer a general procedure that can be applied to any particular style.

Ethnographic context

The analysis presented in based upon fieldwork conducted from November 1966 to December 1967 in San José, a small village in the foothills of the Tarascan Sierra of northwestern Mexico. The village consisted of about forty households; total population was about three hundred people. Most people were bilingual, speaking both Tarascan and Spanish. The majority of households engaged to some extent in pottery making. Usually men and women shared in the work, there being no rigid assignment of any task to one sex.

A variety of vessel shapes and wares were produced. Moulds were used to form vessels, which were then finished by hand. Vessel forms were essentially of two kinds: (1) shallow, bowl-shaped forms, which were made in one piece on mushroom moulds; and (2) more enclosed forms with higher sides, which were made in two pieces inside two-part moulds. The most common kind of pottery made was a plain red utility ware, which was finished on some or all surfaces with a clear glaze. When these vessels were intended for cooking, their primary use, they were not glazed on the outside. Vessels intended for eating were either finished in the same way or glazed on both sides. The second most common ware was the green-glazed decorative ware which is the subject of this study. The most visible surfaces of these vessels were painted with a white slip in intricate designs. The painted area was then covered with a clear green glaze (Fig.

2.1). Because the fired clay was brick red, the result was bright green designs on a blackish background. The other surfaces were usually covered with clear glaze. These dishes served as kitchen decoration and drinking vessels; they were used, with some care, for food, but tended to be reserved for special occasions.

Pottery manufacture was conducted as a household industry, the income from which supplemented that from agriculture. Households varied greatly in the extent to which they engaged in and were dependent upon pottery production. Other factors affecting production and income included frequency of firing, size of kiln, type of ware made, and the kind of market in which pottery was sold. A household that depended heavily on pottery income would usually fire and sell a kiln-load of pottery a week. A medium-sized kiln held about thirteen dozen assorted redware vessels of small and medium size. Under normal market conditions, these would be sold at a profit of about $80.00 (in Mexican currency) at the local weekly market. A kiln of the same size held about twenty dozen greenware vessels of various sizes, which would yield a profit of $125.00 at the same market.[3] In addition to nearby weekly markets, a large number of San José potters made greenware for several important local and regional fiestas. Finally, some households sold pottery at fiestas in more distant towns within or near the Tarascan region; in these cases, family connections usually determined where a potter would go. A few households took their pottery to fairs or shops in more distant towns, in particular, Patzcuaro, Moralia, and Mexico City. These greenware pieces, some traditional, some more recent innovations, were designed for urban and tourist buyers.

An examination of the affinities of San José pottery in general and of the greenware in particular shows that the basic technique of manufacture, using one-part and two-part moulds, is common to most of the Tarascan region. Salient exceptions are the products of Comanja, Zipiago, and Cocucho (West 1948: 63). While the mushroom mould is thought to be pre-Columbian in origin, scholars are less certain about the two-part mould (Foster 1948: 360–2). In form and general mode of finishing, San José pottery is more closely related to the redware and greenware of the western part of the Tarascan region (that of the Eleven Pueblos and Patamban) than to that of the eastern part of the region (that of towns near and around Lake Patzcuaro). Within San José, the vessel forms used for greenware are much the same as those used for redware, although redware is made in larger sizes. San José greenware is most closely related to the greenware of Patamban, described by Pozas (1949), and of Sta. Thomas in the Eleven Pueblos. While the products of these towns can be distinguished stylistically, they share overall similarities of painting technique and organization of design. Historically, the three variants are closely related. The ware was developed in Patamban, was being made in San José shortly before the Mexican Revolution, and was subsequently adopted in Sta. Thomas. In contrast, the greenware made in Tzintzuntzan, which is relatively recent in origin

Fig. 2.1. San José vessels painted with the same design. The vessel on the left has been fired once (Field Museum 167550) while that on the right has also been glaze fired (Field Museum 167556).

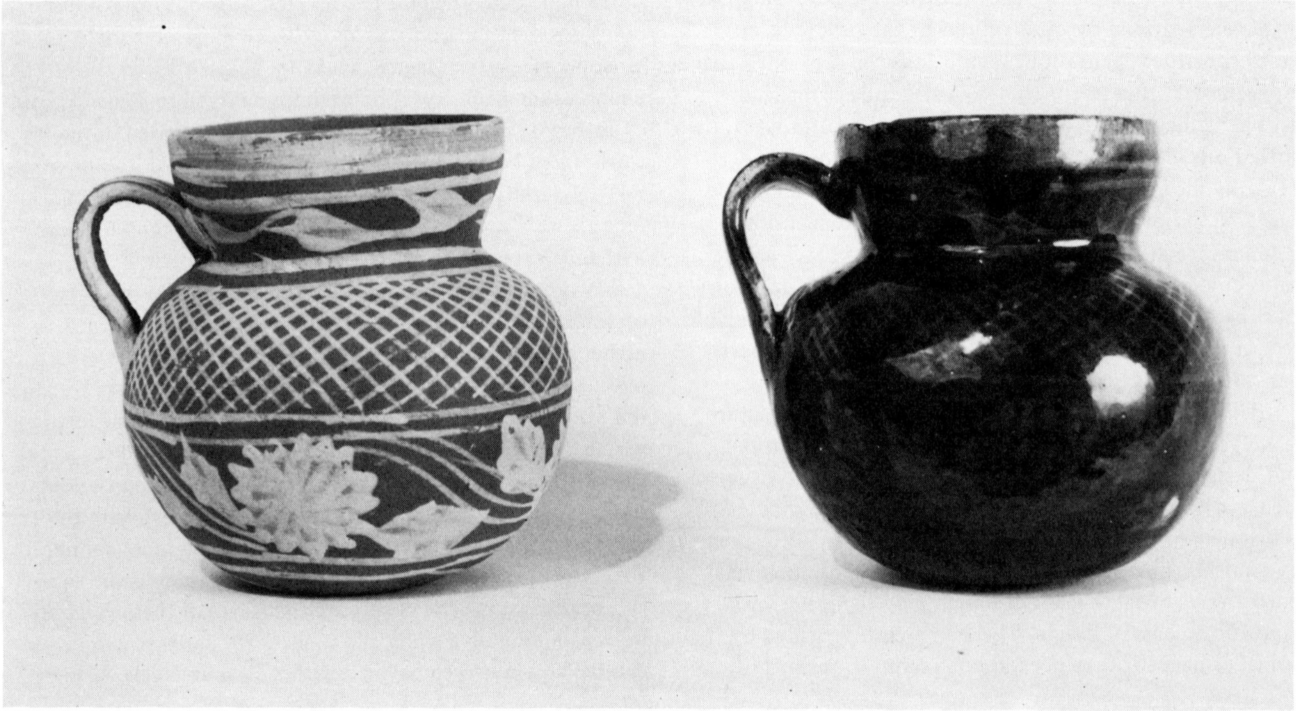

(Foster 1967: 43), is different from that of the western Tarascan area in style, painting technique, and quality of glaze.

Problem and evidence

The purpose of this section is first to delineate the materials to be described in the account of design structure and then to summarize the categories of data upon which this analysis is to be based. While painted greenware is made in a variety of shapes, the olla, a simply shaped pot, usually with one handle, is by far the most common form. This analysis of design structure is limited to olla painting, not only because a larger sample was available than for any other vessel form, but also because designs painted on these vessels have a more complex structure and exhibit a wider range of variation than designs painted on other forms.

Before turning to a summary of the kinds of evidence available, let us briefly describe how these vessels are decorated. In olla painting the vessel's surface is divided into horizontal bands, which may vary in size and number (Fig. 2.2). The designs that occur in the areas marked off by the painter range from geometric forms to arrangements that include floral elements and animals. The large central band may be subdivided vertically to form 'rectangular' areas; in addition, these rectangular areas may then be further subdivided (Fig. 2.3).

The painted designs exhibit a large range of variation. The main factor underlying this variety is the complexity of the style, which affords the painter alternative choices at a number of points in the painting process. In addition, three other factors contribute significantly to the variety that the ethnographer observes. The work of individual painters varies according to differences in both skill and knowledge. Smaller vessels tend to be painted more simply than larger vessels,

Fig. 2.2. San José vessel after first firing, illustrating exclusive use of horizontal spatial divisions (Field Museum 167331).

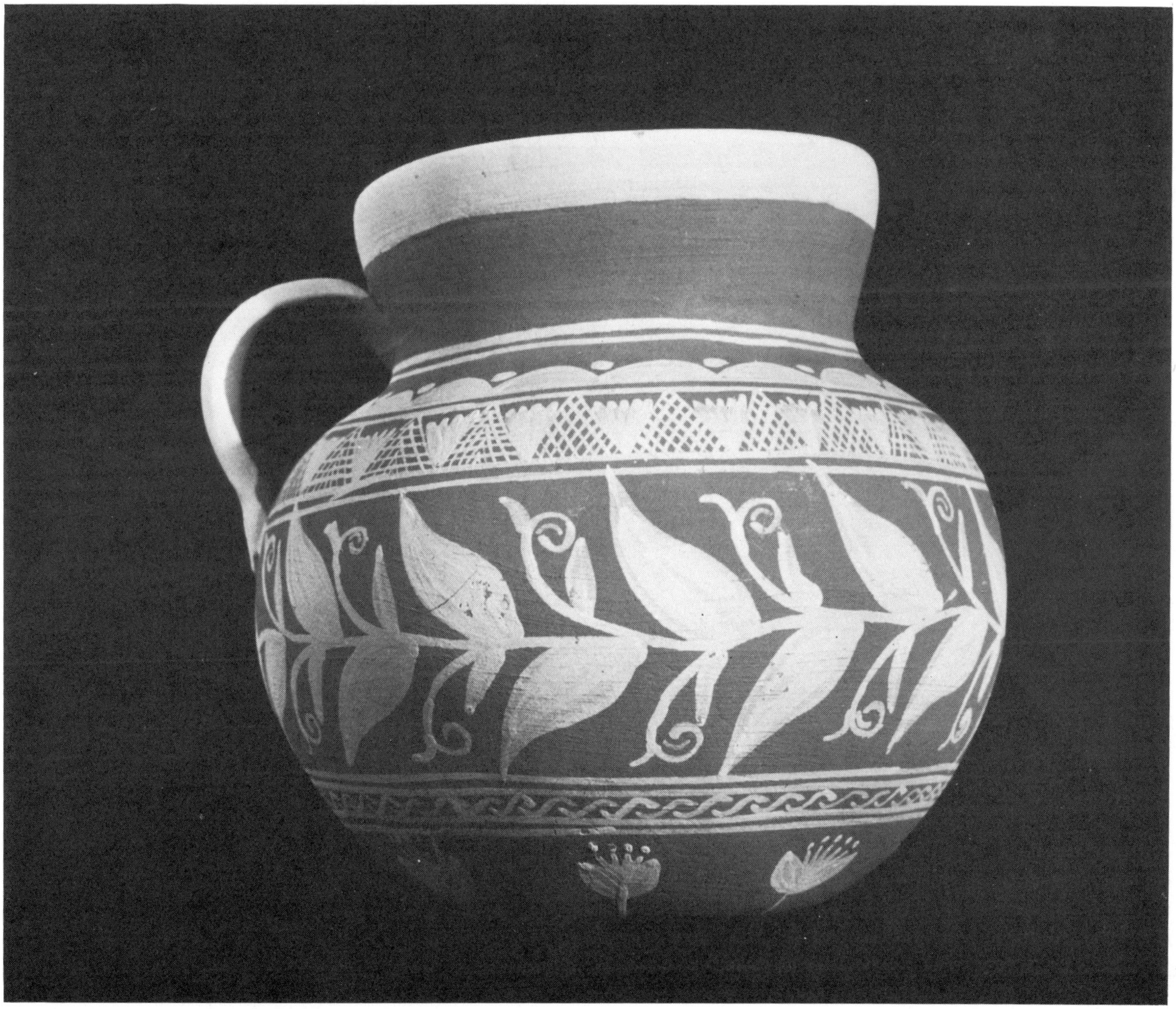

although in technicality, the same system of design is used for vessels of all sizes. Economic factors are also reflected in complexity of painting.

The relationship between this complexly patterned variation and the account of design structure outlined below is not a simple one. A description of graphic style that was essentially a summary and codification of common or widely shared features and relationships provided the basic framework of the analysis. Other categories of data then suggested interpretations of the observed stylistic relationships. The goal of analysis was not to describe behaviour or the products of behaviour, but to make inferences about the organization of information underlying the painter's performance.

The ten categories of evidence used in this paper may be described in terms of the conjunction of two dimensions of variation. The first dimension involves a progression from observations of graphic style (completed vessels, painting sequence), through readily volunteered verbalizations about particular vessels (descriptions of vessels, aesthetic evaluation of vessels, division of vessel surface, description of painting sequence), to responses to more formal sets of questions (aesthetic rankings, triad tests, painting out of context). The first category differs from the other two in its exclusion of verbal behaviour. The distinction between the latter two categories lies in the spontaneity with which the information was given. The first kind of verbal data involves responses to single vessels; it includes several distinct ways of talking about them. Such information was volunteered but could also be easily elicited. The second kind of verbal data resulted from more structured situations; for example, a fixed set of questions would be asked about a specific set of vessels. The second dimension further divides each of the three sets of categories defined by the first dimension. It contrasts dynamic and static views of design; categories involving the preliminaries to painting and the painting process are distinguished from those involving completed vessels.

The evidence categories complement each other; that is, each provides more information about some components of design structure than about others. Similarly, some kinds of data could be systematically gathered from a wide sample

Fig. 2.3. San José vessel after first firing, illustrating both levels of optional subdivision of horizontal central band (Field Museum 167407).

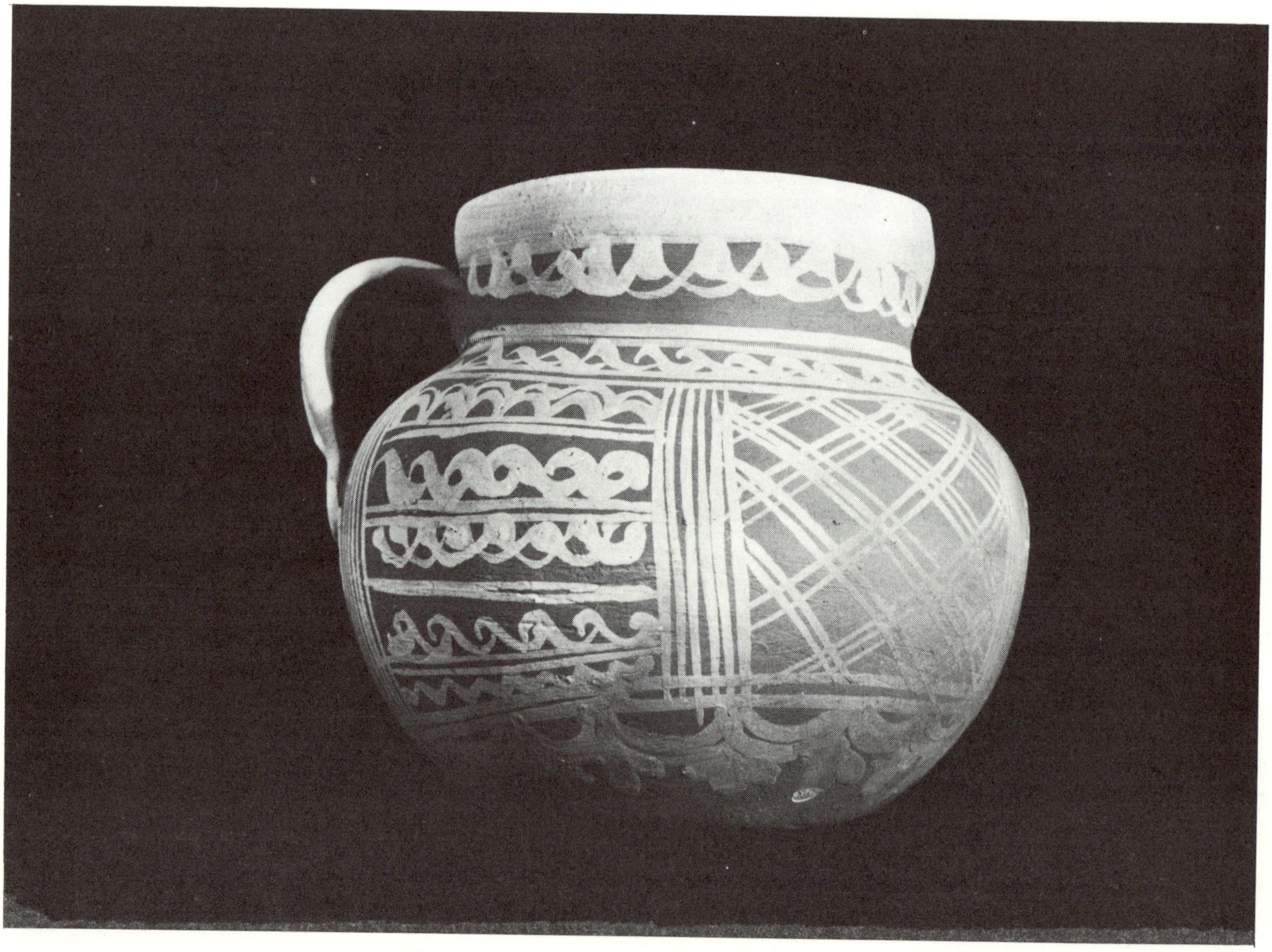

of painters while others could not. The summaries that follow provide a brief explanation of the materials included in each category, touching upon the size of the sample involved, and the use made of this information in the analysis of design structure.

Completed vessels

Drawings were made of about 400 vessels; of these, about 200 were collected and are available for further analysis. The work of all sixteen major painters and of most occasional painters was sampled.[4] In addition, during the course of fieldwork, a much larger number of vessels was seen; these did not contradict or add to what had already been recorded. The importance of the completed vessels is that they form the largest and most representative category of information. This corpus of design provides a framework for understanding more narrowly focused bodies of data. However, painted vessels by themselves do not always provide sufficient evidence of design structure, as alternate interpretations of some designs are possible.

Painting sequence

Knowledge of the pottery painting sequence is based on records made of about two hundred vessels while they were being painted. From these observations it became clear that there was a standardized order in which painting tasks were executed. Although the processual order in which painted decoration is produced must be distinguished from the structure underlying the process, in the San José case, the order did reflect structured relations between various portions of the arrangements being painted.

Description of vessels

Several painters volunteered descriptions of what was painted on a particular vessel; more extensive examples were collected from one painter. All decoded vessels in the same way, agreeing on what parts of the designs covering the vessels should be mentioned. Descriptions of painted vessels were important because decoding strategy, when contrasted with encoding strategy, provided important insights into the way in which the basic decorative problem was defined.

Aesthetic evaluations of vessels

Painters readily offered comments on the aesthetic qualities of specific vessels. These volunteered evaluations provided the information upon which more detailed aesthetic questionnaires were based. Aesthetic evaluations consisted of statements about whether the vessel was well painted rather than statements about whether the commentator simply liked or disliked the vessel for other, sometimes more personal, reasons. Interestingly, although San José painters had definite personal styles, most painters could not recognize the work of all San José painters. The explanation for this lay in differential social contact, for painters did recognize the hands of those whose work they saw most frequently. Thus, the effect of personal feelings on vessel evaluation was lessened both because aesthetic judgement constituted a separate domain and because painters were limited in their ability to ascribe vessels to other painters.

Division of vessel surface

Painters readily divided the surface of unpainted vessels into segments, each of which was referred to by one to four terms. These divisions created four horizontal segments, of which two were further subdivided. The system of named partitions provided information about painters' perception of the vessel prior to painting, and thus about the definition of decorative problem.

Description of painting sequence

Painters were able to describe not only the sequence of steps that they were using to paint a specific vessel but also were able to reconstruct a sequence that might have been used to create the designs on a completed vessel. These descriptions of the ideal process indicated that painters worked from an encoding strategy that corresponded to the sequence that they normally used in painting a vessel. This strategy provided information about the definition of decorative problem and the ruler governing the use of basic units.

Design name questionnaire

The sixteen major painters were asked to identify forty-nine designs painted on portions of completed vessels. The purpose of the questionnaire was to provide a wider range of information about the terms used to describe painted elements and the way in which they were applied than was obtained from descriptions of designs painted on specific vessels. Painters' answers helped to identify the basic unit of design.

Aesthetic ranking

The sixteen major painters were asked to subdivide and rank two sets of vessels, using the common terms of aesthetic evaluation. The first set contained eight vessels decorated by painters of varying skill; the painted decorations were variants of two very common themes. Two things were learned from painters' answers: (1) that the aesthetic terms used represented the end points of three dimensions of evaluation, which will be described in the analysis that follows; and (2) that while these dimensions were independent, they were related to each other in a definite way. The second set contained seven vessels painted by painters of equal skill; a wide variety of designs, some common, some new innovations, were represented. Responses to this questionnaire showed that: (1) aesthetic terms were initially applied to individual areas of decoration; and (2) there was a specific procedure for arriving at an evaluation of the whole vessel. In general, the system of aesthetic evaluation provided information about definition of decorative problem and rules governing the use of basic units.

Triad tests

The triad tests involved a series of nineteen sets of three vessels each. The sixteen major painters were asked to pick the most different vessel from each triad and to give the reasons for their choice. The vessels used were small and simply painted. An attempt was made to minimize the reasons for choice; frequently, two features on which grouping might be based were deliberately tested against each other. In some cases the patterns of response to the tests were neither simple nor elegant, and it was necessary to recognize that some triads provided the painters with no criteria that they found natural for grouping two of the vessels. Responses provided information about the basic units of design and their classification, as well as about the relation of these to the classification of vessel decoration.

Painting out of context

One unusually skilled and innovative young person painted a series of designs out of context, using the white slip on black paper. He placed the designs in groups, explaining the reasons for the grouping as well as the points being illustrated by each design. This series provided valuable information about the nature and classification of basic units.

Analysis of design structure

This section outlines the design structure underlying San José greenware painting. The analysis is divided into four stages, each of which involves determining the exact nature of one of the four components shared by all decorative art styles. Further, the stages can be logically ordered; that is, the formal properties of one component narrow the range of questions that can be asked about other components in subsequent stages of analysis. In the following discussion a section is devoted to each of the components, which are treated in their logical order; (1) decorative problem, (2) basic unit, (3) classification of basic units, and (4) rules for the use of basic units. The analysis of each component is presented in four parts: (1) explanation of what is included in the component; (2) a discussion of its significance; (3) possible forms that the component might take, given the limitations imposed by the other components; and (4) statement of the form taken in the Tarascan example, together with a summary of supporting evidence. The fifth section provides a short summary of the design structure.

Decorative problem

Explanation The definition of decorative problem involves two related aspects of decorative style. First, the area to be decorated must be defined; that is, the boundaries of the field or fields of decoration must be set. Second, a basic procedure for building up decoration must be established.

Significance Decorative problem is concerned with the relation between the form of an artifact and its decoration; obviously, the way that the problem is defined is reflected in the appearance of the embellished object as well as in the general appearance of the designs themselves. More important, the nature of the decorative problem narrows the potential range of variation of other components of design. The basic procedure for building up decoration is closely related to the nature of the basic unit and also affects the rules for its use.

Logical possibilities The ways in which the definition of area to be decorated can vary are quite simple; the decorative field or fields can differ in four ways; number, size, shape, and location. In addition, the boundaries of the areas to be decorated may or may not be marked with painted elements.

Basic procedures for building up decoration can be classified in terms of a continuum with two polar types, analytic and synthetic, which are illustrated with the artificial examples that follow. In the analytic type, space is filled with decoration by a process of division and subdivision (Fig. 2.4a–d); as an area is progressively redivided, it

Fig. 2.4. Polar type of basic procedure: analytic.

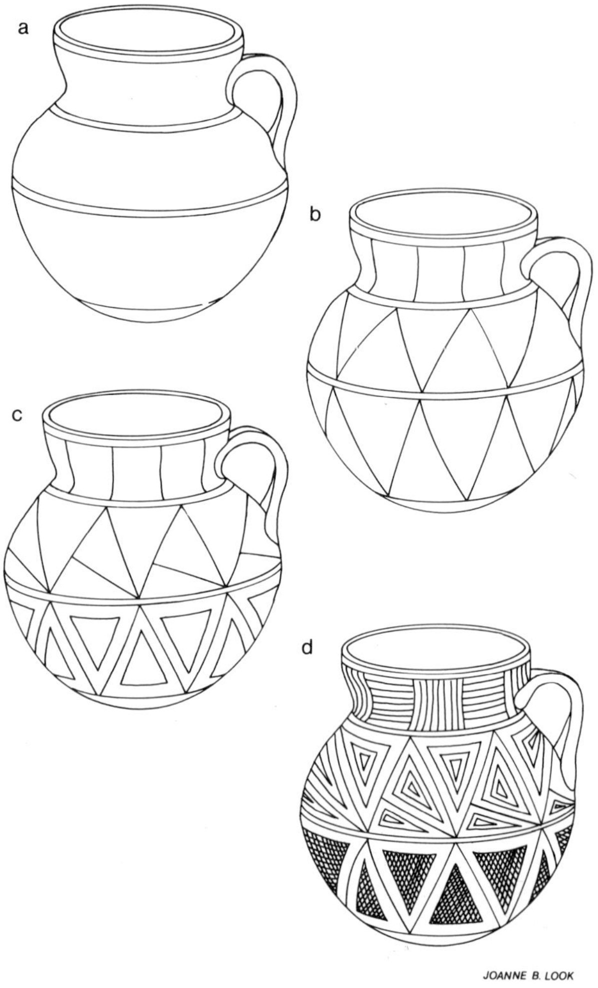

becomes filled with decoration. In the synthetic type, a decoration is built up by the successive addition of elements (Fig. 2.5a–d); as the design grows, the decorative field is filled. Other basic procedures, falling between the two extremes, use varying amounts of the division process and the building process.

The Tarascan case and supporting evidence In San José greenware painting the area that must be decorated includes the outside of the olla, encompassing the bottom of the vessel and the outside of the handle. The boundaries of the area are clearly marked by a different decorative treatment: edges of the decorative field – the vessel's mouth and handle – are marked off with thick bands of white paint.

The basic procedure for creating decoration rests upon two interrelated but distinct systems. The first of these systems is analytic; it consists of a set of spatial divisions; some of these may be further subdivided. The second system is synthetic; it produces an array of designs. These designs, built up of smaller elements, are painted within the divisions.

The normal painting procedure, consisting of three major steps, provides a clear outline of the definition of decorative problem (Fig. 2.6a–d). First, all of the major horizontal spatial divisions are marked although optional divisions and subdivisions may be made later. Second, the areas defined are filled with designs. Third, after all of the spatial divisions have been filled, the mouth and handle are painted, thus marking the edges of the decorative field. Two separate structures become intertwined in the vessel painting process. The first is the system of spatial divisions that presents the painter with a number of choices and optional subdivisions. The second system presents the painter with an array of designs from which he chooses those used to fill each area defined. The edges of the decorative field are dealt with at the end of the painting process. Marking the boundaries of the decorative field is clearly separated from filling it with designs.

The separateness of the two systems of space and design is also illustrated by differences in focus of encoding and decoding strategies. This can be illustrated by summarizing the information given in encoding and decoding the same vessel. In describing encoding, emphasis is placed on the

Fig. 2.5. Polar type of basic procedure: synthetic.

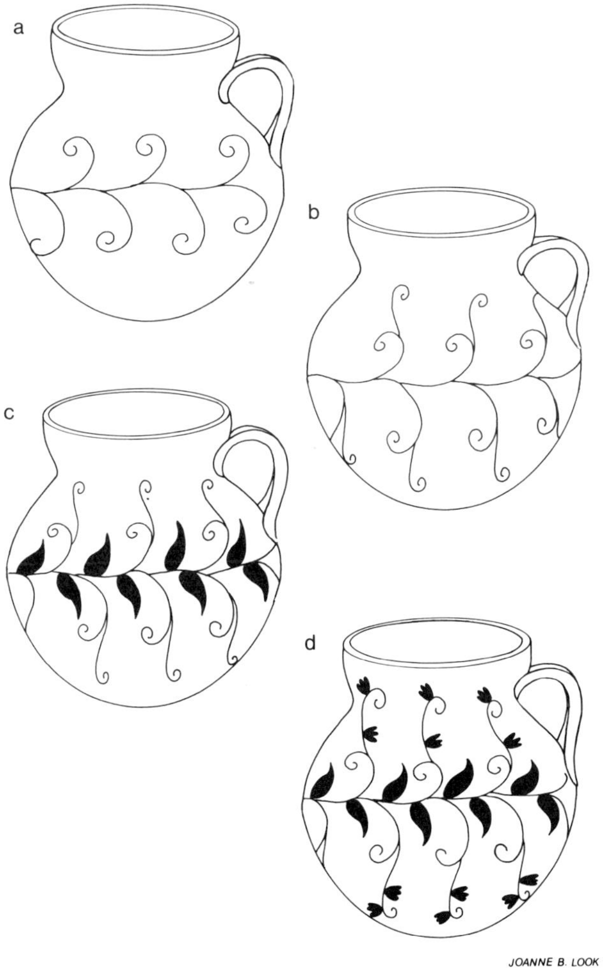

Fig. 2.6. Normal San José painting procedure, illustrating alternation of spatial division and design choice (Field Museum 167407).

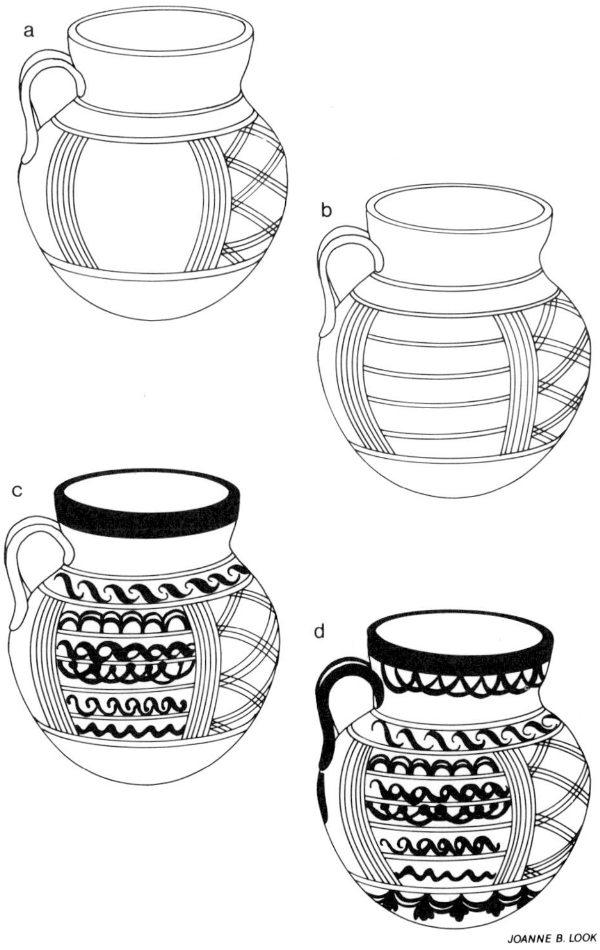

order in which all of the painted elements are placed on the vessel (Fig. 2.7a–e). Complex verbal forms describe the painting of each element or set of similar elements. There are a number of verbal roots, each specifying the kind of painting action and most appropriately used only to describe a narrow range of painted elements. In some cases, information about spatial relationships is provided incidentally by verbal roots. Examples include *wiri-*, 'to go around a horizontal band' and *wana-*, 'to cross' (another painted element). The verbal form used also routinely specifies where on the vessel's surface an element is painted; more precisely, Tarascan has an obligatory grammatical category, a suffix of the verb, which gives the location of the action. Information about what is painted is secondary. In describing decoding, emphasis is placed on what design is painted in each area (Fig. 2.8a–e). Only the designs placed in each area are mentioned; painted elements functioning as boundary markers are ignored. The description proceeds from the top of the vessel to the bottom rather than in the order in which the designs are usually painted.

The conceptual separation of the systems of spatial division and design is further illustrated by two other kinds of verbal data: aesthetic evaluation and triad tests. Aesthetic evaluation provides a framework for judging the designs painted in a specific area. It does not include criteria for evaluating the overall organization of decorated space. Triad tests show how painted decorations are classified. There is a system for judging similarities between designs, but none for similarities between patterns of spatial division. In the first triad (Fig. 2.9a, b, c), vessels were grouped on the basis of the designs painted in the main spatial divisions. In the second triad (Fig. 2.9a, c, d), when the central area did not contain the same designs, there was no basis for grouping. Rather than using spatial division as a criteria, painters said that the vessels could not be grouped.

Basic unit

Explanation The basic unit of design structure is the conceptual category that painters use to organize their knowledge of the system within which they work. Basic units can, thus, be expected to correspond in a regular way with visual complexes representing a particular level of

Fig. 2.7. Vessel encoding strategy (Field Museum 167332).

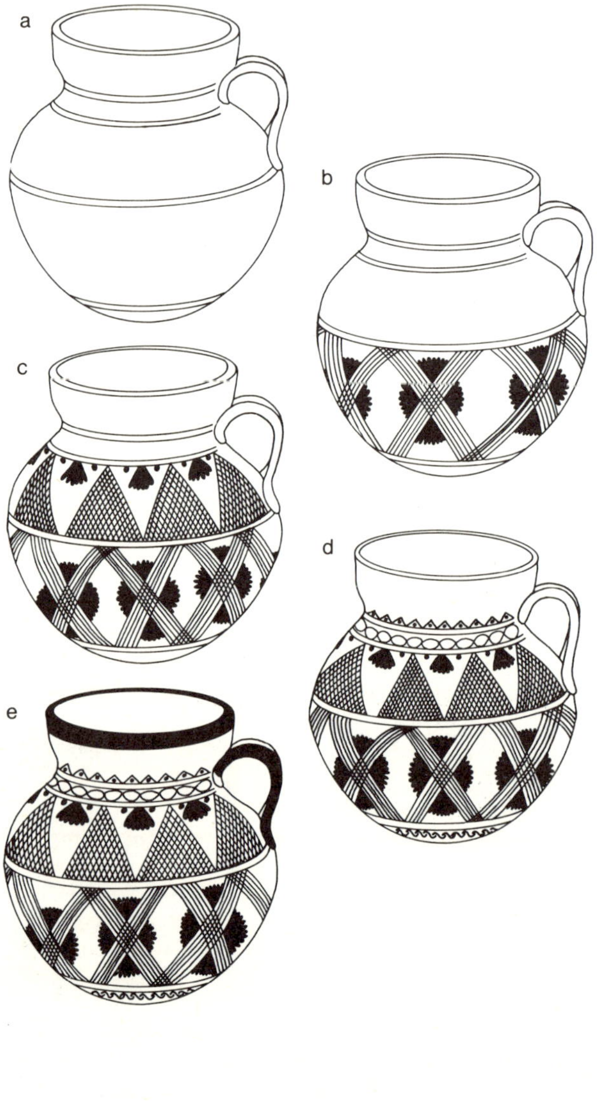

Fig. 2.8. Vessel decoding strategy (Field Museum 167332).

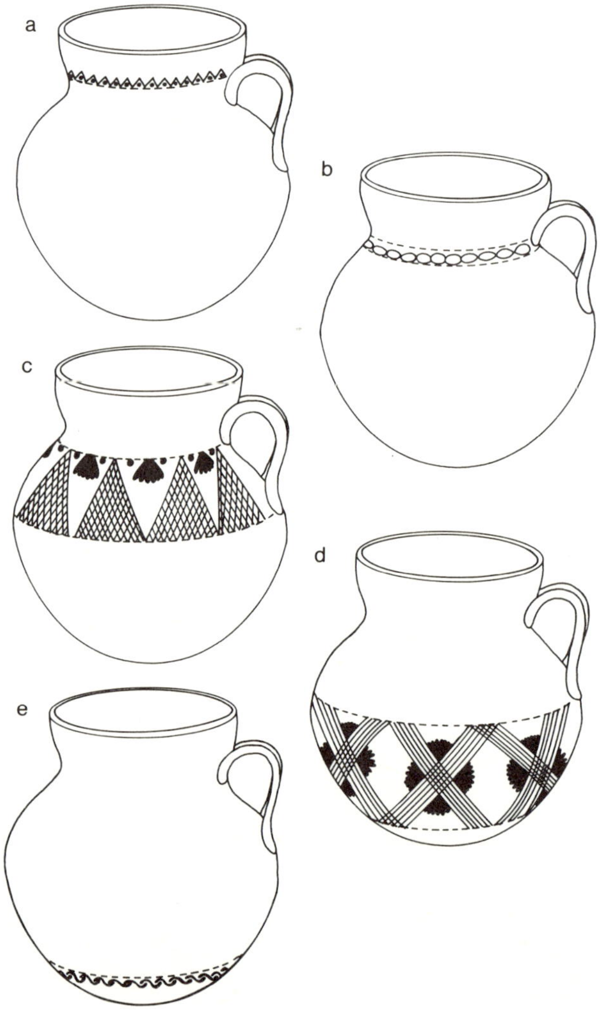

organization in the object's decoration. Obviously, these units may vary in complexity from style to style. Within any particular system, structures of the level of complexity of the basic unit are thought of by painters as basic or primary.

Significance Because information is explicitly organized in terms of basic units, they provide a reference point for the painter's organization of information about other levels of design structure. Visual complexes that correspond to basic units are easily abstracted from their painted contexts – for example, they might be expected to diffuse easily from painter to painter.

Logical possibilities In Tarascan greenware painting the basic conceptual unit might be associated with one of a number of isolable visual complexes. The basic unit could correspond to one of the four levels of organization that may be distinguished in the painted designs used to fill a spatial division: (1) the brushstroke; (2) the design element; (3) the motif; or (4) the design configuration. The simplest level of painted design that may be distinguished is the brushstroke. Design elements (Fig. 2.10a, d, g, j) are always manipulated as a single unit although they may be constructed from one or more brushstrokes (Fig. 2.10d, j). In addition, painters vary in the number of brushstrokes they habitually use to paint the same element. Motifs (Fig. 2.10b, e, h, k) are combinations of design elements that by themselves are not of sufficient complexity to fill a spatial division; they are used as a fixed combination in forming larger arrangements. This level of organization occurs in only a small percentage of San José designs. Configurations are arrangements of sufficient complexity that they might be used by themselves to fill a spatial division (Fig. 2.10c, f, i, l). Alternatively, the basic unit might correspond to some aspect of the system of spatial division.

Tarascan case and supporting evidence In Tarascan pottery painting it is the design configuration that corresponds to the basic unit. The basic nature of the design configuration can be seen by the emphasis, previously discussed, that is placed on it in decoding strategy and aesthetic evaluation, as well as by its importance in the criteria used in responding to triad tests. Also, when arrangements of elements painted in an area are named, the term used identifies the configuration by referring to its essential part.

Fig. 2.9. Triad tests illustrating role of design and spatial division in judgements of similarity (Field Museum 167507, 167509, 167516, and 167525).

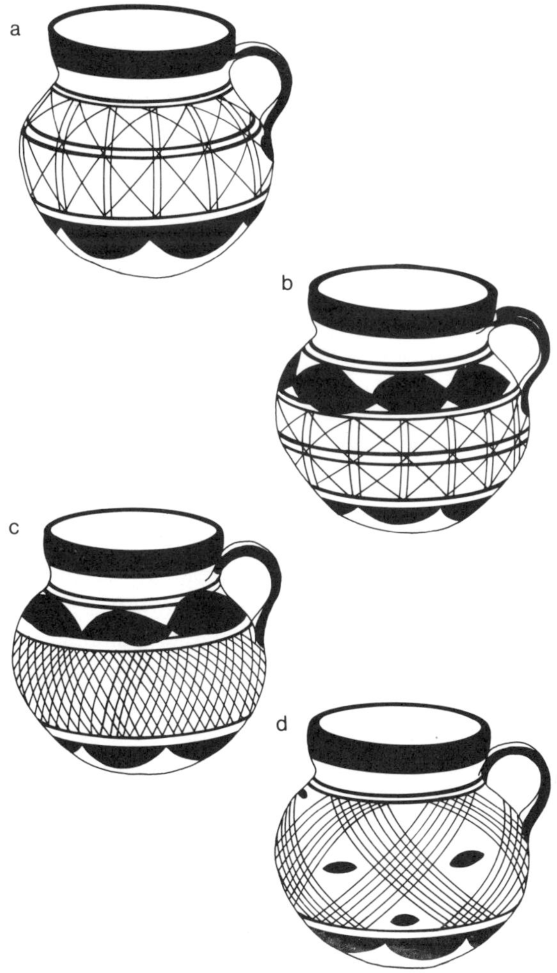

Fig. 2.10. Levels of organization of design.

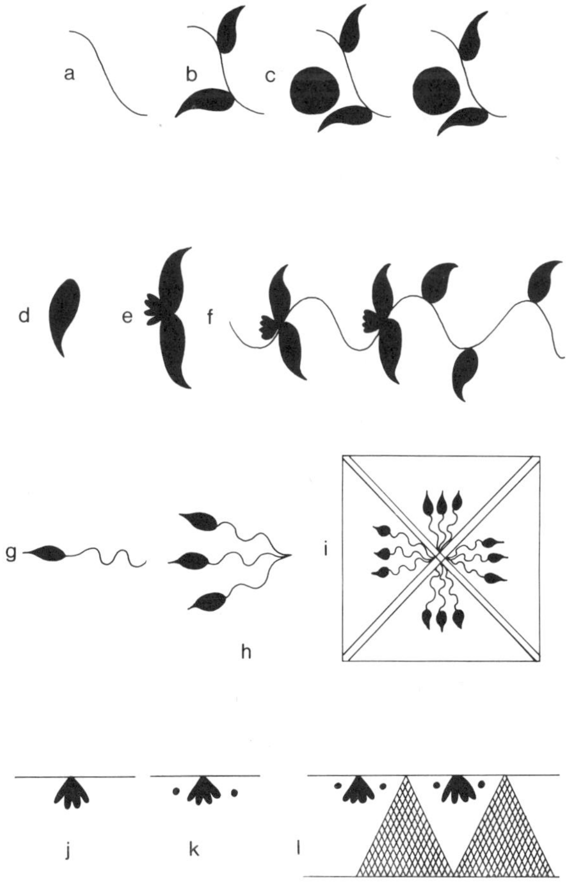

For example, secondary elements are not named. Thus the configuration in Figure 2.11a is named by identifying the essential S-shaped elements, while no reference to the optional leaf-like elements is necessary. Further, it is the configuration itself that is named rather than the elements from which it is constructed. Thus in Figure 2.11b it is the whole arrangement that is named and not the individual lines from which it is constructed.

Configurations can be taken out of context. When painters borrowed from each other, normally it was specific design configurations that were copied. The fact that the designs painted on paper were configurations illustrates their independence as conceptual units from the context in which they are normally used; that is, they are classified and information about them is organized in terms of a cognitive framework that is distinct from the patterns of decoration that appear on painted vessels.

Classification of basic units

Explanation The classification of basic units includes the categories into which they are placed, the relationships between these categories, and their internal organization. In order to understand the system of categories, it is necessary to know what is meant by belonging to the same class, as well as the properties that designs must share if they are to belong to the same class.

Significance Categories used in the classification of basic units are important because the way in which information about design is organized may be related to the ways in which designs are used. The internal organization of classes of units can provide rules for the further elaboration of designs and may be related to style growth; that is, to those processes of style change that lead to a greater complexity of design structure and resultant painted decoration.

Fig. 2.11. Naming of design configurations.

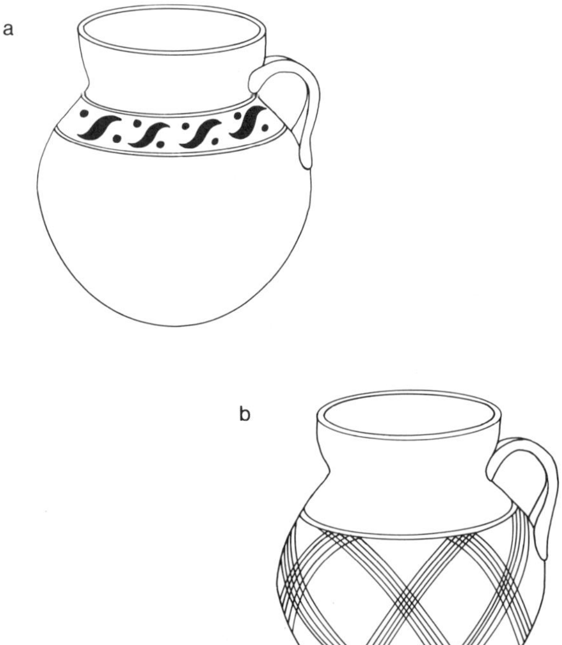

Logical possibilities The basis for class membership may vary. Classification of configurations might possibly be based on the following shared qualities: (1) the shape of the configuration; (2) its complexity; and (3) the units out of which it is constructed. The internal organization of a class of configurations could be based on a similar range of features. Higher level relationships could be based on a similar range of features, including (1) use; (2) shared formal properties (for example, symmetry); or (3) shared internal organization.

Tarascan case and supporting evidence All of the configurations placed in one class have the same basic configuration; that is, they are constructed around the same arrangement of one or more kinds of design element. Configurations within a class vary in the ways in which these basic elements may be elaborated and in the use made of secondary, that is, optional, elements. The internal organization of categories is paradigmatic. There is no explicitly stated higher-level taxonomic organization.

Triad tests provided information about the criteria governing the classification of specific configurations. Responses to triad tests placed vessels together when the designs painted in the central area belonged in the same class. The first triad (Fig. 2.12a, b, c) showed that presence of secondary elements – that is, greater complexity of design – was not a basis for classification. Thus, the vessels shown in Figures 2.12a and 2.12b were grouped together rather than those shown in Figures 2.12b and 2.12c. Variation in the basic configuration was not an important difference. Thus in the second triad (Fig. 2.12c, d, e), vessels were grouped (Fig. 2.12c, d) because they shared main designs even though the basic elements were rendered quite differently. In contrast, the location of the designs did not provide a basis for grouping vessels (Fig. 2.12d, e).

Configurations painted out of context, together with the commentary of the painter, showed how classes were defined and how they varied internally. In examining the examples that follow, it is important to bear in mind that the intent of the painter was not to paint each member of a specific class but to show what constituted a class and to exemplify the ways in which its members might vary – that is, to specify dimensions of variation.

In the first two examples, secondary elements can be used in only one position. The configurations can, however, vary in two other ways: form of primary element and secondary element use. In configurations built around hooks (Fig. 2.13a–f) the basic elements varied in: (1) thickness,

(2) hookedness, (3) size, and (4) doubleness. Two kinds of variation are associated with secondary element use: (1) presence or absence of secondary elements, and (2) kind of secondary element used. The configurations built around leaf-like elements (Fig. 2.13g–i) vary in: (1) the fatness of the thick part of the element; (2) the size of the entire element; and (3) the mode of conjunction of elements. In addition, secondary elements can vary in kind and in the places in which they are attached.

In the next pair of examples (Fig. 2.13j–l and Fig. 2.14a–d) the primary elements do not vary in form. Secondary elements are used in two positions. A wider range of secondary elements can be used in the interstitial areas between primary elements than inside them.

The final examples involve two configuration classes (Fig. 2.14e–g and Fig. 2.14h–k) that are treated in the same way. The primary elements cannot be left empty but must be filled in some way. Two kinds of fill are illustrated: (1) smaller copies of the primary element are placed inside it; or (2) several varieties of cross-hatching are used. Secondary elements are optional in the angle formed by the conjunction of primary elements. Alternatively, a more complicated motif is attached to the opposite boundary of the spatial division.

Rules for the use of basic units

Explanation Rules governing the use of basic units are of two kinds. The first type of rule specifies the framework within which the basic units are to be used. These rules are related to the definition of decorative problem, as their form

Fig. 2.12. Triad tests illustrating basis for classification of configurations (Field Museum 167517, 167506, 167518, 167510, and 167508).

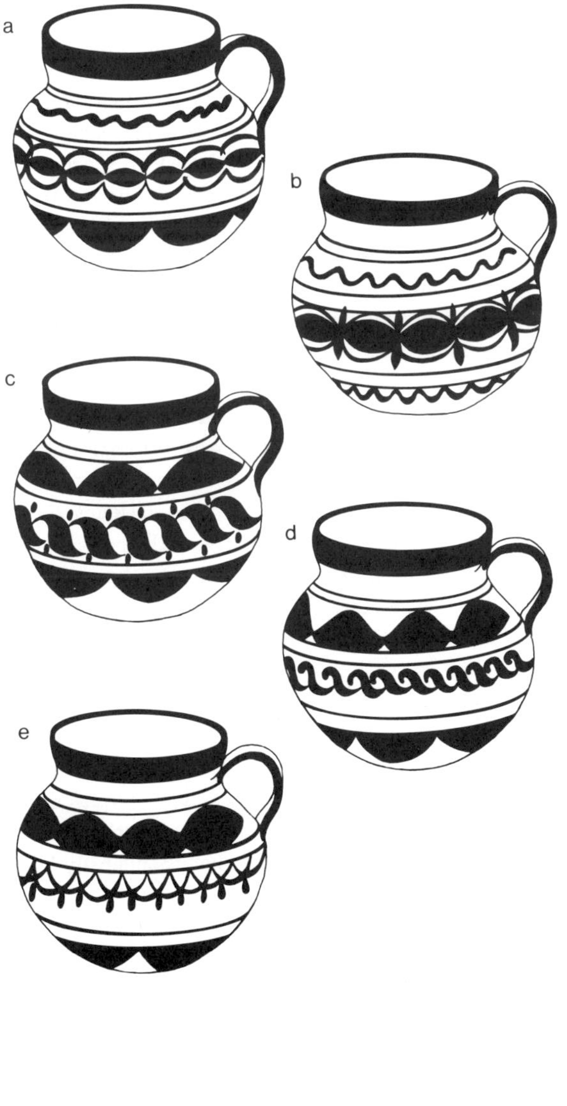

Fig. 2.13. Configuration classes.

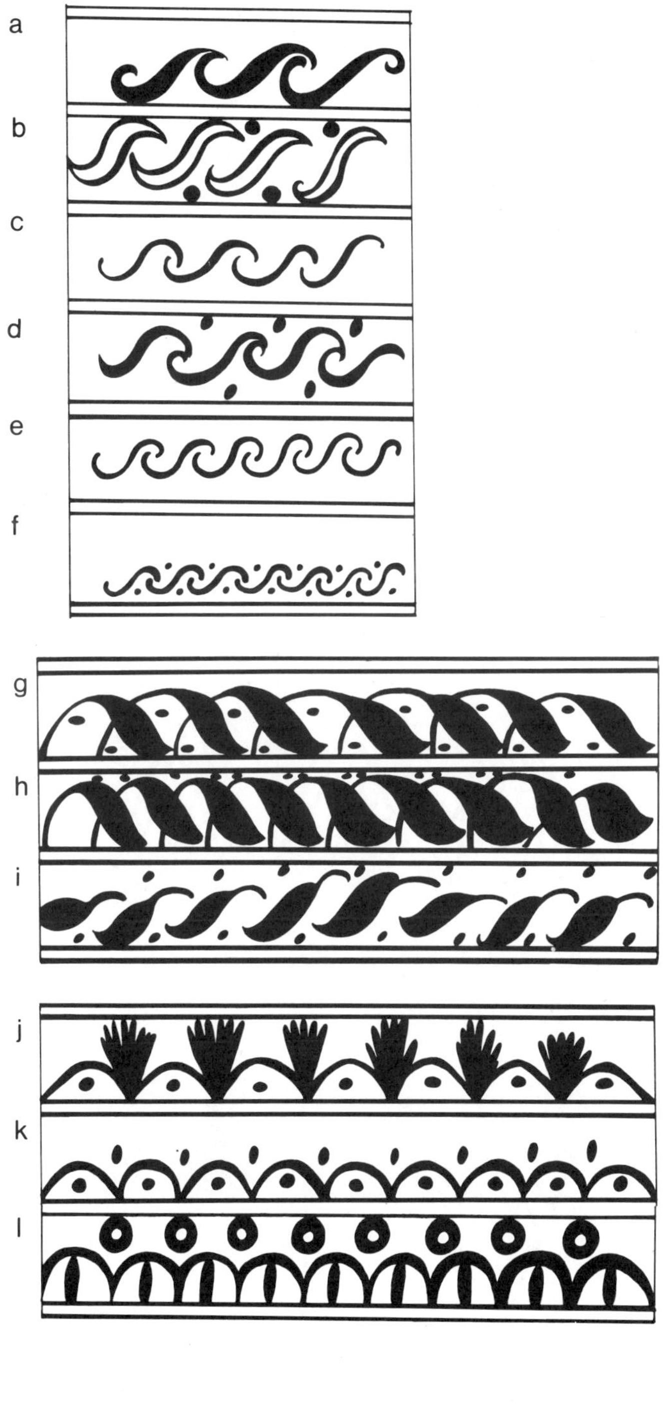

is partially dependent upon the basic procedure used for building up decoration. The second type of rule governs the occurrence of basic units.

Significance These rules involve knowledge about how to use designs rather than knowledge about the designs themselves. They present two sources of stylistic variation: differences in framework and in design choice.

Fig. 2.14. Configuration classes.

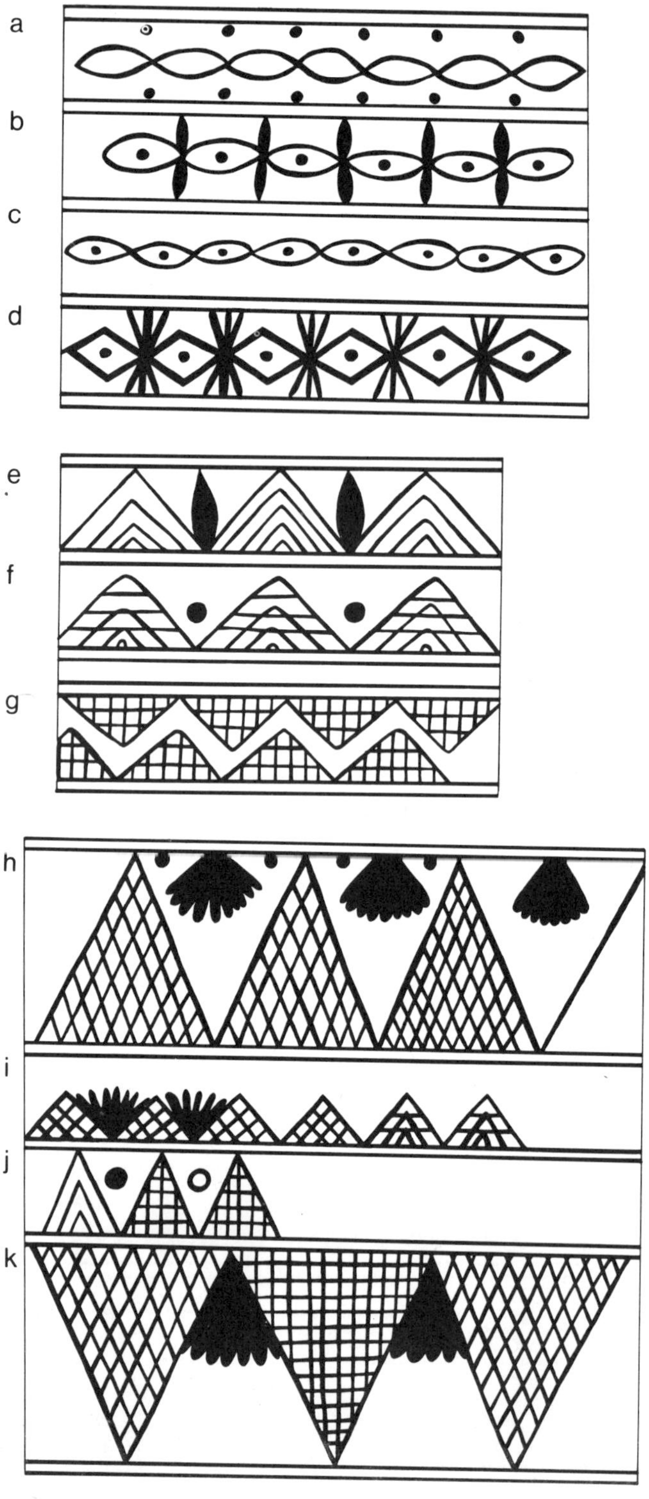

Logical possibilities As the definition of decorative problem implies, in San José pottery painting it is the system of spatial divisions that provide the framework within which design configurations are used. Given this framework, two analytical problems remain. First, the cognitive structure underlying the painted subdivisions must be determined. For example, the organization of space observed might be based on part–whole relations or on a hierarchically organized pattern of subdivision; it is also possible that some combination of these two structures might occur. Second, patterns of subdivisions should be worked out. The various areas may be elaborated equally or unequally through subdivision. Required, alternate, and optional subdivisions should be distinguished and their interrelationships should be worked out.

Rules governing the occurrence of configurations may vary in their explicitness, in how systematic they are, and in the properties of designs or areas on which they are based.

Tarascan case and supporting evidence The framework within which designs are used is provided by the system of spatial divisions. While the divisions of the unpainted vessel provide a basis for this system, it has been greatly elaborated, and a hierarchical organization has been imposed upon it. The result is a multi-level system of part–whole relations: lower level units stand in a part–whole relationship to higher level units (Fig. 2.15). Variation in the use of space is provided by the existence of optional horizontal divisions as well as by two completely optional levels of subdivisions of the central area. The first level can be subdivided in two ways: with perpendicular or slanted boundaries. The second level exhibits three alternative patterns of subdivision: horizontal, vertical, and diagonal. As indicated in the diagram, the number of partitions used in both levels is variable.

There are no explicit rules governing the occurrence of configurations within spatial divisions. Although individual configurations are used in a definite set of contexts, actual patterns of use do not reveal clearcut general rules.

The cognitive structure underlying the painted spatial divisions can be inferred from: (1) the named parts of the unpainted vessel; (2) the painting process and painters' statements about it; (3) the patterns of spatial division observed on completed vessels; and (4) information given about location and spatial relations in descriptions of painted designs. The outside surface of an unadorned vessel (Fig. 2.16a) is subdivided into five named, structurally equivalent parts: four horizontal divisions (Fig. 2.16b–e) plus the handle (Fig. 2.16f). In turn, two of these areas, the neck and bottom of the vessel (Fig. 2.16c, e) have named subdivisions (Fig. 2.16g, h, i, j).

Although there are additional divisions and some variation in exact location, the painted boundaries largely conform to the system of part–whole relations imposed on the bare surface. However, a significantly different hierarchical organization is imposed on the system of part–whole relations by the first painted division. This boundary marker divides the vessel into edge (Fig. 2.16k) and interior (Fig. 2.16l), which are subsequently treated as separate units. Significantly, this boundary is the most elaborated as well as the most variable. Its location can vary from the narrowest part of the neck to a point near the upper attachment of the handle, although the former location is the most common. It can also be painted in a greater number of ways than the other boundaries.

Study of painted vessels and painting sequences indicates the following organization of the interior portion of the vessel's surface. One division is required to define the circular bottom of the vessel (Fig. 2.16q). When the edge–interior boundary is painted near the upper limit of its range, a narrow band (Fig. 2.16m) is also required on the upper neck; its lower boundary falls roughly at the narrowest part of the neck. Optional but equivalent divisions can produce the following narrow bands: (1) the lower neck (Fig. 2.16n); and (2) the lower band (Fig. 2.16p). The latter two divisions have the effect of narrowing the wider band at the vessel's middle. Thus, the middle (Fig. 2.16o) may be residually defined as the area remaining after adjacent optional subdivisions are marked off. Spatial terms associated with boundary markers reflect this relationship. The bottom of the vessel may be optionally divided into bottom band (Fig. 2.16r) and base (Fig. 2.16s).

The edge of the vessel (Fig. 2.16k) has two main parts: the rim (Fig. 2.16u) and the handle (Fig. 2.16t). The rim is further divided into the mouth (Fig. 2.16v), which is painted white, and the band adjacent to it (Fig. 2.16w), which may be optionally decorated with a design near to or dependent from the white border.

Visual evidence and spatial terms used in describing painted decoration are the basis for analysing the first subdivisions of the vessel's middle as a level separate from the system of horizontal divisions. Painting sequence clearly indicates that the second level of subdivision represents a further, optional partitioning of the first level of subdivisions rather than a more complex, alternative variation of the first level of subdivision.

Rules governing the use of designs are not explicitly stated and may not operate in a rigidly systematic way. For example, while definite patterns of use can be seen from examining the occurrence of a few configurations, there is not always a single pattern of use associated with all members of a configuration class.

The principles governing configuration occurrence are of a more general and flexible nature. Aesthetic criteria perform this function by providing negative rules. As has been described, the primary application of aesthetic terms is at the level of individual spatial divisions; thus they deal with the question of whether a particular design was appropriate for the area in which it appears. The treatment of each area is judged in terms of three dimensions: (1) fineness–broadness of painted designs; (2) coveredness–bareness of the area; and (3) well-paintedness–badly paintedness of decoration. The latter is a general dimension, which incorporates the first two

Fig. 2.15. System of spatial divisions (optional divisions are shown in parentheses).

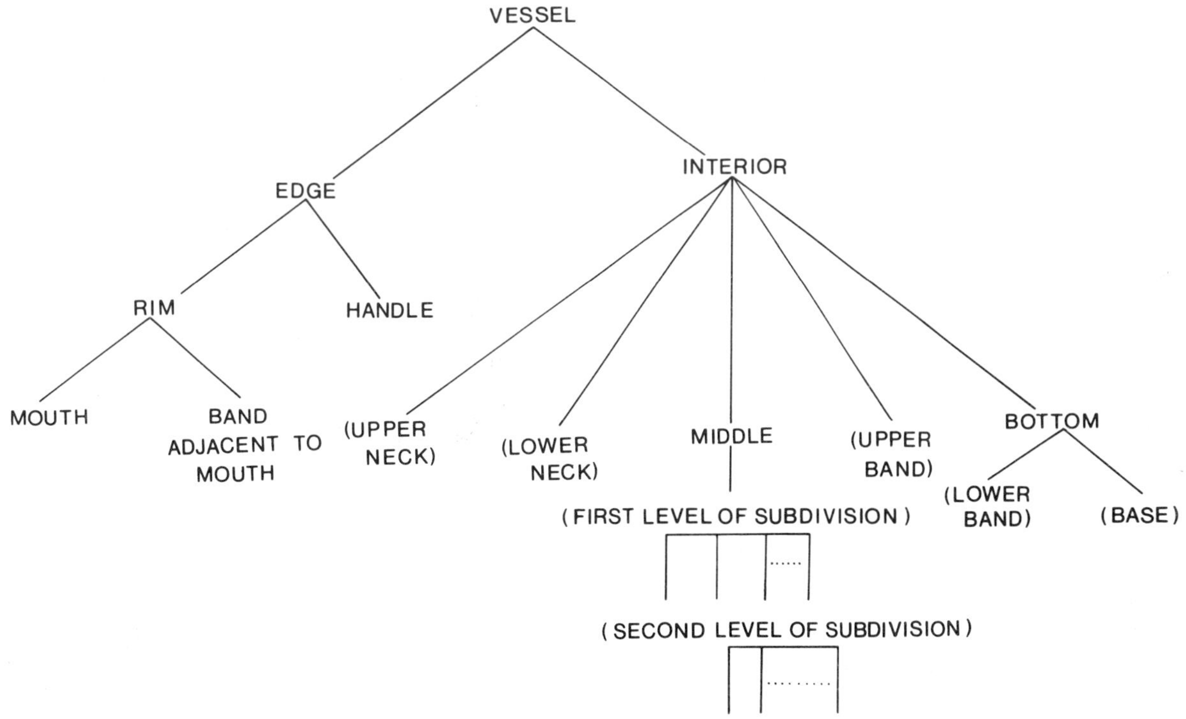

more specific dimensions in addition to other factors.

Let us now turn to some specific applications of these values. Since designs that meet all aesthetic requirements are finely painted and fill the area involved, cross-hatching is highly valued (Fig. 2.17a). When designs leave too much bare space within an area, they are faulted for being bare (Fig. 2.17b). Designs which do not totally fit within an area are criticized, as they lack one of the components of well-paintedness. Frequently, such designs are painted hastily with a large brush and are, thus, too broad (Fig. 2.17c). Interestingly, designs which are carefully painted but deliberately superimposed one on another are also interpreted as overlapping and are criticized (Fig. 2.17d).

Summary of San José design structure

The structure of pottery painting, as it is practised in San José, can now be summarized in terms of its components. The decorative problem requires that a clearly demarcated and continuous area on the outside of the vessel be decorated. This is accomplished through a procedure that draws upon a hierarchy of spatial divisions and a system of design configurations. The basic unit in terms of which design structure is organized is the configuration, which may be defined as that arrangement of painted elements that is of sufficient complexity to fill a spatial division. The explicit classification of design configurations is shallow, consisting of a series of relatively small, narrowly defined classes. Rules for the use of configurations are based on a framework of spatial divisions, which is essentially a multi-level hierarchy of part–whole relations. While there are no explicit rules governing the occurrence of configurations in a spatial division, aesthetic criteria do provide negative rules that govern the relationship between specific configurations and the areas in which they are placed.

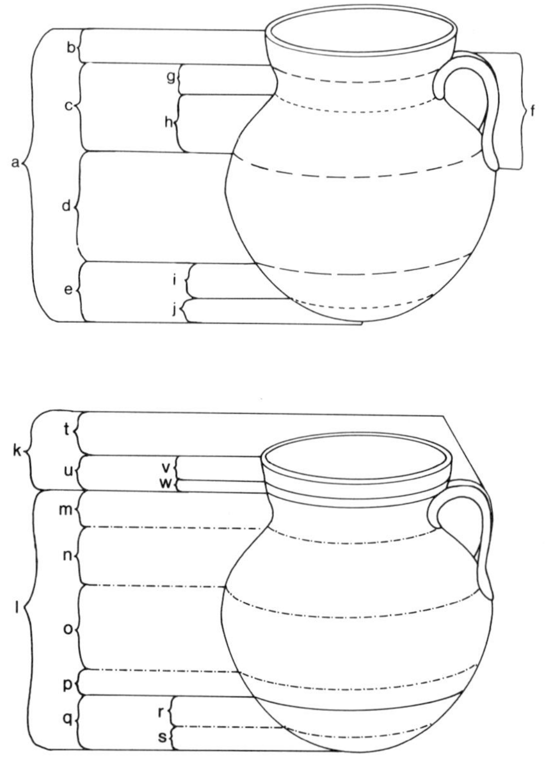

Fig. 2.16. Named vessel parts and structure imposed by boundary markers (boundaries of vessel parts – – –; boundaries of subdivisions of vessel parts -----; required painted boundaries ——; optional painted boundaries · – · –).

Conclusions

A method for determining the design structure associated with graphic style has been presented in terms of the analysis of San José greenware painting. A typology of categories of ethnographic data was offered and the use of each kind of evidence was explained.

The analysis rested upon the assumption that all decorative styles must offer a solution to the same formal problems and have the same set of components. These components were then seen to be ranked: that is, when they were placed in the proper order, the form of one component limited the range of variation of those that followed it in the

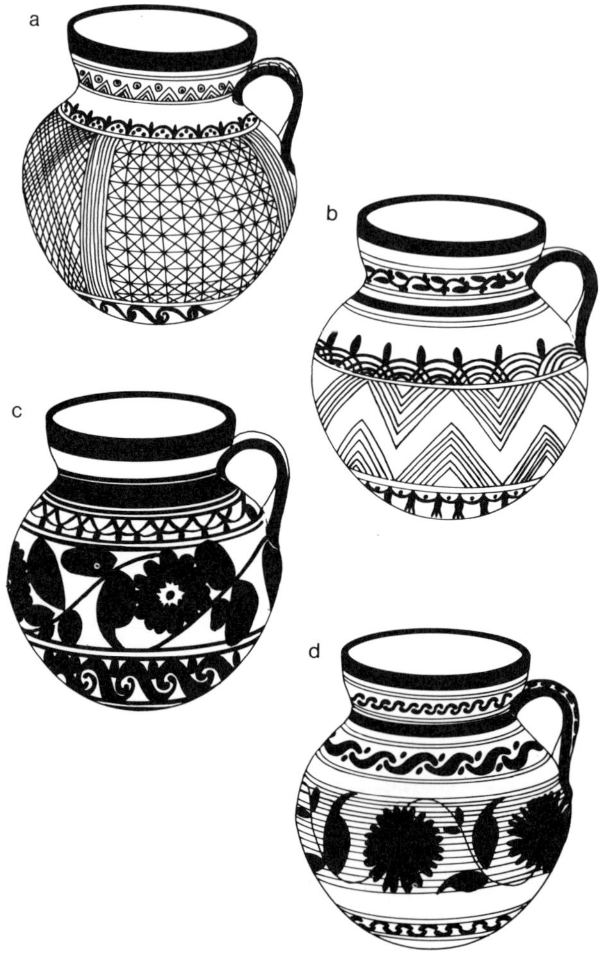

Fig. 2.17. Illustrations of application of aesthetic values (Field Museum 167318, 167311, 167395, and 167308).

ranking. Thus, a consideration of all of the possibilities for each component in turn could be used to produce a general typology of decorative styles, which could then serve as a basis for further specific analyses.

Some general points about the system of knowledge associated with material culture are illustrated by the Tarascan case. Both verbal and visual data about the style were essential to the analysis. The two kinds of information were complementary. On the one hand, verbalizations were narrowly focused and fragmentary, requiring concrete visual referents for their interpretation. On the other hand, inferences of design structure based on visual evidence alone were non-unique: that is, because at times visual evidence lent itself to several interpretations, verbal information was required to dispel ambiguity. This suggests that the learning and maintenance of a system of design as well as of other important segments of material culture must rest not only upon the information obviously gained from observations of patterned behaviour and the resultant objects, but also upon verbal statements, however sparse, which serve to orient the learner toward one of a number of the alternate rules that might be inferred from observation.

The analysis of Tarascan pottery painting presented was not intended as a formal account; nor are the basic units and rules governing their use stated in sufficient detail. Determining the components of design structure is, however, an essential preliminary to producing an account that is useful for further analysis of the behaviour of the painting style outlined as well as that of other active systems of design. Problems that can be fruitfully dealt with using this framework include variation within a style, diffusion within the community of artists of features abstracted from subvariants of the style, and creation of new content and rules within an existing style. A grammar of design that seeks to account for only the form of the artifacts themselves does not constitute an adequate framework unless the style consists of little more than a set of mechanically repeated types. It must be assumed that a shared cognitive structure, which cannot be fully inferred from the material objects themselves, is necessary to maintain stylistic unity. In the Tarascan case, this common design structure supports a high degree of stylistic homogeneity while providing for productivity and regular style growth.

Notes

1 Research on which this paper is based was supported by a Public Health Service predoctoral fellowship (SF 1–MH–32, 844–02) and a Wenner-Gren museum research fellowship at the Field Museum of Natural History in Chicago. The paper was originally read before the Anthropological Society of Washington, D.C., in February 1973 and was revised several times in the next few years. Because it did not prove possible to publish the volume for which the paper was written, it languished. I am grateful to Bill Sturtevant for releasing it and to Dorothy Washburn for giving it a home. While some changes and additions have been made recently, the paper represents my major concerns at the time it was written. It focuses on the internal organization of the style. Space did not permit the expansion of the paper to deal also in sufficient detail with broader questions concerning the formal similarities between natural human language and highly patterned decorative styles. Nor was it possible to lay out the multiple ways in which Tarascan design structure connects painted forms to broadly pervasive systems of culturally specific meaning. I hope that the reader will understand that these must remain to be dealt with in subsequent papers.

I am indebted to Maxine Kleindienst, Maude S. Wahlmann, Donald Collier and John Pfeiffer for reading the paper in manuscript and for providing many helpful comments, and to Phyllis Chock for her comments on aesthetic evaluation. I would particularly express my gratitude to Raymond Fogelson for his support and detailed comments on the paper, to Paul Friedrich for his encouragement and extensive criticism of the paper at several stages in its development, and to William Sturtevant for his helpfulness and many useful comments. I am grateful to Michael Smogor for making the slides used to illustrate my lecture and to Bonnie B. DeZur and Lee-Ann Konrad for typing and editing the manuscript. The vessels illustrated were collected by the author and are in the permanent collections of the Field Museum, which kindly provided the photographs by Ron Testa. I wish to thank Joanne Look for the thoughtfulness with which she approached the task of illustrating the paper and Sam Grove for his invaluable advice to us about the illustrations. Finally, I would like to thank those who contributed to the revision of my paper through their interesting questions and comments after my talk.

2 I am indebted to Dell Hymes for the ideas developed in this and the following section, which grew out of his oral comments on the symposium, Generative Analysis of Art: Iconics, presented at the 68th meeting of the American Anthropological Association (New Orleans, 1969).

3 For purposes of comparison, at the time fieldwork was carried out, the average daily wage for agricultural labour in San José and nearby towns ranged between $10.00 and $12.00 (Mexican currency).

4 The distinction between major and minor painter is an arbitrary one made by the ethnographer. Major painters were those who worked at their craft with some regularity during the period of fieldwork; specifically, they worked on a kiln-load of greenware three or more times during a year. The reason for this cut-off point is simple: many households other than those regularly producing greenware turn to its production twice a year, as it is traditional for people from San José to sell greenware at two fiestas in the annual cycle. Thus, most of the minor painters were those who helped make greenware for these ritual and social occasions or similarly for more distant fiestas or holiday celebrations which they attended because of family ties.

References

Arnold, Dean E., 1971. Ethnomineralogy of Ticul, Yucatan potters: etics and emics. *American Antiquity* 36 (1): 20–40.

Boas, Franz, 1955. *Primitive Art.* Dover Publications Inc., New York (first published 1927).

Bunzel, Ruth L., 1926. *The Pueblo Potter: a study of creative imagination in primitive art.* Columbia University Press, New York.

Conklin, Harold C., 1953. Buhzd pottery. *University of Manila Journal of East Asiatic Studies* 3 (1): 1–12.

DeBoer, Warren R., 1975. The ontogeny of Shipibo art: variations on a cross. Paper presented at the 74th Annual Meeting of the American Anthropological Association, 1975, San Francisco.

Faris, James C., 1972. *Nuba Personal Art.* University of Toronto Press, Toronto.

Foster, George M., 1948. Some implications of modern Mexico mold-made pottery. *Southwestern Journal of Anthropology* 4: 356–70.

1967. *Tzintzuntzan: Mexican Peasants in a Changing World.* Little, Brown & Co., Boston.

Friedrich, Paul, 1970. Shape in grammar. *Language* 46 (2) (1): 379–407.

1971. *The Tarascan Suffixes of Locative Space: Meaning and Morphotactics.* Language Science Monographs No. 9. Indiana University Press, Bloomington and Mouton, The Hague.

Green, Roger C., 1979. Early Lapita art from Polynesia and Island Melanesia: continuities on ceramic, barkcloth, and tattoo decorations. In *Exploring the Visual Art of Oceania*, edited by Sidney M. Mead. The University Press of Hawaii, Honolulu.

Holm, Bill, 1965. *Northwest Coast Indian art: an analysis of form.* University of Washington Press, Seattle.

Hymes, Dell, 1970. Linguistic models in archeology. In *Archeologie et calculateurs*, edited by V.C. Gardin *et al.* Editions du Centre National de la Recherche Scientifique, Paris.

Kaplan, Flora S., 1976. Cognition and style, an analysis based on a Mexican pottery tradition. Unpublished Ph.D. dissertation, Anthropology Department, City University of New York.

Mead, S.M., Lawrence Birks, Helen Birks and Elizabeth Shaw, 1975. *The Lapita Pottery Style of Fiji and its Associations.* The Polynesian Society, Wellington.

Muller, Jon, 1966. An experimental theory of stylistic analysis. Unpublished Ph.D. dissertation, Harvard University.

1979. Structural studies of art styles. In *The Visual Arts. Plastic and Graphic*, edited by Justine Cordwell, pp. 138–211. Mouton, The Hague.

Pozas, Ricardo, 1949. La Alfareria de Patamban. *Anales del Instituto National de Anthropologia e Historia* 3: 115–46.

Roe, Peter G., 1980. Art and residence among the Shipibo Indians of Peru: a study in microacculturation. *American Anthropologist* 82 (1): 42–71.

Rowe, John H., 1962. *Chavin Art: An Inquiry into its Form and Meaning.* University Publishers, Inc., New York.

Shepard, Anna O., 1956. Ceramics for the archeologist. *Carnegie Institution of Washington Publication* 609.

Sturtevant, William C., 1964. Studies in ethnoscience. In *Trans-cultural Studies in Cognition*, edited by A.K. Romney and R.C. D'Andrade. *American Anthropologist* 66 (3, part 2): 99–113.

Van Esterik, Penelope, 1981. *Cognition and Design Production in Ban Chiang Painted Pottery.* Papers in International Studies. Southeast Asia Series No. 58. Ohio University, Athens.

West, Robert C., 1948. Cultural geography of the modern Tarascan area. *Smithsonian Institution Institute of Social Anthropology Papers* 7. Washington, D.C.

Chapter 3

Recent Shipibo–Conibo ceramics and their implications for archaeological interpretation

Donald W. Lathrap

Introduction

This paper is an outgrowth of and a departure from one which I read at the 1969 meetings of the Society for American Archaeology in Milwaukee. At that time I had a conceptual framework which would encompass some but not all of my data. Since that time I have enlarged and altered that framework so that it will now, I think, account for the richness of the data which I have collected. By now, of course, my data are by no means adequate as a check on the validity of the new set of premises. The assumptions I was attempting to validate through my fieldwork were not so much either supported or negated by a confrontation with real data; rather they seemed to dissolve and become something quite different.

During the summer, autumn, and winter of 1967–8, I was engaged in studying present day Shipibo–Conibo pottery-making. Two diverse kinds of problems motivated the observations recorded. On the one hand I was interested in the Shipibo–Conibo's conceptualization of the domain of pottery and in comparing their scheme with my own views on the appropriate analysis of ceramic collections derived from archaeological excavations. On the other hand I was interested in checking the validity of certain assumptions which formed the basis of the early developments of that intellectual movement which has come to be known so resoundingly as the 'New Archaeology'. It was this second set of goals which largely determined the kinds of data which I collected and the extent and nature of my sample.

There were a number of reasons which led me to select the Shipibo–Conibo as the group most appropriate for study. I have a familiarity with the group extending back to initial contacts in March 1956. The pottery they are currently manufacturing forms the last unit in the long and complex ceramic sequence which my students and I have established for the flood plain of the Central Ucayali Basin of eastern Peru. This sequence has at the very least twelve markedly different chronological units and spans a time period of over 4,000 years. Thus we have excellent developmental perspective.

The Shipibo–Conibo ceramic tradition remains vigorous, with much pottery still being manufactured for use within the household. Though production for the tourist trade is starting to affect ceramic output in certain villages with maximum exposure to visitors, the pottery made for the Indians' own use remains remarkably free of decorative motifs or organizational principles which could be derived from the Western industrial tradition; our familiarity with the archaeological background leaves us in an excellent position to detect such influence. Finally, I have had extended opportunity to observe Shipibo pottery in use, both on a day-to-day basis and in ritual contexts.

During 1956 I was privileged to attend the last full-blown girls' puberty ceremony in the vicinity of Yarinacocha, and to photograph the distribution of manioc beer by the host families. On such sacred occasions the sharply conceptualized shape categories of Shipibo–Conibo pottery function in ritual performances as formalized as the Japanese tea ceremony.

What might be designated as the Deetz–Longacre hypothesis (see Brose 1970: 53–9) was worked out by Deetz as early as 1958, with reference to some archaeological collections of Arikara ceramics. His formulations were presented publically in Philadelphia at the 1961 American Anthropological Association meetings. Longacre (1964) applied similar ideas to archaeological pottery from the Southwest. To put the case most baldly, it is argued that pottery produced by the members of a matrilocal extended family should show very little stylistic variation since it is produced by potters who were either taught by the same potter or by closely related potters who were taught by the same potter one generation earlier. This situation should contrast strongly to that in patrilocal extended families where the women will come from a range of outside families and will have been taught by several unrelated potters. Deetz (1965) and Longacre (1964) have suggested that the latter case would lead to a wide range of stylistic variability and no discernible patterning. Brose (1970), in what is the most elaborate and subtle application of this kind of reasoning, suggests that the patrilocal situation may in some cases also result in a recognizable patterning. I was not initially hostile to the hypothesis, and in fact frequently discussed these ideas with Deetz during the period 1957–9 while he was working up the Arikara material. I decided that the Shipibo–Conibo offered the perfect ethnographic setting for testing the hypothesis and it is this fieldwork which has brought me to my present state of scepticism.

Before examining the Shipibo–Conibo data which might bear on the assumptions of Deetz, Longacre, and Brose, it might be well to look at these assumptions more carefully in terms of the total epistemology which they imply.

A critical examination of the Deetz–Longacre hypothesis should not be taken as a general attack on the 'New Archaeology'. One must observe that the key premises and specific research strategies which are being labelled the New Archaeology have changed rather rapidly over the last decade and that thorough and systematic testing of these premises and strategies has not kept pace with the speed at which new premises and strategies are being generated. Furthermore, as Flannery (1973) has pointed out, at least two markedly divergent and potentially antagonistic orthodoxies are currently housed under the blanket term 'New Archaeology'.

I am largely in agreement with the position and tone of the paper by Lewis Binford in the volume *Man the Hunter*. The area of agreement is best expressed in a statement of Binford's which could be taken as a justification for my study of Shipibo–Conibo ceramics. 'However, among contemporary groups, or groups whose residence patterns are known through documents, the proposition may be stated as a testable hypothesis. This illustrates one of the functions of ethnographic data in archeological reasoning. These data may be used for testing hypotheses for which information on one or more relevant variables is not obtainable through archeology' (Binford 1968: 270). I also offer the heartiest endorsement to a more general statement of Binford's: 'Archeologists have worked too long without the benefits of the understandings of ethnology as to the operation of sociocultural systems' (1968: 271).

I disagree, however, with Binford's unqualified reiteration of the Deetz–Longacre hypothesis and his total endorsement of their position: 'We can today state within definable confidence limits the post-marital residence patterns of prehistoric communities' (1968: 270). I also disagree with two of the three assumptions or propositions which Binford feels are true and which by their verity permit him to deduce the model which underlies the foregoing assertion. These assumptions or propositions are: 'Homogeneity of cultural expression within a group varies directly with the homogeneity of the group's composition', and 'Many formal characteristics of pottery are stylistic and tend to vary with tradition rather than utilitarian or mechanical factors' (1968: 270).

My objections to the second statement are not that it is incorrect but that it needs to be both elaborated and made more specific. It is little more than a tautology to state that style varies with tradition rather than functional or mechanical factors, unless one makes some prior assumptions as to the function of style.

The late Robert Redfield has been a highly influential anthropologist and nowhere has his influence been as strong as at the University of Chicago with which he was so long associated. During its 'Formative Stage' the New Archaeology had many of its most vociferous theorists at the University of Chicago. I think there is a relationship between these two facts. One can detect a strong Redfieldian influence on much of the thinking of New Archaeologists. Redfield was fairly consistent in playing down the degree of individualization in 'primitive societies'. He stresses the lower level of personality differentiation and weight of custom. He suggests that much, perhaps most, of what the primitive artist considers artistic creation is in fact mere copying which tends to preserve the tradition without appreciable change (1957: 15). The Redfieldian primitive or peasant functions very well within the hypothetical world created by the New Archaeologists; in fact, just such a primitive is necessary to make that world go round. Whether such a Redfieldian primitive or peasant ever existed in the flesh is a question which has already given rise to a considerable body of anthropological literature (Lewis 1970). I wish to make no additions to that literature beyond the simple observation that I met no Redfieldian types among the Shipibo–Conibo.

A different view on the degree of creativity involved in

the artistic production of so-called primitive peoples is to be found in the writings of Franz Boas, particularly in *Primitive Art* (1927). Boas stressed the importance of playing with techniques and of conscious manipulation of the traditional conceptual units which every culture offers its adherents. Once one recognizes the possibility of play and of conscious attempts at progressive elaboration one also introduces the certainty that successive artistic productions of the same individual will change progressively over the individual artist's creative lifespan. One also introduces the certainty that particularly satisfying solutions of the aesthetic problems which are basic to a particular art style will be appreciated by other artists in the same tradition who are working on the same problems. Such solutions are likely to pass rapidly through all available communication networks. Art thus serves as a form of communication. I have found Bateson's article on art style the most satisfactory discussion of what is being communicated by artistic production within a particular art style (1972: 137).

It is true that one learns a style so that one can be identified as a proper member of one's own group and a nonmember of other ethnic groups of the same general level of inclusiveness. One also learns a style so that one can be identified as an individual different from all other individuals in one's own group. One does not learn a style so that one can ultimately produce exact copies of the stylistic productions of one's teacher (whether the teacher be mother, mother-in-law, grandmother, etc.). One learns a style so that one can produce unique, grammatically correct performances which are within the limits of a particular stylistic tradition. In all groups with styles of a reasonable degree of complexity both group labelling and individual expression must be major functions of stylistic variation. I could cite a large body of observations that support the conclusion that the Shipibo–Conibo potters behave like Boasian artists and particularists rather than like Redfieldian xerox machines.

Binford's proposition concerning group homogeneity also needs very careful examination, even though initially it sounds plausible. Should it prove that homogeneity of cultural expression within a group varies directly with homogeneity of the group's composition and recruitment, then one must accept as a corollary that there can be absolutely no interaction among the members of the group once it is formed – at least no interaction and observation which would lead the individuals to modify their artistic production. The people in a world governed by that proposition would behave like a deck of IBM cards each punched by its teacher at an early age for a limited amount of stylistic variation and each continuing to produce just that amount of stylistic variation for the rest of its productive life. When archaeologists start peopling their now dead cultural complexes with individuals who behave more like IBM cards than responsive humans, it is probably true that such archaeologists have become too familiar with computers and too unfamiliar with the ethnographic record!

There is the further implication in Binford's proposition that the diversity of cultural expression within a group is entirely the result of stylistic differences *among* the members of the group. The possibility that the stylistic diversity within the artistic production of a single member of the group might exceed the stylistic diversity of the pooled products of the other members of her group does not seem to have occurred to the New Archaeologists. Again this would seem to be a world in which the artist or artisan was hard-programmed before marriage, with reference to the range of stylistic diversity which she could produce, so that her production was totally unexpanded by all later interaction.

The Shipibo–Conibo sample

The Shipibo–Conibo inhabit a section of the Ucayali River about six hundred miles long. Their territory lies in eastern Peru within the canopy of dense tropical forest which covers nearly the whole floor of the Amazon Basin, but they conceive of their world in terms of the narrow strip of alluvial flood plain along the Ucayali and a few of its major tributaries, rather than in terms of the broad expanse of jungle back from the river (Lathrap 1968a, 1968b, 1970). Until very recently the huge tracts of interriverine jungle were inhabited by smaller, relatively mobile ethnic groups whose material culture and art style are rudimentary or even childish by Shipibo standards. In a real sense the extreme technological control which underlies Shipibo–Conibo ceramic production and the complex art style which is applied to ceramics, textiles, and certain carved wooden objects is an affirmation of the Shipibo–Conibo's position on the river banks, and a declaration of their right as civilized people to hold this economically superior niche.

The economic basis of Shipibo–Conibo society is a combination of slash-and-burn agriculture, emphasizing manioc and more recently plantains, with a systematic exploitation of the incredibly rich protein resources of the large, white-water rivers. Over the past few decades the population of Shipibo–Conibo has been undergoing a remarkable explosion, and they now (1968) number around 12,000 persons. The ethnogenesis of the group we now call the Shipibo–Conibo is complex, and I have elsewhere written on the subject (Lathrap 1970); for present purposes it is enough to say that ancestors of the modern Conibo can be recognized on the Central Ucayali at least as early as A.D. 800. Contrary to my earlier suggestions (Lathrap 1970) it now seems certain that the ancestors of the riverine Panoans entered the Ucayali Basin from the Mácas area of eastern Ecuador.

It was my interest in the evaluation of the various propositions labelled the Deetz–Longacre hypothesis that focused my research and dictated the kinds of data which I collected: a large body of information which could be used to check the various propositions concerning the relationship of stylistic variation to other factors. The study was conducted in a number of settlements which were selected to sample a wide geographical range of Shipibo–Conibo villages. A complete census of extant pottery was made for the Shipibo communities of San Francisco de Yarinacocha and Nuevo Destino, the Conibo communities of Painaco and Bella Flor, and the Río Pisqui community of Manco Capac. A complete inventory of ceramics was made for a large number of extended family groupings within the Shipibo community of Callaria, at the Conibo community of Caimito, and at the Río Pisqui community of Nueva Eden. The ceramic inventory included the location of each pot within a particular structure, the maker of the pot, the age of the pot, the name of the functional class to which the pot belongs, the occasion (if special) for which the pot was made, and the function which it is now serving. For each pot I measured mouth diameter, maximum diameter, and height. For each painted pot I made a drawing of the design and took from one to four photographs. For each community in which I worked, I have a complete village census and genealogies indicating interrelationships among the various extended families in the community along with considerable information indicating genealogical ties among various villages. For each of the communities where I studied I have a map showing the relative position of all structures including living houses, cooking houses, potting sheds, chicken houses, etc., and the genealogical data is keyed to the distribution of these structures. For each potter who entered my sample I know where she is now living and where she lived for various earlier periods in her life, from whom she learned to make and paint pottery, and, in cases where memory served, from whom her teacher learned to make and paint pottery.

There is no space to discuss at length the conceptual structure which underlies Shipibo–Conibo ceramics and permits the potter to generate a series of pots which are unmistakably Shipibo–Conibo. There are two levels of reality in the Shipibo conception of ceramics. One relates to clearly maintained and widely agreed upon distinctions in clays, temper, horizontal segmentation of vessel form, resin glazes, slip paints, and line width modes within painted design. These units are the building blocks out of which a set of functionally significant, named vessel categories is generated. The presence of this full set of shapes is a diagnostic of Shipibo–Conibo ethnicity, and maps precisely with their territory. These shapes include the *quënti* cooking pot which comes in three sizes; the *mapu ëti*, a kiln for small vessels (both of the former are of a ceramic fabric which is heat resistant and designed to be returned to the fire repeatedly); and a set of serving vessels which includes the *quënpo*, cup, in three standardized sizes; the *shrania*, also a drinking vessel; the *quëncha*, food bowl, in three distinct shapes; and the *chomo*, storage and transport vessel for liquids, in three distinct sizes. These standardized vessel form categories offer the framework on which the Shipibo–Conibo women exercise their artistic impulses.

We shall examine the stylistic diversity observable within various of the extended families which are the typical cooperating social units among the Shipibo–Conibo, and as we go along discuss some of the processes which seem to affect the degree of stylistic diversity within such households or even within the production of a single potter, since the question of household uniformity cannot be considered independently from the productivity of its most variable member.

Most Shipibo–Conibo live as a part of large, extended family groups. Isolated nuclear families may occur as the result of the death of other close relatives, or people with minimal success in coping with their own culture may choose to isolate themselves; but such units are abnormal. The structure of the extended family is variable, but far more individual nuclear families locate themselves with reference to the wife's ties of consanguinity than with reference to the husband's. The statistical norm is the matrilocal extended family, and it is expected as a cultural norm that the families of average, respectable Shipibo will extend matrilocally. The families of the chiefs and the families of a particularly powerful class of shaman known as a *muraya* tend to extend bilaterally with both sons and daughters residing adjacent to their parents' house after marriage.

A mature and smoothly functioning extended family finds its expression in a distinctive grouping of structures. There will be a large living house belonging to the oldest and/or most powerful nuclear family, surrounded or adjoined by several smaller living houses of the younger or less powerful nuclear families who consider themselves part of the extended family. All may share a single cook house, or one or more of the individual wives may demand her own cook house; again, the number of potting sheds per extended family is a matter of considerable variation. In its early stages of development the extended family may all reside in a single very large house. The architectural setting of the extended family thus relates to a maturational cycle, and we will presently see that the same maturational cycle strongly affects stylistic diversity.

The exact arrangement of the houses comprising such a cluster is highly variable. They may be spread out along a half a mile of lake shore or river bank or they may be crammed in together to conform to the demands of a Spanish-style grid plan. In neither case are the limits of the cluster of a particular extended family formally marked off from those of adjacent extended families by greater intervening space or other kinds of boundary indicators. If one approached the problem from the archaeological point of view, one would have to limit the extended family units on the basis of the similarity of their ceramic content, a procedure which would introduce a high degree of circularity into the argument.

When one looks at the vicinity of a Shipibo–Conibo dwelling and notes the pattern of refuse deposition beyond the edge of the well-swept plaza, one realizes just how futile it would be to attempt to define activity areas on the basis of what would remain from a Shipibo dwelling one hundred years after it was abandoned. The New Archaeology can be most effective when it is studying the cultural debris of slobs. The refined and highly convincing reconstructions of the spatial organization of specialized activities which Brose (1970) has made for the Summer Island site are possible only because no one ever took out the garbage; the leavings of various food processing and manufacturing procedures were allowed to rest eternally wherever they originally fell. The situation is very different in the house of the Tropical Forest Indian. The house floor and all of the cleared plaza area is swept once or twice a day, so that all refuse is thoroughly mixed and comes to rest a broom stroke beyond the edge of the plaza. The cleanliness of the Shipibo–Conibo house is in part a matter of family pride and an aesthetic consideration; but these practices are also highly adaptive in terms of group health and prophylactic against the various diseases which are endemic to the tropical forest setting.

The effect of visiting on stylistic uniformity

Though most Shipibo–Conibo households are matrilocal, the sheer fact of matrilocality does not shield the individual potter from stylistic influences emanating from outside the matrilocal family. It is considered proper for each Shipibo nuclear family to visit the husband's parents for a month or so each year, and other family ties may initiate extended visits to distant points. Major ceremonies such as girls' puberty ceremonies may bring people together for extended periods of time and from a radius of over one hundred miles. The Shipibo artist frequently returns from such a visit potting comfortably in the style of the other household or community. She may gradually revert to her previous set of stylistic habits; or her stylistic vocabulary may be permanently expanded. In either case the process greatly increases the amount of stylistic variability in the nuclear household and in the extended family, yet it has no relationship to the makeup or homogeneity of the extended family. I can document this process both for impressionable newlyweds and, most spectacularly, for a culturally swinging great-grandmother who, in her Picasso-like virtuosity for picking up and practising a wide range of stylistic variants, has left enough cultural diversity in the refuse of her house to be interpreted as the work of a whole patrilocal extended family.

The effects of adoption

One might expect that adoption would have a minimal effect on stylistic variability within matrilocal extended families. If the individual is adopted young, she should receive the same instruction as her adoptive sisters and should grow up to be culturally similar even though she is genetically more divergent. Things don't work out that way among the Shipibo–Conibo. In the first place adoption is extremely common. It operates freely to absorb orphans, but its most typical pattern of operation is completely unrelated to the needs of the child. The successful Shipibo mother and housewife who has gone through menopause and who no longer has any small children of her own to enculturate will adopt a child just to keep things lively around the home. One may demand a child from a wide range of relatives but the demand is most frequently made and most frequently honoured in the case of one's sibling's child or one's child's child. Actually, grandchild adoption is most common, and while there is a strong matrilocal bias in residence, there is no preference as between daughter's child and son's child. The availability of a child of proper age, 2–5, and desired sex seems to be the only consideration; so in about 50 per cent of the cases the child will be taken out of the extended family and even out of the community into which it was born. The child if a girl will then be instructed in the art of pottery-making by her adoptive mother. Women clearly regard the giving of such instruction as among the most pleasurable aspects of their life.

If, as is highly likely in cases of grandchild adoption, the adoptive parents die before the biological parents, the biological parents will reestablish the claim of parenthood on their daughter, who by now may be thoroughly trained as a potter. The daughter will come to live in a matrilocal extended family along with her biological sisters, though she may pot in a quite different variant of the stylistic tradition. In one example of this situation the daughter trained by an adoptive parent was technically an extremely skilful potter, artistically inventive and able to incorporate a great amount of new stylistic elements without a loss of stylistic integrity; on the other hand the sister, trained by her biological mother, was during the study technically incompetent and stylistically disorganized. These characteristics seemed to relate to a period of depression in the potter's life cycle, and were not learned directly from her mother, who was in every respect a brilliant potter, in fact the culturally swinging great-grandmother mentioned above.

There is another way in which adoption strongly affects stylistic variability among Shipibo–Conibo potters. Until very recently the Shipibo–Conibo have maintained a state of constant warfare with the culturally simple groups occupying the stretches of jungle away from the major rivers. Shipibo–Conibo raiding parties would attack the settlements of the forest Indians, attempting to kill as many adults as possible and to capture children, especially female children. If the female child were very young, she would be adopted into a household and fully trained as a Shipibo–Conibo. If she were somewhat older, her acceptance would be less complete, and she would become a household drudge in a Shipibo–Conibo family. Such slave girls would frequently become the mistresses of mature men in the household or partners in early sexual experimentation on the part of the growing boys in the family. The offspring of such irregular unions were adopted into Shipibo–Conibo households and thoroughly trained as Shipibo–Conibo. It would appear that the training of these jungle Indians and of their illegitimate children was rather more rigorous than that of a legitimate girl. On the average such women end up as technically superb potters with a rather low degree of stylistic variation among their own products. They will exert more than usual rigour in training their own children in art and technology, and if they are not blessed with a large number of female children, they are likely to adopt several and train these with special care. These adoptive families of Shipibo by adoption are likely to show far less intra-familial variation in style than an ordinary extended family. This phenomenon might be called the Cinderella or Avis effect, and is best illustrated by a large and artistically productive family in the Río Pisqui town of Nueva Eden (Fig. 3.1).

The effect of genius

I have elsewhere discussed the career and influence of the remarkable Conibo artist Wasëmëa (Lathrap 1968c). By elaborating on the curvilinear elements in her design layouts she evolved a distinctive personal style much admired by her fellow artists. In the course of her active creative life, she resided in several Conibo communities and in each left a group of artists who were consciously emulating her artistic innovations. Her disciples were not recruited according to any principle of kinship or residence but through their own personal conversion to the 'New Style'. Because of her personal magnetism, which related both to artistic skill and an ability to communicate with the supernatural, pockets of stylistic uniformity were spread over three hundred miles of the Central Ucayali drainage. The differential acceptance of the 'New Style' led to stylistic diversity within villages and even within extended families. If the New Archaeologists have contemplated their own intellectual history, they should not be surprised that a peregrinating genius could establish pockets of stylistic uniformity in a number of far-flung locations.

Wasëmëa unfortunately had died before my fieldwork and most of my information about her came from her elder sister Valentina, who in 1967 was still actively maintaining her sister's heritage in Painaco. Valentina was a most knowledgeable and sympathetic informant, eager that the nature of her sister's genius be recorded. I could well have worked a month with her; unfortunately my research design allowed a couple of hours. I have recorded several surviving examples of Wasëmëa's work and many examples of the production of

Fig. 3.1. Designs from the bottom of open food bowls, *quëncha*. All are from a large extended family in the Río Pisqui community of Nueva Eden. The elder potter and dominant personality of this social group is a vigorous woman named Antonita, about 65 years old. She is the daughter of a captive Cashibo who was early adopted by a Shipibo mother and trained in the art of pottery-making. She, in turn, has taken a number of adoptive daughters and trained them most rigorously in potting. A to D are the work of Antonita; E to G are the work of her eldest adoptive daughter, Rosa. H to J are the work of a somewhat younger adoptive daughter, Ilsa. This particularly large and stable extended family is based largely on ties of adoption, and potting seems to be a major cohesive element.

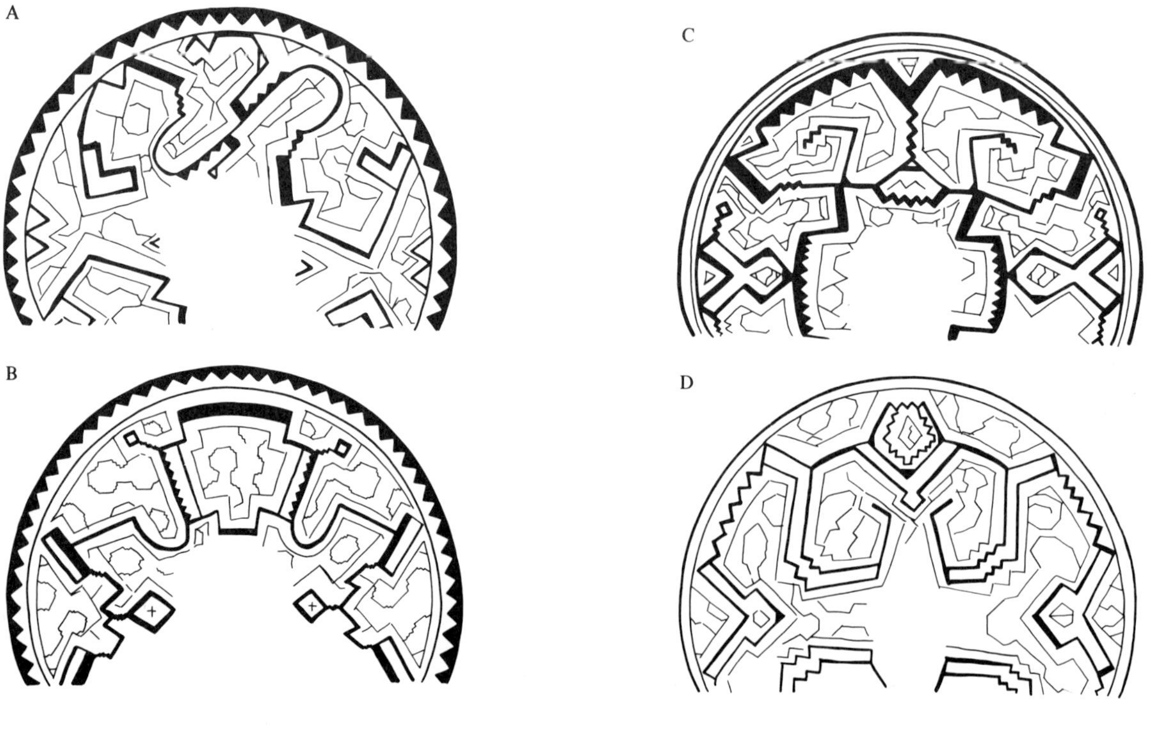

her adopted daughter, but the design from a *chomo* made by Valentina strikes me as the most satisfactory embodiment of Wasëmëa's school (Fig. 3.2).

Individuals of low stylistic variability

There is little in the data I have reviewed which suggests that forced exposure to a number of divergent stylistic variations will *of necessity* lead to a high degree of stylistic diversity in the products of the mature potter, or necessarily cause her production to diverge markedly from the products of the other potters in the extended family in which she resides. The case of Mercedes Agustín is a good illustration. Mercedes' father was a Shipibo born in San Francisco de Yarinacocha. He married a Conibo girl of Caimito and, as was proper, resided with his wife's family until she died. Mercedes, the only child of this union, was about ten years old at the time of her mother's death. She was officially adopted by her father's mother and for the next four years rigorously trained in art by her adoptive mother, who in turn died when Mercedes was about fourteen. Her father had by then remarried. His wives were two sisters in a large extended family in San Francisco de Yarinacocha and he was now residing with that family. Very shortly after the death of her adoptive mother, Mercedes married a brother of her father's new wives. Since the family into which she and her father were now married was the family of a *muraya*, it was considered proper that the family extend bilaterally, so she ended up living in a house adjacent to that of her biological father. Since she was only fourteen, she continued to receive instruction in pottery-making, this time from her stepmothers or sisters-in-law (depending on how one cared to figure the relationship) and from their mother and grandmother. Today she is a fine potter whose pottery shows remarkably little stylistic variation from one example to the next (Fig. 3.3) and whose production conforms well stylistically to the production of the other women of the extended family in which she continues to live, though the production of each of the other potters in the extended family shows more internal variation than does that of Mercedes. Interestingly enough, Mercedes is outspokenly hostile to stylistic innovation emanating from outside San Francisco de Yarinacocha.

The marked and unusually strong stylistic uniformity which characterizes Mercedes' artistic production would

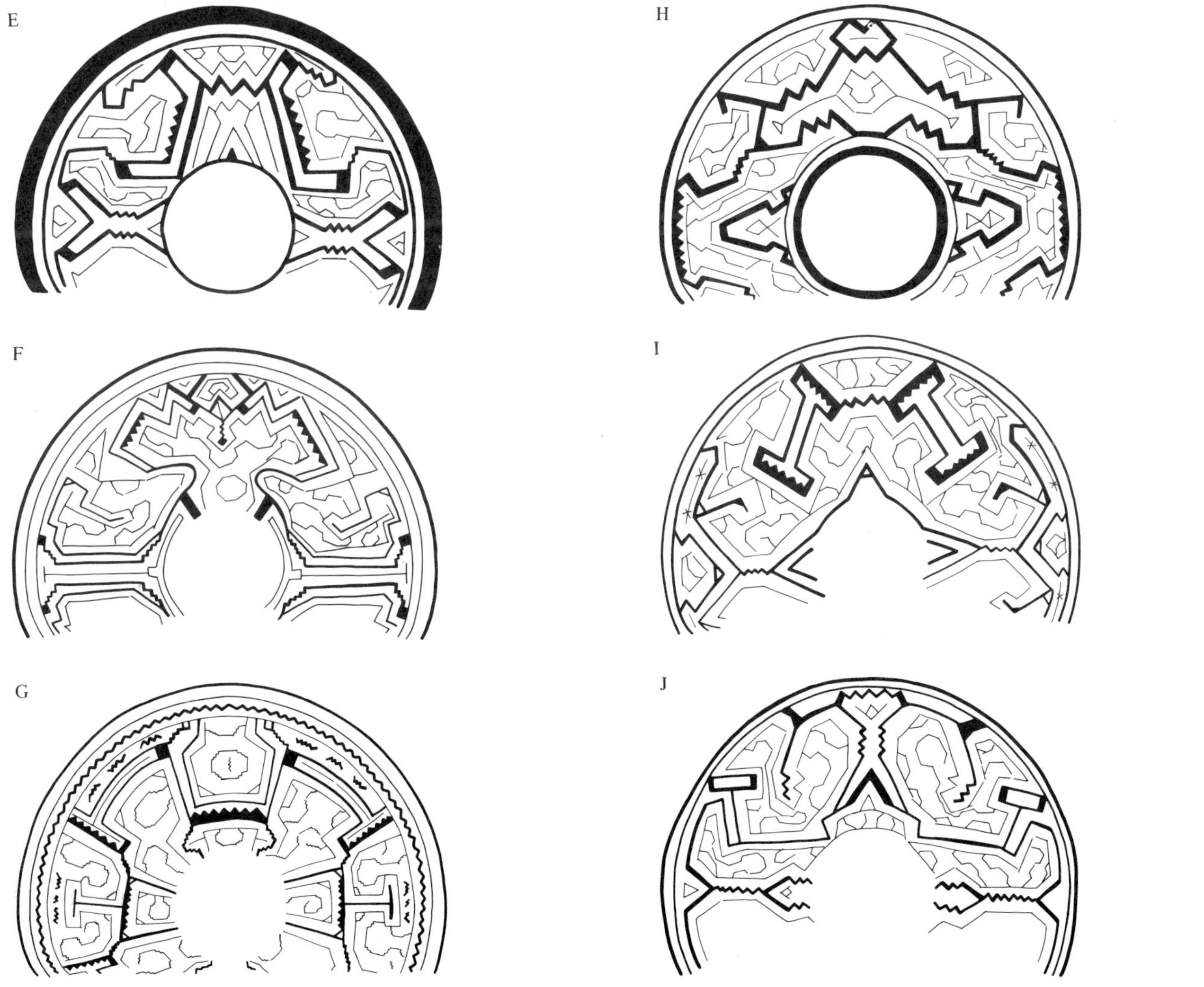

seem explicable only in terms of her unique life history and her personality structure. One could hypothesize that the unusually large number of enculturative influences to which she was subjected during the second decade of her life were more than she could easily assimilate and structure so that she has become hostile to further outside influences impinging on her. Such an hypothesis could be examined only through an in-depth study of Mercedes as a personality structure, a study far beyond what my original research design envisaged. Though she is the least experimental artist in her extended family, she is by far the most prolific potter. During 1967–8 her output was over one half of the total output of the extended family.

Stylistic variability and the maturational cycle of the extended family

It is the Shipibo ideal that the matrilocal extended family should expand and flourish through several generations. The death of a key figure in the family, an irresolvable quarrel between two of the nuclear families, or deviations in the sex ratio of one or two of the nuclear families so that there is a superabundance of boys and no girls, usually truncate such a growth before it reaches full maturity. There are, however, a few extended families in the sample which fulfil cultural expectations completely. The large matrilocal extended family at Nuevo Destino is the most instructive, containing six very active potters and spanning four generations. Asunsiana, the dominant figure in the family, is now between seventy and eighty years old. She has two daughters, Ana and Jesusa, living in the extended family. Ana's daughter Juana also lives in the extended family and has two daughters who are already starting to pot. One of these is being trained by her mother, Juana, while the other has been formally adopted by her grandmother, Ana. This extended family has flourished in the same location for

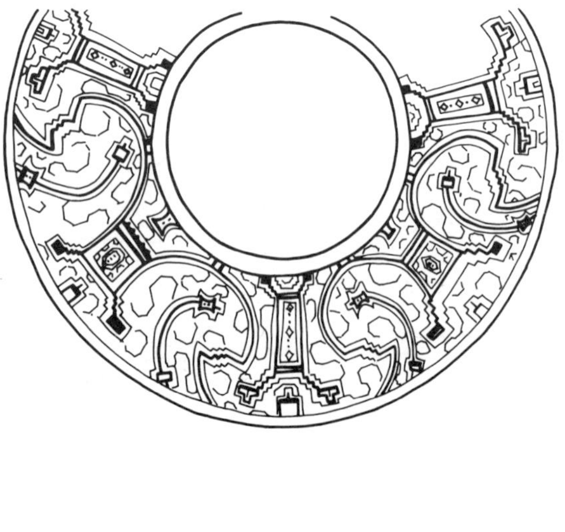

Fig. 3.2. The design from the shoulder of a *chomo* collected at the Conibo settlement of Painaco. It is a particularly fine example of the kind of extreme curvilinear design developed by the famous Conibo artist, Wasëmëa, and subsequently spread to a number of Conibo communities. This particular specimen is the work of Wasëmëa's elder sister, Valentina.

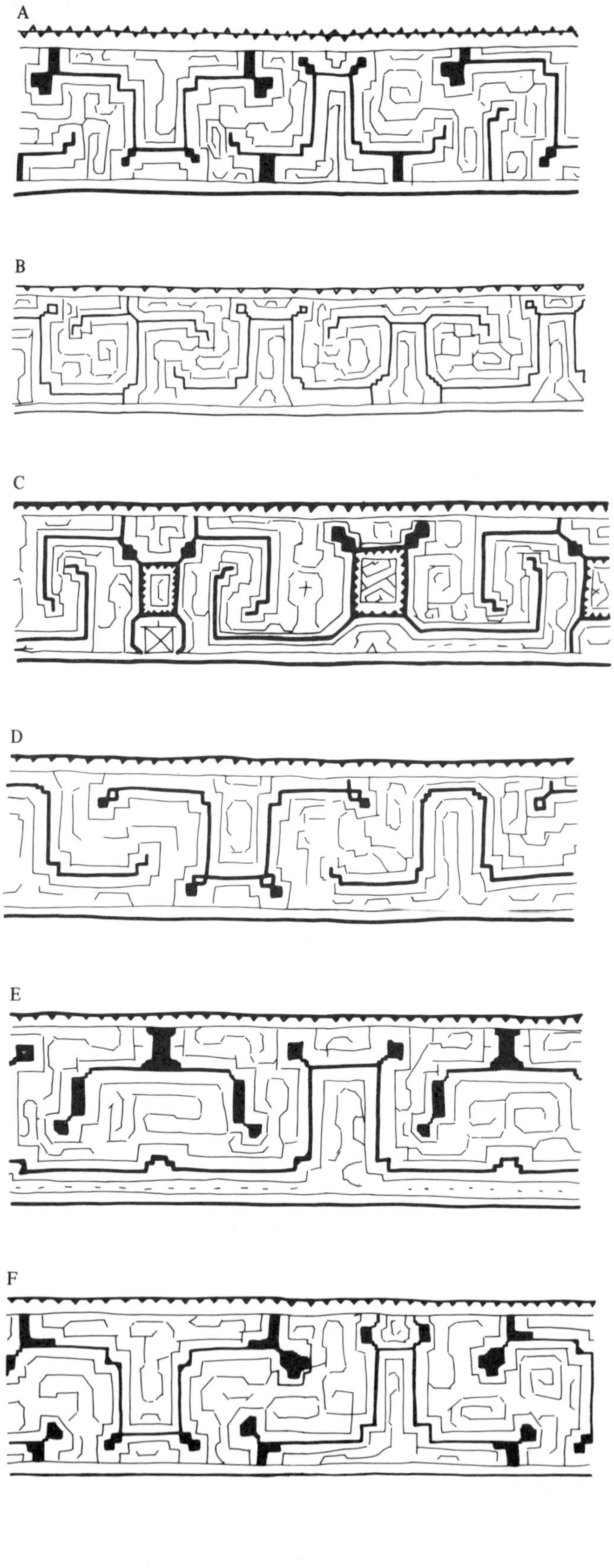

Fig. 3.3. Band designs taken from the ceramics of the Shipibo artist, Mercedes Agustín de Bardales, showing the limited range of design motif and execution typical of her total, very considerable artistic output.

thirty-four years. It is a paragon of group homogeneity and cultural propriety. If any family should exemplify the Deetz–Longacre hypothesis, this one should. Let us examine its stylistic variability as of late 1967.

Asunsiana's style is markedly divergent from that of all of the other potters in the group. The broad line elements are simpler and the fine line fillers are carelessly drawn and widely spaced. Her vocabulary of design motives is shrinking, for as she grows older she is progressively eliminating stylistic innovations which were unknown during her youth but subsequently acquired during middle age. There is a childish, unfinished look to her recent production which hints at the onset of senility.

Her two daughters are both at the height of their power as potters; both were trained by Asunsiana; both have spent all of their life in the same extended family; both pot in the same potting shed; and each is appreciative of the stylistic accomplishments of the other. Yet the production of the two sisters diverges remarkably from the point of view of style, and the production of each taken individually shows a remarkably wide range of stylistic variation. Ana favours restrained curvilinear designs; is experimenting with the effects of rotational symmetry, a kind of design layout which I rarely noted elsewhere; and occasionally attaches small human effigies to her beer urns, *chomo ani*. Jesusa favours a bold, rectilinear style; on occasion includes Cocama-derived motifs in Shipibo design layouts; and is given to making pots in the shape of ducks and other odd forms. Ana's daughter Juana is also a virtuoso artist who shows characteristics of both her mother and aunt, and maintains both a traditional style and a simplified style for the tourist market. The extensive production of both of Juana's children is predictably childish since neither has fully mastered the techniques of painting, nor the rules of design layout. The range of stylistic variability within this extended family could scarcely be greater (Figs. 3.4 and 3.5).

There are two other households relatively close to this large extended family. Both are remnants of once-larger extended families, which have mostly died out or moved away. The men marrying into the smaller households have come from the large extended family next door. The female members of these two smaller households were taught by their mothers, who were not closely related to the extended family headed by Asunsiana. Neither household pots with

Fig. 3.4. Band designs showing the wide range of stylistic variation in the four generations of the particularly large potting community at the Shipibo colony of Nuevo Destino. A is by the matriarch of the group, Asunsiana, who is now between 70 and 80. B, C, and D are by her elder daughter, Ana. E and F are by her slightly younger daughter, Jesusa. E is typically Shipibo in style, while F shows marked influence from the modern ceramic style of the neighbouring Cocama. G is by Ana's daughter, Juana; while H is the still childish production of Isabella, the 10 year old daughter of Juana, who has been officially adopted by her grandmother, Ana.

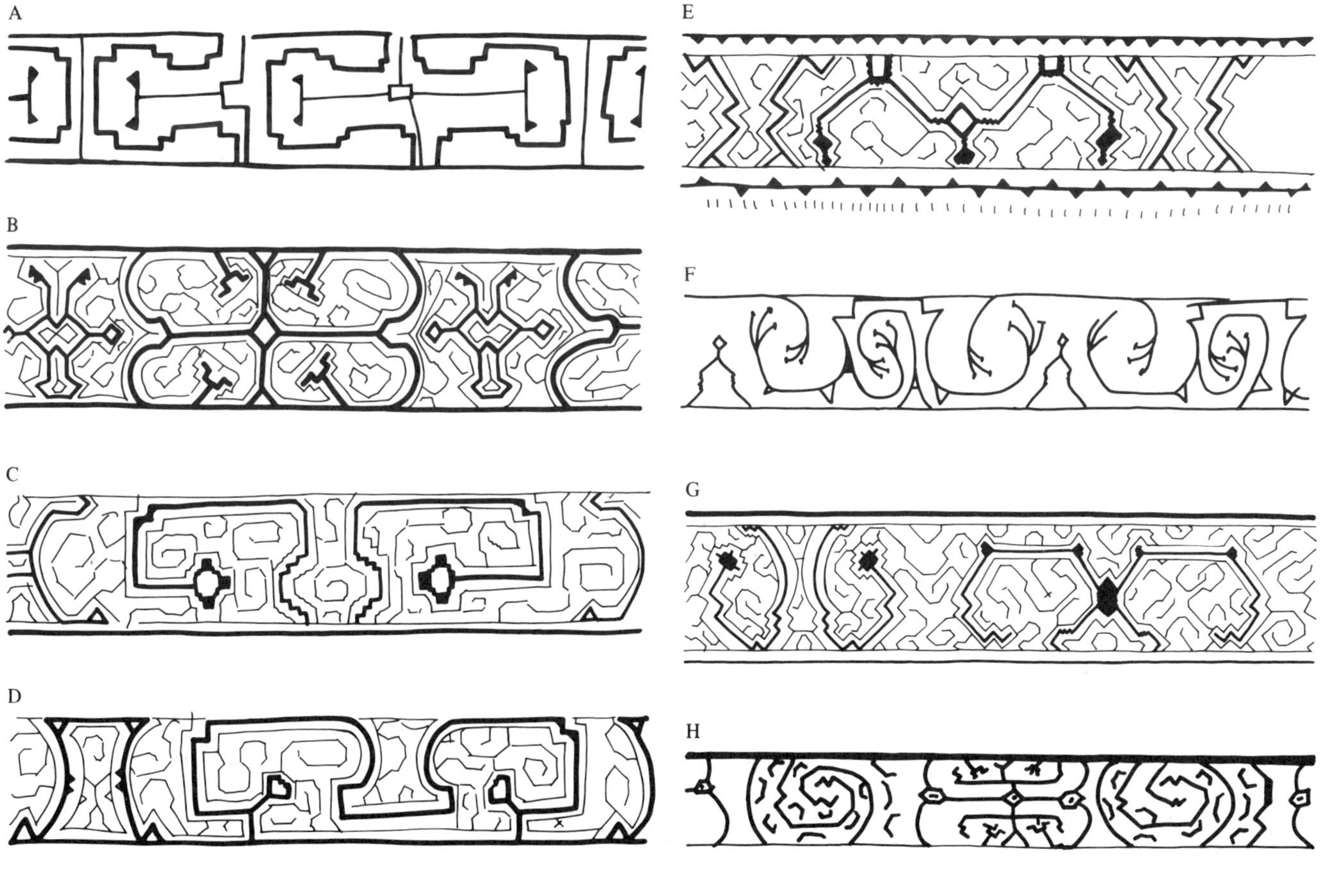

Fig. 3.5. A range of circular designs from the large, stable, extended family at Nuevo Destino. A and B are the work of the matriarch, Asunciana. C and D are the work of Asunsiana's eldest daughter, Ana. E and F are the work of the slightly younger daughter, Jesusa. G to I show the range of decoration in the ceramic production of Juana, Ana's daughter, with I showing the kind of simplified Shipibo design made for sale to tourists. J is the work of Juana's 7 year old daughter, Ermelinda, who is learning potting from her biological mother; while K is the work of Juana's 10 year old daughter Isabella, who has been adopted by her grandmother, Ana.

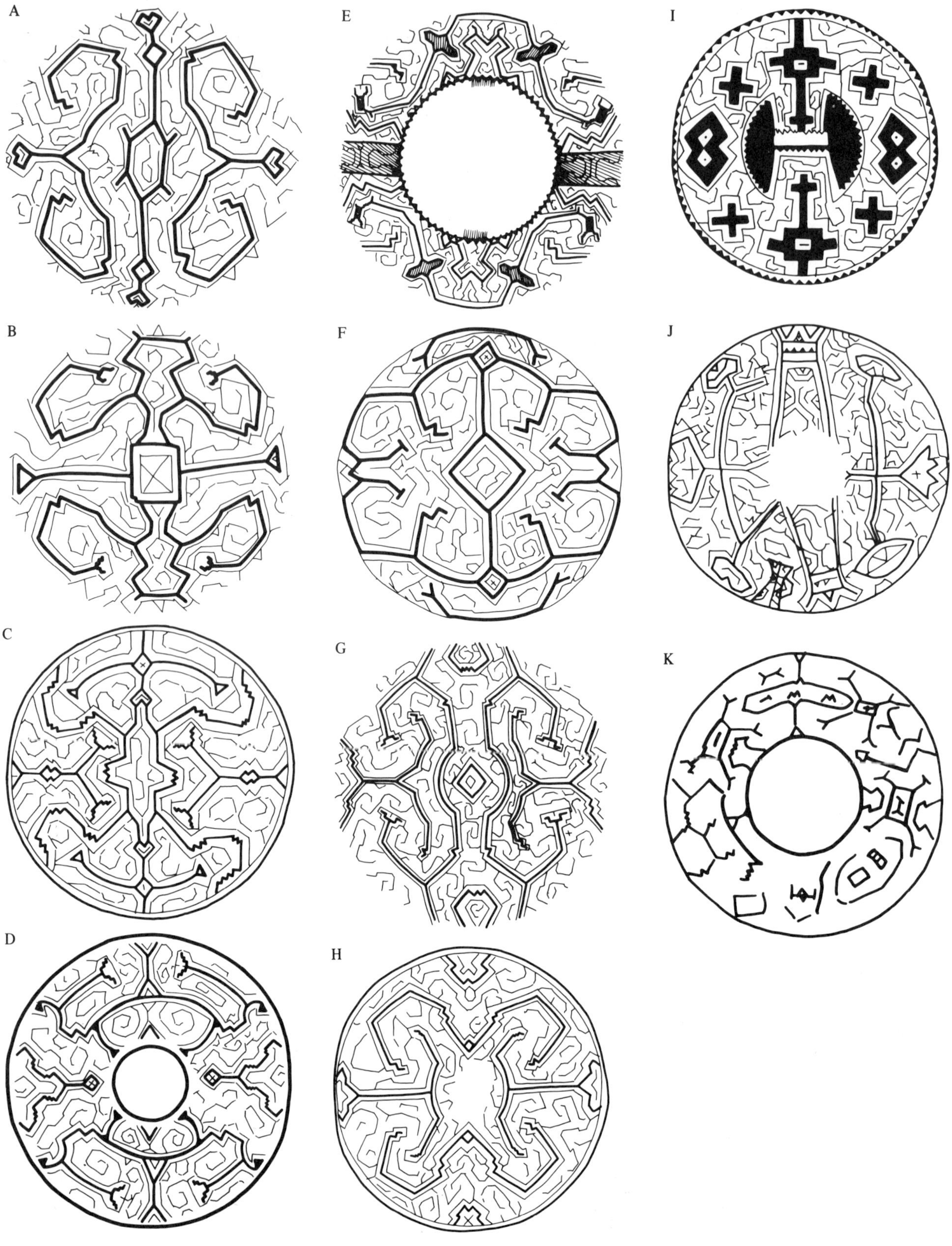

the frequency and vigour of Asunsiana's extended family. At present most of the stylistic characteristics of the products of these two households suggest a strong affiliation with the more conventional aspects of the flourishing ceramic tradition next door. Most look like simplified imitations of Ana's least experimental productions. I suggest that shared artistic activity is serving to bind these isolated families progressively closer to the extended family of Asunsiana.

None of the above observations supports the contention that uniform adherence to matrilocal residence *in itself* will ensure stylistic uniformity in the extended family unit. It has already been observed that Shipibo–Conibo women enjoy teaching children to pot. A day at Nuevo Destino impresses one with the amount of stylistic variability which can be introduced into a sample by the copious productions of incompletely enculturated children.

The marked stylistic divergence between Ana and Jesusa also deserves further comment. I would hypothesize that this results from a perhaps unconscious rivalry between the two women. There is the obvious question as to who will become the leading figure in the extended family once their mother has died. The intensity of their potting activity suggests that we are viewing the long-term result of an ongoing process, the process which Bateson has labelled symmetrical schismogenesis (Bateson 1958: 177). I suspect that this process is likely to occur and to create marked stylistic diversity in precisely the most mature, uniformly recruited and stable extended families. To verify this hypothesis I would have to make long-term observations of the patterns of personal interaction between Ana and Jesusa and on a number of other similar pairs of sisters, a kind of data not envisaged in the original research design.

There is in my Shipibo–Conibo data little support for the proposition of Binford that 'Homogeneity of cultural expression within a group varies directly with the homogeneity of the group's composition.' I feel confident that no more fully quantitative analysis of the data will uncover less obvious patterns of stylistic uniformity to give comfort to that proposition.

But then there is the Cruz family

In all of my sample there is a single matrilocal and not very extended family which could be offered as the ideal Deetz–Longacre family, who seem as representative of that hypothetical world as Archie Bunker is of Middle America. The mother, Clara Cruz, is about forty years old. She is an avid potter and a superb artist. Her older daughter Maria is about twenty-two and *is only recently married*. She is an equally superb potter and artist. The younger daughter Teolinda is about eighteen and *still unmarried*. Her fine line brush work is perhaps the most intricate of any of the members of the family. Clara's son Leonardo lives in a house about one hundred yards away, and his thirteen-year-old daughter Celia is learning to pot and paint from her grandmother. Though not quite yet an expert at design layout, Celia is already doing designs which are emphatically *Cruz*. Except for the childishness of Celia's production, the Cruz family shows less stylistic variation than any other family of similar size and even less than most individual mature potters. The family's involvement in pottery-making is intense; the four artists are extremely aware of and appreciative of each others work; and, what is most interesting, no other family in the Conibo town of Caimito makes pottery which could possibly be mistaken for a Cruz product (Fig. 3.6).

One might attribute the stylistic uniformity of the Cruz family simply to its stage of maturation. One would expect to find maximum uniformity in a family where the mother had just finished teaching her two daughters all she knew about pottery-making; such a family, in theory, should have a mother aged about thirty-two and the daughters about thirteen and fifteen. The Cruz family is a bit over-ripe to fit such a model. There are other odd things about the Cruz family. The fact that Maria reached twenty-two before getting married and that Teolinda has reached eighteen and is still not married is a public scandal in terms of the Conibo views as to the proper age of marriage. While I was recording the voluminous ceramic production of the Cruz family, my compadre Catilino was having a long discussion with the father, Clarino Cruz. Clarino spent most of the time complaining about the numbers of pineapples his Conibo neighbours were stealing from him. I was unfortunately too busy measuring mouth diameters to get all of this in my notes, but my memory of the conversation is clear. Such is the Shipibo–Conibo abhorrence of theft, that I have seen a mother attempt to cut off the hand of her kleptomaniac son. If the other Conibo were indeed ripping off pineapples from Clarino it could only mean that they had written him off from membership in the human (Shipibo–Conibo) race.

Caimito is the only town in my sample which had a resident missionary. The rest of the Conibo in Caimito were reasonably well behaved *evangelísticos* as long as the missionary was looking and engaged in appropriate fiesta behaviour whenever the missionary turned his back. By Clarino's choice his house occupied the one point in town which was fully visible from the missionary's house. In Clarino's life the missionary was always looking. The missionary on his part was lavish in praising the 'good Christian behaviour' of the whole Cruz family.

Confirmation would require long-term observation of the interaction patterns of the Cruz family, but I hypothesize that the stylistic uniformity of the Cruz family's pottery and the failure of the Cruz style to affect other ceramic production in Caimito is a precise measure of the degree to which the Cruz family is alienated from the other extended families of Caimito. If, as I have already insisted, art is a form of communication, then the Cruz family is simply not communicating with its neighbours.

On one non-trivial level of exposition one can suggest that among the Shipibo–Conibo the degree of stylistic uniformity and isolation exhibited by the Cruz family can always be taken as a symptom of social pathology. It is pathology only from the Indian point of view; to the missionary the Cruz family appears the best fruit of his good works. I think, however, that we can now put these observations in an even broader framework. The stylistic diversity observable within Shipibo–Conibo extended families would seem to relate to a number of dynamic ongoing processes which are in a real sense adaptive. These include processes which relate the individual to the extended family, processes which relate to the maturational cycle of the whole extended family, and processes which permit articulation and cooperation among family groups. The Cruz family is unique in my sample precisely in the fact that its artistic activity is serving to isolate it from rather than integrate it into the rest of the community. We will return to the broader implications of this observation shortly.

Summary

The data on Shipibo–Conibo pottery-making which we have just reviewed offer the basis for a redefinition of the problem of stylistic variation as it occurs in ethnographic or archaeological contexts. We are observing and attempting to account for the quantity and quality of communication within specialized kinds of communication networks. I would suggest that the single most important generalization which can be drawn from these data is that the nature of communication within a particular network at a particular point in time can be explained only in terms of long-term, ongoing processes within the network; particular 'causal factors' such as matrilocality or patrilocality offer little explanatory power. How long has the network been in operation? How intense has artistic communication been within that network? Have particular dyadic relationships within the network been infused with a sense of continuing rivalry (symmetrical schismogenesis in Bateson's terminology) or a sense of ongoing emulation by a self-perceived inferior toward a recognized artistic innovator (complementary schismogenesis in Bateson's terminology)? These questions are likely to provide more insights than reference to any model of linear causality, no matter what causal factors are invoked.

Fig. 3.6. The extremely detailed and precise style of ceramic painting characteristic of the Cruz family at the Conibo colony of Caimito. A to C are the work of the mother, Clara, about 38 or 40. D and E are the work of the elder daughter, Maria, about 22 and only recently married; while F to H are the work of the younger daughter, Teolinda, still unmarried at the age of 18.

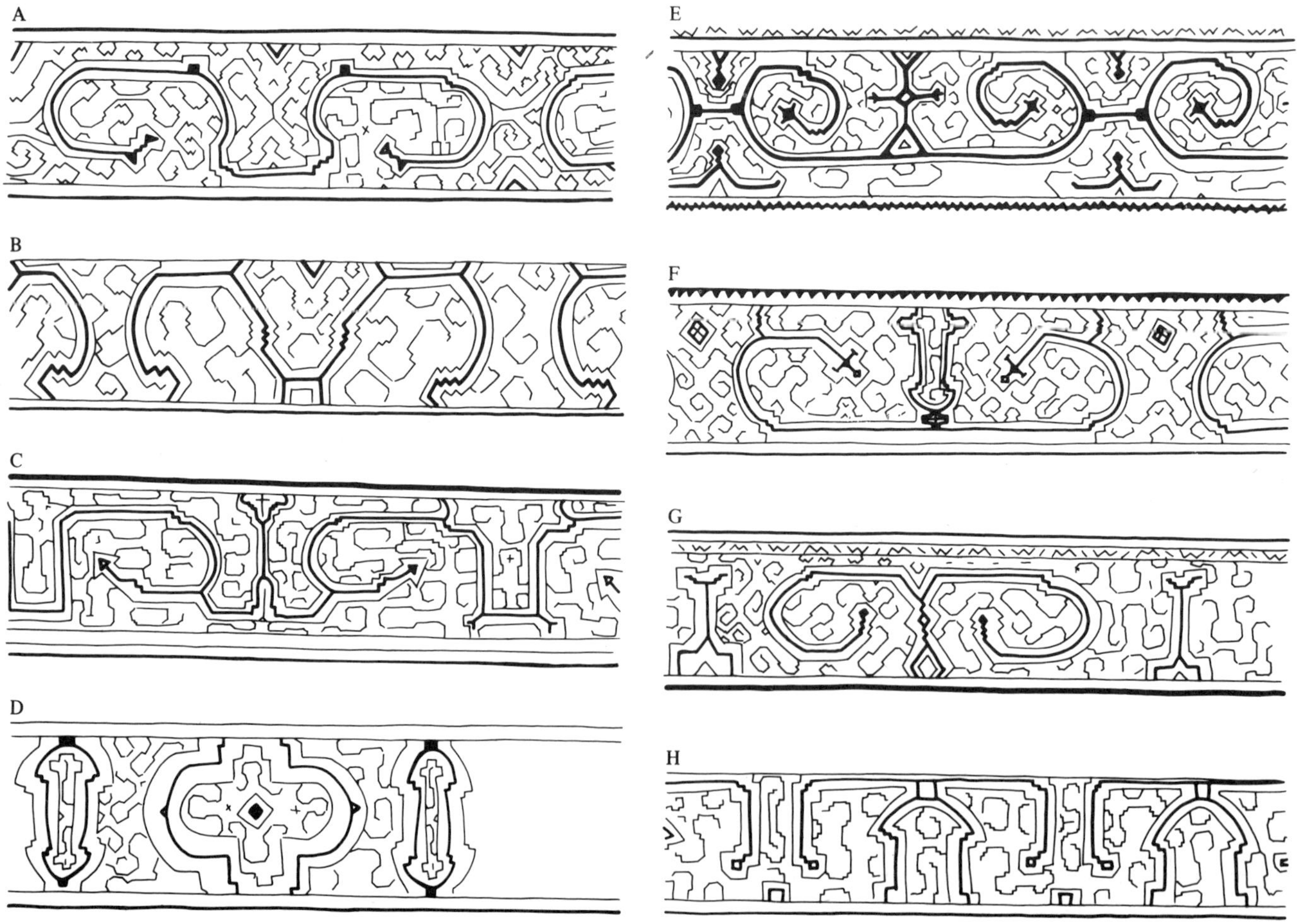

The preceding comments are merely a specific case of the more general observation that one can understand most of the peculiarities in the current state of a system only in terms of the processes operating during the past history of the system. This is an idea which recently has had acceptance among some New Archaeologists (Flannery 1972, 1973), though they prefer to speak of the trajectory of a system rather than of its history.

It is also very clear from the Shipibo–Conibo data that if we examine the problem of stylistic uniformity or diversity within particular extended families we cannot disregard the effect of the personality of the individual artists within the family group. Here is another lower level of ongoing, coherent systems which can only be understood in terms of their past trajectories.

In many ways I find Brose's monograph (1970) the most satisfying exposition of the Deetz–Longacre hypothesis. The logic of this set of ideas is pushed to its limits; and the nature of the archaeological sample with which Brose was working makes it possible to assign particular batches of pottery to particular definable familial units, and then to examine the degree of stylistic variation within each of these units. The Middle Woodland occupation at the Summer Island site consisted of four familial units, one possibly nuclear, three almost certainly extended. It is probably that this particular community represents a seasonal summer occupation which endured no more than two or three consecutive summers. There is no evidence of the moving of familial dwellings which would mix the refuse and make it difficult to assign particular groups of pottery to particular family units. The kind of short-term discrete occupation resulting in the Summer Island site is most appropriate to a fine-grained, intensive application of New Archaeology. In such circumstances one has the best chance of identifying activity areas, and even patterns of traffic flow. The opportunities are greatly increased if, as was the case at Summer Island, refuse was allowed to accumulate in and around the houses where it initially fell. Much of Brose's reconstruction of familial units and activities strikes me as of a high level of probability.

Even when dealing with archaeological sites that are the result of short-term occupation by small groups, in which there has been minimal disturbance and redistribution of refuse, there are difficulties in achieving an archaeological interpretation which approaches the complexities of ethnographic reality. Bonnichsen's (1973) experimental use of a recent camp site of a size and duration not dissimilar to the Summer Island site should stand as a healthy warning that a complete reconstruction of past events will always elude even the most imaginative archaeologists.

Bonnichsen's warning is a general one. The warning inherent in the Shipibo–Conibo data is specific and relates to precisely the kinds of stylistic variability examined by Brose. Brose notes that there are differences in stylistic variability among the ceramic units which he assumes were the products of particular extended families. He interprets these differences in terms of the working out of a particular form of cross-cousin marriage (1970: 59). The explanation is ingenious and plausible in terms of all that is known about Algonkian kinship systems. I would argue from my own experience that just these kinds of differences are as likely to arise from more specific and idiosyncratic reasons. Perhaps in one instance the two potters had been working side by side for the past 15 years while in the more diverse household the two women had worked together for only one year. It is to Brose's credit that he notes that this kind of explanation is conceivable (1970: 59). Perhaps the greater diversity in the one familial setting relates to the stylistic virtuosity of a single potter. I submit that both explanations have a plausibility equal to that of the explanation offered by Brose, and the archaeological record is most unlikely to give us any criteria for selecting among them.

When one is examining the ceramic production of five or six potters over a span of two years, one must expect that the effects of personality differences and differences in the maturational cycle of particular extended families will be maximally visible. The situation is rather like using an inappropriately high level of magnification on a microscope: one is looking through the level of structuring for which one has appropriate models to a level where the necessary data for model construction will always be lacking. Conceivably in this kind of situation one might even zero in on the disordering effects of a particular potter's menopause.

Long-term, intensive interaction must inevitably affect the stylistic variability in any pair of potters who work together for a protracted period of time. This is as clear from Friedrich's data (1970) as from my own. If the intensive artistic interaction always worked so as to produce progressively greater uniformity with the passage of longer periods of time, the task of interpreting the archaeological record would be less desperate, but the situation at Nuevo Destino suggests that intensive long-term interaction, when infused with rivalry, can produce just the opposite effects. The personalities of the individual potters in an extended family are a range of data forever unavailable to the archaeologist, but it is at just this level that the explanation of observed variability lies.

In a study such as Deetz's (1965), a much larger data base is used and the differences in stylistic variability among whole villages are the basis for examining the hypothesis. My data offer a less direct check against this form of argument from large pooled samples. Even here, though, the eastern Peruvian situation suggests that a basic reformulation of the hypothesis is in order.

My own observations and the observation of Friedrich indicate that there are groups of potters who share stylistic innovations because they interact artistically at a high level of intensity. These networks of intensive artistic interaction do map on units of observed stylistic similarity. Once we admit the existence of such units of intense artistic communication, we must reformulate the Deetz–Longacre hypothesis. This hypothesis will be true if and only if these networks of artistic interaction are as enduring as the units of economic cooperation and social interaction which are generated by consanguinity, marriage, and residence pattern, and if the networks of artistic interaction map *precisely* on the units of cooperation generated by consanguinity, marriage, and residence. These conditions do *not* hold for the Shipibo–Conibo sample as a whole – in fact the unique situation where they do hold, the Cruz family, appears as a social pathology. To put it another way, if we view cultures as evolving and ecologically rational systems, is it sensible to expect that the Deetz–Longacre hypothesis should always be true?

We must return again to the function of intensified artistic communication and the function of the networks within which such communication operates. One can mention two views of the primitive world and its social equilibrium. We have already noted the position of Redfield (1957) who argues that the forces within primitive society all work toward changelessness and stability, and that this stability is broken only by the impingement of the modern industrial world. There is another view of primitive society that pictures such societies and indeed all societies as existing in a totally dynamic and unstable condition with survival dependent on constant readjustment and an elaborate set of controls and negative feedback mechanisms. The view that the world is but one step away from chaos and can be maintained in balance only by continuous readjustment and positive action is not rare in 'primitive' cosmologies, as the studies of Reichel-Dolmatoff on the Kogi (1949–50) and Desana (1971) indicate. This view is given the most systematic exposition in Bateson's magnificent monograph *Naven* (1958).

Bateson in discussing the function of the Naven ceremony among the Iatmul has summarized this complex state of affairs as succinctly as is possible:

> The reality of the integrating effect of *naven* might still be doubtful if the Iatmul communities were limited in size by some factor other than the weakness of their internal integration. It is conceivable, for example, that a community whose size was limited by its physical environment would never reach that size at which every contributory integrating factor becomes relevant. But actually, in Iatmul culture, it is clear that the factor which limits the size of the villages is the weakness of their internal cohesion. The larger villages are continually on the point of fission and the fissions which have taken place in the past are always ascribed to quarrels which have split the parent community. More than this, these fissions when they occur invariably follow the lines of the patrilineal groups – a clan, a phratry or a moiety splitting off from the parent community and thereby rending the system of affinal linkages. From this pattern of cleavage it is evident that the patrilineal linkages are stronger than the affinal, the latter presenting as it were a plane of weakness of the community. Under these circumstances the importance of any factor which strengthens the affinal links becomes apparent and we are justified in saying that the villages could not be as big as they are if it were not for *naven* ceremonies or some analogous phenomenon.

Transferring Bateson's insight to the Shipibo–Conibo, we would observe that the natural planes of cleavage are between the largely matrilocal extended families. If the networks of artistic communication were consistently coterminous with these extended families, as they are in the one aberrant case of the Cruz family, these patterns of communication would work to emphasize the potential planes of weakness and to facilitate the fragmentation of the society. If they cut across such cleavages they will exert a positive, cohesive force on the society.

Under certain conditions it may be adaptive for an ethnic group to fragment down to the smallest unit which is economically feasible, and one would expect that unlimited availability of the appropriate kind of land would be one characteristic of the ecological setting of such societies. But considering that the Shipibo–Conibo adjustment is to a highly restricted ecological setting, the immediate flood plains of the major rivers, and considering that the population size of contact period Conibo communities was 2,000, one can see that 'every contributory integrating factor becomes relevant', and art to the Shipibo–Conibo is such an integrating factor.

I would suggest that the Deetz–Longacre hypothesis be rewritten somewhat as follows: units of stylistic uniformity, whatever their pattern of recruitment, will map on units of consanguinity, residence, and economic cooperation, in those situations where it is ecologically feasible for the society to fragment into the minimal viable units of economic cooperation. In total ecological settings where it is necessary for the society to maintain social units which are larger and more elaborate than the minimal units of economic cooperation, units of stylistic uniformity and communication will cross-cut the more basic social units, serving as one of several communication networks to bind across the units most likely to break away, and thus strengthen the total fabric of the larger society.

As well as being supported by Bateson's formulation, this set of generalizations is precisely what Chagnon (1973) has observed concerning group size and outward colonization among the Yąnomamö, of Venezuela. A vast area of Venezuela is occupied by groups of these rather primitive tropical forest agriculturists. Those groups near the boundaries of Yąnomamö territory tend to move outward and fission down to minimal economically feasible size in response to aggression from other Yąnomamö groups. In the course of this outward migration, behaviour involving intense interaction with other groups is weakened or discontinued.

On the other hand, groups in the centre of Yąnomamö territory cannot move out, and the response to the problem of military aggression is to develop larger group size and to intensify all forms of affective communication with several other allied groups, so that there is a tendency to fuse into even larger social units. Thus feasting, trading, and patterns of mock combat are all intensified so as to bind together several groups into powerful military alliances. I suspect that if the Yąnomamö had visual art of even moderate complexity this too would intensify as a communication network. Unfortunately they do not.

I am in total agreement with Chagnon that the total ecological setting must be conceived broadly, including all other human groups with which the subject group is in competition. It cannot be conceived merely as the physical environment: 'First the concept of cultural ecology should be broad enough to embrace inter-group social relationships as a component' (Chagnon 1973: 136).

To summarize: units of stylistic similarity can be viewed only as the result of networks along which artistic communication is intense. Such networks in turn can be understood only as the result of total societal adaptation, ongoing repetitive process, and notions of negative feedback; in other words in a systemic model. Art as communication is a subject of such complexity that it must be handled in the context of systemic models (serutan archaeology in Flannery's (1973) terminology). Attempts to handle these problems with models based on linear causality (law-and-order archaeology in Flannery's categorization) must inevitably give partial or more probably trivial answers.[1]

Note

1 This paper has greatly benefited from the criticism of my wife, Joan W. Lathrap. Because she remained in the village of San Francisco de Yarinacocha for the full eight months of fieldwork, her observations on ongoing familial interactions were more extensive than my own. I have made free use of her insights on these matters, but take full responsibility for any faults in the interpretation. The final form of the paper has also been sharpened as the result of a seminar on cognition and culture taught jointly with Klaus Witz. The paper was originally submitted in 1974 for a volume to be published by the Anthropological Society of Washington. I thank the staff of the National Museum for executing the drawings and William Sturtevant for his support and release of the paper.

References

Bateson, Gregory, 1958. *Naven*, 2nd edn. Stanford University Press, Stanford.

1972. Style, grace, and information in primitive art. In *Steps to an Ecology of Mind*, pp. 128–52. Ballantine Books, New York.

Binford, Lewis R., 1968. Methodological considerations of the archaeological use of ethnographic data. In *Man the Hunter*, edited by Richard B. Lee and Irven DeVore, pp. 268–73, Aldine, Chicago.

Boas, Franz, 1927. *Primitive Art* (reprinted 1951). Capitol, New York.

Bonnichsen, Robson, 1973. Millie's Camp: an experiment in archaeology. *World Archaeology* 4 (3): 277–91.

Brose, David S., 1970. The Summer Island Site. *Case Western Reserve University Studies in Anthropology* No. 1, Cleveland.

Chagnon, Napoleon A., 1973. The culture-ecology of shifting (pioneering) cultivation among the Yąnomamö Indians. In *Peoples and Cultures of Native South America*, edited by Daniel R. Gross, pp. 126–42. Natural History Press, New York.

Deetz, James, 1965. *The Dynamics of Stylistic Change in Arikara Ceramics.* Illinois Studies in Anthropology No. 4, University of Illinois Press, Urbana.

Flannery, Kent V., 1972. The cultural evolution of civilizations. *Annual Review of Ecology and Systematics* 3: 399–426.

1973. Archeology with a capital S. In *Research and Theory in Current Archeology*, edited by Charles L. Redman, pp. 47–53. John Wiley and Sons, New York.

Friedrich, Margaret Hardin, 1970. Design structure and social interaction: archaeological implications of an ethnographic analysis. *American Antiquity* 35 (3): 332–43.

Lathrap, Donald W., 1968a. The 'hunting' economies of the tropical forest zone of South America. In *Man the Hunter*, edited by Richard B. Lee and Irven DeVore, pp. 23–9. Aldine, Chicago.

1968b. Aboriginal occupation and changes in river channel on the Central Ucayali, Peru. *American Antiquity* 33 (1): 62–79.

1968c. Wasëmëa and the rise of Mayakënë. Paper read at the Annual Meeting of the Society for American Archaeology, Santa Fe.

1970. *The Upper Amazon.* Thames and Hudson, London.

n.d. The transmission of Shipibo–Conibo art style: stylistic similarity and the structure of households. Paper read at the 34th Annual Meeting for the Society for American Archaeology, Milwaukee, 2 May 1969.

Lewis, Oscar, 1970. Tepoztlan restudied: a critique of the folk–urban conceptualization of social change. In *Anthropological Essays*, pp. 35–52. Random House, New York.

Longacre, William A. 1964. Sociological implications of the ceramic analysis. *Fieldiana: Anthropology* 55: 155–70. Chicago, Field Museum of Natural History.

Redfield, Robert, 1957. *The Primitive Worls and its Transformations.* Great Seal Books, Ithaca.

Reichel-Dolmatoff, Gerardo, 1949–50. Los Kogi. *Revista del Instituto Etnológica Nacional* 5 (1a) and (2a). Bogotá.

1971. *Amazonian Cosmos: The sexual and religious symbolism of the Tukano Indians.* University of Chicago Press, Chicago.

Chapter 4

Where two dimensions meet: the Kuba of Zaire

Marie Jeanne Adams

Introduction

The physical form of African sculpture has received considerable attention in twentieth-century scholarly work. Freudian theory stimulated interpretations of form emphasizing the sexual elements, such as von Sydow's influential notion (1927) that the pole-like character he perceived in African sculpture signified its underlying phallic meaning.

The more valuable early work established stylistic canons for various ethnic groups on the basis of art works of secure provenance, so that the great number of pieces in museums and private collections could be grouped and identified as to place of origin. Frans Olbrechts' studies of the 1,525 pieces of Belgian Congo sculpture in the 1937–8 Brussels exhibition (published in Dutch 1946, in French 1959) supplies the fundamental document on African art styles. He noted the emphasis on the single, monochromatic figure, the neglect of natural proportions, the exaggerated size of the head, and the frontal pose as consistent general features of the sculptured human body. He (1959: 29–35) distinguished individual ethnic works according to the shape and position of the limbs and by comparing details of hairstyle, eyes, ears, mouth and nose (see his Figs. 12–15, p. 34), thereby establishing criteria still in use today.

Art scholars in the fifties and sixties extended Olbrechts' efforts and gave more attention to context (Wingert 1950, Trowell 1954, Paulme 1956, Leuzinger 1960, Fagg 1965), although not offering more than naming the type of ritual in which an object appeared and assigning some general functionalist label such as ancestor or fertility figure, or mask of social control.

Papers at a 1965 conference at Columbia University, organized by Douglas Fraser, marked a significant advance in attention to form because several Africanists pointed to the specificity of materials and features of art objects used in political contexts and, generally, to the significance of the objects according to the people making and using them. In commenting on the papers, Fraser and Cole (1972) emphasized that in regard to physical properties, elite arts are distinguished from those of lesser leaders or of the common people by contrast which may take varied forms such as elaboration, miniaturization or monumentality. The elite corpus is further characterized by more complex techniques of fabrication, more imported materials, more complex iconography, and a proliferation of types and varieties of objects. Fraser and Cole also note *some* correlation between the extent of (idealized) naturalism and the degree of sociopolitical differentiation. Pasztory (1971) then strengthened the link between political context and forms by showing that in the region of southern Nigeria characterized by centralized leadership, artists developed hierarchical group compositions

– a more complex arrangement than the single sculptured figure type of neighbouring societies organized by less articulated political structures.

These essays helped subsequent scholars to break away from a tradition of interpretation in which a work of art is assumed to convey the total character of the social world, and led them to specify the proximate context and its sponsors. In this way, one learns which segment of society the arts speak for and toward what end – that is, how art is structured within the larger social context. After collecting evidence from specific contexts, one can attempt to formulate preferences that may operate over several domains.

The first scholar to see African principles of structuring physical form as part of a broader organizational preference was an anthropologist, James Fernandez (1966, 1977), who worked among the Fang of Gabon. For him and some of his informants, the carved statuettes that guard the bones of important dead show the principles of balance and opposition valued by the Fang. In the statuette these principles are evident in the general bilateral symmetry and in the co-occurrence of child-like and adult features. He observed balanced opposition also in the layout of confronting rows of village houses, in the male and female character of the dwellings, in the concept of the ideal mature person who combines forceful initiative with reasoned restraint. It was just the balance of opposites that, according to the Fang, gave vitality to social interaction and to the sculptured figures.

Robert Thompson, who began to investigate explicit aesthetic preferences by questioning various classes of Yoruba people in Nigeria about their sculpture in the early sixties, gradually developed a position (1974) that dance and music are clearly structured by certain strong shared canons of form to which Thompson gave such lively titles as 'swing every note and every color strong', 'simultaneous suspending and preserving of the beat', 'a get-down quality', and 'call and response'. The contrast, powerfully felt by the Yoruba, between hot and cool states, established the ultimate effect sought in their art forms. He discusses these preferences for certain kinds of rhythm and expression as factors shaping Yoruba and other African sculptural forms.

Lévi-Strauss's emphasis on binary sets (1963, 1969) is directly acknowledged as an inspiration for analysing form in *African Art as Philosophy* (1974) in which Douglas Fraser and several of his students point to complementary usage as a way in which Africans structure artistic efforts. Interesting examples include seed and fruit motifs among the Dogon, beauty and the beast images among the Ibo, and expressions of creative and destructive forces among the Yoruba. In a brief but brilliantly developed essay in the book, DeMott points out, on the basis of ethnographic reports, the contrasting usages for spiral forms and for chequerboard designs among the Dogon. She concludes (p. 19): 'The Dogon describe the beings, energies and qualities of the supernatural world by curvilinear or spiral forms, and they represent the products and actions of human life and the basic human order by horizontal/vertical systems.'

A more detailed working out of dualistic categories as expressed in art forms can be found in Vogel's work on the Baule (1973, 1977). Contrasts between the wild bush and the controlled village domain, between youth and elders, and between men and women as social groups are exemplified in sets of masked figures with either coarse or refined features. Particularly interesting for us is that the Baule identify sculptured figures as mischievous bush spirits or as spirit mates for humans not according to formal style but according to surface effects resulting from the way the figures are given offerings. Food offerings are placed in bowls before the spirit mates, who eat in human fashion, while offering mixtures are simply poured over the bush spirits. Thus, the distinctive formal feature for interpretation is the opposition of cleanly polished and dull, uneven surfaces.

Another approach to form was suggested in the sixties by the French aesthetician, Jean Laude (1966). Using a series of works in relief from different ethnic groups in West Africa, he contrasted the realization of form and compositional order in what he called the mythic and historic modes.

In the mythic mode, found in acephalous societies, actors only are depicted, not events. Elements of myth carved on door panels are figured in an abstract style and they are not arranged in a sequential, narrative order but according to some kind of conceptual schema. Mythic action takes place outside ordinary space, so the artist does not seek to reproduce ordinary depth nor imagine a perspectival point of view. In the historic mode, in centralized kingdoms in which the king as a person is prominent, as in the former Dahomey and Benin courts, imagery is presented in naturalistic form, and figures on textile appliqués and bronze plaques are juxtaposed as in a real event, thus creating recognizable scenes.

These several investigations reaffirm that form itself – shape, size, arrangement of parts, surfaces, and style – indicate category boundaries, not simply of artistic, ethnic or cult groupings, but also those of greater and lesser political power, of male and female or older and younger groups, and, in imaginative domains, of spirit and human nature and of mythic and historic situations. Revelation of category boundaries derives from studied observation of objects, from outsiders' insights into native practice, from elicitation or from some combination of these methods.

Building on this body of work, I will consider yet another aspect of form. An hitherto unexamined aspect of art objects in a cultural context is their dimensionality, that is, the degree of depth or thickness of objects. The art of the Bushoong, the former ruling ethnic group of the Kuba kingdom in central Zaire, provides an interesting example of the structuring of dimensionality within a political context. It is my thesis that the distribution of works of two and three dimensions among the population signalled Bushoong attitudes toward access to political authority. Fully rounded human-figure sculpture was rare, appearing only in the royal sphere. In contrast, the artistry expressed in flatwork – that is, in two dimensions – such as woven cloth or designs on mats and textiles and in scarification, was available to most of the population. The most telling point is that objects which combine these two dimensions, that is, the great quantity of carved decorated boxes and winecups, which are three-dimensional objects covered with a profusion of low-relief designs from the two-dimensional inventory, and the elaborate bulky costumes built up from flat, two-dimensional textiles, functioned in the dynamic sphere of political competition. Such objects, elaborated by professionals, were an integral part of the competitive activities by which men won political appointment and gained renown.

The Kuba, the Bushoong and their arts

Most of our knowledge about the Kuba people of Zaire derives from the reports of the ethnographer, Emil Torday, who in the early twentieth century led an expedition to this central African region for the British Museum, and of the historian, Jan Vansina, who studied Kuba society in the field between 1953 and 1956.

The Kuba number about 75,000 and occupy the territory between the Kasai and Sankuru Rivers in central Zaire. Their earlier development as a kingdom seems to fit the pattern of a number of other, larger 'empires' in central Africa, in which a conqueror organizes a number of agricultural village communities into a state having at its centre a sacred ruler and a royal court with supporting aristocracy. In the late nineteenth century this aristocratic kingdom comprised twelve ethnic groups dominated by the centrally located Bushoong. The hereditary chief of the Bushoong was the acknowledged sovereign of all other ethnic chiefs. Kuba society seems to have been a stable and prosperous one in which values emphasizing work and wealth stimulated a development of material culture of a richness and diversity not found among surrounding peoples of Zaire (Vansina 1967–8). The Bushoong developed a unique constellation of art objects: wood sculpture, embroidered textiles and decorated architecture.

Visitors to the capital, Mushenge, in the late nineteenth century found a planned court layout, and a large population (approximately 4,000), consisting of the king with his hundreds of wives, relatives, officials and nobility, along with a number of specialized craftsmen, such as tailors and sculptors. The Kuba maintained extensive trade links at border markets, but the king forbade entry of foreigners under penalty of death to anyone who assisted them.

The first person to penetrate the capital of this well-ordered kingdom was a remarkable black American Presbyterian missionary to the Congo, William Sheppard, who was received in 1892 by the king as a putative descendant of a past ruling family (Sheppard c. 1918). Although Sheppard and his successor learned the Kuba language, the mission was short-lived and had to move out of Kuba territory. In the next decade Torday's two-volume description of Kuba institutions (1910) impressed the Belgian Government, which after 1910 became the colonial authority, so that the Kuba territory was allowed indirect rule until the independence of Zaire in 1960. In the 1950s, when Vansina came to study, Kuba society provided an exceptional opportunity to glimpse a traditional African kingdom and its relationship to art.

Kuba art objects, like most African art, are made to be used, to be handled; they are made for some specific purpose, to be manipulated or to be worn. Even statuary in black Africa is handled a great deal; it is taken out of its resting place, rubbed with oil, colouring, and often danced with. These usages help account for the small scale of so many of the objects. They serve as personal insignia, such as staffs or ceremonial weapons, or function within the sphere of the person, like hand-held musical instruments or small carrying stools, as part of the bearer's social image.

Another striking feature of the arts of either village or court is the intensity, dignity and seriousness of craftsmanship and statement, so that we can say there is no folk art, none of the objects we associate with European villages that are charming, cheerful, frivolous or just cute in character. We do not find this genre in villages of central Africa because African works are associated with serious spiritual aims and important secular concerns.

Although we do not see the familiar European contrast between court style and folk art, the existence of royal courts does give an impetus to the production of art works in terms of abundance and elaboration.

The Kuba king belongs to the African category of sacred rulers, who are believed to enjoy special powers of fertility and destruction to which the well-being of the kingdom as a whole is linked (Vansina 1958; 1964: 98–103). Photographs of the Bushoong court from the early twentieth century into the 1970s show the great attention to regalia as symbols of this sacred kingship. Much of this regalia is shared with court officials and regional chiefs who support the Bushoong king (Fig. 4.1). As a whole, the character of the Bushoong court exemplifies the arts of leadership, as these arts are set forth by Douglas Fraser and Herbert Cole (1972).

First, the ruler is distinguished by special space, the royal capital which is segregated from the small common settlements. The capital is the king's personal domain, each successive section is enclosed by walls. In public appearances, the king is spatially segregated (Fig. 4.2). He is shaded and elevated. He is marked by contrast. His shell-covered costume appears white in contrast to the red garments of the wives, officials and nobles who surround this sphere. His costume is far more elaborate than any others, with a greater number and variety of designs. The materials are more precious. The king wears garments of leopard skin as a royal prerogative. The red cloth of the other men's and the women's skirts is made of local palm fibre, dyed with redwood imported from neighbouring peoples, but the cowrie shells that decorate the king's garments and his insignia are imported from the Indian Ocean.

The king had important powers of political appointment including the officers of several grand councils who determined policy (Vansina 1964: 126–34). The king stood at the apex of an intricate and elaborate system of title-holders to whom he delegated his powers. They administered courts, represented the regions or the villages, and exercised police and religious authority. The greater part of the offices were reserved for men but community titles, including chiefly ones, existed for women (Vansina 1964: 127). In contrast to the neighbouring Lele society, whose members acquired prestige by passing into older age sets, the Kuba associated prestige with political position. Because of the prestige and profit that were attached to political authority, these positions were much sought after. All brought economic benefit in the form of fines, fees, and other rewards. Above all obtaining political title was the mark of success and public recognition of prestigious status (Vansina 1964: 127).

In this black African kingdom there was no discernible ancestor cult in family households (Vansina 1958: 745).

Fig. 4.1. Kuba chief in regalia. Domiongo, 1974. (Photo: J. Cornet)

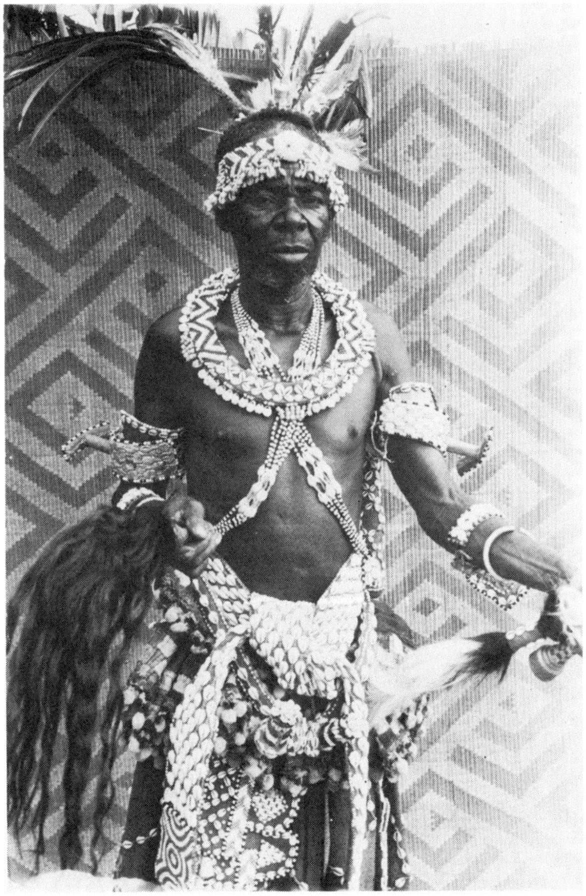

However, kings and some chiefs did preserve carved images of their predecessors. The most famous type of Zairian art is the Kuba king statue (*ndop*). Five of these, collected between 1909 and 1913 from the Kuba court, are said to represent past Kuba kings (Torday 1910: 30–1; Olbrechts 1959: 57). These figures, about 50–5 cm in height, are carved of a hardwood, which is unusual in African art. Each depicts a human figure sitting crosslegged on a throne-base, with a wooden object carved in front of it (Fig. 4.3). At the first public audience witnessed by William Sheppard, the king displayed four figures of his predecessors near him on an earthen platform. Sheppard (c. 1918: 113) was informed of the identity of the kings according to the emblematic object carved in front of the figure.

We know little of the ritual surrounding these commemorative figures. Upon ascension, a king commissioned an *ndop*, a royal drum and a special design, which were announced to the public. During his lifetime the figure was believed to house a counterpart of the king's soul. Kept in the women's quarters, the statue would be placed near a wife in childbirth to ensure safe delivery (Vansina 1972: 44–5). This link between a leader and the fertility of his wives (as an indication of the prosperity he is able to bring the kingdom) is clearly stated in the special hairstyle projecting in two mounds, like horns at the forehead, which was traditionally worn by leaders. This hairstyle is similar to the one worn by a woman who is carrying her first baby (see Figs. 4.4 and 4.5).

The statue could also serve as a substitute for the king. In his absence, his wives would anoint, stroke and fondle it (Vansina 1972: 44). After the king's death the figure was used in rites to establish continuity of his spirit with the new king, who slept with it at his side (Maesen 1960: pl. 19). Then it was stored away in the special hut, presumably to be brought out on important occasions.

Four of the early figures are so similar in style as to suggest that they are the product of one hand, probably carved in the early nineteenth century, after the destruction of earlier ones, or as a response to more emphasis on the cult of sacred kingship (see illustrations and discussion of history and style in Rosenwald 1974: 26–31).

The *ndop* figure represents the king's body in rounded form as in nature, the upper part of the body larger in proportion than the lower limbs, in a manner we can term 'descending perspective'. To carve this figure, the royal sculptor works with a simple tool, the adze, which has a wooden handle to which a metal blade is attached at an acute angle. It takes great skill of the hand and the eye to bring out fine details with this tool. In addition to the organic shape of the facial features and body parts, the sculptor reproduces realistic detail on the body, such as the line across the chest, the outline of the lips and the dip in the hairline, a style favoured by Bushoong men, perhaps a reference to the more traditional jutting hairstyle.

The king, Kot a Pe, who gave the now best-known

Fig. 4.2. Kuba king seated in state. Mushenge, 1970. (Photo: E. Elisofon)

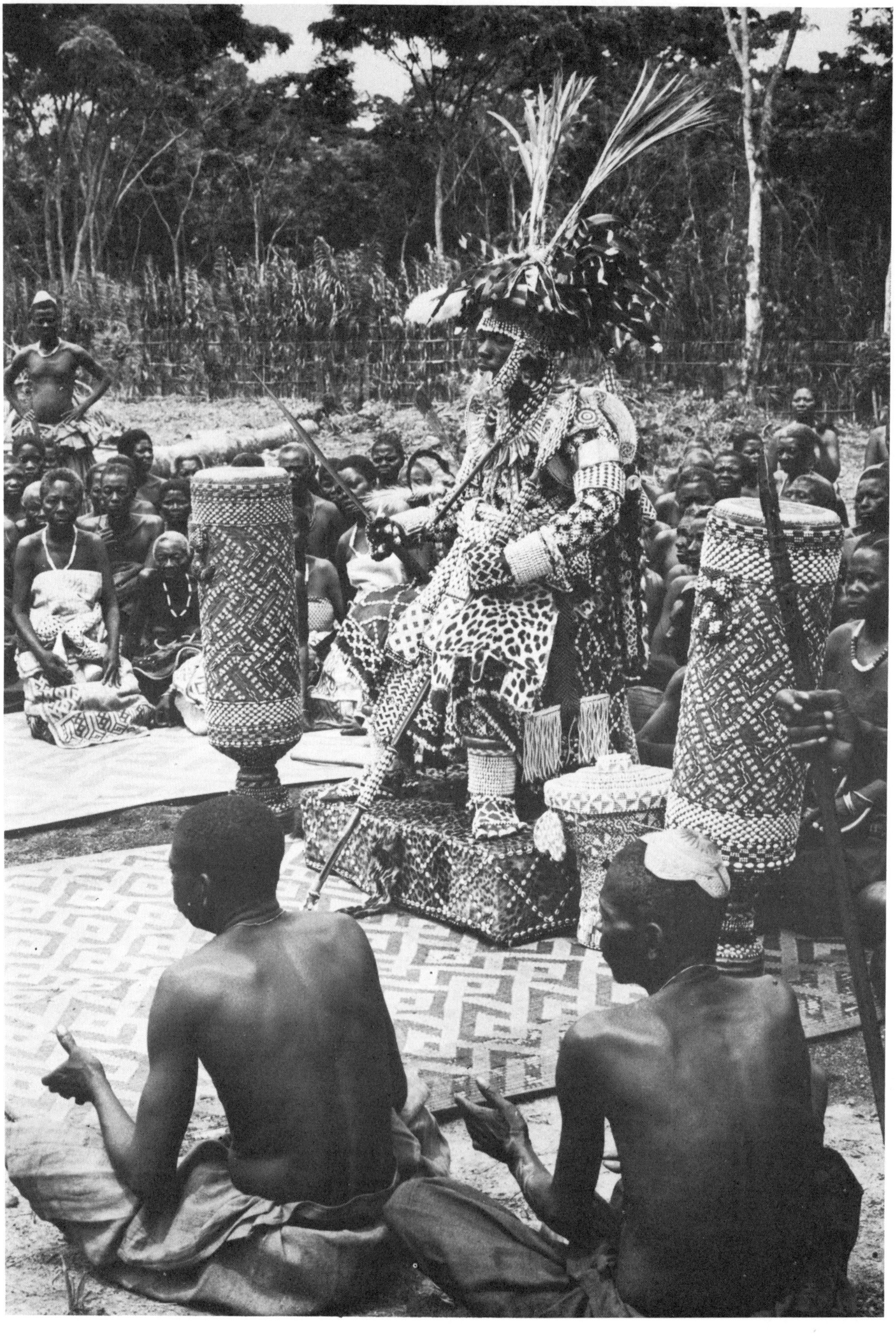

Fig. 4.3. Statue of Kuba king Shyaam. (Museum of Mankind, London)

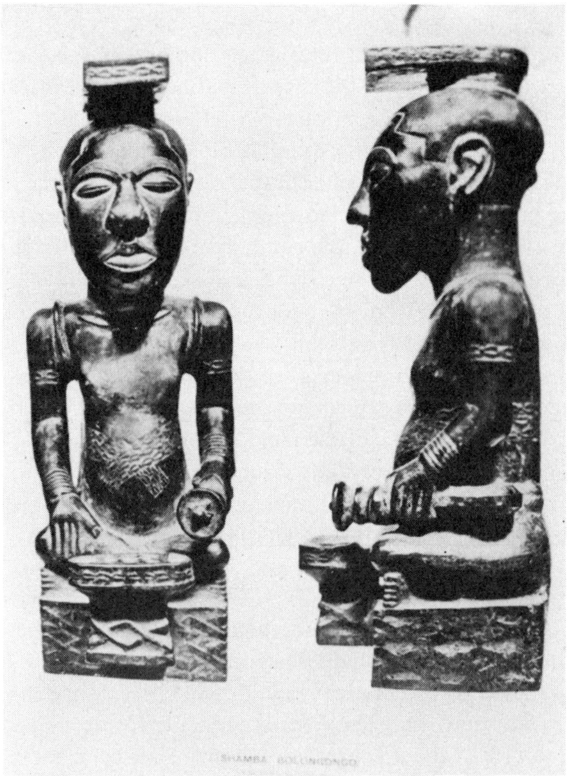

Fig. 4.4. Kuba chief with special hairstyle. (Torday photo)

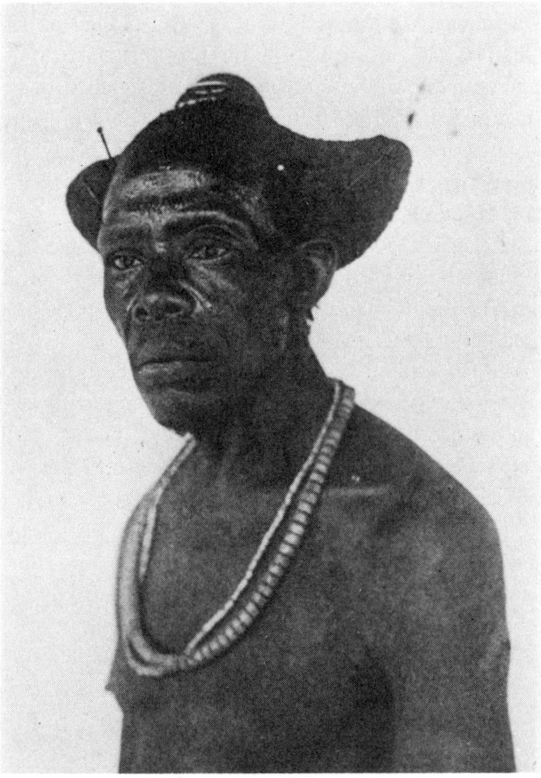

Fig. 4.5. Pregnant woman with special hairstyle. (Torday photo)

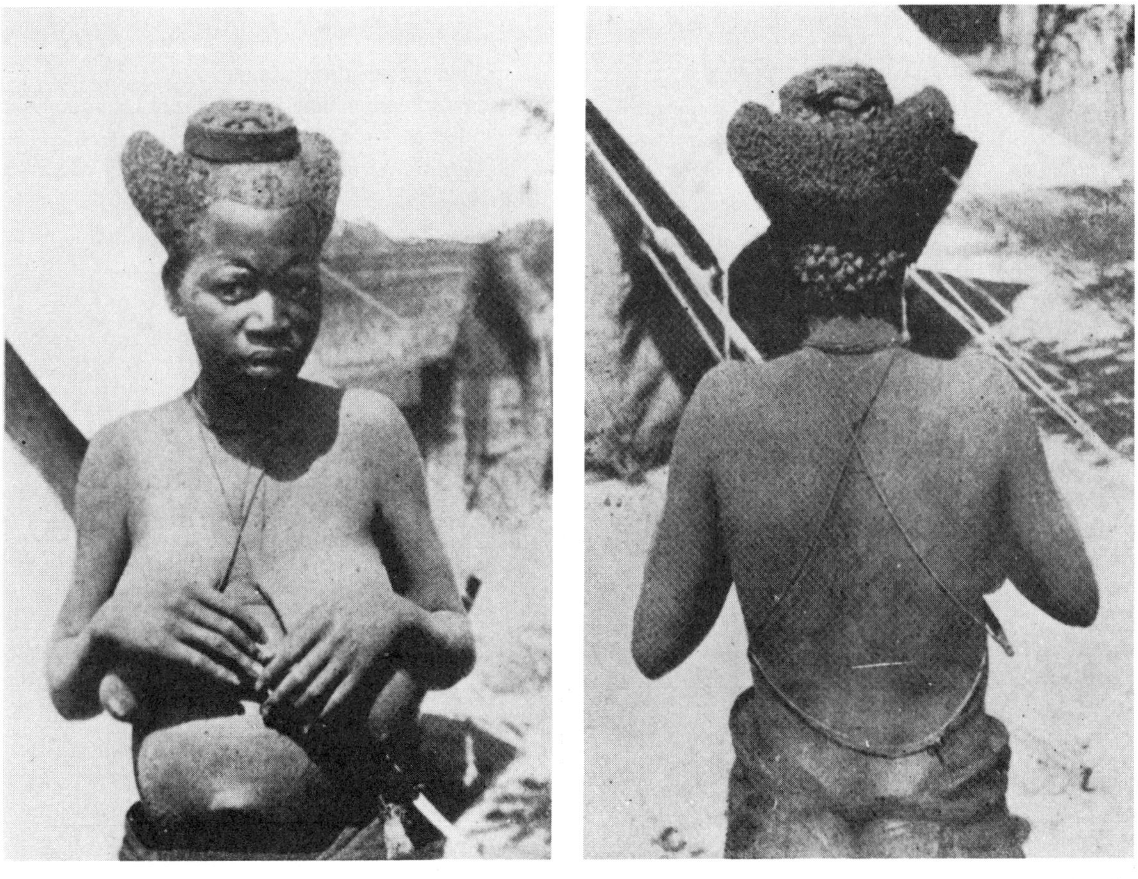

figure (Fig. 4.3) to Torday for the British Museum in 1908, said it represented King Shyaam who reigned, according to other data, early in the seventeenth century (Vansina 1972: 54). Shyaam is a culture hero to the Kuba. He instituted the political councils and taught the use of new plants for food and the making of cloth from raphia palm. He is remembered for his wisdom, and people continue to quote his sayings. In giving this figure to Torday (1910: 27) the king quoted Shyaam as saying to his people:

> When they look at this statue they will be able to remember me, and think that I watch over them, consoling them when they are sad, giving them inspiration and courage anew.

The Kuba identify this figure as the king by the essentials of royal regalia (Torday 1910: 202–3). Starting at the bottom, we can list these recurrent features. The square base replicates the padded rectangular throne-seat of Kuba kings. The object in front of the base is a symbol chosen by the king to represent his reign. For Shyaam, this object is a game board which he is said to have introduced to reduce disputing. In front of another king figure, the object represents an anvil, for that king was noted as a great smith.

The king figure (*ndop*) holds in the left hand a short parade sword. Across the buttocks lies a woven cloth plaque only worn at royal ceremonies. The plaited belt identifies him as a member of the crown-council and the highest judicial court. The cowrie shell belt, wristlets and armstrings are insignia of high nobility. The shoulder hoops of cane are especially reserved for kings. The projecting panel shading the king's face refers to the brim of a pillbox hat, worn by chiefs and the king (Vansina 1972: 51, and see his fig. 3.1), that is still part of the royal costume inventory at the capital. With this particular set of features on the sculpture we recognize the conventional portrayal of a king. The size, impressiveness, material and cues from the regalia signify these figures as royal art.

Another aspect of a human figure as a visual statement is its mood, tone, expression – that is, the personality that conditions the work. How does the form itself convey this, and how does this relate to the political context of the subject matter? The seated crosslegged pose conveys a relaxed calm and a motionless image. The body position, with large head placed near the chest and the arms held alike close to the torso, conveys an impression of compactness, containment and stolidity. The object in front of the figure forms a visual barrier that adds further detachment.

Two important areas of the composition as indicated by the clustering of elements occur in the upper part of the body and at the base. In between, the body is recessed and the carving is understated, the surfaces marked by very shallow designs. In the upper part the projecting face is dominant, its features organic in proportion and perfectly symmetrical. Its physiognomic quality is of calm immobility. The large, oval shape is a quiet form, the eyes are closed, the lips relaxed. There is no dynamic given to the expression by the direction of a gaze.

These obvious features are reinforced by qualities of a more abstract character. The intangible outline that we feel encloses the total figure is rectangular, and a rectangle is a stable form. Within that rectangular outline, the substance of the figure fills most of the space, creating a massive effect. The dense grain of the wood contributes to the sense of compact heaviness. The unity of impression is enhanced by the sombre monotone and smooth surfaces. Except for the hat brim in profile, there are no strong, interrupting contrasts.

In the lower part, the combination of decorated surfaces and the mass formed by the crossed legs, the thick base and the object in front of it convey an impression of bulk and weight that adds a stolidity to the figure. If we compare this statement with the image of the king in photographs of the 1920s, we see a similarity in the massive dignity and immobile appearance of the king. According to Vansina (1967–8: 24–5) and readily evident in the filmed scenes of the king in 1970 (Fig. 4.6), there is an ideal of deportment. The king walks with slow ponderous movements and, as expected, he maintains a majestic calm throughout his ritual appearance.

This ideal of composure runs through Kuba society. Visitors in the early twentieth century and later have been struck by the aristocratic restraint of all classes going through their daily activities. This ideal is explicitly formulated and epitomized in the proper way of dying – in a calm and unruffled manner. Kuba ceremonies have a quite elegant character. They have a fondness for restrained, long, slow mimed pageants (Vansina 1967–8: 26). The king figures can be seen as embodying certain ideals of kingship and behaviour held by members of this society.

Reports of earlier times tell us that this mode does not tell the whole story of Kuba kingship or behaviour. This mood of measured tranquility has the placidity of a volcano (Vansina 1967–8: 25). There are eruptions in the intense competition for titles and for positions of power. The open display and flaunting of wealth and rank creates jealousy, a leading cause for the use and accusations of sorcery. This undercurrent of tension comes to vivid public expression in the agonizing poison ordeals for witchcraft or sorcery (Vansina 1969: 246), which were reinstituted as independence neared in 1959.

As for the king, there is in addition a negative ideal attached to kingship. The people believe that kings are sorcerers (Vansina 1964: 102–3). Kings are associated with filth, *nyec*, and a lack of shame, *bushony*, because upon installation they repudiate their kin group and commit ritual incest (Vansina 1964: 109), thus violating the two imperatives that restrain the ordinary man. The king possesses supranormal powers by virtue of going beyond the basic norms of Kuba society. In addition the king gains an omniscience and authority beyond his limited constitutional powers by the expectation that he possesses *paam*, the power to exercise arbitrary and violent authority. However he must do these violent things in secret, or lose face (Vansina 1964: 104–5). The art form of elite sculpture seems restricted only

Fig. 4.6. At a public ceremony, the Kuba king moves ponderously. (Photo: E. Elisofon)

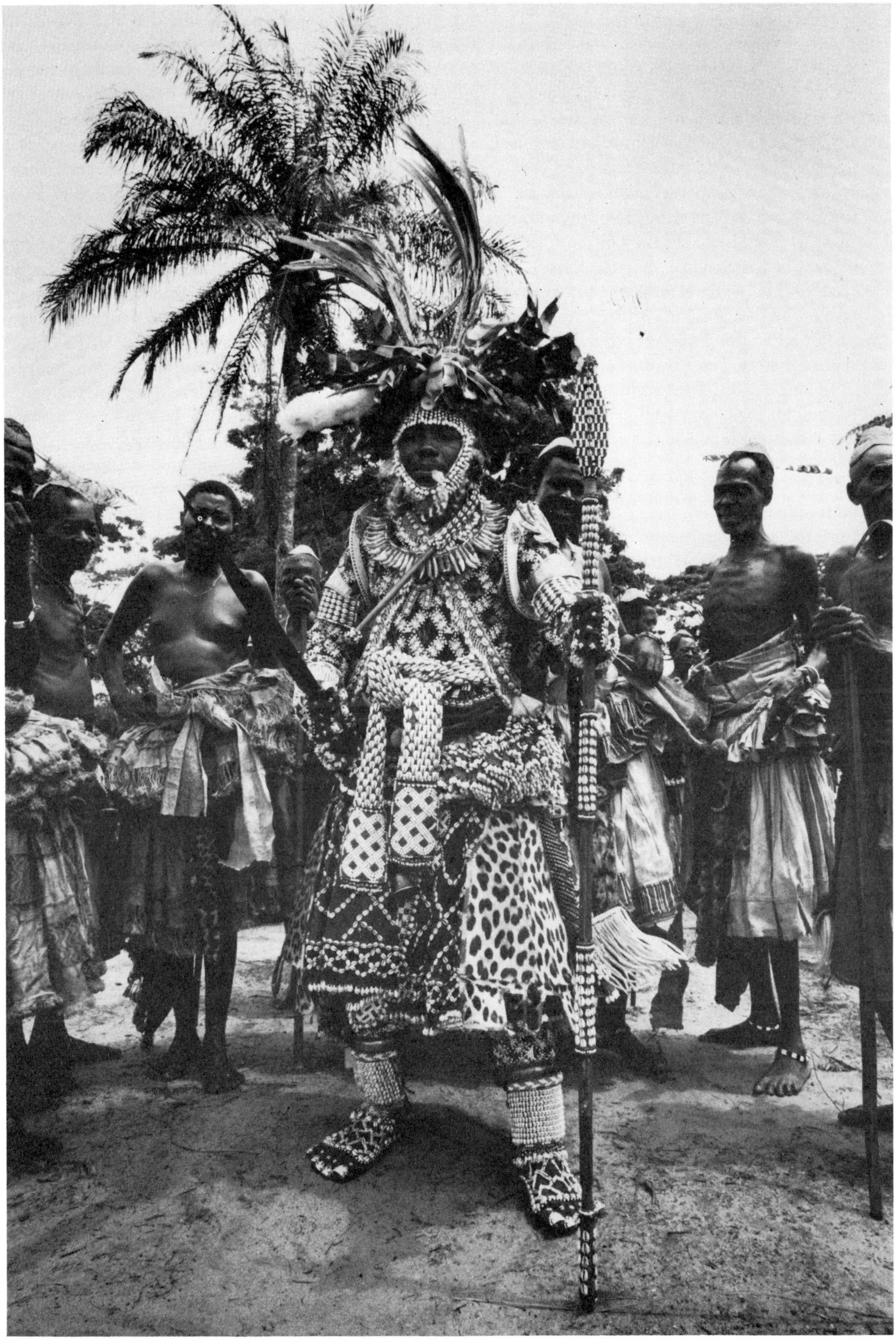

to the positive ideals that are identified with the king. Even if that sphere is important we should recognize the specificity of the artistic statement, that the art of the statues is limited to that sphere.

Rarely does the king wear his royal mask, one made not of wood like other Kuba masks, but of animal hide in hood form, which is covered with cloth, feathers, beads and shells. Wood is used for the attached ears, nose and mouth. The king dons this mask only at his installation or on very special occasions. When the king appears in his royal mask, masked 'fool'-dancers come out and whip arbitrarily into the audience (informant, Kwete Mwana, nephew of previous king; 'fool' mask identified at National Museum, Kinshasa 70.5.434, in Adams 1976). The royal mask presents evidence of the king's power in the special animal pelts and eagle-feather crown, and of his wealth in the imported beads and shells. I would suggest that the unusual ritual action accompanying the masked king stands for the secret powers he should possess of exercising whatever arbitrary or violent action is needed to maintain his position and the integrity of the society.

Two- and three-dimensionality

Kuba carvers produced figural sculpture other than the *ndop*, but the Bushoong lacked the ubiquitous wooden images related to cults elsewhere in black Africa. One of the earliest travellers through the Kuba territory, William Sheppard (c. 1918: 113) noted that only the king possessed human figure sculpture: 'I have seen in no Bakuba village an idol.' However, at each new moon, on behalf of the country's well-being and harvests, the king sprinkled the blood of a sacrificed animal over 'the big idol in his own fetish house'.

Olbrechts (1959: 59), who studied the vast collections stored in the royal colonial museum at Tervuren, Belgium, was struck by the limited number of Kuba figures, other than the royal statues:

> It would be vain to search in this region for the function or the forms with which other stylistic regions of the Belgian Congo are so richly endowed: no ancestor statues, no funerary statues, almost no fetishes, and where by chance one finds any, they manifestly bear the imprint of their foreign origin, either Songe, Tetela or Bena Lulua; figurines of divination are scarcely more numerous.[1]

The initiation process for boys inspired an array of small carvings that appeared on or near a temporary high fibre wall that separated the village from the bush for the duration of the ritual period (Vansina 1955). These included various figure carvings such as monkeys, birds and masks, and at the base of the wall stood a large (approximately 50–70 cm) female figure with a painted face, as a fertility symbol. However this initiation took place only once a generation at the capital and at specified royal villages. Although elite women wore elaborate insignia, the few known examples of large female statues are nude and unadorned, their black monochrome surface interrupted by only a few scarification marks.[2] Among elite families, a young girl might be given a small figure of a female with a child that after her marriage was believed to help her give birth without mishap (Vansina 1967–8: 18), and a few of these can be found in various collections.[3] The identification of figures according to their pre-colonial usage is complicated by the developments in the 1920s of a syncretic cult that encouraged the use of paired male and female figures (Vansina 1959: 87), and by the encouragement given during the colonial period to carvings for sale (see for example Anon. 1954, 5: 11–12, 18–19).[4]

Most of the human images of early date are either very small, sharply angular and schematic in shape, or have incomplete bodies. For example, in the British Museum, a partial human figure attached to a base shows a rounded head, neck and shoulders, but the central part of the torso is hollowed out to a square space.[5] (This feature recalls the framed hollow that marks Luba divination figures.) The most numerous and typical form of the human figure occurs as one of the many types of small household and personal charms. In this form a partial or complete human figure, about 5–8 cm in height, terminates at the lower end in a spike (Olbrechts 1959: pl. 65), so that it could be stuck in a hairdress, a house wall or other support.[6]

The testimony of Olbrechts and the small number of figurative sculptures collected by Torday and other early travellers show that, except for the special female fertility figures and the king statuary, the sculpted body is not fully defined and its forms are fragmentary or schematic. We can conclude that the large, well-articulated, organic human figure with regalia is limited to the narrow elite leadership level.

Another art for which the Kuba are famous among collectors and museums and which the Kuba produced in quantity is of a two-dimensional character: flat, linear designs. Coming into the capital village laid out in two rows of houses, travellers were impressed with the myriad designs on the plaited walls of houses. Groups of men were seen lashing attractive mats with coloured linear designs (Fig. 4.7). Women were busy with their needles designing orderly embroideries and adding appliqued patches to palm-fibre skirts. Another notable two-dimensional art form was the elaborate low-relief scarification on women's torsos.

In contrast to the restricted possession of the three-dimensional human figure statues, these two-dimensional arts belonged to everyone. Since this was the case it is fitting that the people worked on these art forms openly in the central plaza, men making mats (Fig. 4.7) or weaving fibre cloth, and women gathering to embroider cloth designs.[7]

These products moved into a widespread series of internal markets in which both men and women participated (Vansina 1962). The Bushoong also imported wood and plain cloth from neighbouring ethnic groups and applied skilful decorations to these materials in order to exchange them in external markets for still other desired products. In these markets small pieces of flat (two-dimensional), finely woven textiles served as a major form of currency until about 1910. This emphasizes the commonality of the two-dimensional forms. At enthronement ceremonies, the king-designate indicated a geometric pattern of decoration that would be his sign and would be carved on his official drum (Vansina 1972: 44). Most of the houses in the capital had plaited walls and an inventory in the early 1950s showed that every household held decorated textiles. Any group of men or women could be drawn into discussion of design names; waiting porters drew the two-dimensional designs in the ground (see Himmelheber 1960: 365, fig. 289), and children played sand-drawings and string games based on the designs (Torday, 1910: 97, 204).

Where the two- and three-dimensional forms meet, that is, where the combination of two-dimensional designs and three-dimensional objects appears, we find another major and abundant corpus of Kuba artistic work. This combination occurs most prominently in the form of decorated wood carvings and in bulky ritual costumes. The wood carvings are mainly in the form of boxes and cups 15–25 cm in height, of high artistic value (Fig. 4.8, and Himmelheber 1940). They are three-dimensional forms whose surface is elaborated with the two-dimensional design inventory. The boxes are used to hold precious things, and especially for mixing redwood powder into an oily paste used to paint the body. Painting the body is essential to proper appearance at public gatherings. Boxes also hold razors which are used for hairdressing and for scraping the skin, activities which are part of friendship rituals that are important for maintaining social support. The beautifully carved Kuba cups are for the serving and drinking of palm wine (Fig. 4.9). One does not ever drink alone but only at a palm wine gathering. Another kind of elite drinking cup is a buffalo horn; their surfaces are also covered with linear designs in relief.[8] The wooden cups particularly have captured wide attention as they range from simple graceful cylindrical forms to well-defined head cups. On these objects of three dimensions, the Kuba carve a selection of motifs from the rich two-dimensional design inventory, also seen on textiles and mats (Torday 1910: 209).

Plain woven cloth, the material for the distinctive Kuba costume, is the two-dimensional art form par excellence. Over the surface the Kuba like to add embroidery or appliqué. The highest valued decoration, however, is a form of embroidery that creates a pile about 5 mm thick on the surface (see Adams 1978). In Bushoong style, the pile traces linear designs which are juxtaposed with thick rows of

Fig. 4.7. Recent scene of Kuba men lashing a large mat, 1974. (Photo: J. Cornet)

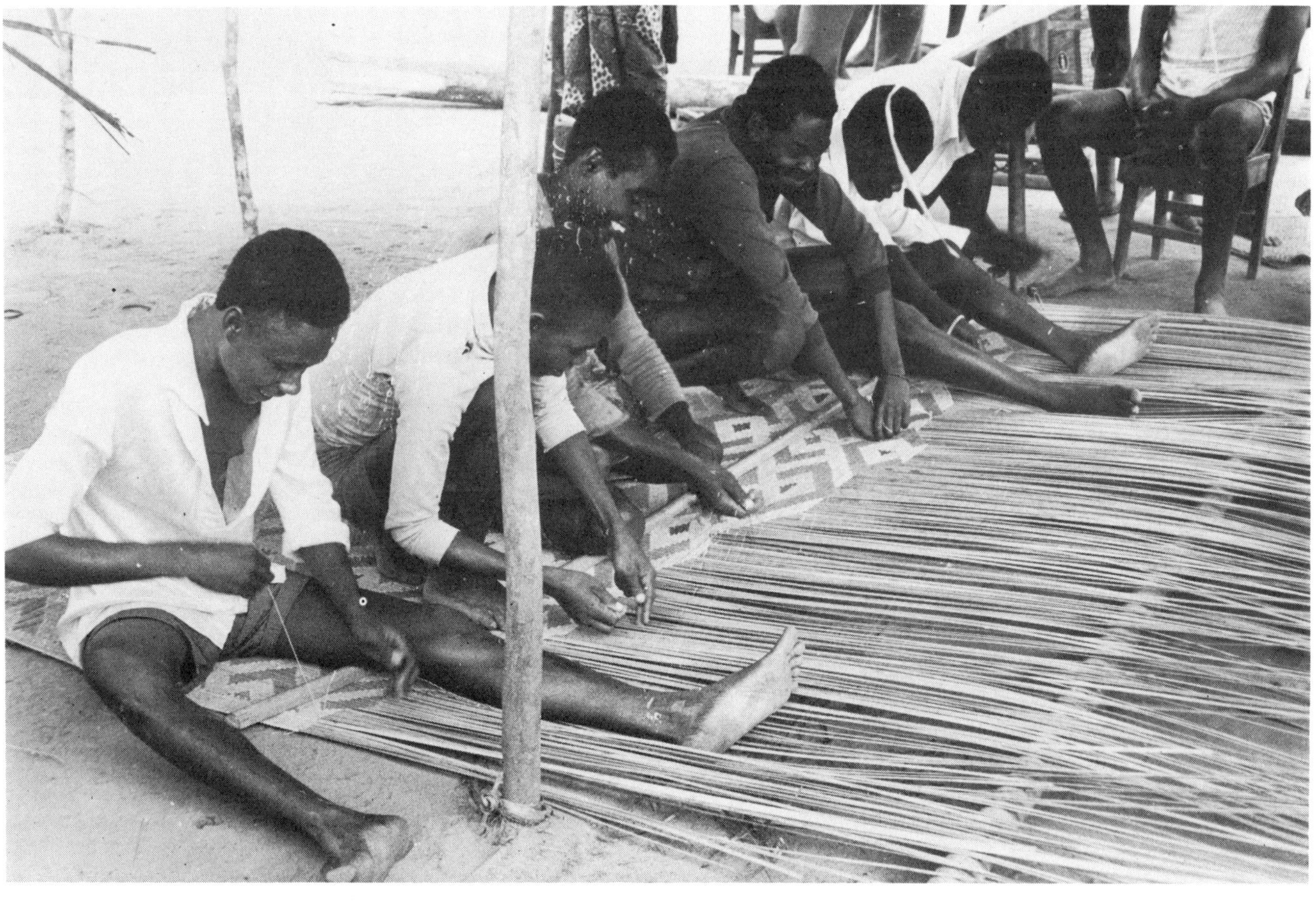

embroidered lines, altogether covering most of the surface of the cloth. These forms of ornamentation create heavy, thickly layered cloth (Fig. 4.10).

In creating costumes, the Bushoong arrange flat cloths so that they acquire a three-dimensional character in depth. The distinctive daily wear of the free Bushoong man was a plain red cloth gathered to form a thick skirt, held by a cord at the waist, with the upper ends pulled out over the cord creating a bulky effect (Fig. 4.11). For major festival occasions, the men donned an extra voluminous skirt, thickly gathered at the waist, displaying varied ornamentation including plush borders and fringes of plush balls at the upper and lower edges (Fig. 4.12a, b). Women increased the number and size of skirts they wore, typically decorated with appliqued designs. Their outermost skirt displayed a border that flared up to 10 cm in depth (Fig. 4.13). This pressure toward three-dimensional bulk is well illustrated by the special belt worn only by high royal men and women: a thick plaited band from which is hung a number of objects in the round decorated with cowrie shell designs (Fig. 4.14). Special performers at rituals added panels of plush cloth to their outfits. Thus the character of the costume created an aggrandized, imposing figure.

The path of access to these composite objects is narrower than to the common two-dimensional skills. Prior to colonial times, it seems likely that among the Bushoong, the wives of the elite were the main suppliers of the plush decoration, while simple embroideries could be done more widely (Vansina 1980). Tailoring of costumes in the capital continues to be one of the specialized crafts. While every man knows how to weave or to lash the Bushoong mats there were only one or two sculptors to a village (Fig. 4.15). Sculptors were professionals who belonged to a guild whose representative had the highest standing among craftsmen represented in court councils (Vansina 1964: 141, 144). Thus social and economic considerations entered into the effort to obtain these objects.

Before Vansina's studies of Kuba cultural values (1954, 1964, 1967–8), decorated wood carvings and textiles found in many households were considered simply utilitarian objects illustrating the African artists' love of decoration or a horror of empty spaces. But there is more to this possession of decorated objects in the household than these trivial observations would suggest.

To appreciate the social significances of these objects, we need to consider the luxuriant proliferation of symbolism linked with political structure. When the king was installed, he announced a decorated drum and an emblem for his reign,

Fig. 4.8. Carved cup, wood. Mushenge Museum, 1971. (Photo: J. Cornet)

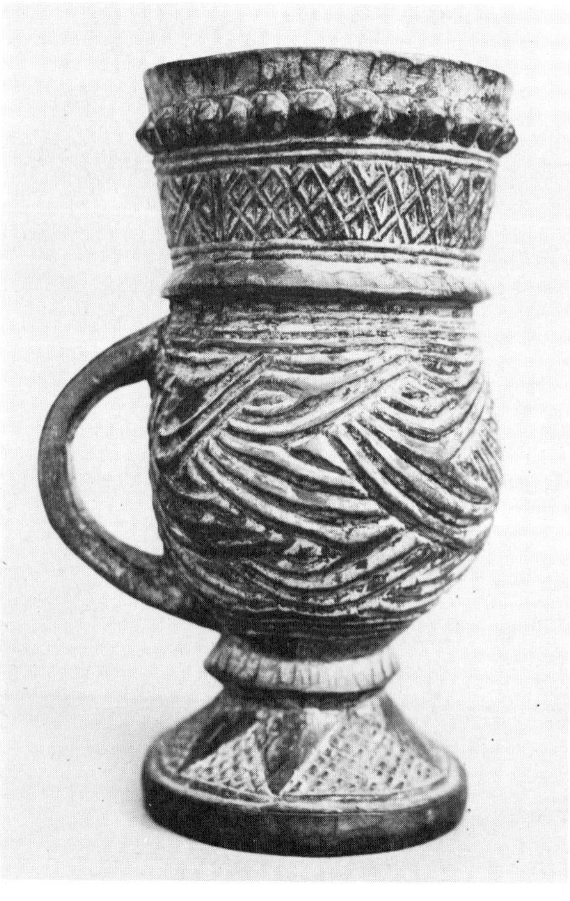

Fig. 4.9. Kuba man drinking palm wine. (Photo: J Cornet)

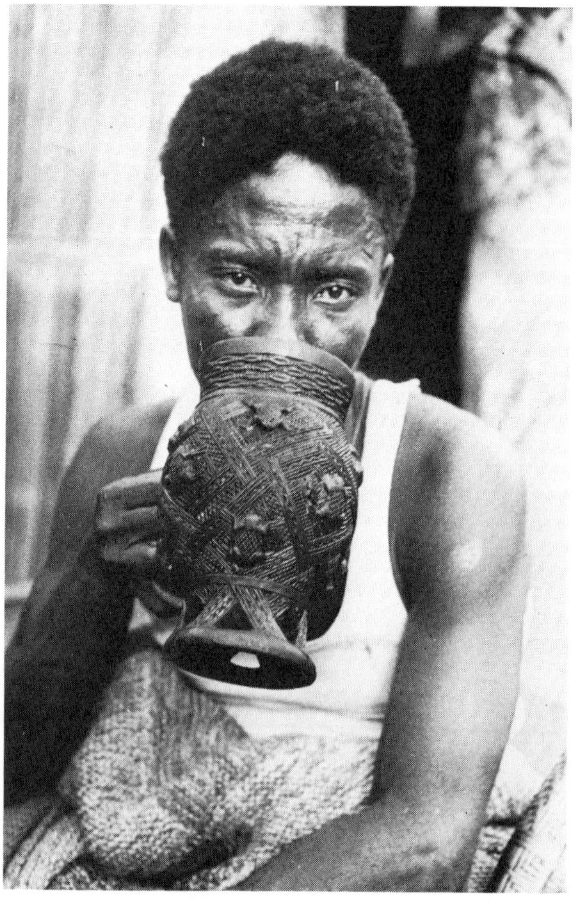

Fig. 4.10. Embroidered cloth of raphia palm fibre, owned by the sculptor son of the former king Mbop a Mabiinc. The borders are covered with thick lines of black and beige embroidery; the plush designs and the embroidered lines in the centre are dyed dark red. Bushoong, Mushenge, 1971. (Photo: J. Cornet)

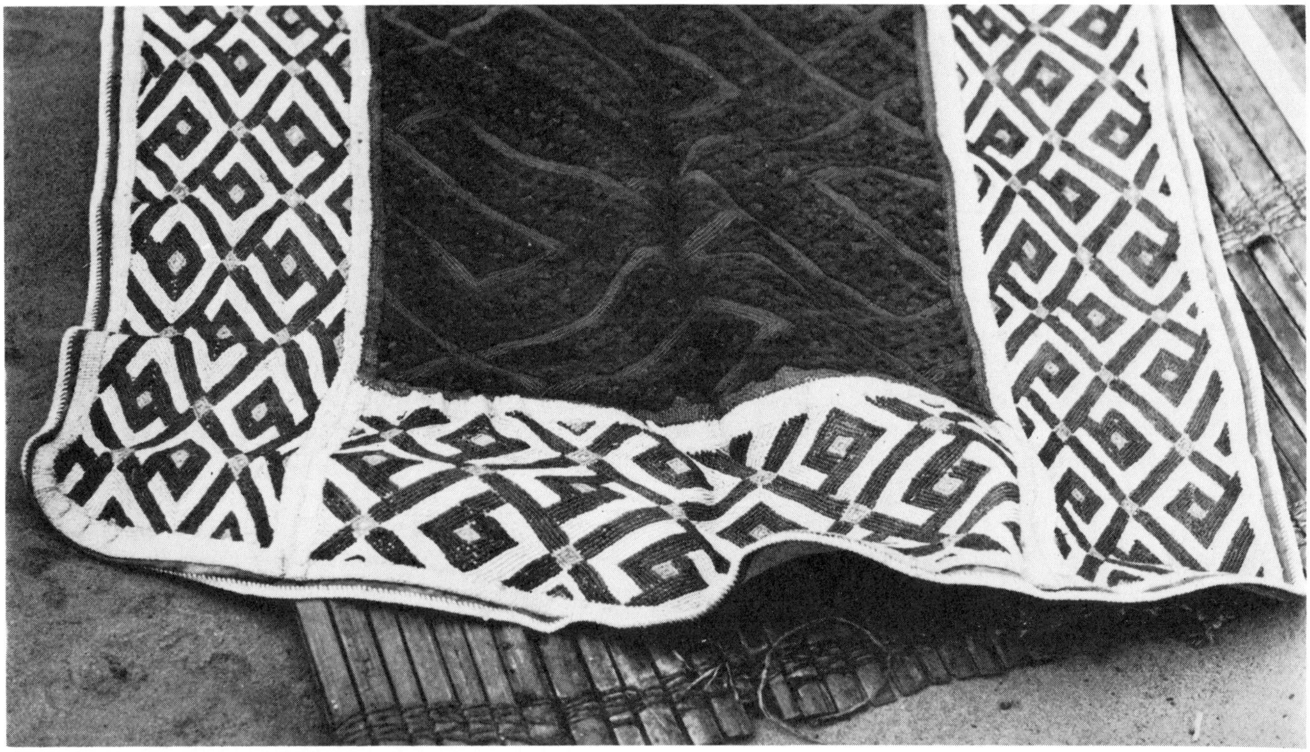

Fig. 4.11. In the foreground a man wears the full, gathered skirt, dyed a dark red, typical for the Kuba. Men and women perform in the *itul* festival in front of the king, who wears an official costume ornamented with leopard skin, shells and a headdress of eagle feathers. Mushenge, 1974. (Photo: J. Cornet)

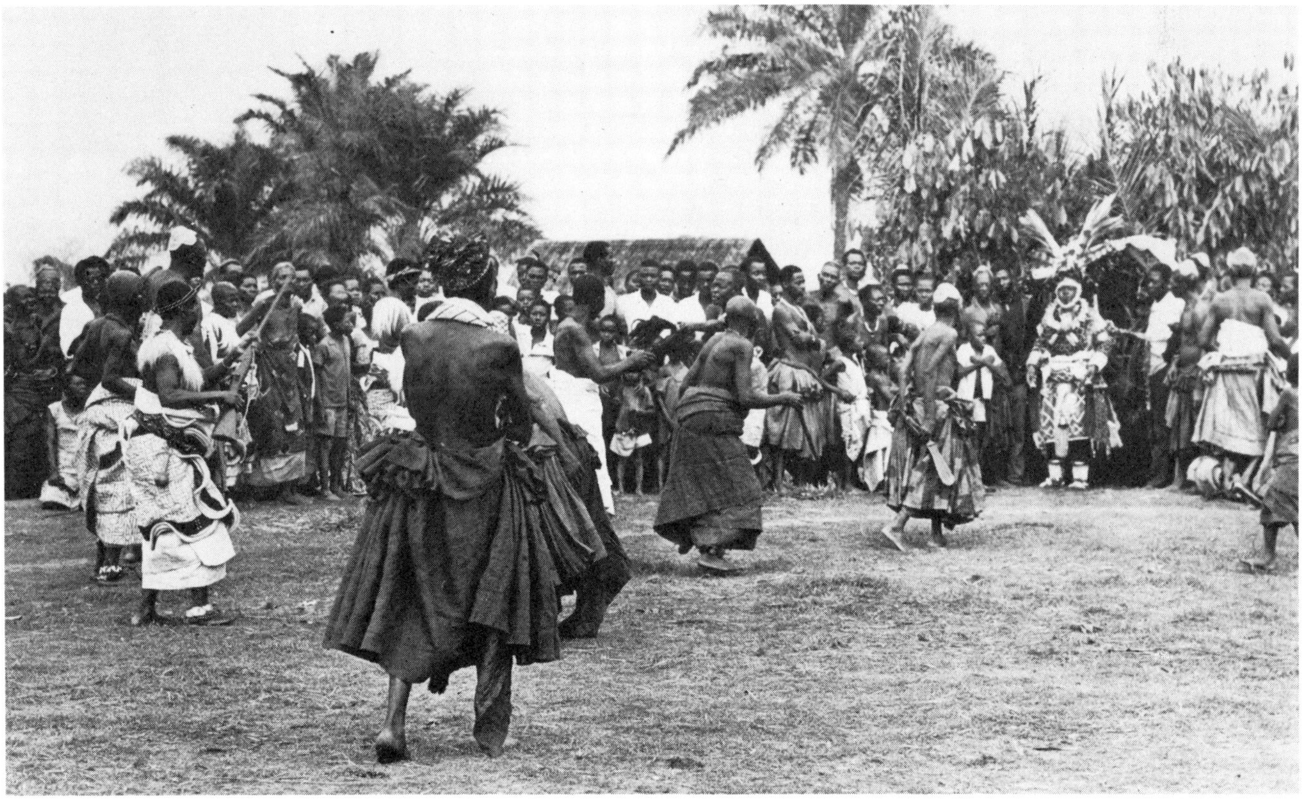

invented an official design motif (Vansina 1964: 108), and attached literally dozens of praise names to his person, to his new capital and to every street in his capital. Visual symbolism abounded throughout the ranks of the political hierarchy. Vansina considered the profusion of insignia as an indication of the deep interest this society had in the exercise of political authority (1964: 109). The Bushoong dreamt of an ever-increasing status and glory for their society as a whole and for all the people in it (Vansina 1967–8: 21).

This dream was expressed in one of the most exuberant systems of title-holding known in black Africa (Vansina 1964: 103–9; 1967–8). By grace of the king there were over two hundred title-holders in the capital, who in turn could bestow titles to others at lower ranks. Even at the village level, one out of two men by the age of forty could acquire a title. Through these titles people participated in the political regime. Free men were eligible for most political posts. Only the king's position was strictly hereditary. Certain posts were filled from hereditary groupings, such as the successors or founder clans, but generally this kind of restriction was avoided. There was also no accumulating of titles in one person. The king could create new titles, and at the capital level, appointments were made at the pleasure of the king. Theoretically he could revoke a title, but in practice this was rarely done, so that titles were held for life.

Titles gave the right to attend councils which formulated policy and promulgated rules about division of land, division of tribute and judging cases. Titles gave authority over a fraction of the territory and population; title-holders were specialists in political office, each with different functions and with particular concerns to oversee at the local, village, canton, provincial or court level.

There was intense competition to obtain title appointment. Even after appointments were made, competition remained intense, because title-holders sought to expand their prestige by augmenting the privileges of the office and increasing their participation in policy by the king's favour. The title system, accessible to all free persons, was a central value and a dynamic force in Kuba culture (Vansina 1964: 127).

A certain wealth was required to obtain nomination and one had to acquire the ceremonial costumes, objects and

Fig. 4.12a, b. Kuba costume for men. Ngeende, 1974. (Photo: J. Cornet)

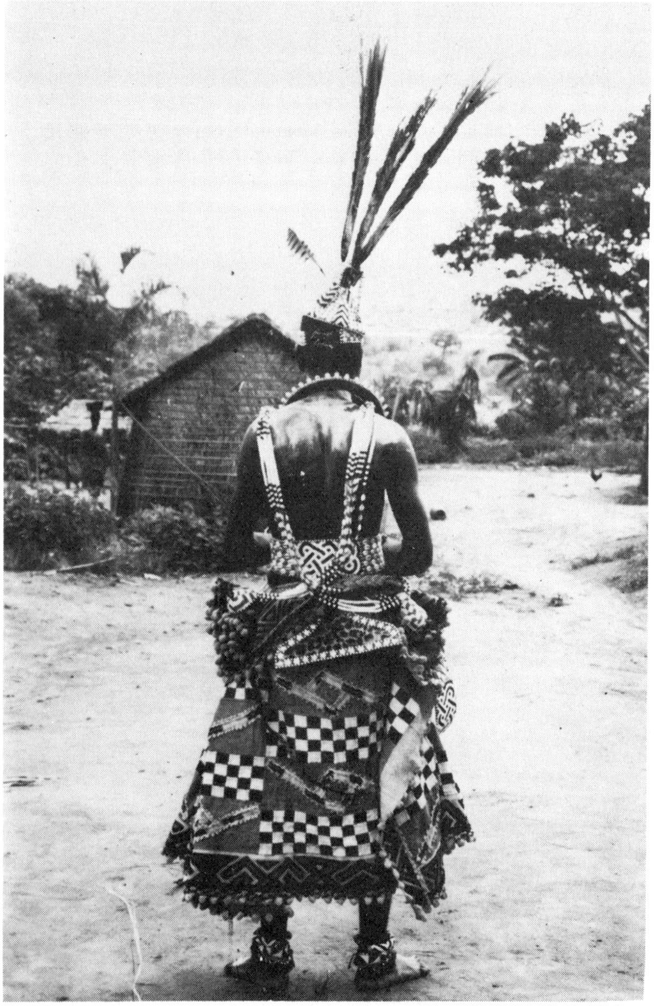

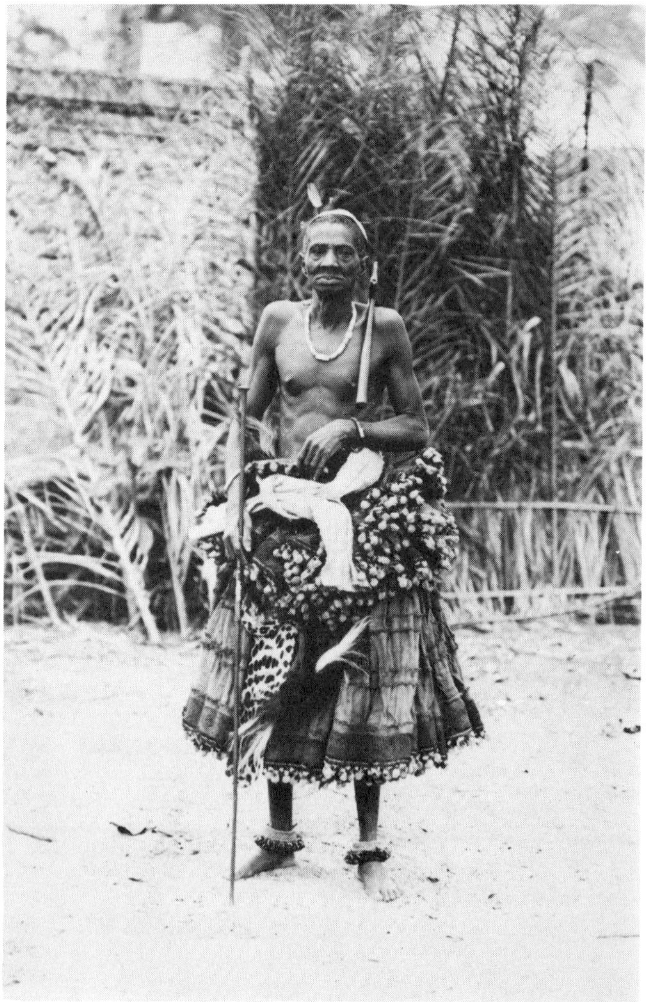

Fig. 4.13. Kuba women in ritual dress. Mushenge, 1974. (Photo: J. Cornet)

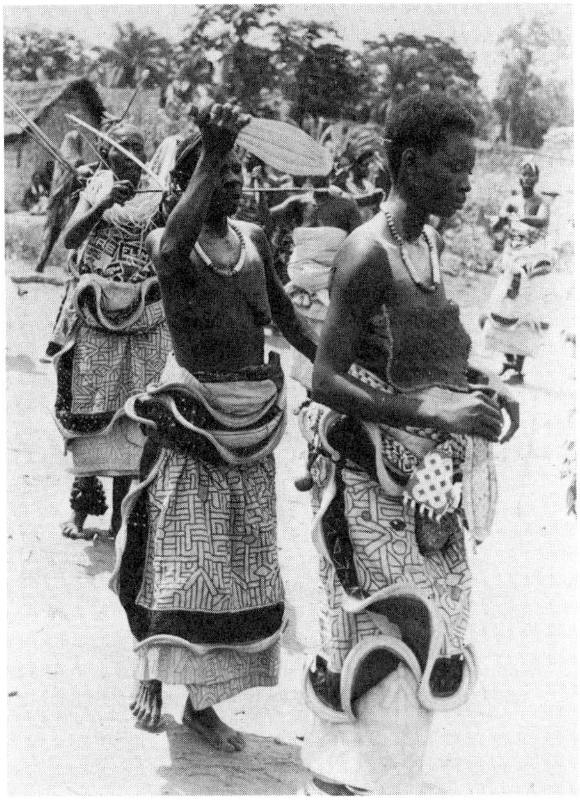

insignia appropriate to the rank; these could be obtained through production, family, influence or favour. Raw wealth was not enough, whether in cowries, coppers or cloth (Vansina 1964: 125–6). To rise in status, one had to acquire prestige through the display of rich clothing, furnishings and hospitality. It was important to create prestige by distributing largesse and inviting friends and clients to drink palm wine – strong sentiments were attached to this activity – and thus create a following (Vansina 1954: 904).

The status of court nobility had to be maintained by sponsoring public festivals (Vansina 1964: 122) which also displayed wealth in the form of elaborated costumes and fine service objects. Wealth and power had to be flaunted, made visible to all by the clothes one wore, the objects one handled and the emblems one acquired (Vansina 1967–8: 19; 1964: 125). This extensive use of prestige symbols explains why the Kuba turn so many of their household objects into decorated forms (1967–8: 903). The significant point is that among the Kuba, artistically made objects were components of political prestige. Possession of decorated costume and utensils brought the prestige which was essential to acquiring authority and political appointment.

The artistic elaboration itself was the instrument of qualitative advancement. The palm wine cups, other utensils or containers, and the tailored costumes were all objects that combined two- and three-dimensional forms. In terms of form and in terms of social competition they stand between

Fig. 4.14. Ritual costume belt, *yeet*, for Kuba royals. Mushenge, 1971. (Photo: J. Cornet)

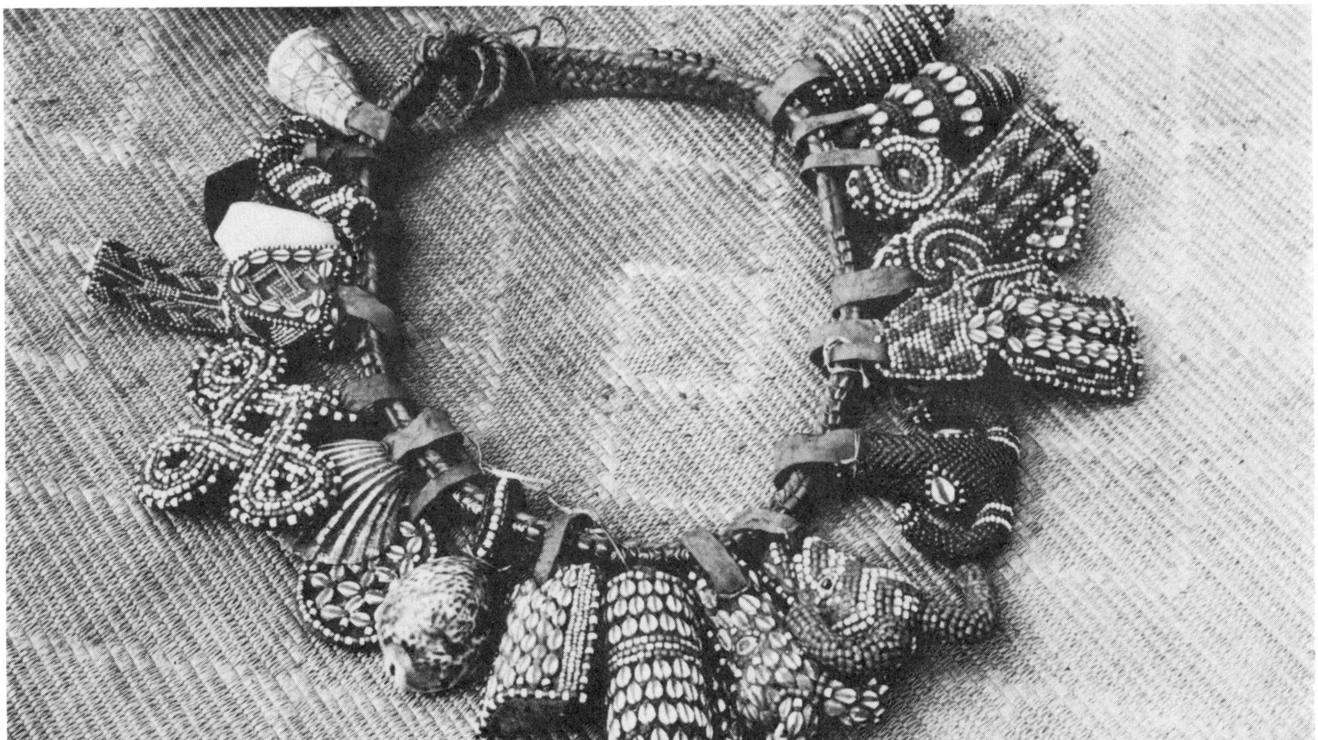

the exclusive royal statues and the accessibility of the two-dimensional works. The two- and three-dimensional combination appears on objects that are intimately associated with manual manipulation, and they are used in manipulating progress from lower to higher status. Even if upon investigation elsewhere, this systematic distribution of dimensionality proved unique to the Bushoong, it supplies another illustration of the refined structuring of artistic effort within a specific cultural context.

Notes

1 The figures seen in the capital by Torday (1910: figs. 18, 19, and 102) are from the Songe, ordered as charms a few years earlier after they won a battle over the Kuba. Most of the several figures collected by Torday, now in the Museum of Mankind, London (such as 1908–TY 148, 157, 158, 159, 160, 161, 162, 163 (Adams 1977)) derive from the Ngongo, including those at Lusambo, outside the Kuba kingdom (on the Ngongo as a peripheral group, see Vansina 1964: 6–7).

2 A few such female figures, in kneeling pose, were collected in the early 1970s by the staff of the National Museum in Kinshasa in the following sizes: 70, 71, and 72 cm (Adams 1976). In form they resemble the figure photographed by Vansina at a 1953 initiation screen. A small (26 cm) figure at Tervuren shows a pregnant woman ready to give birth (illustrated in *Geburt-Krankheit-Tod in der Afrikanischen Kunst*, by E. Haaf and J. Zwerneman, 1975, Stuttgart), a subject appropriate for the initiation screen figure. Vansina (1967–8: 19) learned of one case in which a man had carved a female statue as a memorial to his daughter, who had died in childbirth. The Shobwa at the northwestern border of the Kuba kingdom, who have their own language and distinct culture, treasure small female figures known to be used in funerary rites (see Vansina 1972: 345). These are extremely rare; one example can be found in the National Museum at Kinshasa: 75.119.1, 44.5 cm in height.

3 For examples, see at the Museum of Mankind, London, figures 1904–125, 21 cm; 1909–5–13–314, 21.3 cm; at the Tervuren Museum, Plate 36, no. 16, 29 cm, in *Annales du Musée du Congo Belge*, Ser. 6, Vol. 2, no. 3, 1939.

4 Various figure carvings of the 1950s are shown in fig. 92, p. 120 of *African Crafts and Craftsmen*, by Rene Gardi, 1969, New York: Van Nostrand Reinhold. In 1971, a councillor to the king held a large plain wooden, male figure, wearing a raphia skirt and hide skull cap, said to be a fetish of the hunt (J. Cornet, photograph no. 968). This function recalls the Ngongo hunting fetish collected by Torday, now in the Museum of Mankind, 1908–TY 148, a half figure covered with dried plants and charms.

5 This figure (92231/41293, 28.8 cm) was registered in 1928, acquired from M. Pareyn, a Belgian dealer who earlier collected many nineteenth- and early twentieth-century objects from the Belgian Congo.

6 Vansina (1980) considers that the use of rounded small figures (up to about 40 cm) as charms is probably fairly old – that is, prior to the rise of revitalist cults beginning in 1925; but he

Fig. 4.15. Two sculptors at work on carvings for sale. Mushenge, 1971. (Photo: J. Cornet)

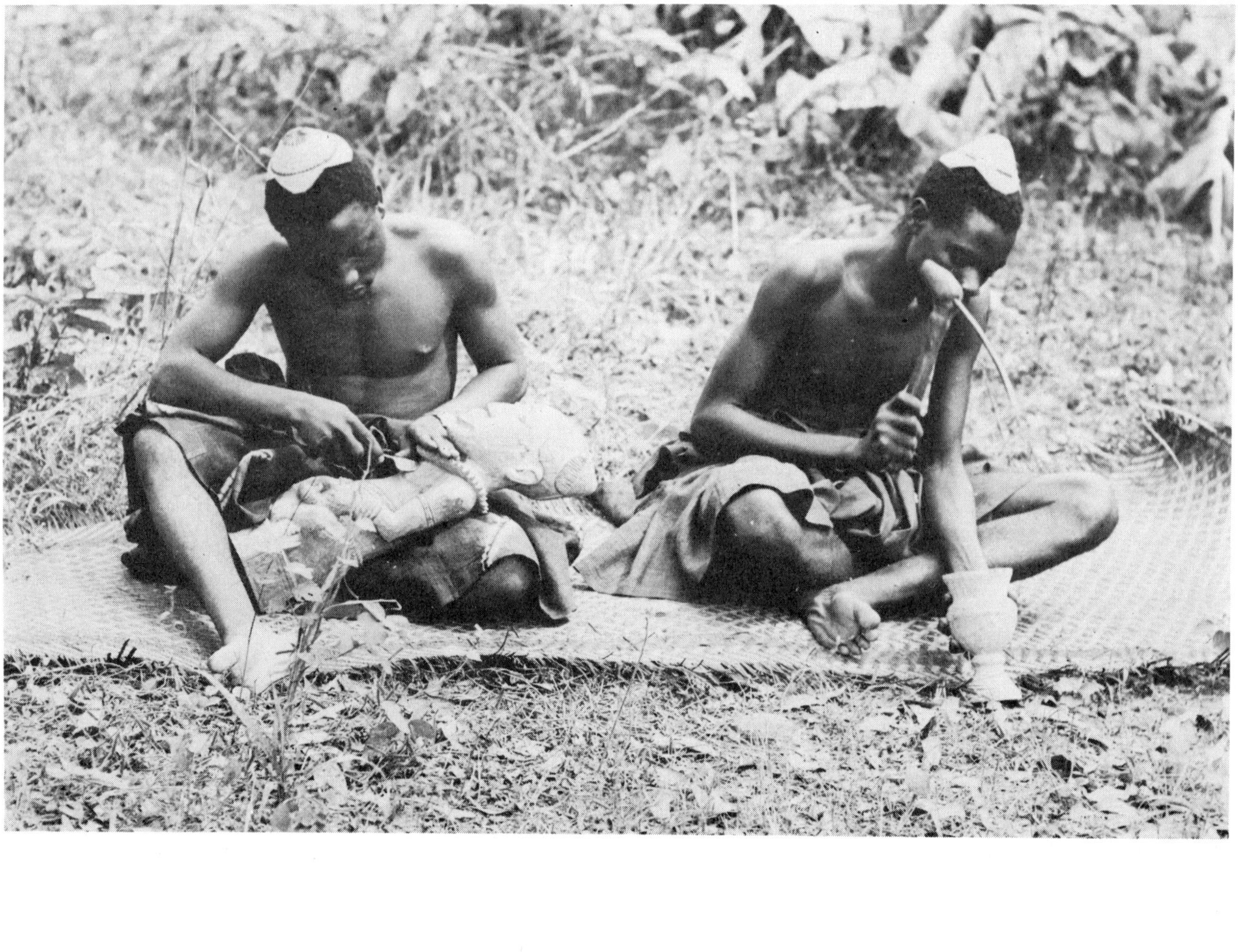

points out: 'It is remarkable that *nobody* comments on seeing them.'

7 G. de Macar, an ivory merchant, reporting in 1895 on his visit to the capital from his station at Luebo, noted that at the centre of almost all the Kuba villages, there was a large covered area where weaving was done. He commented on this feature because he did not find it elsewhere (*Le Congo Illustré*, Vol. 4: 174, 1895).

8 Other types of Kuba carving combine the dimensions, such as the decorated gourds used for enemas, an object important also for friendship rituals (Vansina 1954: 900). Various carved posts in the capital are covered with relief designs (see J. Cornet, photograph no. 956). The important sculptured items, *mboong itool*, that are displayed at elite funerals, imitate objects and human forms, their surfaces enhanced by relief designs. Women make these sculptures from a mixture of redwood powder and sand, which is then dried in the sun. (See illustrations in Himmelheber 1960: figs. 287–8, pp. 363–4.)

References

Adams, Marie Jeanne, 1976. Journal, Research Visit. Kinshasa, Mushenge.
1977. Journal, Research Visit. Museum of Mankind, London.
1978. Kuba embroidered cloth. *African Arts* 12 (1): 24–39, 106–7.
Anon., 1954. Biennale des art Conglais du Kasai, *Brousse* 5: 11–12, 18–19.
Fagg, William, 1965. *Tribes and Forms in African Art.* Tudor, New York.
Fernandez, James W., 1966. Principles of opposition and vitality in Fang aesthetics. *Journal of Aesthetics and Art Criticism* 25 (1): 53–64.
1977. Fang architectonics (paper read at 1970 Conference on Traditional African Architecture). ISHI, Philadelphia.
Fraser, Douglas, 1974. *African Art as Philosophy.* Interbook, New York.
Fraser, D. and H. Cole, eds., 1972. *African Art and Leadership.* University of Wisconsin Press, Madison.
Himmelheber, Hans, 1940. Art et artistes Bakuba. *Brousse* 1: 17–30.
1960. *Negerkunst und Negerkünstler*. Klinckhardt and Biermann, Braunschweig.
Laude, Jean, 1966. *Les arts de l'Afrique noire.* Le Livre de Poche, Paris.
Leuzinger, Elsy, 1960. *Africa: The Art of the Negro Peoples.* McGraw-Hill, New York (first published 1959).
Lévi-Strauss, Claude, 1963. *Structural Anthropology.* Basic Books, New York (first published 1958).
1969. *The Raw and the Cooked.* Harper and Row, New York (first published 1964).
Maesen, Albert, 1960. *Umbungu, Musée Royale de l'Afrique Centrale.* Cultura, Brussels.
Olbrechts, Frans M., 1959. *Les arts plastiques du Congo Belge.* Erasme, Brussels.
Pasztory, Esther, 1971. Hieratic composition in West African art. *Art Bulletin* 53 (4): 299–306.
Paulme, Denise, 1956. *Les sculptures de l'Afrique noire.* Presse Universitaire, Paris.
Rosenwald, Jean B., 1974. Kuba king figures. *African Arts* 7 (3): 26–31, 92.
Sheppard, William H., c. 1918. *Presbyterian Pioneers in the Congo.* Presbyterian Committee of Publication, Richmond, Va.
Sydow, E. von, 1927. *Primitive Kunst und Psychoanalyse*, pp. 100–1, 103, Internationaler Psychoanalytischer Verlag, Leipzig.
Thompson, Robert F., 1974. *African Art in Motion.* University of California Press, Los Angeles.
Torday, Emil, 1910. *Les Bushongo.* Musée du Congo Belge (Tervuren), Annales ser. 4, Vol. 2.
Trowell, Margaret, 1954. *Classical African Sculpture*. Faber and Faber, London.
Vansina, Jan, 1954. Les valeurs culturelles des Bushong. *Zaire* 8: 899–910.
1955. Initiation rituals of the Bushong. *Africa* 25: 138–53.
1958. Les croyances religieuses des Kuba. *Zaire* 12: 725–58.
1959. Miko Mi Yool, une association religieuse kuba. *Aequatoria* 22 (2): 7–20; (3): 81–92.
1962. Trade and markets among the Kuba. In *Markets in Africa*, edited by Paul Bohannan and George Dalton, pp. 190–210. Evanston, Ill.
1964. *Le royaume kuba.* Musée Royal de l'Afrique Centrale (Tervuren), Annales, Sciences humaines, No. 49.
1967–8. Kuba art and its cultural context. *African Forum* 3/4: 13–27.
1969. The Bushoong poison ordeal. In *Man in Africa*, edited by Mary Douglas and Phyllis Kaberry, pp. 245–60. Tavistock Publications, London.
1972. Ndop: royal statues among the Kuba. In *African Arts and Leadership*, edited by Douglas Fraser and H.M. Cole, pp. 41–55. University of Wisconsin Press, Madison.
1980. Pers. comm. to M. Adams, 28 July.
Vogel, Susan M., 1973. People of wood: Baule figure sculpture. *The Art Journal* 33 (1): 23–5.
1977. Baule art as the expression of a world view. Unpublished Ph.D. dissertation, University Microfilms, Ann Arbor.
Wingert, Paul, 1950. *The Sculpture of Negro Africa.* Columbia University Press, New York.

Chapter 5

Design structure and community organization in Quinua, Peru

Dean E. Arnold

Archaeologists traditionally have used ceramic design to formulate sequences of technological history in order to develop chronologies, infer culture history (see Adams 1979) and postulate cultural diffusion. Since the development of systems archaeology in the 1960s and the pioneering work of Deetz (1965), Longacre (1970) and Hill (1970), archaeologists have had a great deal of interest in using ceramic design to reconstruct the social patterns of ancient societies.

These studies raise two important issues: first, what is the nature of ceramic design? Bunzel (1929), Rowe (1959), Lathrap (1962) and Roe (1980) have all used the analogy of language to describe ceramic design. This analogy is a useful one because design, like language, is made up of units which are structured into higher level patterns. In language, these basic units are sounds which are structured into phonemes, syllables, morphemes, phrases, sentences and larger units of discourse like the paragraph. Similarly, ceramic design also consists of basic units which are structured into sequences in a particular area of the pot and juxtaposed with sequences in other areas.

Some of the archaeological work dealing with ceramic design (e.g. Longacre 1970; Hill 1970) has focused on design elements and their frequencies as the aspect of the design which carries social information. Elements, however, are only one small part of the entire structure of the design. Like language, it is not the elements themselves that carry information, but the way in which they are patterned and structured.

A second issue, and the major theme of the present paper, concerns the relationship of ceramic design to the society of which it is a part. How does ceramic design relate to the social structure in a society? Allen and Richardson (1970) have shown that archaeologists' views of social structure are based upon Murdock's (1949) classification and are thus 'ideal' statements of what descent and residence patterns should be rather than what they actually are in terms of 'real' behaviour. Related to this issue is whether patterns of learning pottery-making follow a descent and/or residence model and whether the subsequent interaction of potters reinforces these basic patterns. Stanislawski (1977; 1978; Stanislawski and Stanislawski 1978), however, has shown that the Hopi learning patterns do not correspond to any one social structural pattern (such as a descent, family or clan model) that accounts for the transmission of the pottery-making skill from generation to generation.

The potential of relating pottery design and social data does not lie in the 'ideal' patterns of social structure, but rather in the patterns of social interaction as suggested in a pioneering paper by Hardin (1970). Like Bunzel (1929), she noted the importance of design structure on pottery and found that design structure reflects potters' interaction patterns and their intensity more than design elements.

Hardin found that design elements and their configurations diffused through a community quickly with very little social interaction. Hardin's work suggests that the structural analysis of both archaeological and ethnographic pottery design may reveal structural patterns which are products of the social interaction of corporate groups of potters such as a family, extended family, barrio, or community.

If archaeology is to relate the structure of ceramic design to corporate groups that have regular social interaction, it is important to know the design correlates of these groups. One such social group is the community of potters. The community is particularly important to study because: (1) it is probably the largest group of potters with some social interaction, (2) it is probably small enough to have interaction often and regularly, and (3) it is a discrete entity in space; spatial discontinuity exists between different communities of potters. Structural similarities of pottery design within a community would not only be useful to identify ancient communities by direct historical analogy, but if such studies were extended in space they would provide the basis for a cross-cultural theory of ceramic design which relates kinds of design structures to particular social interactional groups and provides a guide for identifying the design correlates of different levels of social interaction.

A previous paper (Arnold forthcoming) has argued that the community of potters has a number of stylistic correlates, including high frequencies of particular structures of decorative space and motif and band symmetry patterns. This paper argues that these high frequency patterns correspond to fundamental structural principles which the community uses to organize space apart from pottery design. Thus, these design patterns are a 'real' behavioural manifestation of patterns of spatial organization and utilization in the community that are apparently the result of reification of 'real' patterns of social interaction.

Conceptual approach

One of the basic ways a community adapts to its environment and organizes its participants for social and cultural ends consists of categorizing, organizing and utilizing space. Space is often a continuum with few boundaries, so its organization into discrete units involves one of the most basic cultural processes. Culturally organized and defined space consists of at least three components. First, environmental space involves the way the community conceives of and differentially exploits the ecological setting around the community. Many communities have access to a variety of ecological zones, each of which provides varying resources. In order effectively and efficiently to exploit this resource potential, the community must have ways of categorizing and identifying the ecological zones and their potential for subsistence. The people in a community represent a second kind of space – social space which the social structure organizes into positions, groups and their interrelationships for the performance of cultural ends. A third type of space is symbolic space, which involves the organization and structure of symbols in a community which includes ritual, religion, mythology, and design on such media as ceramics and textiles.

The categorization and organization of space in a community need not be consciously conceived or linguistically labelled by its inhabitants. Some spatial categories will be emic, while others may be etic and defined behaviourally by non-linguistic criteria.

The kinds of cultural space are not restricted to these classes, but any kind of cultural space can have either a vertical or a horizontal orientation. Vertically oriented space consists of space in which the vertical dimension is emphasized and subdivided and in which the vertical dimension exceeds the size of the horizontal dimension. Horizontally oriented space consists of space in which the horizontal dimension is emphasized and subdivided, and exceeds the extent or magnitude of the vertical dimension.

Since every culture is systematically interrelated, the organization and utilization of one kind of space will be reflected in the organization and utilization of other kinds of space in a community. Conversely, principles that structure decorative space are not arbitrary, but reflect basic structural patterns that organize other kinds of space in the community. Specifically, the principles of organizing and utilizing environmental and social space will also occur in the organization and utilization of the symbolic space in a community. Thus, the basic principles of spatial organization in a society are so important to the structure and maintenance of the society that they are reified and reinforced in symbolic space such as ritual, religion, art, textiles and pottery. Adams (1973), for example, noted that the same structural principles were responsible for patterning the social organization of the Island of Sumba and the design on the textiles made there. This paper argues that the organization of the environmental and social space in a community is also reified symbolically in the organization of decorative space on pottery. It is thus the purpose of this paper to show how the basic principles of organizing and utilizing environmental and social space in Quinua, Peru, are reflected in the organization and utilization of decorative space on four of the most frequently utilized painted vessels produced in the community.

Ceramic vessels provide an excellent medium for the expression of such spatial patterns. Although the plasticity of the clay permits a wide range of vessel shapes, the shapes produced (at least for utilitarian uses) are largely influenced by technological and utilitarian variables. Cooking pots, for example, should have a round bottom to minimize breakage from thermal shock (Rye 1976). Narrow-mouthed bottles in which the mouth is considerably smaller than the maximum diameter of the vessel are ideal for transporting liquids because they minimize spills. Vessels with mouth diameters equal to or exceeding their maximum diameter are ideal for serving vessels. Moreover, while the local environment provides the ranges of materials available for ceramic production, painted decoration is sufficiently flexible to permit the execution of virtually any design. The possibilities are almost endless. Thus painted design provides an extremely flexible and variable medium which can reflect a wide range of spatial patterns in a community.

The community of Quinua

The village of Quinua lies in the south central Andean highlands fifteen kilometres northeast of the city of Ayacucho. With the elevation of slightly less than 3,396 metres, Quinua is located on the upper portion of the gentle slopes of the eastern edge of the Ayacucho Basin (Fig. 5.1), Immediately behind the village the mountains rise abruptly to elevations exceeding 4,300 metres. Since detailed descriptions of the community already exist (Mitchell 1972; 1976a; 1976b; 1977; 1979; forthcoming), this description will

Fig. 5.1. The Quinua area, showing the relationship of the principal towns in the central portion of the Ayacucho valley, the extent and placement of the ecological zones, the location of potters, and the principal archaeological sites. The boxed symbols labelling ecological zones are abbreviations of Tosi's Spanish labels: tp-A, alpine rain tundra; pmh-SA, subalpine wet paramo; bh-M, montane prairie or moist forest; bs-MB, lower montane savannah or dry forest; ee-MB, lower montane thorn steppe. The map was produced by projecting Tosi's zones onto the map of the Ayacucho quadrangle (scale = 1/200,000). Boundaries of the zones in the Quinua region have been established by applying Tosi's criteria to the author's data.

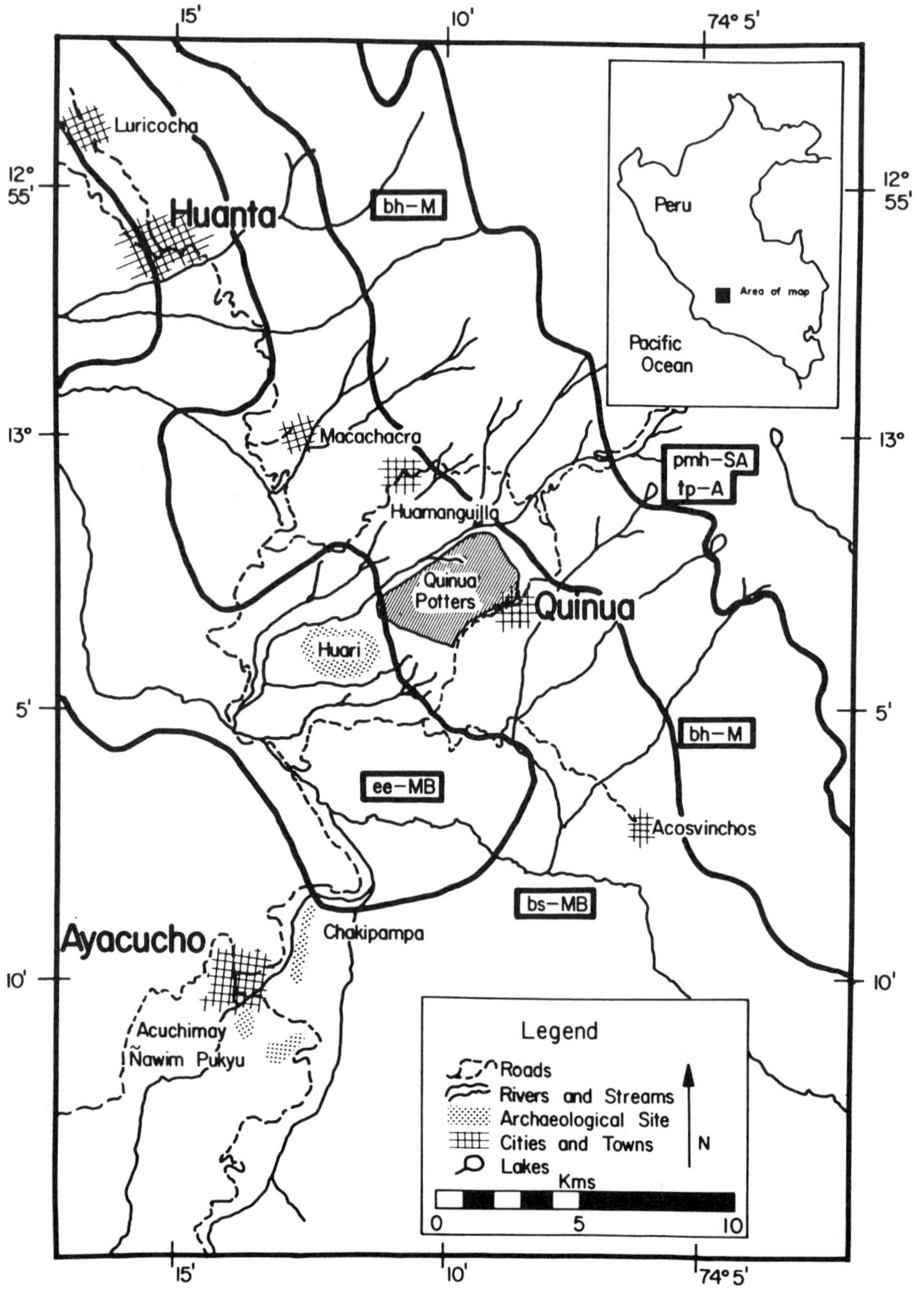

emphasize only the most important principles of spatial organization in the community.

Probably the most important organizing principle of environmental space in Quinua consists of the subdivision of the area around the community into a series of successive horizontal zones arranged vertically on the eastern slope of the basin (Fig. 5.2). Because of the great difference in altitude from the top of mountains to the bottom of the basin, different elevations have different mean temperatures and amounts of cloud cover, sunshine and rainfall. These differences create major ecological zones at different elevations, and these different zones produce varying resource potentials for human exploitation.

The alpine rain tundra/subalpine wet paramo zone dominates the high mountainous area directly east of Quinua. Although this zone does not support agriculture because of its low mean annual temperature, it serves as grazing land for llamas and alpacas.

Immediately below this zone lies the montane prairie. This zone covers the upper parts of the steep slopes east of Quinua. Consisting mostly of bunch grasses, it is an important food resource for the animals which graze there. The inhabitants of the zone practise agriculture in addition to herding, but there is a fallow time of five to seven years for every two years of cultivation. In the upper portion of this zone, bitter potatoes (*Solanum* sp.) are the only crop, while in the lower portion of the zone other kinds of potatoes, oca (*Oxalis crenata*), mashua (*Tropaeolum tuberosum*) and ullucu (*Ullucus tuberosus*) are grown (Mitchell forthcoming).

Below the prairie, the montane forest consists of dense underbrush, mostly small trees and shrubs 2½ to 3 m in height. It covers the lower portions of the mountain slopes, from about 3,700 m down to 3,400 m, where the terrain becomes more level. While agriculture in the prairie is limited to root crops, crops in the moist forest include a high altitude variety of quinoa (*Chenopodium quinoa*) and a variety of Old World crops including wheat (*Triticum* sp.), barley (*Hordeum* spp.), peas (*Pisum sativum* var. *avense*) and broad beans (*Vicia faba*). Much of the land is uncultivated and requires one to five years of fallow time for every three years of cultivation (Mitchell forthcoming). Considerable amounts of wild vegetation also occur in this zone and are used for fuel for firing pottery, making baskets and for culinary and medicinal herbs (Mitchell forthcoming).

Fig. 5.2. The central portion of the Ayacucho Basin looking northeast, showing the location of Quinua, the most important ecological zones, and the ancient site of Huari.

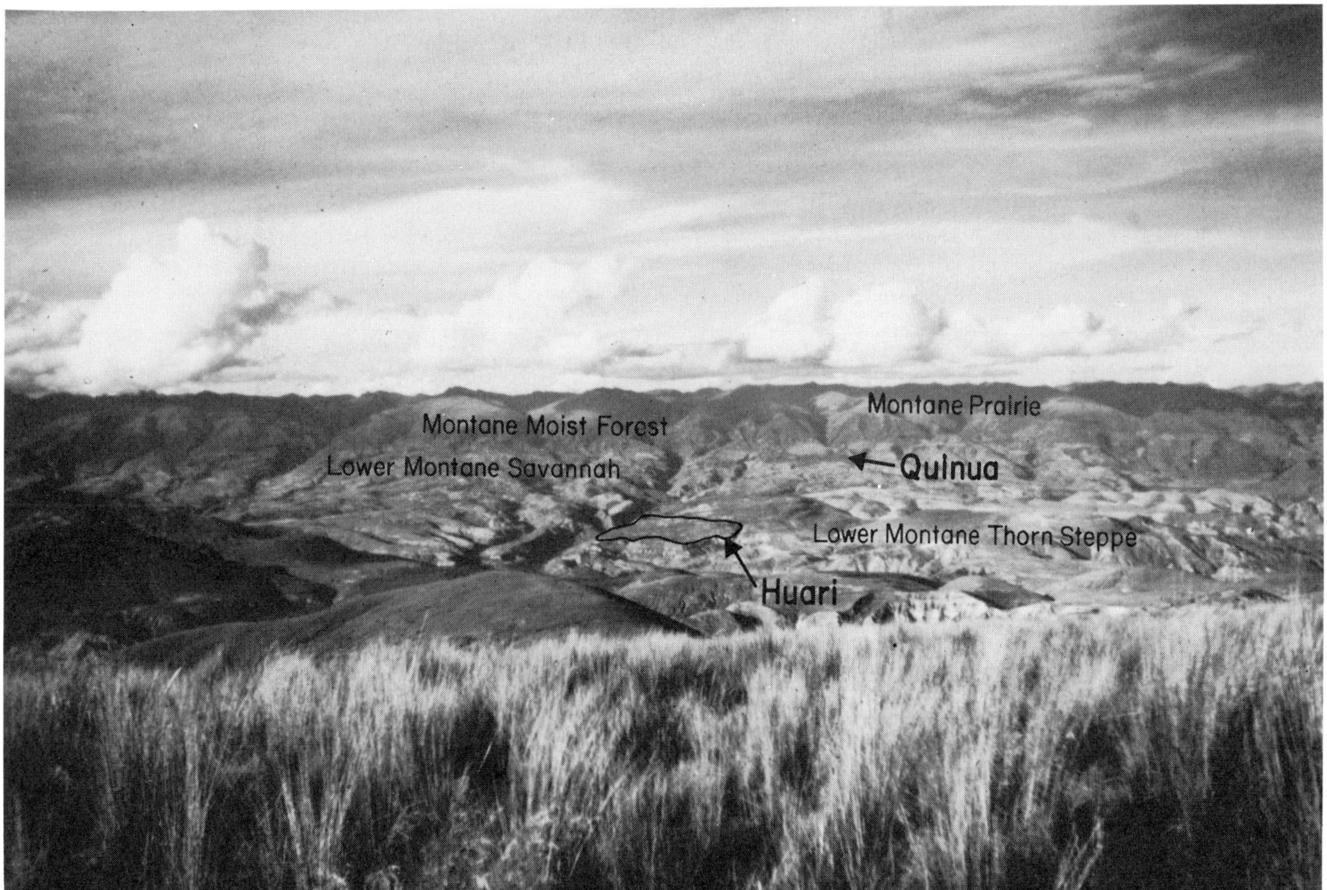

Moving down the slope, the lower montane savannah begins at the base of the steep slopes of the mountains. This zone receives approximately the same amount of rainfall annually as the zones above, but because of more sunshine, higher temperatures and a lower altitude, it has a higher rate of moisture loss from the soil. This zone is the primary agricultural zone in the Quinua region. It includes almost all of the agricultural land around Quinua, as well as the village itself. It is the highest zone in which maize can be cultivated. Other crops grown in this zone include potatoes, oca, mashua, wheat, oats (*Avena sativa*), peas, quinoa, habas (broad beans), squash (probably *Cucurbita maxima*) and beans (probably *Phaseolus vulgaris*).

The lower montane savannah has both the highest population and greatest population density of all the ecological zones of Quinua. This zone contains the nucleated settlement of the village of Quinua and a highly dispersed rural settlement distributed in a variety of hamlets. Furthermore, the savannah is the most important zone for irrigation; no irrigation exists in the zone above and very little in the zone below, except in the alluvial bottom land.

The lowest ecological zone in the region is the lower montane thorn steppe. Few people inhabit this zone, except for the alluvial bottom land. In comparison with the zones farther up the slope, this zone has less rainfall and more moisture loss from the soil. Because of these factors, less agriculture occurs here, except in the alluvial flood plain which is intensively irrigated. Outside of this niche, the most common crops in the steppe are wheat, quinoa, chick-peas and a type of squash. All of these crops require less rainfall than most of the Andean crops grown farther up the slope and can be grown here without irrigation.

The boundaries of the District of Quinua are arranged so as to include all of these zones. Each zone is differentially exploited etically. The Quinua population has access to the products of each zone through trade and/or market exchange in order to achieve community self-sufficiency. Nevertheless, these major zones are not distinguished emically, but are terminologically collapsed into two areas: the *Puna* or the upper zones consisting of the montane, alpine or subalpine zones, and the *quechua* or the lower zones consisting of the lower montane zones and the alluvial river valley (see Figs. 5.1 and 5.2).

This multizonal pattern occurs widely in the Andes (Webster 1971; Brush 1977; Isbell 1978; Bastien 1978) and provides a crucial adaptation to the complex Andean ecosystem in order to provide community self-sufficiency. Murra (1972) first called attention to this pattern and called it 'vertical control' – the simultaneous exploitation of a series of ecozones occurring at different elevations. This same organization of vertical space also occurs in dreams, mythology, ritual and cosmology in the Pampas River valley to the south of Ayacucho (Zuidema and Quispe 1968; Isbell 1978) and in highland Bolivia (Bastien 1978). The widespread occurrence of this principle indicates its great significance not only as an adaptive pattern in the Andes but also as an important principle organizing behaviour in other areas of culture.

The second major pattern of spatial organization in Quinua consists of the division of the community into two barrios on the basis of the two irrigation systems in the community. These irrigation systems begin in the moist forest above the community and extend into the steppe below, but they principally serve the lower montane savannah. Since the system is gravity-fed, each irrigation system corresponds to the drainage area of the ravine on either side of the community. A low ridge running down the slope divides the drainage of one ravine from that of the other (Fig. 5.3). More importantly, the two drainage areas correspond to each of the major subsections of the community; one drainage area corresponds to the Lurinsayuq barrio and is served by one irrigation system and the other drainage area corresponds to the Hanansayuq barrio and is served by the other irrigation system (Fig. 5.4). The irrigation pattern thus subdivides and organizes environmental space in the savannah, and is oriented more towards subdividing space along a horizontal dimension.

Until recently, each major section of the community had its own native political organization (the *varayoq*) whose function it was to administer the irrigation system. At the present time, the local district officials have assumed this function for both barrios (Mitchell 1972: 174–206; 1976b: 195; 1977: 50).

In addition to the bisection of the rural community into two barrios, the irrigation system also subdivides each barrio into administrative subsections. In the barrio of Lurinsayuq, for example, the irrigation system subdivides the land into the three subsections (called *pagos*) of Muya, Lurinsayuq and Llamahuilca. Each of these subsections (except Lurinsayuq) has a very small nucleated settlement as its focus (see Fig. 5.4).

Irrigation is important in the savannah because it expands the amount of land in which maize can be successfully raised at this altitude. In spite of a wide variety of crops available, maize is the most highly valued crop because it is an important source of protein (William P. Mitchell, personal communication), can be stored for long periods of time, and has a wide variety of uses (Murra 1973). In the lower montane savannah, climate and rainfall combine to make maize cultivation impossible without irrigation except in a narrow horizontal band. In the upper portion of the savannah, colder temperatures prolong maize maturity to a total of nine months. Since rainfall at the beginning of the rainy season (September–November) is insufficient for maize germination and growth, it must be planted in December, when the regular heavy rains begin. The six months between the December rains and the night frosts in June, however, do not provide sufficient time for the maize to mature before the frost occurs. In order to permit maize cultivation, people in the upper portion of the savannah plant maize in September, and thus utilize irrigation to extend the growing season into the time of insufficient rains before the heaviest rains begin. The lower portion of the savannah, however, presents a different problem for maize cultivation. There, maize requires only six months to reach maturity because the climate is warmer and sunnier. The people in this subzone plant their maize in December when the heavy rains begin, which allows the maize to mature before the frosts come in June. The amount of rainfall in the lower savannah, however, is insufficient for successful maize agriculture, so in this area, irrigation supplements rainfall during the rainy season. The irrigation system, then, has complementary functions in the savannah. In the upper savannah, it extends the growing season backwards into the period of insufficient and erratic moisture before the heavy rains begin in December. Then, irrigation water is sent down the slope to the lower savannah to supplement moisture during the heavy rains. Thus, the difference in climate between the upper and lower parts of the savannah create a two-fold division of vertical space in the zone as reflected in the etic function of the irrigation system (Mitchell 1976a; 1976b; 1977).

The distinction between the urban district centre and the rural portion of the community represents a division of horizontal social space which is one of the basic distinctions in the Quinua world view and is also reflected in social class (Mitchell 1979; forthcoming). Local people describe the inhabitants of the nucleated centre of the community as *vecinos* and those of the rural portion of the community as *campesinos* or peasants. This distinction occurs elsewhere in Latin America in general and in the Andes in particular as the difference between mestizos and indians. Mestizos are more acculturated to the national hispanized culture in terms of language, literacy and dress, while the indians are less acculturated and more traditional in terms of native language and dress, and in ability to read, write and speak Spanish (Mitchell 1972: 75–127; 1979). While these distinctions in Quinua are clear geographically and from the point of view of ideal behaviour, the stratification system has a number of attributes which are sometimes difficult to apply to any one individual because of the change and fluidity in the system. Indeed, Mitchell (1979) reports that there is considerable status inconsistency in the system.

The last significant kind of space used in the community consists of another kind of social space: kin group affiliation. In Quinua, as in other parts of the Andes (Isbell

Fig. 5.3. View of the town of Quinua from above, showing most of the area covered by the Quinua irrigation system. The central portion of the Ayacucho Basin and the city of Ayacucho are in the background.

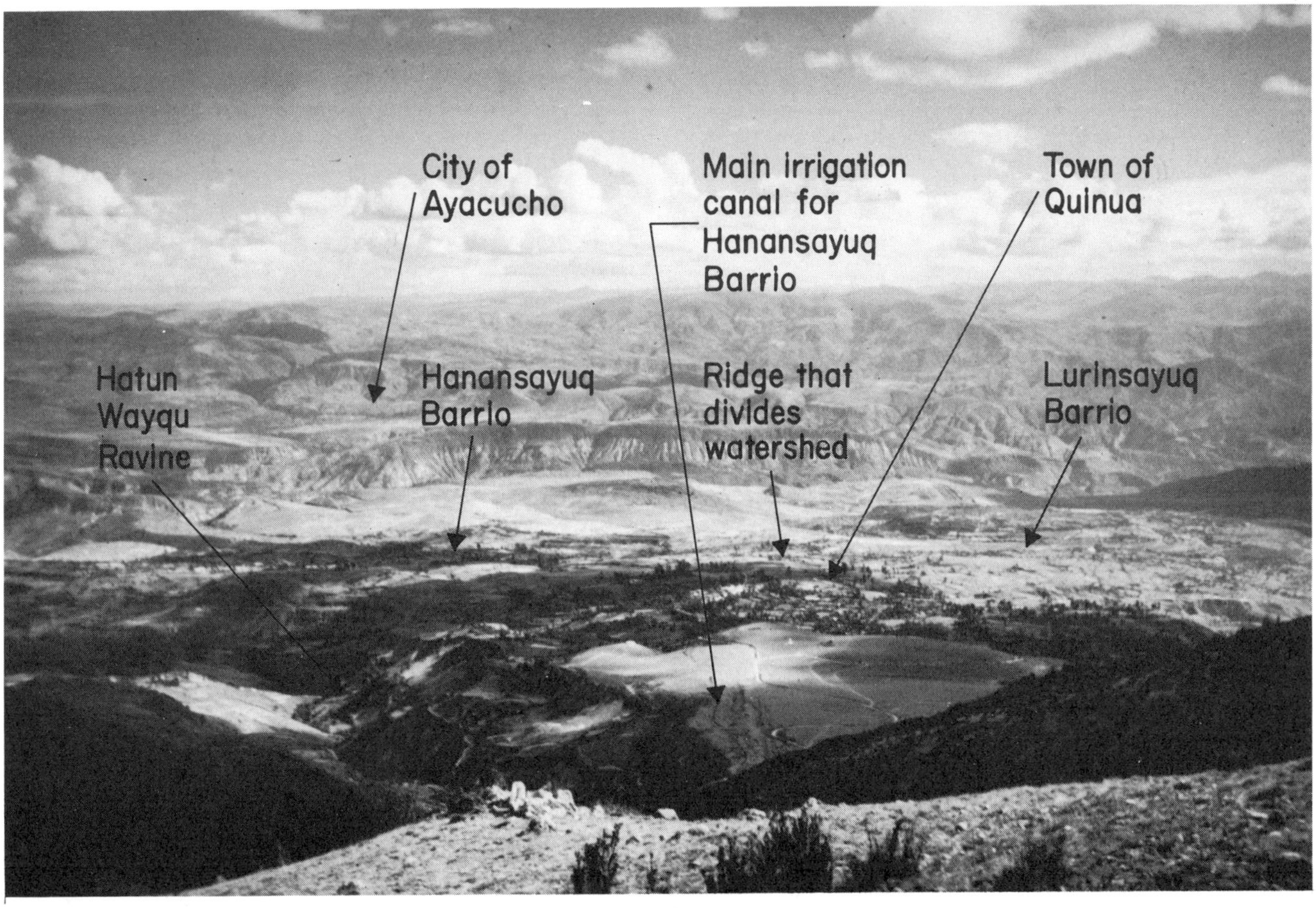

Fig. 5.4. Map of the irrigation system of Quinua, showing the pattern of the major canals and their division of the community into two barrios. (Reproduced by permission of the American Anthropological Association from *American Anthropologist* 78 (1): 31, 1976.)

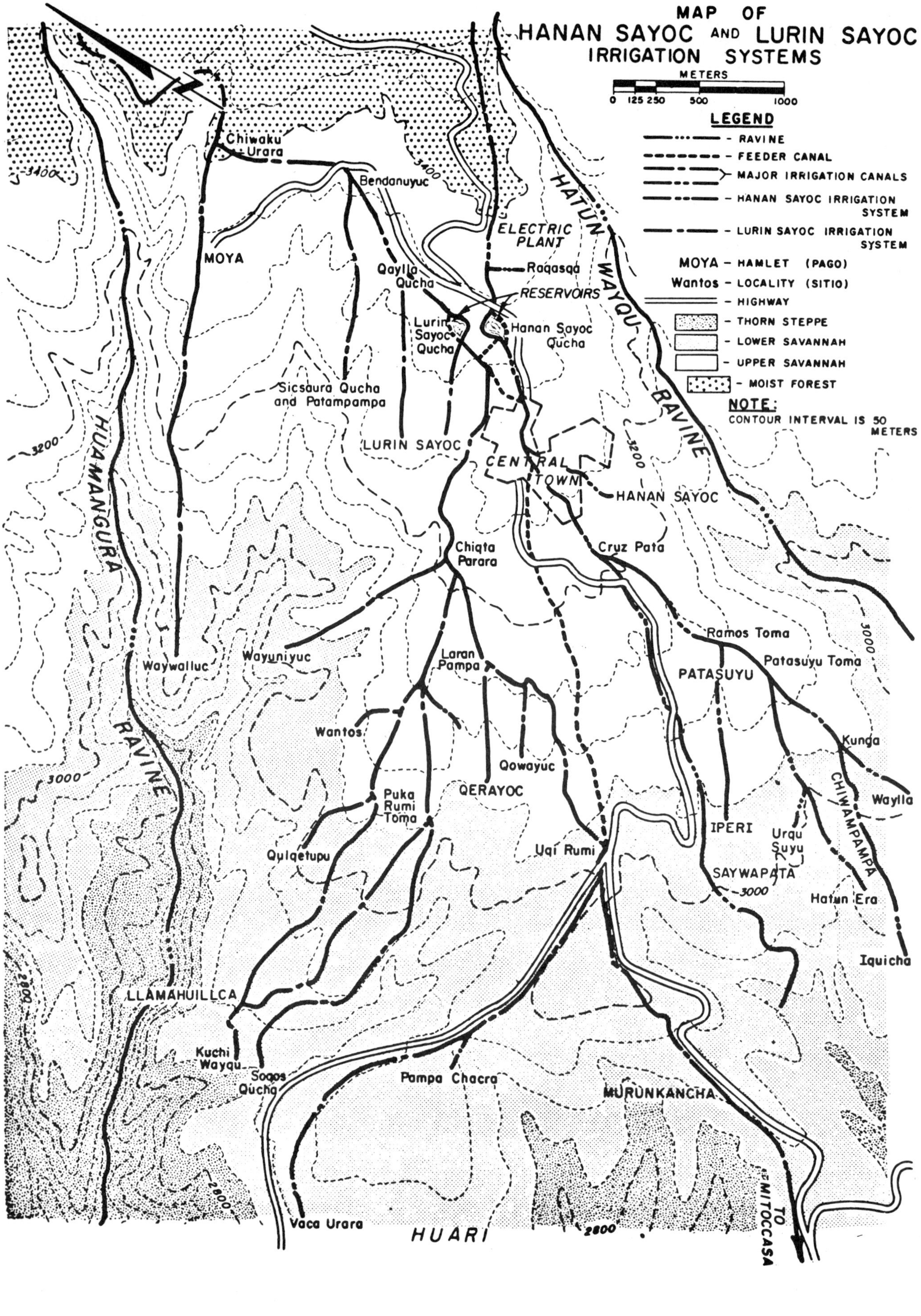

1978), each person belongs to two kin groups called kindreds – one on his mother's side and one on his father's side (William P. Mitchell, personal communication). Kindreds are descent groups reckoned from one's grandparents, and include all consanguineal relatives in three successive generations (Isbell 1978). In Quinua, the patrilineal kindred is more important than the mother's kindred and is extended to all people with the same patronym. This larger group, as well as the smaller well-defined patrilineal kindred, are exogamous (William P. Mitchell, personal communication).

The ceramics of Quinua

In 1967, except for the three potters in the artisan school who lived in the central town of Quinua, all of the potters lived in the rural section of the community in the barrio of Lurinsayuq. There are important ecological reasons for this residence pattern and these are detailed in another paper (Arnold 1975).

Quinua potters produce a wide variety of ceramics with a complex technology which is unique within the Ayacucho Basin and within Peru as a whole. A number of factors contribute to this complexity. First, potters utilize two distinct pastes for making pottery (see Arnold 1972a; 1972b). One is behaviourally untempered with naturally occurring non-plastics and used for undecorated pottery, and the other is behaviourally tempered with volcanic ash and used to make the decorated pottery (Arnold 1972a; 1972b). Second, potters use vessel-forming techniques (modelling and modified coiling) to produce a repertoire of approximately forty shapes which originally were used for utilitarian, decorative and ritual purposes. These vessel-forming techniques have provided the flexibility necessary for producing new shapes for the tourist market, which, along with traditional shapes, are exported widely to import shops and department stores abroad in places like Chicago and New York. Thirdly, Quinua potters decorate their pottery in three painted styles (two polychrome and one bichrome). Each of these styles occurs on certain vessel shapes and each has its own set of designs and paint, polish, and slip combinations (Arnold 1972b). Each vessel shape in each style generally has more than one structure of design space. Several of these structures utilize a variety of design zones and often have a wide range of designs and symmetry classes. Besides extensive descriptions of Quinua pottery by Arnold (1970; 1972a; 1972b; 1975; forthcoming), Spahni (1966) and Litto (1976) also briefly describe it.

This study is based on a sample of 172 vessels of four shapes (Figs. 5.5–5.8) which were observed during field work in the Quinua region from February to July 1967. These four shapes include a low open bowl (*plato* – 36 vessels) and three globular bottles: (1) a wide-necked vessel with a circular mouth (*tachu* – 46 vessels); (2) a narrow-necked vessel with a small circular mouth (*yukupuyñu* – 44 vessels); and (3) a narrow-necked vessel with a mouth moulded into a pouring spout (*puyñu* – 46 vessels).

Fig. 5.5. Principal organization of design space for the *yukupuyñu*.

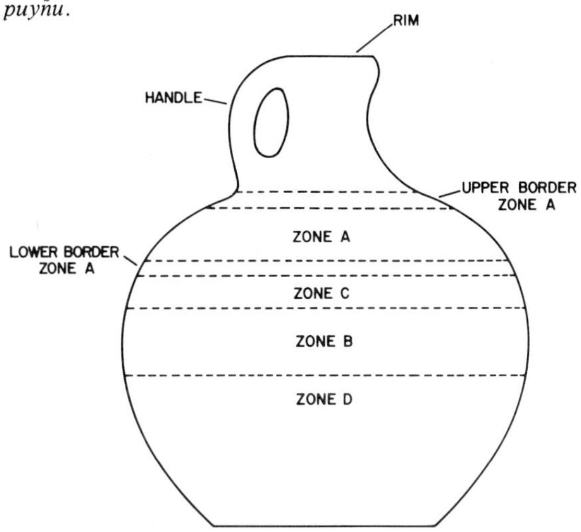

Fig. 5.6. Principal organization of design space for the *puyñu*.

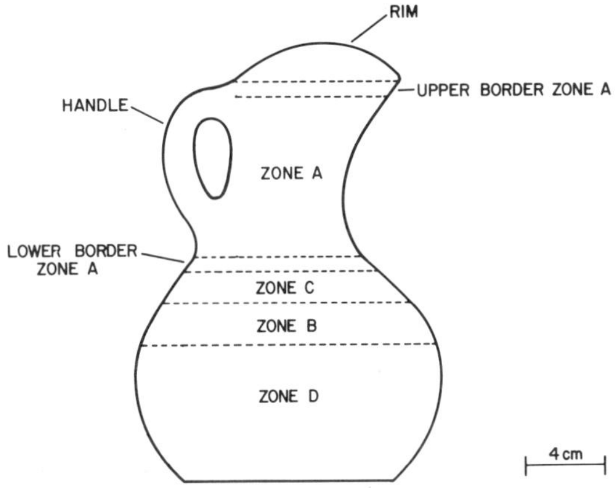

Fig. 5.7. Principal organization of design space for the *tachu*.

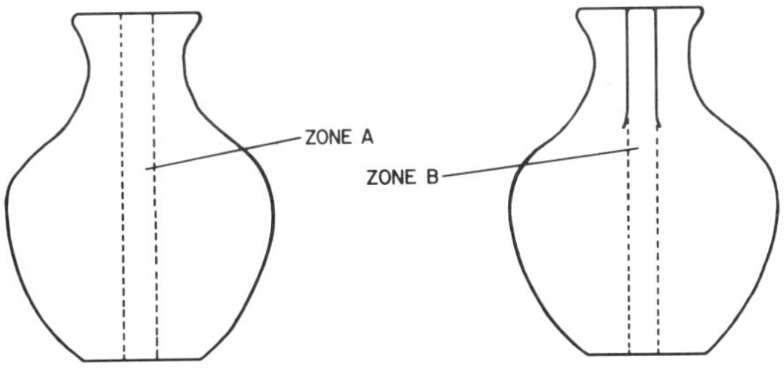

Fig. 5.8. Principal organization of design space for the *plato*.

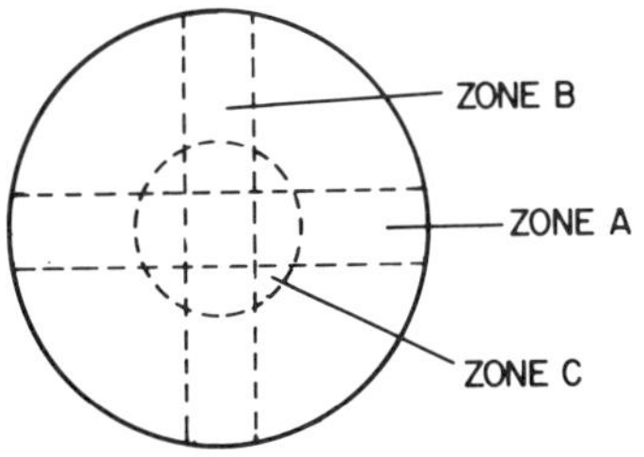

These shapes were selected for three reasons. First, they are decorated utilitarian shapes which were observed being used most frequently by the natives in Quinua. The *tachu*, *puyñu*, and *yukupuyñu* are all forms of a pitcher used for holding water or other liquids. Specifically, the *tachu* was observed to have the following uses: (1) a container for carrying water from irrigation ditches to the house; (2) a container for holding water for washing hands and dishes at the stands of roadside food vendors; and (3) a vessel for transferring *chicha* (a maize beer) from a larger vessel into the cups of individual consumers at the stands of roadside vendors. The *puyñu* has similar uses, but, in addition, smaller-sized *puyñus* serve as individual containers from which people drink *chicha* at fiestas. The *yukupuyñu* was observed only as a container for water used by market vendors. The *plato* is utilized as a container for holding hot food (like boiled ears of fresh corn) at the stands of roadside food vendors, but other uses are likely. Second, Quinua potters produce these four shapes almost exclusively for local use and consumption. These vessels occasionally find their way into the tourist market but this outlet is a minor one. Potters who produce ceramics for the tourist market made very few, if any, of these vessels. On the other hand, pottery vendors from Quinua were observed selling these four shapes, and only these shapes, in the local markets in Quinua, Ayacucho, Huanta and Huamanguilla. Third, these vessels are made exclusively by Quinua potters and they thus represent a unique product of the Quinua region sold to the other populations in the valley. Since these vessels are made for utilitarian use and their production is aimed at the native population of the valley, they are affected more by the shared decorative tradition of the community than the changing responses of individual potters to the tourist market.

The organization of the space on these four utilitarian vessels varies according to each vessel shape. Three of the vessels (the *puyñu*, the *yukupuyñu* and the *tachu*) are vertically oriented vessels and have vertically oriented decorative space. Only the *plato* (the bowl) is a horizontally oriented vessel and has horizontally oriented space. Each of these shapes has two or more different organizations of decorative space, but this paper will only deal with the most frequent and widely used patterns of organizing and utilizing decorative space in the community. Because of their high frequency in the sample, these patterns are assumed to be community-defined patterns of decoration. The derivation of these patterns and their variability is described in another paper (Arnold forthcoming).

The narrow-mouthed bottle (*yukupuyñu*) and the pitcher (*puyñu*) both have their vertical space divided into multiple horizontal zones (Figs. 5.5 and 5.6) and this organizational type represents 89% (39/44 of the *yukupuyñus* and 41/46 of the *puyñus*) of the total sample of each of these vessels.[1] All of the horizontal zones do not occur on every vessel, although each shape has an obligatory zone (Zone A) and a lower boundary which occurs on every vessel in the sample (Tables 5.1 and 5.2).

The *tachu* has three organizations of decorative space which includes the total lack of decoration (23.4% or 11/46) and no decoration except for a white rim (36.2% or 17/46). The most frequent organization (40.4% or 19/46) of decorative space on the *tachu* consists of white strips four to five centimetres wide. Subsequent decoration is placed on these strips. There are three additional organizations of design space which involve the location of these strips (see Arnold forthcoming: fig. 1). On the most frequent type (36.2% or 17/46), potters place the strips vertically from the rim to the base in two locations: (1) on the back of the handle down to the base; and (2) directly opposite the handle on the opposite side of the vessel (Fig. 5.7).

The decorative space on the *plato* includes the rim and either the outside or the inside of the vessel.[2] There are five different organizations of decorative space (see Arnold forthcoming: fig. 5). On the most frequent type of spatial organization (58.3% or 21/36), two bands cross at right angles in the centre of the interior of the vessel (Fig. 5.8). A third zone lies at the intersection of these bands, and a single finite motif occurs within it.

The most frequent organization of decorative space on the *tachu* and *plato* does not have percentages as large as the predominant patterns on the *puyñu* and *yukupuyñu*. There are different reasons for this lack of a high frequency type for each of these shapes. The *plato* is the only shape of the four described here which has no Quechua name, and thus its decoration is not as integrated into the decorative tradition of Quinua as the other shapes. The probable reason for the lack of a Quechua gloss and lack of integration is that formerly gourds were used for bowls, but have begun to be replaced in recent years by pottery even though gourd bowls were still sold in the Ayacucho area in 1967. As for the *tachu*, the variation in the types of spatial organization and the lack of any one predominant high frequency type may be due to a different phenomenon. Some Quinua potters suggested that one type of spatial organization was made in Moya, one of the major subdivisions (*pagos*) of the barrio of Lurinsayuq. Furthermore, groups of *tachus* with a design organization other than the most frequent in the sample were being sold by the same vendor in nearby markets. These data suggest that the lack of a high frequency organization of decorative space on the *tachu* may indicate that there is no single community pattern of spatial organization but rather that the design organizations reflect social groups below the level of the community. This kind of variability occurs in distinct contrast to the *yukupuyñu* and the *puyñu*, on which the only deviation from the predominant type of spatial organization occurs on vessels made by the same potter.

The second kind of organization and utilization of decorative space on Quinua ceramics consists of patterns of symmetry (Shepard 1948; 1956) or what Zaslow and Dittert (1977) have called 'pattern mathematics'. Shepard defines

Table 5.1 *Variation of designs and symmetry classes in obligatory and optional design zones on the* puyñu. *(Frequency is percent of all vessels (total = 46) in predominant type of spatial organization)*

	Obligatory zones			Optional zones			
	Zone A		Lower Border Zone A	Upper Border Zone A	Zone B	Zone C	Zone D
Frequency of zone (%)	97.6[1]		97.6[1]	4.9	70.0	7.3	14.6
Total no. of designs in zone	Central panel	Right, left panels					
	3	1	3	1	7	3	4
Type of design (Freq. in %)	Floral (80.5)[2] Fern (17.1)	Fern (48.8)	Double line (73.1) Symmetric band (14.6) Single line (9.8)	Solid white band (4.9)	Symmetric bands (19.6) Finite Motif (2.4)	Symmetric bands (7.3)	Solid white band (7.3) Single line (2.4) Double line (2.4) Symmetric band (2.4)
Total no. of motif symmetry types	1[3]		0	0	3	2	1
Types of motif symmetry (Freq. in %)	Bilateral[1] (97.6)		None (97.6)	None (4.9)	None (46.3) Radial (9.8) Bilateral (7.3) Rotational (2.4)	None (2.4) Bilateral (2.4) Radial (2.4)	None (8.2) Bilateral (2.4)
Total no. of band symmetry types	0		1	0	4	3	1
Kinds of band symmetry (Freq. in %)	0 (97.6)		None (82.9) HR+VR (14.6)	None (4.9)	HR+T (43.9) HR+VR (7.3) VR (4.9) BR (2.4) None	VR (2.4) VR+BR (2.4) HR+VR (2.4)	VR (2.4)

1. One vessel had no data for this zone.
2. This includes all recognizable variants.
3. The floral design may have flowers that occasionally are radially symmetric.

symmetry as the type of motion inherent in repetition and says 'there is no other quality of design that lends itself as readily to precise definition as symmetry' (Shepard 1956: 267). She discusses symmetry in relation to the three spatial categories of design: finite design, band patterns, and surface patterns (Shepard 1948: 217–26; 1956: 268).

> Elements and motifs are symmetric with respect to a single axis (a line), or a point, or intersecting axes, and are referred to as finite designs. If a series of axes is taken to repeat the figure again and again along a straight line, a band pattern is produced . . . We can go further and repeat the fundamental part in two directions to form a surface or all-over pattern.
> (Shepard 1956: 268–9)

All of these spatial categories of design are not relevant to an analysis of the Quinua style. Finite designs and band patterns are the only spatial categories used in Quinua. In the four vessels under consideration here, most designs occur as band patterns.

This analysis of symmetry first involves determining the fundamental unit (Shepard 1948: 217; 1956: 268–9) of the individual motif. This fundamental unit:

> may be an unsymmetric area or part of an area or a segment of a line, but it is always the unique part of the pattern from which the entire composition can be generated by regular repetition of motion.
> (Shepard 1956: 268)

Second, when a design is repeated again and again along a straight line to form a band pattern (Shepard 1956: 268), the analysis must also determine the fundamental unit of the band pattern as well as the motion of repetition.

Shepard (1956: 275) points out that although perfectly symmetric designs are straightforward, symmetry may be rendered imperfect because of: (1) the adaptation of a symmetric design to the curved surface of a pot; and (2) the lack of skill or carelessness in the execution. Since virtually all of ceramic design needs to be applied to a curved surface in one way or another, all the symmetry of ceramic design is imper-

Table 5.2 *Variation in designs and symmetry classes in obligatory and optional design zones on the* yukupuyñu. *(Frequency is percent of all vessels (total = 39) that have the predominant pattern of spatial organization in the sample)*

	Obligatory zones		Optional zones			
	Zone A	Lower Border Zone A	Upper Border Zone A	Zone B	Zone C	Zone D
Frequency of zone (in %)	100	100	69.2	46.1	5.1	2.6
No. of designs in zone	4	3	4	7	2	1
Type of design in zone (Freq. in %)	Lollipop (92.3)	Double line (59.0)	Single line (41.0)	Symmetric bands (46.1)	Unsymmetric band (2.6)	Single line (2.6)
	Lollipop (5.1) variants	Single line (33.3)	Double line (23.1)			
	Other (2.6)	Symmetric band (7.7)	Symmetric band (5.1)		Symmetric band (2.6)	
Total no. of motif symmetry types	1	0	1	2	1	0
Types of motif symmetry (Freq. in %)	Bilateral (100)	None (100)	Bilateral (2.6)	Bilateral (25.6) Radial (10.3)	Bilateral (2.6)	None (26)
Total no. of band symmetry types	2	1	2	4	1	0
Types of band symmetry (Freq. in %)	VR (97.4) VR+HR (2.6)	VR+HR (7.7)	VR (2.6) VR+HR (2.6)	VR (20.5) HR+T (15.4) VR+HR (5.1) T (5.1)	VR (2.6)	None (2.6)

fect and the design on the Quinua pottery is no exception. Sloppiness of design execution also plays an important role in producing imperfect symmetry in Quinua design, but this aspect of the design will not be discussed here.

The symmetry patterns of motifs and bands on the vessels in the sample were analysed using Shepard's criteria (see Arnold forthcoming: figs. 6a–c). Symmetry frequencies were then tabulated and compared for each vessel and for the total repertoire and the total number of designs in the sample. 68% of the total repertoire and 85% of the total sample of motifs use bilateral symmetry as the predominant pattern of repetition for motif construction (Fig. 5.9; Table 5.3). Almost all of this motion occurs along a vertical axis. As for band symmetry, vertical reflection and a combination of vertical and horizontal reflection are the most common patterns (Fig. 5.10). Vertical reflection constitutes 24% of the total sample and 36% of the total repertoire of band patterns, while a combination of vertical and horizontal reflection occurs in 10% of the total repertoire and 36% of the total sample of band patterns (Fig. 5.11; Table 5.4).

The *tachu* bands consist of a combination of three straight and/or zigzag, red and/or black lines drawn on top of the white strip along its entire length. These band designs are produced according to the following principles: (1) the band must consist of three lines of red and/or black paint; (2) the centre line must be zigzag and be framed by two lines which

Fig. 5.9. Percentage of each motif symmetry type found in the total sample of designs in the total repertoire of designs and percentage of each motif symmetry type found on the total sample of each vessel shape. For total repertoire, the total number of motifs is 34.

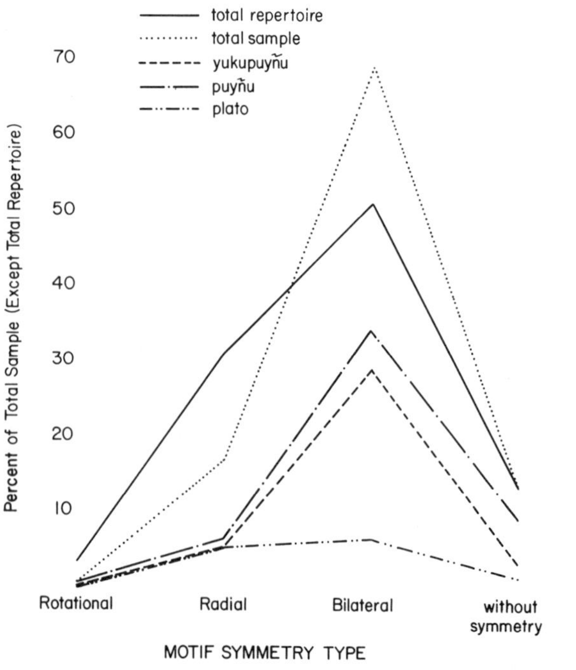

Table 5.3 *Symmetry characteristics of all motifs on all vessels. (Percent of sample)*

	Rotational (Ro)	Radial (R)	Bilateral (B)	Motifs without
Platos				
Total (25 total motifs = 100%)	0	11 (44)	12 (48)	2 (8)
Highest frequency spatial organization	0	8 (32)	6 (24)	0
Others	0	3 (12)	6 (24)	2 (8)
(Percent of total sample of motifs)	0	(5)	(6)	(1)
Puyñu				
Total (105 total motifs = 100%)	1 (1)	13 (12)	72 (69)	19 (18)
Highest frequency spatial organization	1 (1)	13 (12)	72 (69)	19 (18)
Others	0	0	0	0 (0)
(Percent of total sample of motifs)	(.05)	(6)	(34)	(9)
Yukupuyñu				
Total (79 total motifs = 100%)	0	11 (14)	61 (77)	7 (9)
Highest frequency spatial organization	0	11 (14)	61 (77)	7 (9)
Others	0	0	0	0
(Percent of total sample of motifs)	0	(5)	(29)	(3)
Totals (from all vessels)				
Total sample of motifs (209 = 100%)	1 (.05)	35 (17)	145 (69)	28 (13)
Total repertoire of motifs (38 = 100%)	1 (3)	12 (31)	20 (51)	5 (13)

Table 5.4 *Symmetry classes on all bands on all vessels. (Percent of sample)*

	HR+T	VR	HR+VR	SR	BR	T	Without symmetry
Platos							
Total (33 total bands = 100%)	0	6 (18)	8 (24)	6 (18)	0	0	13 (39)
Highest frequency spatial organization	0	6 (18)	6 (18)	0	0	0	13 (39)
Others	0	0	2 (6)	6 (18)	0	0	0
(Percent of total sample of bands)	0	(2)	(3)	(2)	0	0	(5)
Puyñu							
Total (85 total bands = 100%)	18 (21)	5 (6)	10 (12)	0	1 (1)	0	51 (60)
Highest frequency spatial organization	18 (21)	5 (6)	10 (12)	0	1 (1)	0	41 (48)
Others	0	0	0	0	0		10 (12)
(Percent of total sample of bands)	(7)	(2)	(4)	0	(.05)		(20)
Yukupuyñu							
Total (134 total bands = 100%)	6 (4)	50 (37)	8 (6)	0	0	2 (1)	68 (51)
Highest frequency spatial organization	6 (4)	50 (37)	8 (6)	0	0	2 (1)	64 (48)
Others	0	0	0	0	0	0	4 (3)
(Percent of total sample bands)	(2)	(20)	(3)	0	0	(1)	(27)
Total (from all vessels)							
Total sample of bands (252 = 100%)	24 (10)	61 (24)	26 (10)	6 (2)	1 (.05)	2 (1)	132 (52)
Total repertoire of bands (22 = 100%)	1 (5)	8 (36)	8 (36)	2 (9)	1 (5)	1 (5)	1 (5)

may be straight (most frequent) or zigzag; (3) the framing lines must mirror one another in colour and shape (e.g. being straight or zigzag); and (4) all straight lines must be parallel. (The symmetries of *tachu* bands are not analysed in this paper.)

A third kind of organization and utilization of the space on the vessels consists of the variability of the motifs

Fig. 5.10. Two band patterns (from the *yukupuyñu*) produced using bilateral symmetry (B) for motifs, and vertical reflection (VR) and a combination of vertical and horizontal reflection (VR + HR) for band patterns. The chart shows how each pattern in the sample was analysed (see Arnold forthcoming: fig. 6a–c).

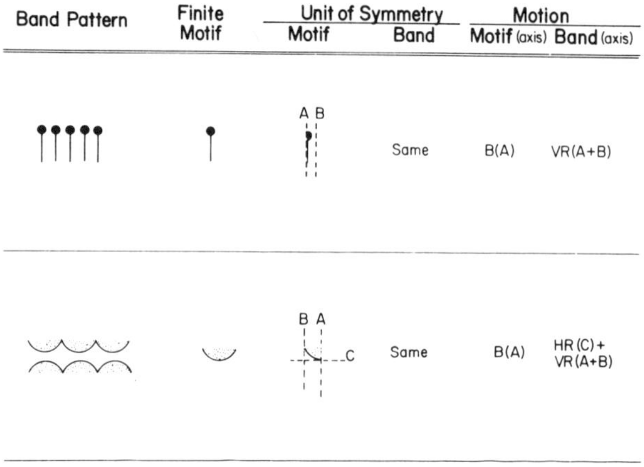

and symmetry patterns in the obligatory design zones. In the most frequent spatial patterns on the *tachu* and *plato*, all of the zones are obligatory zones. The *puyñu* and *yukupuyñu*, however, have a variety of zones of which only one zone is obligatory (Tables 5.1 and 5.2). On these vessels, obligatory zones are associated with specific motifs which do not occur elsewhere in any other zone on these or any other of the four vessels. On the *yukupuyñu*, the predominant motif associated with the obligatory zone (Zone A; see Fig. 5.5) is the 'lollipop motif' (Fig. 5.10) alone or in combination with other motifs. On the *puyñu* shape, the obligatory zone (Zone A; see Fig. 5.6) contains one central panel which occurs below the spout (opposite the handle) and is often (63.4% or 26/41) flanked by designs in a smaller panel on each side of it. The central panel almost universally (80.5% or 33/41) contains a large bilaterally symmetric floral motif (Fig. 5.12) or a variant of it. On rare occasions (9.9% or 4/41), a vertical line or leaf is added to either side of the central panel. The two subsidiary panels usually contain at least one fern-like motif (Fig. 5.12), alone (24.4% or 10/41) or occasionally (39.0% or 16/41) in combination with another motif such as vertical lines (39.0% or 16/41) and/or another fern (4.9% or 2/41; see Fig. 5.12). Besides the axis of bilateral symmetry for the floral motif in the central panel of the zone, the same axis serves as an axis of bilateral symmetry for the entire zone, with one side being the mirror image of the other. Thus, on the *puyñu*, there is no band symmetry pattern in

Fig. 5.11. Percentage of each type of band symmetry (HR – horizontal reflection, VR – vertical reflection, SR – slide reflection, BR – bifold rotation, T – translation) found in the total sample, the total repertoire of the designs, and percentage of each type of band symmetry type found on the total sample of each vessel shape (see Table 5.2). For the total repertoire, 100% equals 28. The bands without symmetry consist mostly of single and double lines.

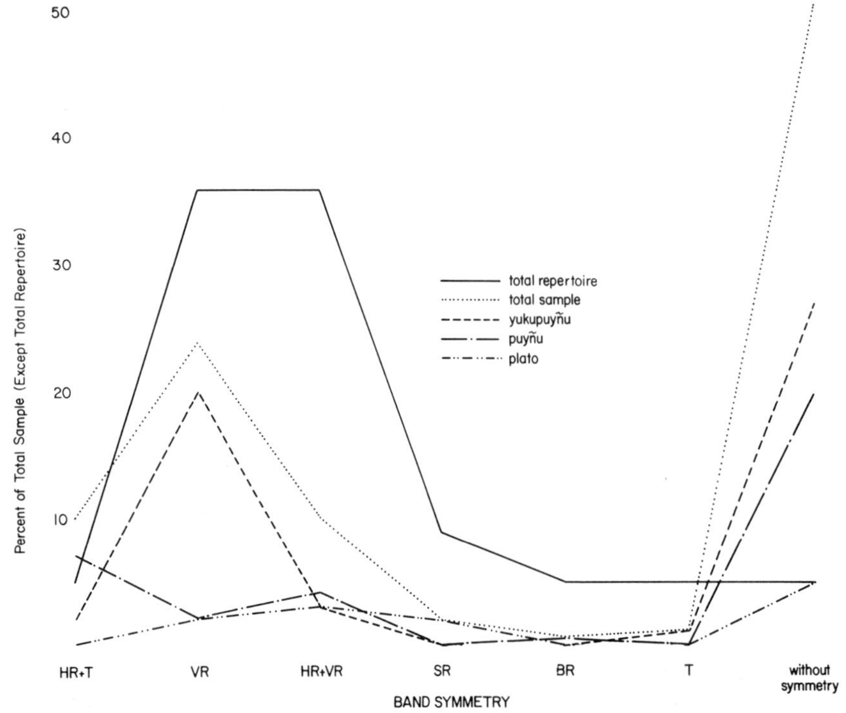

the obligatory zone; only one motif symmetry pattern (bilateral symmetry) occurs there.

The relationship of decorative space to environmental and social space

The most comprehensive spatial pattern in Quinua is the organization of the environmental space around the community into a series of techno-environmental zones which are differentially exploited. This pattern is reflected in two of the three vessels with vertically oriented decorative space (the *puyñu* and *yukupuyñu*). The most frequent organization of decorative space on these vessels consists of dividing the vertical dimension into a series of vertically arranged horizontal zones like the organization of the environmental space around the community.

The second most comprehensive pattern consists of the division of the lower montane savannah into two sections based on the topographic and hydrological prerequisites of the irrigation system: the drainage into the major ravines on either side of the community. Although the system begins in the ecological zones above the community, it has no utilitarian nor classificatory function until it reaches the savannah, where it subdivides the horizontal space in that zone into two barrios. This division of horizontal space into two complementary sections manifests itself in the division of horizontal space on Quinua ceramics in three ways: (1) in the bifurcation of the space on the *tachu* by a single vertical plane created by the two vertical bands of decoration; (2) in the mirroring of the colour and shape of the framing lines on the *tachu* bands; and (3) in the high frequency of bilateral symmetry as the predominant motion of repetition for motifs on the other vessels. All of these patterns are a two-fold subdivision of horizontal space along a vertical axis similar to the two-fold division of the community. A weaker analogy, but still a two-fold pattern produced in a horizontal direction, is the high frequency use of a motion which repeats a motif many times along two axes in a horizontal direction (i.e. vertical reflection; see Fig. 5.10) to produce a band pattern.

Fig. 5.12. The two major motifs used in the obligatory design zone (Zone A) on the *puyñu* reproduced by using bilateral symmetry (B) along a vertical axis (A).

Band Pattern	Finite Motif	Unit of Symmetry		Motion	
		Motif	Band	Motif (axis)	Band (axis)
None	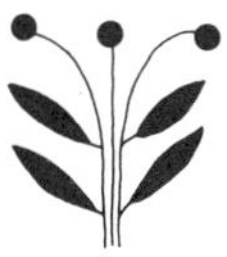	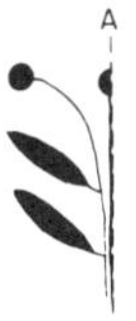	None	B(A)	None
None	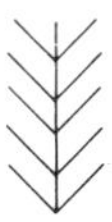	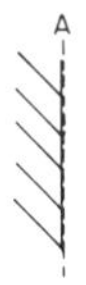	None	B(A)	None

Related to this two-fold division of horizontal space into barrios is the complementary function of the irrigation system in the upper and lower parts of the savannah. Because of the different climates and rainfall along the slope and the inability of the system to supply water to all the people in the community who want it at the same time, the irrigation system has two complementary functions. These functions divide the vertical space within the savannah into two parts: an upper and lower section. This pattern is reflected in the ceramics in the use of horizontal reflection along with vertical reflection as the second most frequent symmetry pattern used to form the band patterns. The subdivision of the savannah into upper and lower portions has lesser importance than the barrio division, and there are no clearly obvious or stated social structural correlates to this division. From the spatial point of view, the vertical division of the savannah into upper and lower is weaker than the two-fold horizontal division into barrios. This relative weakness is reflected in two ways: (1) the lesser frequency of horizontal reflection combined with vertical reflection in the sample compared to vertical reflection; and (2) the fact that the generation of band designs by means of horizontal reflection occurs only once on a horizontal axis in the vertical dimension, while the generation of band designs by means of vertical reflection emphasizes movement along multiple axes in the horizontal dimension. The combination of vertical reflection and horizontal reflection in the designs thus combines the reification of subdivision of horizontal space in the savannah into two barrios by the irrigation system with the subdivision of the vertical space in the savannah based on the complementary functions of the system in the upper and lower portions.

The third most comprehensive pattern consists of the division of horizontal space into the urban nucleated settlement of the village itself and the more dispersed rural area. This division constitutes the basis for the two social classes in the community; the villagers are considered as a higher class than the rural inhabitants. This class distinction is also reflected in the ceramics in the spatial organization of the only vessel with horizontally oriented social space (the *plato*). The most frequent organization of space on this vessel consists of two bands intersecting at right angles with a design zone at their point of intersection. This central zone is analogous to the village, which is a nucleated settlement that is smaller in size and more compact than the dispersed and larger settlement around the village. Being located in the savannah, the village is in the approximate geographical and ecological centre of the community. The intersecting bands also have analogies with the other structural patterns in the community. The two-fold division of horizontal space of the vessel by one of the bands represents the two-fold division of horizontal space in the community into barrios based on the irrigation system. The other band intersecting it represents a division of a kind of pseudo-vertical space. Although the vessel is horizontally oriented and one band divides this horizontal space into two parts, another band at right angles to it must then represent a division of vertical space, since there is no division of horizontal space in the community that cross-cuts the division into barrios. Thus, this division may represent the distinction between the irrigation functions in the upper and lower savannah. This latter division, however, does not cut across the barrio division in the village but rather occurs well below it. Another possibility is the division of the multiple ecological zones in the community into two emic zones (the *puna* and the *quechua*). The subdivision of horizontal space into barrios does not cut across any other zone except the savannah, however, which is part of the *quechua*. So, the relationship of the *plato* structure to the spatial organization of the community is not as clear as it could be, and is also a consequence of its lack of clear integration into the ceramic tradition in the community as manifested in the lack of a Quechua gloss for the vessel. Nevertheless, the pattern on the *plato* provides an example of the use of the two-fold principle for organization already seen in spatial patterns in the community and in the pottery design on other vessels.

An equally important division of social space in the community consists of the corporate descent groups ascribed by kinship. Each individual in Quinua is a member of two descent groups – one on his mother's side and one on his father's side. This bilateral pattern is also reflected in the high frequency of bilateral symmetry as the repetitive motion for motifs. Just as individuals are the smallest units of social space in the community, so the motifs are the smallest units of decorative space. Thus, the membership of each individual in a descent group on each side of his family is reflected in the bilateral symmetry of the motifs; each basic unit of space consists of two parts. This complementary pattern is also reflected in the repetition of a band motif (vertical reflection) along two axes to form the band pattern.

Besides the analogy of the structure and organization of space in the community and in the ceramics, there is also an analogy between the most important ecological zone in the community and the obligatory decorative zones on the *puyñu* and *yukupuyñu*.[3] The location of the ecological zones is fixed and the location of the decorative zones is fixed. Furthermore, some of the ecological zones have great variability in the way they are utilized. The montane prairie and moist forest zones have a variety of exploitative techniques including herding and the cultivation of a variety of crops. Much of the land is in fallow and not being cultivated at any one time. In the forest zone, both brush and other wild vegetation are exploited for a wide variety of uses. Similarly, the lower montane thorn forest is mostly unexploited except for grazing, occasional dry farming and the wild products of the zone like the fruit of the nopal cactus and the pepper (molle) tree, used for making *chicha*. The lower montane savannah contrasts with all of these zones in its importance and in the lesser degree of variability in exploitation. While there is some variation in exploitation in this zone, most of it is intensively cultivated. Maize is the most valued crop in the community and the irrigation system is geared to its production in this zone. Variability in crops cultivated is largely due to the limits of irrigated land; fields in the savannah that are too high or otherwise inaccessible to irrigation are planted with other crops besides maize, like root crops, wheat and barley (Mitchell 1976a). While the other zones vary in the techniques used to exploit them, the savannah has a relatively fixed exploitative activity that is geared to irrigation and maize production.

This relatively fixed nature of the exploitative aspects of the savannah is reflected in the relative lack of variability in the motifs, motif symmetry and band symmetry in the obligatory zones on the two vessels (the *puyñu* and *yukupuyñu*) that model the vertical multizonal ecological pattern in the community. First, the existence of a single obligatory zone on the vessels is a manifestation of the importance and general value of the savannah to the community. Second, there is less variability in the motifs in these obligatory zones than there is in the optional zones on the vessels (Tables 5.5 and 5.6). The relatively fixed designs (the 'lollipop', fern and floral motifs) in these obligatory zones are analogous to the importance of the fixed exploitative activity of maize cultivation in the savannah. This interpretation is reinforced by the fact that informants refer to the fern-like design which occurs in this zone as 'maize'. Third, the lack of variability in motifs carries over into lesser variability in the symmetry patterns in the obligatory zones. On the *yukupuyñu*, bilateral symmetry is the predominant pattern for motif production and vertical reflection is the most frequent symmetry pattern for band production in this zone (Table 5.2). For the obligatory zone of the *puyñu* (Table 5.1), bilateral symmetry is the only pattern of motif symmetry present. The strength of this bilateral pattern, however, does not occur merely with the presence of this type of motif symmetry, but also in the bilateral structuring of the zone itself. The vertical axis of symmetry for the floral motifs in the zone corresponds to the axis of symmetry for the placement of other designs in the zone.

The smaller amount of deviation from bilateral symmetry for motif production and in vertical reflection for band production in these zones on the *puyñu* and *yukupuyñu* suggests the importance of these two-fold patterns in the savannah. These symmetry patterns correspond to the basic structural patterns of spatial organization in the savannah – a two-fold division. Thus, since the obligatory zone on the *puyñu* and *yukupuyñu* occurs within a structure analogous to the vertically arranged ecological zones in the community, has fixed motifs which are analogous to the fixed exploitative activity in the savannah, and has symmetry patterns which correspond to the principles of organizing this zone, the obligatory zones are analogous to the location and great importance of the savannah. The savannah has the

Table 5.5 *Summary: all obligatory and all optional zones combined on the* puyñu

	All obligatory zones	All optional zones
Frequency in %	97.6[1]	0–70.0
No. of different designs	2[2] (excluding vertical lines and vertical leaves that occasionally border the floral motif)	14
No. of different motif symmetry types	1[3]	3
No. of different band symmetry types	1	5

1. One vessel had no data for this zone.
2. This includes all recognizable variants.
3. The floral design may have flowers that occasionally are radially symmetric.

Table 5.6 *Summary: all obligatory and all optional zones combined on the* yukupuyñu

	All obligatory zones	All optional zones
Frequency (in %)	100	0–69.2
No. of different designs	4 (including two variants of the lollipop motif)	11
No. of different motif symmetry types	1	2
No. of different band symmetry types	2	4

Table 5.7 *Analogies of the lower montane savannah to the obligatory decorative zone on the* puyñu *and* yukupuyñu *in comparison to other zones*

Characteristics of the savannah	Characteristics of the obligatory zone
The most important zone in the community with the highest density of population; the political, economic and urban centre of the community.	Most important decorative zone; always present on the vessels.
Relative fixed exploitative activity with focus on irrigation and maize cultivation; less variability in exploitative activity in comparison to other zones.	Relatively fixed designs and least variability in symmetry types: (1) Designs which occur here only occur in this zone and nowhere else (2) Least variability in: (a) number of different designs (b) in types and frequency of: i. motif symmetry ii. band symmetry
The bipartite division into barrios based on the irrigation system.	Very high frequencies (very close to 100%) of two-part (motif) or two axis (band) symmetry patterns (a) motif symmetry: bilateral (two complementary halves) (b) band symmetry: vertical reflection (two complementary axes)

highest density of population, is the centre of political power, and utilizes intensive maize cultivation made possible by the irrigation system. Thus, the obligatory zones on these two vessels are symbols of the savannah on the pottery (Table 5.7).

Since the irrigation system distributes water and three of the four vessels discussed here are used to carry and distribute water, it is not surprising that the organization of space by irrigation system parallels the utilization and organization of the decorative space occurring in certain areas of water-carrying vessels. Just as the irrigation system distributes water throughout the lower montane savannah, the *puyñu*, *yukupuyñu* and *tachu* distribute water from the irrigation system to the houses and the people within them. Thus, the common function of water distribution in the pottery and the spatial organization of the savannah appears to provide the symbolic link between the spatial organization of the savannah on the one hand and the decoration on the water-carrying pottery on the other.

Conclusion

Within the great amount of variability in the Quinua style (Arnold forthcoming), there are high frequency patterns of design structure and organization. These patterns consist of the organization of decorative space, high frequencies of motif and band symmetry and the existence and the lesser variability of the fixed motifs and symmetry patterns that occur within the obligatory zones. In deriving these design patterns, another paper (Arnold 1981) has argued that these patterns were the product of a distinct community of potters. This paper reinforces this conclusion by demonstrating that these patterns are organized by the same structural principles that organize the environmental and social space in the community (Table 5.8). Thus, the interacting community of potters reifies the basic structural principles that organize the community in the decorated

Table 5.8 *Summary: relationship of spatial organization and decorative space in Quinua*

Spatial orientation	Community pattern	Decorative space	Vessel shape
Vertical	Vertical set of ecological zones	Set of vertically arranged decorative zones on vessels with vertically arranged space	*puyñu* *yukupuyñu*
Horizontal	Division of savannah into two barrios based on the irrigation system	High frequency use of bilateral symmetry for motifs	All except the *tachu*
		Bifurcation of space by a vertical plane created by two narrow bands	*tachu*
		Mirroring of colour and shape of framing lines on bands	*tachu*
		High frequency use of vertical reflection to form band patterns	All except the *tachu*
		Division of design space into two parts by one band	*plato*
Vertical	Division of savannah into upper and lower zones based on the complementary functions of the irrigation system	Use of horizontal reflection in conjunction with vertical reflection as the second most prominent band pattern	All except the *tachu*
Horizontal	Bilateral membership of individuals (the smallest unit of social space in the community) in each of two descent groups	Predominance of bilateral symmetry for production of motifs (the smallest unit of design space in the community)	All except the *tachu*
	Social classes: higher class in the village, lower class in the rural area	Inner versus outer spatial organization	*plato*

pottery that they produce. Perhaps even more important is the observation that the relationship of spatial organization and pottery design occurs most strongly on utility vessels which have a common function with the spatial organization of the community. The similarity of structural principles on pottery and society are strongest when they are related to a common function – water distribution.[4]

Notes

1 Design zones on these vessels also include the rim and the handle. These data are not relevant to the theme of this paper and are also very incomplete in the sample.

2 Data on the rim decoration are not relevant to the present paper, are rather incomplete in the sample and therefore are not discussed here.

3 Since all the zones of the *tachu* are obligatory, a discussion of them is not relevant here.

4 This paper is a synthesis of two separate studies about Quinua which analysed separate sets of data and were written independently. The first was a design analysis of the four utilitarian vessels (Arnold 1970; forthcoming) and the other was an analysis of the relationship of potters and their environment (Arnold 1975). The raw data for this study can be found in Arnold (1970). William P. Mitchell generously shared his facilities with me in Quinua and has been especially helpful and generous with data that has made this paper possible. I am grateful to Dorothy Washburn who asked me to write this paper and James Vreeland who finally convinced me (after much initial scepticism) that my design data did indeed fit spatial patterns in other communities around the Andean city of Ayacucho. The fieldwork for this report was supported by National Defense Foreign Language Fellowship and the Depart-

ment of Anthropology of the University of Illinois, Urbana. I a am grateful to R.T. Zuidema and D.W. Lathrap for their guidance, encouragement and support which made the fieldwork possible. The Department of Sociology and Anthropology of Wheaton College, the Wheaton Alumni Faculty Development Fund and a Wheaton Alumni Association grant all provided support for the preparation of the present manuscript. Rich Nickel made the drawings, Melinda Korell and Pauline Roelofs provided typing assistance, and Alva Steffler made the high contrast photostats from the drawings.

References

Adams, Marie Jeanne, 1973. Structural aspects of a village art. *American Anthropologist* 75 (1): 265–79.

Adams, William Y., 1979. On the argument from ceramics to history: a challenge based on evidence from Medieval Nubia. *Current Anthropology* 20: 727–44.

Allen, William L. and James B. Richardson III, 1970. The reconstruction of kinship from archaeological data, the methods, and the feasibility. *American Antiquity* 36: 41–53.

Arnold, Dean E., 1970. The emics of pottery design from Quinua, Peru. Unpublished Ph.D. dissertation, Department of Anthropology, University of Illinois, Urbana.

1972a. Mineralogical analyses of ceramic materials from Quinua, Department of Ayacucho, Peru. *Archaeometry* 14: 93–101.

1972b. Native pottery making in Quinua, Peru. *Anthropos* 67: 858–72.

1975. Ceramic ecology in the Ayacucho Basin, Peru: implications for prehistory. *Current Anthropology* 16: 185–203.

Forthcoming. Social interaction and ceramic design: community-wide correlates in Quinua, Peru. To appear in a Festschrift for Frederick R. Matson, edited by Prudence Rice.

Bastien, Joseph W., 1978. *Mountain of the Condor: metaphor and ritual in Andean Ayllu.* American Ethnological Society Monograph No. 64. West, St Paul.

Brush, Stephen R., 1977. *Mountain, Field and Family.* University of Pennsylvania Press, Philadelphia.

Bunzel, Ruth L., 1929. *The Pueblo Potter: a study of creative imagination in primitive art.* Columbia University Press, New York.

Deetz, James, 1965. *The Dynamics of Stylistic Change in Arikara Ceramics.* Illinois Studies in Anthropology No. 4, University of Illinois Press, Urbana.

Hardin Friedrich, Margaret, 1970. Design structure and social interaction: archaeological implications of an ethnographic analysis. *American Antiquity* 35: 332–43.

Hill, James N., 1970. Broken K Pueblo: prehistoric social organization in American Southwest. *University of Arizona Anthropological Papers* 18. Tuscon.

Isbell, Billie Jean, 1978. *To Defend Ourselves: ecology and ritual in an Andean village.* University of Texas Press, Austin.

Lathrap, Donald W., 1962. Yarinacocha: excavations in the Peruvian Montana. Unpublished Ph.D. dissertation, Department of Anthropology, Harvard University, Cambridge, Mass.

Litto, Gertrude, 1976. *South American Folk Pottery: traditional techniques from Peru, Ecuador, Bolivia, Venezuela, Chile and Colombia.* Watson Guptill, New York.

Longacre, William A., 1970. Archaeology as anthropology: a case study. *University of Arizona Anthropological Papers* 17. Tuscon.

Mitchell, William P., 1972. The system of power in Quinua: a community of the Central Peruvian Highlands. Unpublished Ph.D. Dissertation, Department of Anthropology, University of Pittsburgh.

1976a. Irrigation and community in the central Peruvian highlands. *American Anthropologist* 78: 25–44.

1976b. Social adaptation to the mountain environment of an Andean village. In *Hill Lands: Proceedings of an international symposium*, edited by J. Luchop, J.D. Cawthon and M.J. Breslin, pp. 187–98. University of West Virginia Press, Morgantown.

1977. Irrigation farming in the Andes: evolutionary implications. In *Peasant Livelihood: Studies in Economic Anthropology and Cultural Ecology*, edited by Rhoda Halperin and James Dow, pp. 36–59. St Martin's Press, New York.

1979. Inconsistencia de status social y dimensiones de rango en los Andes Centrales del Peru. *Estudios Andinos* 15: 21–31.

Forthcoming. Multi-zone agriculture in an Andean village. In *Ayacucho archaeological-botanical project*, Volume 1, edited by Richard S. MacNeish, University of Michigan Press, Ann Arbor.

Murdock, George Peter, 1949. *Social structure.* Macmillan, New York.

Murra, John E., 1972. El 'vertical control' de un maximo de pisos ecologicos en la economia de las sociedades Andinas. In *Vista de la Provinica de Leon de Huanuco en 1562, Inigo Ortiz de Zuniga, visitador.* Documentos para la Historia y Ethnologia de Huanuco y la selva central, tomo II, pp. 427–76. Universidad Nacional Hermilio Valdizan, Huanuco, Peru.

1973. Rite and crop in the Inca state. In *Peoples and cultures of native South America*, edited by Daniel R. Gross, pp. 377–89. The Natural History Press, Garden City. (Revised version of an article published in *Culture and History*, edited by S. Diamond, pp. 393–467, 1960.)

Roe, Peter G., 1980. Art and residence among the Shipibo Indians of Peru: a study of microacculturation. *American Anthropologist* 82: 42–71.

Rowe, John H., 1959. Archaeological dating and cultural process. *Southwestern Journal of Anthropology* 15: 317–24.

Rye, O.S., 1976. Keeping your temper under control: materials and the manufacture of Papuan pottery. *Archaeology and Physical Anthropology in Oceania* 11: 106–37.

Shepard, Anna O., 1948. The symmetry of abstract design with special reference to ceramic decoration. *Carnegie Institution of Washington Publication* 547.

1956. Ceramics for the archaeologist. *Carnegie Institution of Washington Publication* 609.

Spahni, Jean-Christian, 1966. *La ceramica popular del Peru.* Peruano Suiza, S.A., Lima.

Stanislawski, Michael B., 1977. Ethnoarchaeology of Hopi and Hopi–Tewa pottery making: styles of learning. In *Experimental Archaeology*, edited by Daniel Ingersoll, John E. Yellen and William MacDonald, pp. 378–408. Columbia University Press, New York.

1978. If pots were mortal. In *Explorations in Ethnoarchaeology*, edited by Richard A. Gould, pp. 201–27. University of New Mexico Press, Alburquerque.

Stanislawski, Michael B. and Barbara S. Stanislawski, 1978. Hopi and Hopi–Tewa ceramic tradition networks. In *The Spatial Organization of Culture*, edited by Ian Hodder, pp. 61–76. Duckworth, London.

Webster, Steven, 1971. An indigenous Quechua community in exploitation of multiple ecological zones. *XXXIX Congresso Internacional de Americanistas Actas y Memorias*, Vol. 3, pp. 176–83. Lima.

Zaslow, Bert and Alfred E. Dittert, Jr, 1977. The pattern technology of the Hohokam. In *Pattern Mathematics and Archaeology*, edited by G.A. Clark. Arizona State University Anthropological Research Paper 2.

Zuidema, R.T. and U. Quispe, 1968. A visit to god. *Bijdragen* 124: 22–39.

Chapter 6

When the map is the territory: art in Maori culture

F. Allan Hanson

It would not be wide of the mark to characterize the cultural process as a sort of ongoing dialogue between human beings. Spoken and written words, music, bodily gestures, material objects: all these are messages which people communicate to each other about mundane affairs, the shape of reality, the criteria of human responsibility and happiness, the entire range of information people need to exchange if they are to coordinate their activities as members of society. The term 'art' is often reserved for those messages which have been articulated with exceptional care, imagination, and skill. Therefore art is a particularly rich territory for the exploration of culture. The only difficulty is that anthropologists are often at a loss as to how art might be interpreted, or translated into a form which is intelligible to their audience. This essay suggests a conceptual scheme for the analysis of art and applies it to the art of the New Zealand Maoris.[1] Our focus will be on Maori culture after European contact but before that event had changed the culture out of recognition, the period from 1770 to 1840.

When iconography fails

Gilbert Archey, in one of the more thoughtful essays published on the interpretation of Polynesian art (1965: 42–9), distinguishes quite sharply between meaning and the aesthetic in art. It is not a distinction which we will ultimately accept, but consideration of its advantages and drawbacks is a good avenue to the position which we will espouse. For Archey, the distinction between the aesthetic and meaning is isomorphic with that between form and content. The meaning of an art object is to be found in its content, which Archey understands as something outside the object and which the object represents. The meaning of the innumerable depictions of the crucifixion in Western art, for example, is the historical event of the execution of Jesus and, more generally, God's love and redeeming grace for mankind. Meaning is a matter of cognition: we know it (if, indeed, we know it at all; someone completely untutored in Christianity would be ignorant of the meaning of a crucifix) intellectually.

The aesthetic in art relates to form. People apprehend or respond to it not intellectually but with feeling. Archey distinguishes three kinds of aesthetics. The 'aesthetic of function' concerns the relation of the form of an object (a knife, an auditorium) to its use. The 'aesthetic of meaning' refers to the way in which an object's form conveys its meaning. 'This is not the *understanding* of the meaning, our intellectual response', stresses Archey, 'but a *feeling-response* to the aptness of expression of meaning' (1965: 44; Archey's italics). Two paintings of the crucifixion may have the same meaning, but divergent uses of colour or rendering of the droop of the head or sag of the body would make them quite distinct so far as the aesthetic of meaning is concerned. Finally there is the 'aesthetic of form' or 'essential form'. This refers to the harmony, rhythm, balance of form in an art object considered quite apart from the object's use or what it means (represents). This last aesthetic, Archey says, is that quality which Roger Fry and Clive Bell term 'significant form': form which refers to or signifies absolutely nothing outside itself (Archey 1965: 44, 46; see also Fry 1947: 194–9).

One of Archey's goals in his expansion of aesthetics beyond pure form to include the aesthetics of meaning and function, and also in his concern with meaning as grasped intellectually, is to provide room – infinitely more than is available in Fry's and Bell's approach – to talk about art in its social and cultural context. From our perspective this is a great advantage, because an anthropology of art by definition is concerned with art as part of a larger matrix. At the same time, for a second important advantage of Archey's scheme, the emphasis he continues to place on aesthetics (including an aesthetic of pure form) avoids an unfortunate tendency in anthropology to reduce art by more than half by attending exclusively to that cognitive aspect of art which Archey treats as content or meaning.

Archey's scheme also has certain difficulties. One of these is in his notion of meaning. He seems to think that the meaning of an art object is like the meaning of a word: you may know it more or less accurately or not at all, but you are conscious of this knowledge (or ignorance) and are able to say what it is. Archey's example is the meaning of the carved Maori meeting house. Maoris often say that the house represents an illustrious ancestor of the tribe, or perhaps the tribe itself, in the form of a human body: the head is carved at the gable, the bargeboards are outspread arms (sometimes with fingers depicted at the ends), the ridgepole is the backbone, the rafters represent ribs (Archey 1965: 45). The problem with this iconographic notion of meaning – so far as Maori art is concerned, at least – is that precious little in Maori art yields to analysis of this sort. As Hamilton and Rowe have both observed, Maori art is primarily decorative rather than representational (Hamilton 1901: 6; Rowe 1928: 8). Those elements of Maori art which can be understood as depicting things outside themselves can be numbered in a few sentences. One is the protruding tongue which so commonly adorns the human figures carved on house posts and door lintels, canoe prows, weapons, and many other objects. An out-thrust tongue is the characteristic posture Maoris adopt in the war dance, so the carvings doubtless represent persons in the highly honoured role of fierce warriors. Again, the carved human figures staring out from the palisades of fortified villages probably represent the alertness of their inhabitants against any attack. A conventional design carved on the bargeboards of decorated storehouses is said to depict a group of men hauling in a whale. A stranded whale is a windfall of immense proportions, so this scene may represent the abundant provisions ideally contained within the house. Fecundity may also be symbolized by the copulating human figures sometimes carved on storehouses. Lizards, depicted more naturalistically than any other form in Maori art, are also carved on some storehouses. Lizards were thought to be forms which gods commonly adopted when visiting the physical world, so their representations on storehouses were probably symbols of – or perhaps actual abodes for – the gods which protected the houses and its contents. Another carved lizard faithfully protected the bones in a burial cave at Waimamaku, near Hokianga. Once a man who had entered the cave to deposit some additional bones there happened to step over the slab with the lizard carved on it rather than prudently passing around it. He lived (but not long) to regret his carelessness, for he 'was bitten by the spirit of the lizard. He felt sick when he got out; went home, and died' (Cheeseman 1906: 454).

The foregoing list demonstrates that iconography does exist in Maori art, but that list also essentially exhausts its extent. Large areas of design remain untouched by the question of representation: rafter painting, textile border design, the intricate wood carving on treasure boxes, food funnels, and other objects. If we hold to Archey's concept of meaning as what an object depicts, much of Maori art must be set down as having no meaning. Archey himself recognizes this situation, accepts it, and has a reason for it. This reason, like the rest of his theory, is grounded in the form/content distinction. The public at large, he holds, tends to be most closely attuned to content, while artists are primarily interested in the exploration and development of form. Over time it is possible for a gulf to open up between artist and audience. The artist's passion for the aesthetic of form leads to works in which the content (what they represent) is increasingly difficult to detect. Eventually the objects communicate no content at all, at which point one might say that their meaning is lost, or has been forgotten.

> We have sometimes wondered if the Maori *tohunga* [artist] may not sometimes have lost touch with his public. I feel sure that in his involved complexities of highly stylized *manaia* and spirals, in a canoe sternpost for example, decorative form had gained ascendancy over meaning. (Archey 1965: 45)

Archey goes on to confess his inability to detect meaning in the complex and beautiful Maori door lintels (*pare*), but expresses the confidence that they once had a meaning, now lost.[2]

We need to recognize the tacit assumption underlying Archey's remarks: that visual art (or, at the very least, Maori visual art) is originally representational. It is a *picture* of something, and the thing depicted is its meaning. From this it follows that if we cannot make out what it pictures, the reason is that form has prevailed over content in this particular art tradition, the artists have lost touch with their public, and the meaning of their art has been lost. The researcher's mandate is to figure out what it is that is so formalistically pictured and thus to retrieve the meaning – if, indeed, formalism has not progressed so far as to make that task impossible.

Several investigators have made efforts to exhume iconographic meanings from Maori art, with results of varying plausibility. Among the earliest was Thomas Kendall, a fallen missionary who 'had been almost converted to the ideas of those whom he had come to save' and who, in the early 1820s, held that the principles of Maori cosmology were depicted in the motifs of wood carving (Binney 1968: 126, 133–5, 138, 143, 144–7). Other interpretations include Archey's own of the *manaia* as a human figure in profile and the double spiral as a derivation from interlocking *manaia* jaws (Archey 1960: 10–19; 1977: 40–2); Barrow's rival interpretation of the *manaia* as a being with a human body and the head of a bird (Barrow 1969: 20); the suggestion by Lévi-Strauss and others that the male facial tattoo design depicts a human face done in 'split representation' – two profiles staring at each other across a vertical central line (Lévi-Strauss 1963: 257; Jackson 1972: 69, 71–2; Schwimmer 1974: 92); and Gathercole's (1974) interpretation of door lintels as 'unwrapped' godsticks. Among the most ambitious efforts, and certainly the least convincing, is the fantastic book *Maori Symbolism* (Rout 1926), in which art is analysed almost as a form of ideographic writing. The difficulty is that the messages which the objects considered in the book are supposed to convey bear no relation to what is known about Maori culture.

Interesting as some of these interpretations may be, it must be borne in mind that they all rest on the tacit assumption mentioned above that Maori art designs are – or at least originally were – representational: pictures of things outside themselves. Insofar as that assumption is inaccurate, the enterprise of seeking meaning in Maori art by reconstructing a representational iconography is misdirected.

One reason to be wary of representational meaning in Maori art, even when Maoris themselves identify what an object or motif depicts, is their tendency to establish an iconic link *after* the object has been made. In decorated meeting houses, for example, the rafter support posts are carved as human figures and are said to represent particular tribal ancestors. But McEwan (1966: 415) writes of these:

> In most cases there is nothing to identify the ancestor represented. Indeed, it is not uncommon for the figures to be named after the house is finished.

Obviously in that circumstance there could be nothing in the 'content' of a carving to identify the particular ancestor it is designated to represent.[3] Something roughly similar happens with rafter paintings (*kōwhaiwhai*), woven wall panels (*tukutuku*) and textile border design (*tāniko*). While such designs have names, the designs were not produced to represent the thing named. On the contrary, the name came after the design, and was selected because of a coincidental resemblance. The *tukutuku* design *ara moana* (ocean path), for example, was so named because its chevrons resemble waves (Mead 1968: 63; Phillipps 1960: 14, 28; Hiroa 1926: 224). One wonders, indeed, if even the notion that the decorated meeting house represents the body of a tribal ancestor did not get started in the same way.

My conclusion from all this is that representational meaning in Maori art is sharply limited. Therefore new insights may be anticipated only from fresh analytic approaches. One useful step in this direction has been taken by Michael Jackson. His concern is to go beyond native exegesis in the analysis of Maori art and to investigate, in terminology borrowed from Victor Turner (1967: 51), its operational and positional meanings. These terms refer, respectively, to the use of a symbol and to the place of a particular symbol in a constellation of symbols. This analytic approach enables Jackson provocatively to link carved door lintels and a few other elements in Maori art to a general cultural pattern of dualism: the different social roles people play in the intimacy of the household and the larger world of the village, and so on (Jackson 1972). A number of my own interpretations of Maori art are close to Jackson's. Before turning to them, however, it is necessary to develop the particular analytic approach I will follow. This can be done by shifting our attention to the side of Archey's dichotomy not yet considered: from meaning to aesthetics, from content to form.

Meaning in form

For Archey, it will be recalled, 'aesthetics' refers to the feelings evoked by an object's form. The aesthetic of function concerns form in relation to use, the aesthetic of meaning deals with the link between form and what the object is intended to represent, and the aesthetic of form refers to the quality of pure form, quite apart from any consideration external to the object itself. Probably the last of these was foremost in Archey's mind when he wrote: 'aesthetic attributes are within the object, its aesthetic self, and do not point to a referent' (1965: 47).

Not content to leave it at that, Archey goes on to consider the basis of people's aesthetic response to art. 'Is it not in large part customariness? The aesthetic is what we are used to' (1965: 47). Furthermore, it is 'the already familiar, assurance salted through . . . with novelty to break the monotony of exact repetition' (1965: 47). In this vein he quotes a felicitous passage from Galsworthy – 'the soul of good expression is an unexpectedness which still keeps to the mark of meaning and does not betray truth' – and Archey comments that truth in this context means 'the content they [the audience to which the object is directed] understand and something at least of the form they have come to expect' (1965: 45).[4] To pass from here to the analytic perspective I wish to espouse requires an argument of two steps. The first is to modify Archey's view of aesthetics as internal to an art object. If we reflect a moment upon his useful notion of aesthetics as the combination of familiar and unexpected form, it becomes clear that Archey's statement quoted above – that aesthetic attributes are within an object – is somewhat misleading. Even if we focus exclusively on his aesthetic of form, it is obvious that the form of any object can be familiar (or unexpected) only in its relationship of similarity (or difference) with other things. Therefore, while holding to Archey's association of aesthetics with familiarity and novelty of form, we need to amend his exposition to read that the aesthetic quality of an object is bound up with its formal relation to other things in the same tradition.[5]

The second step is to close the gap which Archey opened between aesthetics and meaning. This can be done most easily by briefly comparing Archey's attitudes toward modern art with those of Lévi-Strauss. While they both hold that much of modern art has lost its meaning, their reasons for this opinion differ in interesting and instructive ways. For Archey, as is readily understood from the foregoing discussion of his general scheme, it is because much of modern art is non-representational and therefore devoid of content (1965: 45). For Lévi-Strauss, on the other hand, the meaning in art is to be found in messages communicated in a 'language' or style of conventional form. Because many contemporary artists replace such a 'language' with a private system of signs which each one creates for himself and changes frequently, messages intelligible to others cannot be communicated in their art (Charbonnier 1969; see especially pp. 60–90).

It is clear from this that Lévi-Strauss does not share Archey's dichotomy between meaning and aesthetics; for him meaning is closely bound up with form. Specifically, within the rules of conventional form of some artistic 'language', art conveys its meanings via 'profound homology between the structure of the signified and the structure of the signifier' (Charbonnier 1969: 89). Still this position is not radically divergent from Archey's. We have already established that Archey's grounding of aesthetic response in a combination of the familiar and the unexpected in form entails a relationship between an art object and things outside it. That relationship, I suggest, is the same as the one identified by Lévi-Strauss as a homology between signifier and signified. If that is correct, then the main difference between them is that Archey views the relationship as aesthetic and quite separate from meaning, whereas Lévi-Strauss, while agreeing that it is a formal, aesthetic relationship, holds that it is precisely through such relationships that art conveys its meanings.

The basis of that difference is probably to be found in the ways of apprehending art. Archey is quite careful, as we have seen, to point out that meaning is apprehended with the intellect and aesthetics with feeling. Lévi-Strauss seems not to make this distinction; one might even wonder if his focus on messages conveyed in languages of conventional forms does not overly intellectualize art. Certainly I am in agreement with Lévi-Strauss that no gap exists between meaning and aesthetics, but I do not think this position should be bought at the price of banishing feeling from the apprehension of art. Nor do I think it is necessary, for Susanne Langer adopts a point of view very much like that of Lévi-Strauss, but one which still stresses feeling. In terms reminiscent of Lévi-Strauss' homology, she holds that symbol and the thing symbolized have a common logical form (1953: 27). In the case of visual art, where the symbol is material and spatial, she stresses the primacy of form over content by insisting that the identity of objects represented is not so important as the way they are used by the artist to organize space. Like Lévi-Strauss, she would therefore claim that the meaning of an object, what it symbolizes, is located in its aesthetic quality, its formal organization of space. Yet this does not put her entirely at odds with Archey's notion of aesthetics, because for Langer intuition and feeling are of crucial importance both in what art symbolizes and in how it is apprehended. Thus Langer (1953: 82) characterizes a work of art as:

> a presentation of a highly articulated form wherein the beholder recognizes, without conscious comparison and judgment but rather by direct recognition, the forms of human feeling: emotions, moods, even sensation in their characteristic passage.

To this I would add only that art may recapitulate the forms of cognition and of cultural categories and institutions as well as feelings.

This completes the construction of the theoretical perspective I intend to apply to Maori art. It is an amalgamation of the contributions of Archey, Lévi-Strauss and Langer. It holds that an art object stimulates an aesthetic response due to its presentation of a combination of familiar and unexpected forms. Those forms are familiar because they bear a homologous relationship to things outside the object itself, including other art objects and, beyond the realm of art, natural or artificial objects, emotions, ideas, social and cultural institutions of all sorts. The meaning of an object is located in the constellation of formal relationships in which it participates. While it is logically possible that members of society may be able explicitly to formulate both sides of the homology – the art object and that to which it is related – this is not common. The relationship is usually diffuse or multivocal (an art object is homologous with a number of other things) and the aesthetic response to it is a matter of feeling or intuition which a person is usually hard put to articulate. Therefore the analyst can rely on native exegesis only to a limited extent in the task of interpreting art by identifying those things to which it is related by formal homology. The analysis of Maori art which I will offer is anthropological, meaning that it is especially tuned to formal links between art and cultural institutions.

The organization of lineal space

When the Maori artist was called upon to decorate a long panel, one of his most common strategies was to carve it in bas-relief with alternating full-face and profile human figures (*tiki* and *manaia*). Often these figures are depicted as moving in the direction which the *manaias* are facing. All figures might be going in the same direction, as when in canoe wash strakes they all seem to be rushing toward the bow. In other cases, such as porches or walls of decorated meeting houses or storehouses, the figures on either side of the composition may be moving either toward or away from a central *tiki* (see Fig. 6.1).[6] Archey identifies the alternation of *tiki* and *manaia* forms as a major compositional theme in Maori art. He considers that pattern – with numerous variations but often taking the form of a central *tiki* and flanking *manaias* – also to inform the composition of the beautifully carved Maori *pare* or door lintels (Archey 1960: 14–18).

Archey contends that the pattern of alternating, moving *tiki* and *manaia* forms is one source of rhythm and dynamism in Maori art (1960: 14, 21). Certainly that insight is correct. The theoretical approach to art developed above enables us to carry on with the analysis and to detect further significance in this compositional form. Langer, it will be recalled, claims that what forms represent is less significant than the way they are related to each other in the organization of space. *Tikis* and *manaias* organize a linear continuum dualistically by the alternating occurrence of two forms, and Langer's observation invites us to seek a similar structure in other conventional patterns of Maori art. As soon as the issue is posed in this way, a number of examples spring to mind. One, as Jackson has noted (1972: 63–4), is the design of the interior walls of decorated meeting houses. These consist of rafter support posts (*poupou*) carved as large *tikis* alternating with wall panels woven with geometric designs (*tukutuku*).

The most elaborate organizations of linear space, however, are *kōwhaiwhai* patterns. Occasionally found in cenotaphs and other objects such as canoe paddles, these are most commonly seen as painted designs on rafters of meeting houses. Structurally they are similar to panels of alternating *tikis* and *manaias* and to interior meeting house walls in that these designs tend also to organize the space in terms of paired forms in alternation. One difference is that the other cases we have considered utilize two distinctly different forms in alternation, while rafter patterns use the same form differently presented. The difference may be carried by colour: typically the designs are done in black, red, and white, and adjacent forms may differ only in the reversal of black and red (Fig. 6.2). Or the difference may be positioning (often conjoined with colour shifts also), so that in alternate depictions the form is upside down (Fig. 6.3).

Rafter designs are an especially fruitful area for investigation because of their intricate and challenging structures. If one approaches them with the question in mind of how art organizes space, it is impossible to escape the conclusion that they are studies of nearly mathematical precision in bilateral symmetry. Virtually all types of bilateral symmetry are represented in these patterns. Some have the structure of mirror reflection across one axis, or across several axes simultaneously. The design in Fig. 6.4, for example, reflects across a central longitudinal axis and also across latitudinal axes located at different points in the pattern. Others are done in the sort of symmetry known as slide reflection – where a figure and its mirror image alternate along a line – often combined with a reversal of red and black colours (Fig. 6.5). Still others are organized according to bifold rotation. The design depicted in Fig. 6.6 manifests bifold rotation around two different axes. One is the straight, latitudinal white line which divides the figure into panels, and the other is the white serpentine line connecting the opposite corners within each panel. Finally, many designs feature the simultaneous use of two or more different sorts of symmetry. Referring

Fig. 6.1. Threshold (*paepae*) of the carved storehouse Te Oha. With permission of the Auckland War Memorial Museum.

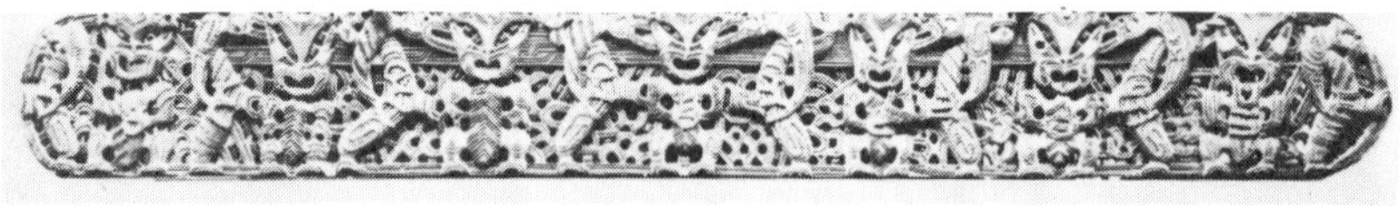

Fig. 6.2. Rafter pattern. On actual rafters the designs are much longer than these fragments, but enough is depicted here to give the structure of each pattern. All rafter patterns illustrated are taken from Hamilton (1901).

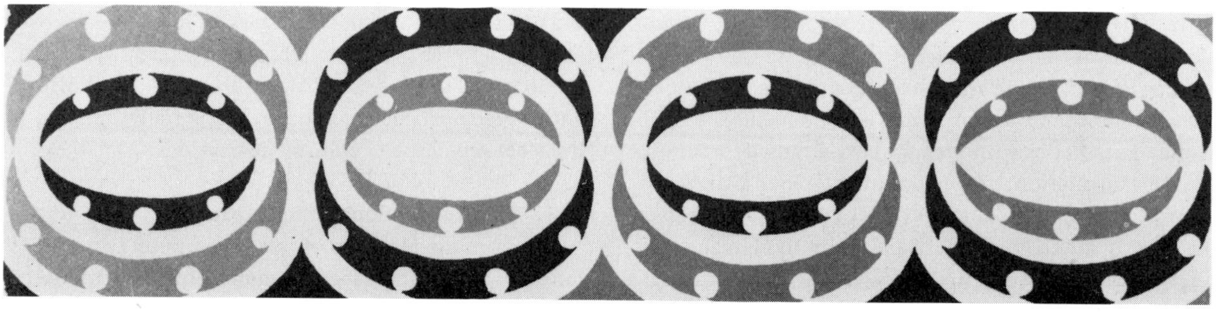

again to Fig. 6.6, in addition to bifold rotation the pattern also yields to analysis by translation (the same pattern being simply repeated) across the straight latitudinal axis. About the only form of symmetry which does not appear in rafter designs is radial, in which – as with a starfish or a kaleidoscope – the same figure is represented several times at regular intervals around a central point. The rich expressions of bilateral symmetry found in rafter designs link them structurally to the interior walls of decorated houses, with their carved rafter support posts and intervening woven panels, as well as to the alternating *tiki* and *manaia* forms found on canoe wash strakes, thresholds of decorated houses and storehouses, bargeboards and exterior walls of storehouses, and in other places. Taken together, all these demonstrate the Maori use of art to organize linear space dualistically.

Dual forms in Maori culture

Our theoretical model directs us to seek homologous relations between artistic forms and other structures or patterns of culture. The dual organization of linear space is one aspect of Maori art which is clearly homologous with other parts of the culture. Large segments of Maori myth, religion, traditional history, and social, economic, and political behaviour can be understood as organized in terms of duality. The duality itself had two basic forms, depending upon whether the paired elements were different or similar. Dual relationships of the first sort I will term complementary; those of the second, symmetrical.

Complementarity refers to the sort of relationship which obtains between pairs of unlike relata. The root metaphor upon which many complementary relationships were modelled is the relationship between the sexes. Maoris were explicit about this, attributing sexuality to nearly all things, biological or not. 'Everything', wrote Elsdon Best, 'has its male and female element' (Best 1921: 2; see also Best 1914: 133). The Maori sage Nepia Pohuku confirmed the point: 'all things have their female counterparts . . . nothing stands alone without a mate' (Smith 1913: 32, 137; I have modified the translation slightly).

Complementary relationships have a syntagmatic structure; that is, they pass through a developmental career. To summarize its stages briefly, as with male and female, complementary relata of all sorts are mutually attracted. They unite and their union is creative, the female entity producing offspring of some sort. Eventually, however, the state of union proves to be confining to some party to the relationship – either one of the relata or one or more of their offspring. As a result the original pair separates. But separation has its deficiencies as well: frustration, impotence, ineffectuality. This is followed by mutual attraction and a new union, thus closing the circuit and putting the relationship into a new 'generation'.

Here I can give only two instantiations of the complementary structure, one relatively specific and the other very general. The more specific example is the Maori creation myth. It begins with the male sky, Rangi, pressed close against the female earth, Papa. Their union produced a number of sons, the major gods of the Maori pantheon. Confined in darkness between their parents, the sons of Rangi and Papa resolved to separate them. When this was accomplished

Fig. 6.3. Rafter pattern.

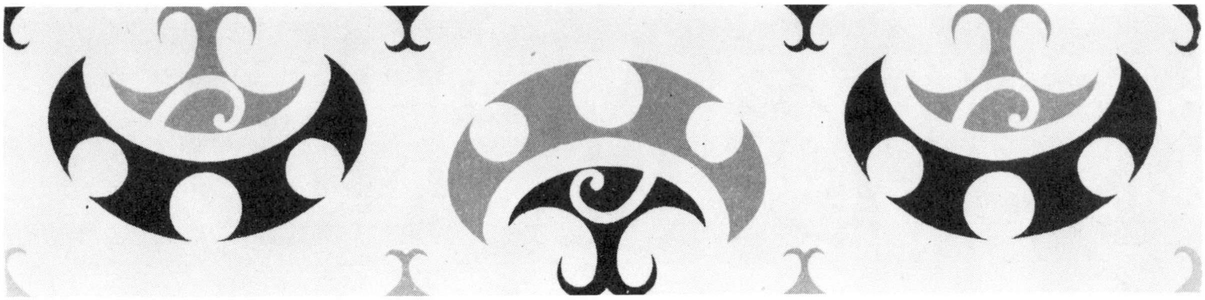

Fig. 6.4. Rafter pattern.

one of the sons, Tāne, desired to create mankind. However, he was impotent to do so without the collaboration of some female entity. There follows a series of unions and separations as Tāne copulates with a variety of female beings. All these unions are productive – water, plants, birds, insects and other furnishings of the world were born of them – but Tāne separated from each of his mates because his driving design to create mankind was not accomplished. Finally he moulded a female form from the earth itself, breathed life into her nostrils, and copulated with her. She bore a daughter. One more passage through the syntagmatic structure of complementarity was necessary, however, because Tāne separated from the woman he had made from the earth and incestuously united with the daughter she had borne. From that union, at last, sprang mankind (Grey 1956: 1–3; 1971: 1–2; Smith 1913: 35–8, 139–43; White 1886–90, I: 158–60 [English], 142–4 [Maori]; Best 1924: 73; 1925: 765).

In my other example of complementarity – Maori religion – the relata were conceptualized not so much in terms of the sexes as according to a more abstract model of active and passive. Maoris divided reality into two realms: the physical world of human existence called *te ao marama* (the world of light), and the world of gods, ghosts, spirits of all sorts, comprising both *rangi* (the heavens) and *po* (the underworld). Communication between the two realms was common; any events in this world for which no physical cause was apparent were attributed to *atuas*, gods or spirits from the other realm. These included thunder and lightning, the growth of plants, physical and mental illness, fear which grips a normally brave warrior, the skill of an artist – even, after the arrival of Europeans, the operation of a windmill (Best 1924: 121–4, 128; 1925: 1002; 1929: 39; Goldie 1904: 3, 73, 88; Shortland 1856: 82; Cruise 1824: 31; Earle 1966: 196–7). 'Atuas', as Dieffenbach (1843, II: 118) summarized it, 'are the secret powers of the universe.' Anyone or anything which was under the influence of *atuas*, under stimulation from the other world, was *tapu* (a term taken into English as 'taboo'). Conversely, things and people not *tapu*, not under the influence of *atuas*, were *noa* (Shortland 1856: 102; Best 1922: 32; 1925: 1123).

The developmental career of relationships between *atuas* and things of this world adhered to the syntagmatic structure of complementarity as outlined above. *Atuas* were the active agents, people and things of this world the more passive relata. Their union was creative: when someone or something of the physical world was *tapu*, under the influence of *atuas*, something would *happen*. The person would fight bravely, create art, fall ill; menstruation would occur, the muscle twitch, the plant grow, the windmill turn. Often, however, it was desirable to separate oneself from *atua* influence. This might be because the *tapu* was intrinsically harmful, like illness, or because after its beneficial purpose had been accomplished one wished to be released from the restrictions *tapu* placed on normal activity. Much of Maori ritual can be understood as concerned with controlling these union and separation phases of the complementary relationship between humans and the gods. *Tapu* was ritually instilled into persons and things where it was desired (such as planted fields, to stimulate the growth of

Fig. 6.5. Rafter pattern.

Fig. 6.6. Rafter pattern.

crops), and it was ritually removed from places where it was not, or no longer, wanted. Complementarity characterized many parts of Maori culture other than the creation myth and religious belief and practice, and the way it worked in religion of course had many intricacies not touched upon in this summary.[7] But I hope that some appreciation of the pervasive importance of the syntagmatic form of complementarity in Maori culture can be derived from what has been said.

The other dual form in Maori culture – that between relata which are like each other – may be called symmetry. The hallmark of symmetry is equivalence. The core transaction in symmetrical relationships – exchange – should be equivalent, and the entities entering into a symmetrical relationship are equivalent, or at least they should be. Probably the most stable sort of symmetrical relationship was the exchange of qualitatively different goods, such as the trade of seafood for forest food between coastal and inland dwellers. Here equivalence of exchange and of partners can be maintained indefinitely, with both partners realizing palpable benefits from the relationship.

In other cases, such as the exchange of feasts, the items which passed between symmetrical relata were of basically the same type. Little social work is accomplished by the exchange of precise equivalents – say, a canoe for a canoe of the same type and size – so in these circumstances the difference between what was received and what was given was quantitative. There was, in other words, a tendency for the exchange to escalate as each side tried to outgive the other (Firth 1959: 423). This constituted an internal contradiction in symmetrical relationships. On the one hand the relata should be equivalent, and Maoris were very much on their guard against any effort by their partners to assume a dominant position in the relationship. On the other hand, they were quite willing and anxious to secure a superior position for themselves. Efforts to outgive their partners were efforts to do precisely that, and they were perceived as such. Therefore symmetrical relationships tended to be unstable. One party would feel affronted by an action on the part of the other, would launch an insult in return, and the whole relationship would turn bitter. Note that the symmetrical relationship was not thereby terminated, because the exchange of equivalents persisted. Only its mood changed from positive to negative as the exchange of feasts or other gifts gave way to the exchange of insults and injuries.

Like complementarity, then, Maori symmetry had a syntagmatic structure. Although in some cases cordial exchange might continue indefinitely, often symmetrical relationships transformed from cordiality to hostility. From that point any one of three quite distinct steps might be taken. The relata could reconcile, thereby closing the circuit by returning the relationship to a cordial mode. Or they could separate, thereby terminating that particular relationship, although one or both of them might subsequently enter into relationships with other entities. Or one of them might utterly subjugate the other.

A great many examples of symmetry may be found in Maori culture, but again we must limit ourselves here to a very few. One is the fable accounting for why the sun shines in the day and the moon at night. At first they wanted to stay together, and the sun urged that they live in the day while the moon championed the night. They argued earnestly but neither would give in (which, after all, would have been to cede a dominant position in their relationship to the other). Finally they cursed each other. The moon told the sun to go to the day, where people would use his heat and light to dry out menstrual cloths, and the sun retorted that the moon should go to the night where men would make cooking ovens by his light. (In Maori culture to link someone with cooked food was a great insult.) Thus each went to its preferred element, terminating their symmetrical relationship by separation (Smith 1913: 48).

The creation myth affords an example of the termination of symmetry by subjugation. After the earth and the sky had been separated, a series of wars broke out among their sons. Some of these were the attacks by Tu, who represents mankind in this myth, against his brothers. He defeated them one by one, and ate them – a series of acts which established the human food supply. Tu's devouring of his brother Tangaroa, god of the sea, provided mankind with seafood of all sorts. That of Tāne, god of forests, was the source of edible birds. His victories over Rongo and Haumia secured cultivated and uncultivated plants for humans to eat. Thus the symmetrical relationship between the divine brothers ended by subjugation, in fratricidal cannibalism (Grey 1956: 7–10; 1971: 3–5). And, of course, cannibalism continued well into the nineteenth century to be a favourite means by which Maoris would terminate their symmetrical relationships with subjugated enemies.

Enough has now been said about dual organization in Maori culture for the homology between its artistic and other instantiations to be evident. One must be careful, however, not to be excessively specific in making these connections. I have found nothing in the art, for example, which corresponds to the syntagmatic careers outlined above for complementarity and symmetry. Doubtless the claim could be made that panels decorated with alternating *tikis* and *manaias* and interior house walls correspond, as dual organizations composed of different forms, to complementarity. One might then go on to claim that rafter designs, which achieve duality with the same forms differently presented, correspond to symmetry.[8] In my judgement, however, the most important point is the more general one that in Maori culture reality in a great many of its aspects was conceptualized dualistically: relations between human individuals and groups, between gods and humans, cosmology, human history, the landscape, those objects and spaces created or reworked by artists. The frequency and variety of its concrete instantiations, both in art and in other institutions, indicates that dualism is an ordering principle of pervasive importance in Maori culture.

Bilateral surfaces

So far our consideration of Maori art has been limited to linear composition. Confidence in the generalization just made would be increased if other Maori art forms could also be shown to be structured dualistically. This is readily done, for nearly all of Maori art in fact has this structure. The elaborate carved funnels, used to feed persons who, while in the state of *tapu*, may not touch food or drink with their hands, typically have the structure of bilateral symmetry; canoe bailers and the carved ends of clubs (*taiaha*) do also. One of the high points of Maori art is represented by carved 'treasure boxes' (*waka huia*). These shallow boxes, generally oblong in shape and ranging from about 35 to 80 cm in length, were used to store feathers, greenstone ornaments, and other small, valuable articles. Carving usually covers their entire surface; since they were commonly hung from rafters they were as likely to be viewed from the bottom as from the top. Here again, the basic structure of design is bilateral. From one perspective, treasure boxes rank with rafter patterns in interest and significance because the structure of their decorative designs invites the conclusion that they too are studies in symmetry. Compare, for example, a treasure box in the Peabody Museum of Salem (Massachusetts) with one in the National Museum, Wellington. Both use *tikis* and *manaias* as design elements, in very much the same way. The difference between them is that one of them employs these forms to organize space into a symmetrical structure of mirror reflection, while in the other it is bifold rotation (see Fig. 6.7).

Maoris considered their own bodies to be spaces for cultural organization by means of art, and they accomplished that by tattooing. Maori tattooing might more appropriately be termed skin carving (see Hall 1920: 217). The pigment was introduced into incisions cut deeply into the skin with a blade such as a sharpened albatross bone which was set in a handle in the manner of an adze and struck with a light mallet. These incisions might be deep enough to pierce the cheek entirely, 'so that when the person undergoing the operation took his pipe, the smoke found its way out through the cuttings' (Taylor 1855: 151). Pigment was made from the burnt resin of *kauri* or pine. The soot so obtained might be mixed with dog fat (Tregear 1904: 259). In a more complicated process, the soot from burnt *kauri* and pine resin was mixed with bird fat and given to a dog to eat, and the dog's faeces were later collected and kneaded with bird's oil and water to form the pigment (Colenso 1891: 449–50). The pigment was black, but in a completed tattoo the skin had the appearance of being 'deeply excavated' (Forster 1777, I: 220) with blue lines.

The tattooing process was excruciatingly painful and the healing period long. Still, Maoris considered tattooing to be an essential mark of adulthood. The missionaries, however, moved to strip them of this 'savage and debasing' custom (Yate 1835: 150). As a result, male tattooing (which covered the entire face and thighs) died out around the middle of the nineteenth century – although there was a brief revival, using somewhat truncated designs, among rebellious *hauhau* warriors in the 1860s. On the other hand

Fig. 6.7. Two treasure boxes (*waka huia*). With permission of the Peabody Museum of Salem, Massachusetts (the upper box) and the National Museum, Wellington (the lower box).

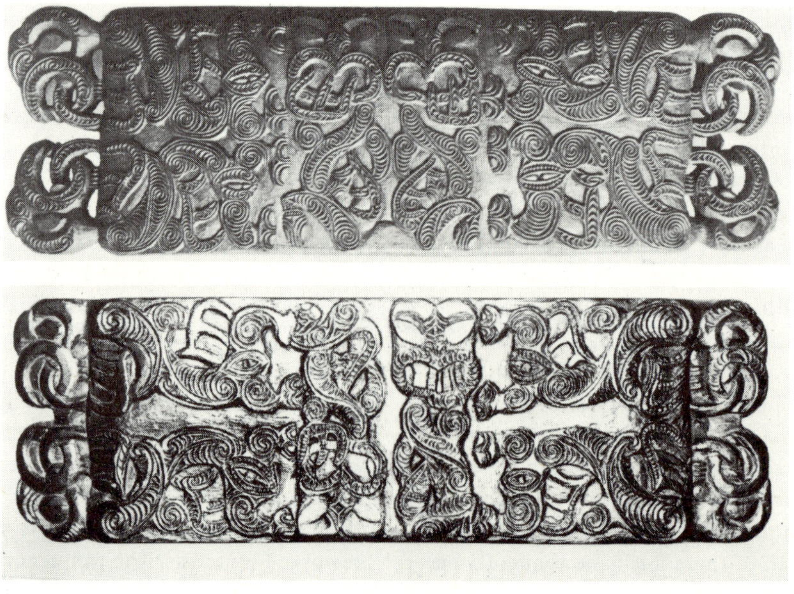

women's tattooing – which was limited mainly to the lips and chin – persisted well into the twentieth century (see King 1972).

Here we are particularly interested in men's facial patterns, which unquestionably must rank among the outstanding achievements of Pacific art. The controlled creativity of these designs is remarkable: each is singularly unique and yet they all adhere closely to a style defined basically by a line of untattooed skin down the centre of the face, arched bands on the foreheads, and spirals on the nose and cheeks.[9] The design, incidentally, is done in the negative, with the identifiable shapes (such as the bulbed *koru*) being formed in the unmarked skin surrounded by tattooing (Hamilton 1901: 308).

One interpretation of the male facial design is that it is the depiction of a face on a face – or rather, two faces, done in split representation. One can pick out their profiles staring at each other, with mouths gaping, across the central vertical line (Lévi-Strauss 1963: 259; Jackson 1972: 71–2; Schwimmer 1974: 92). While the resemblance may be only coincidental, it is an intriguing possibility. We have already noted that a gaping mouth signified the warrior's defiance and that human figures carved in wood are commonly depicted in that posture. It certainly does not stretch the imagination to suppose that a Maori male would have his ideal image of himself – as a fierce warrior – permanently etched on his face (see Fig. 6.8).

Remember, however, that our approach directs more attention to the relationship among figures than to what they may represent. Regardless of what a facial tattoo design depicts – if, indeed, it depicts anything outside itself at all – there can be no question that in literally every example of the dominant style on record a vertical line of untattooed skin passing down the centre of the design bisects the face into highly symmetrical halves. The tattoo therefore enhanced the natural symmetry of the face, making it a more elaborate and more perfect instantiation of the Maori construction of reality as bilateral. In this way tattooing transformed the individual into a more fully cultural being. It marked him (or, much less elaborately, her) as an adult and as an individual whose unique appearance by cultural design eclipsed the singularity which the untattooed face owed to the haphazard workings of nature.

Even a figure like the spiral, which initially seems utterly alien to binary structure, turns out in the Maori making of it to be yet another means of organizing space dualistically. Equable spirals[10] abound in Maori art: as surface decoration on carved human figures, on door lintels, in facial tattoos; among the finest are those on canoe prows and sterns (see Fig. 6.9). So fine was the execution of spirals that one student of Maori art was moved to declare: 'I would define the Maori people as the one race in the world which has exalted the spiral conception in design to its highest level' (Phillipps 1948: 30). Certainly the spiral contributed to the

Fig. 6.8. Male facial tattoo. A drawing by the Maori Te Pehi of his own tattoo. From Robley (1896).

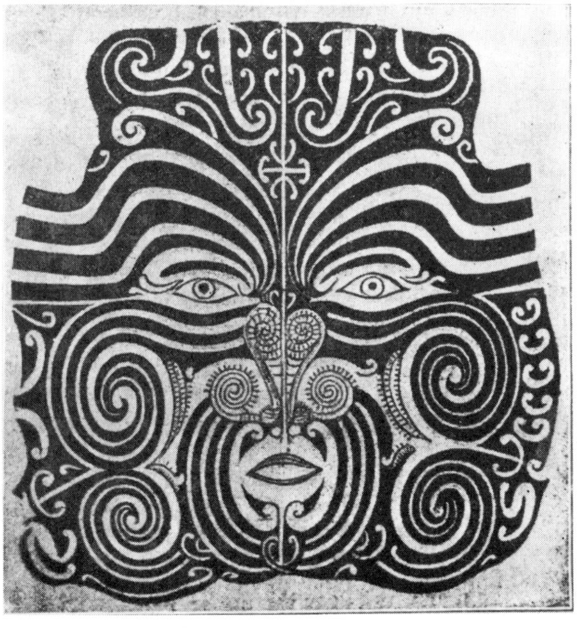

Fig. 6.9. Canoe stern piece (*taurapa*). With permission of the Wanganui Regional Museum.

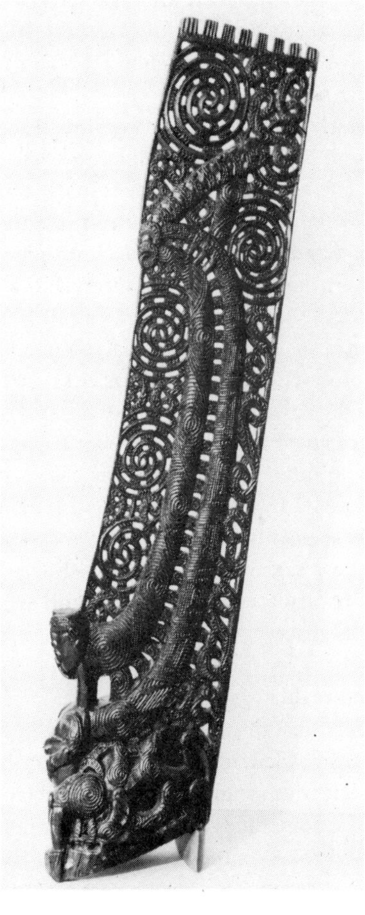

dynamism of Maori art; its swirling form lends movement and interest to whatever it adorns. From the perspective of this analysis, however, the intriguing thing about Maori spirals is that they are nearly always double. They are made, that is, of two lines rather than one. And if one separates those two lines, it is immediately apparent that they form two separate spirals related to each other by bifold rotational symmetry. Hence it emerges that, even by means of the spiral, Maori art organizes space dualistically. The spiral's uniqueness is that the duality it creates is not one of adjacent spaces but rather a dual division which intertwines and grows within the *same* space as the two arms of the spiral revolve outward from (or, if you prefer, inward towards) a common centre point.

While dual organization is widespread in Maori art, I do not wish to create the mistaken impression that it is universal. Carved stone images placed in *kumara* gardens as resting places for the *atuas* believed to be so active there during the growth of the crop – images at once the most sacred of all Maori art objects and the most crudely fashioned – show no particular dual composition. Nor do carved wooden palisade figures. Combs do not have a dual structure, nor do the intricately carved bird snares and knife handles (which were fitted with sharks' teeth for the blade). Finally, the beautifully worked greenstone ornaments – *tiki* figures and an occasional *manaia* – are not organized dualistically.

But if not all parts of visual art are organized in dual forms, it is also true that some sectors of Maori art other than the visual do have such a composition. Of Maori vocal music Mervyn McLean wrote:

> The form is clearly strophic, with two phrases, of which the second is usually longer than the first, to each strophe. The end of the strophe is marked by the leader solo, and the end of the song itself is marked by a characteristic expulsion of breath accompanied by a glissando drop of the voice over the interval of a third or fourth. (McLean and Orbell 1975: 16)

Moreover, McLean informs me (in a personal communication) that a large proportion of these songs exhibits a pattern of exactly eight vowels in each of the phrases of a pair. One of the concerns of music, it seems fair to say, is to lend organization to an interval of time. In the case of Maori music this is accomplished by breaking the continuum of time into identifiable segments marked by strophes, and then structuring each of these segments dualistically. Hence the dual organization of reality accomplished by Maori art invades time as well as space.

Appearance and reality

I have laid a great deal of stress on symmetry in Maori art. It must now be acknowledged that the symmetry is rarely perfect. The reflective symmetry of men's facial tattoo designs, for example, is sometimes broken on the forehead or chin, and is invariably broken in the area just before the ears. The symmetry of wood carvings is likewise commonly broken. One clear example is the threshold of the storehouse Te Oha (see Fig. 6.10). While the composition of a central *tiki* flanked by alternating *tikis* and *manaias* is entirely symmetrical, the surface decoration on the forms and the interstitial carving is quite different on the two sides of the threshold. Te Oha is particularly interesting for its side walls. At first glance the two sides seem identical, with the normal alternation of *tikis* and *manaias*. Closer inspection reveals, however, that the *manaias* on one wall all face toward the central *tiki* while on the other wall they face away from it. Symmetry is suspended in most Maori art forms, so that if one part of the experience of viewing Maori art is to determine the sort of symmetry it represents, another part is to detect how the symmetry is broken.

Of course, most art traditions which feature symmetry relieve it with occasional breaks. In the terms of Archey's aesthetics, these constitute the novelty which seasons the familiarity of the symmetry, preventing it from becoming tedious (see p. 76 above). While this is as true of Maori art as of any other, it seems also that breaks in symmetry combine with other characteristics of Maori art to form a pattern of particular significance in this culture.

The pattern may be expressed quite simply by the proposition: 'things are not what they seem'. The pattern is instantiated in the issue we have just been discussing, of course, by the fact that compositions which initially appear to be entirely symmetrical turn out not to be so. Another expression of the pattern is the fact that some compositions seem to be purposely misleading, so that one's initial formulation of their structure is mistaken. Rafter patterns provide especially good examples. The design reproduced in Figure 6.11, for example, seems at first glance to be organized according to mirror reflection across the longitudinal axis and also across any of several latitudial axes. But closer inspection reveals that such an analysis cannot account for the *koru* (bulbed figures) along the upper and lower edges of the design. From them it is clear that the symmetrical structure of this design is not reflection at all, but bifold rotation. It even occurs in some cases that the first impression turns out to be mistaken and closer study reveals that *no* single analysis of the forms is possible. A wood carving from Taranaki, for example, seems initially to be structured according to mirror reflection across a central axis (Fig. 6.12). While that is true for its *tiki* forms, the lattice-like carving between them is organized in terms of translation.[11]

A third characteristic which contributes to the patterns we are discussing is that in Maori art superficial complexity often masks underlying simplicity. Some rafter patterns and treasure boxes are immensely convoluted, so replete with florid detail in paint or wood that the eye and mind boggle upon initial encounter. But then, after one has spent some time looking at the object, forms begin to detach themselves from the jumble (in the case of treasure boxes, usually *tiki* or *manaia* forms, and often engaged in copulation) and an overall pattern of design emerges. Nearly always it is a dual

Fig. 6.10. Detail from the threshold of the carved storehouse Te Oha. With permission of the Auckland War Memorial Museum.

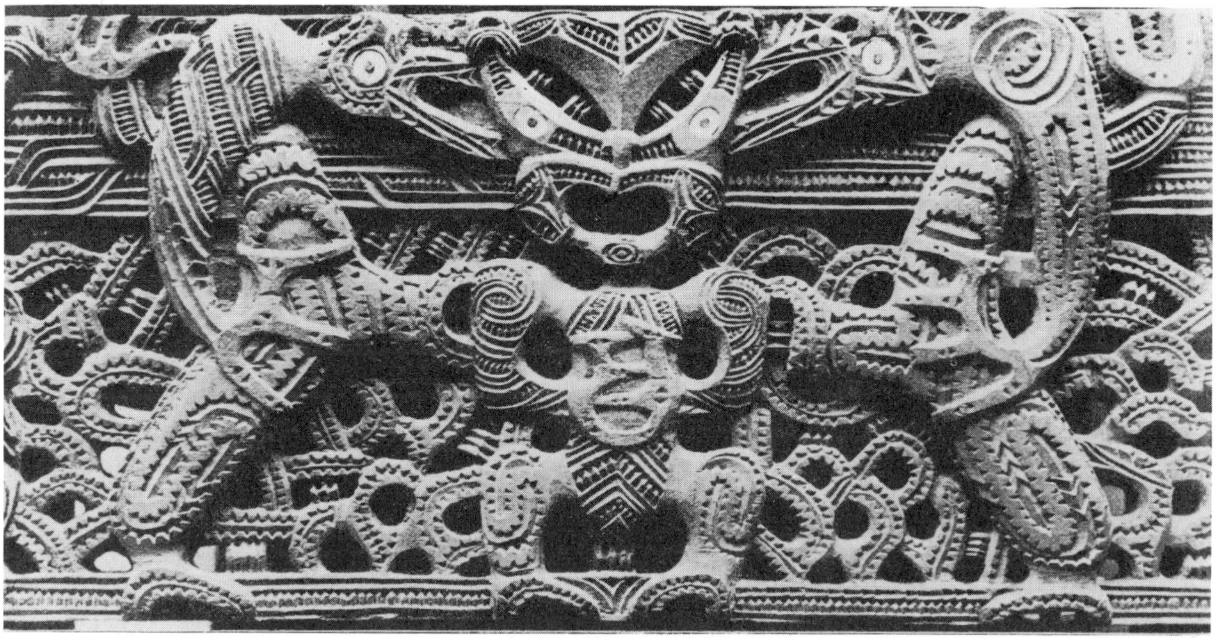

Fig. 6.11. Rafter pattern.

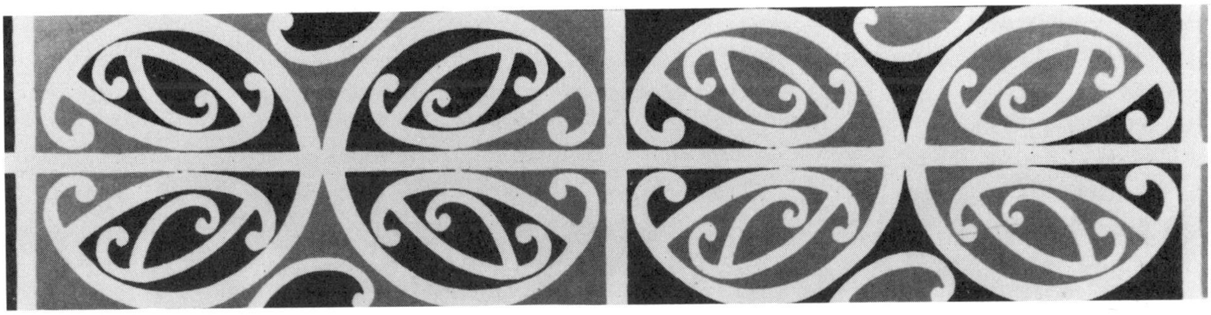

Fig. 6.12. Wood carving from Waitara. With permission of the Taranaki Museum.

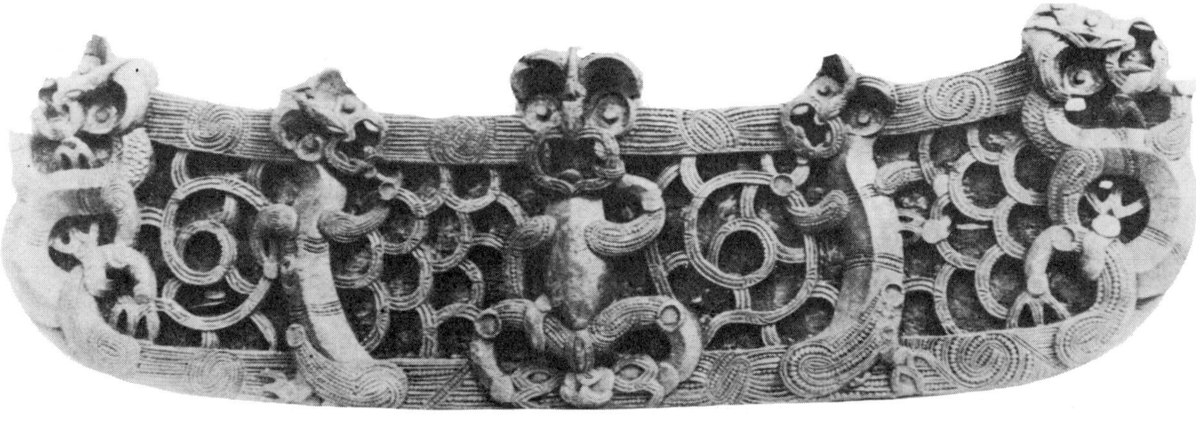

pattern, with the segments of design related in some sort of symmetry.

Finally, the notion that things are not what they seem is instantiated in Maori art by the fact that designs which are superficially very different turn out to be structurally identical. Once again, rafter patterns afford many examples. Despite their apparent differences, the three designs in Figures 6.3, 6.13, and 6.14 are structurally the same. In each case, the step from one design element to the next is accomplished by bifold rotation plus a reversal of red and black.

Maori Cartesianism

The common discrepancy in Maori art between the surface and the structure, between what seems to be and what is, bears a homologous relationship with certain other aspects of Maori culture. Generally speaking, these can be combined under the assumption that overt events have hidden causes. One example of this, already mentioned, is the notion that thunder, the growth of crops, illness, muscular twitches, and all other events for which physical causes are not immediately apparent stem from the invisible activities of *atuas* (gods, spirits).

Formally consistent with the idea that *atuas* are unseen animators of visible events is the Maori theory of mind; a theory which in philosophical parlance would be called Cartesian dualism. In accord with Descartes, 'Maori philosophers regard the body and the mind as separate entities' (Goldie 1904: 73). They also affirmed the Cartesian corollary that publically visible bodily activity results from the hidden intentions, plans or passions of the mind. So sharply did Maoris distinguish between overt physical acts and covert mental causes that they accounted for a traveller singing at night in these terms: 'it was your spirit (*wairua*) making you do it as a sign of danger to you' (Tregear 1904: 213).

Maoris regularly explained human behaviour in terms of inner drives. Violence was attributed to an inner thirst for revenge, itself described as a physiological feeling of one's heart swelling. When the missionary Samuel Marsden in 1823 urged a chief of the Ngapuhi tribe to make peace with their enemies, he replied that his brother had recently been killed by them and that 'his heart was so big when he thought of his brother that he could not keep it down, and satisfaction he must have before he could rest' (Elder 1932: 388).[12]

A Cartesian distinction between sequestered activities of mind and overt behaviour is conducive to the somewhat cynical notion that people's true motives are often at variance with their public representations. This is evident in a great deal of Maori folklore, where the protagonist often achieves his end by deception. Proverbs testify to the same attitude. One compares the hidden purposes of the mind to the tangled roots of a particular plant: 'The many roots of the convolvulus creep below the ground' (Brougham and Reed 1963: 103). Less subtle is the proverb that warns: 'A crooked reed may be seen but a crooked heart is concealed from view' (Shortland 1856: 197). Maori songs also acknowledge a divergence between inner feelings and outer

Fig. 6.13. Rafter pattern.

Fig. 6.14. Rafter pattern.

appearance. The following excerpts are from a song composed by Te Paea when she was deserted by her husband (Ngata and Hurinui 1961: 210–11):

With the fall of eventide I lay me down to sleep,
Within me, alas, is like the raging seas
For the loved one now estranged.
. . . .
Why did you not in my native soil,
Gently put me aside then, dear one?
You let our idyllic time linger on,
Now my slave body is to be returned
To my parents of whom I do now dream.
. . . .
O friends all! What a grievous thing;
Only my outward part you do see,
When all within is in a turmoil, alas, ah me.

Especially in their corollary that the inner wellspring may be quite different from the outer appearance, these Cartesian notions about mental causation of physical behaviour, and the more general metaphysical ideas about divine production of worldly events, recapitulate in religion and psychology the artistic pattern of discrepancy between surface manifestation and underlying structure. Hence we discover a second formal homology between art and other parts of Maori culture. It is, however, not entirely distinct from the principle of dual organization identified earlier. The homology at present under investigation deals with the play between the covert and the overt, the inner and the outer aspects which are found in art, in human behaviour, and in reality in general. But the division of things and events into surface appearance and underlying form, or public happening and private cause, is, of course, nothing other than an additional set of instantiations of the dualism which so thoroughly permeates Maori culture.

The map is the territory

It is often held that art 'reflects' or 'expresses' other parts of culture – cosmology, ethics, social stratification, and so on. This is certainly true; the present essay is one demonstration of it. It is important to recognize, however, that this is not a one-way process on the model of independent and dependent variables such that, say, the political organization somehow produces a certain style in art which reflects or expresses it (see Fischer 1961). My position is that all institutions – political, economic, religious, artistic, etc. – are instantiations or consequences of structural principles which underlie any culture. The link between institutions is therefore not direct but indirect, passing via the structural principles (see Hanson and Hanson 1981). So if a particularly close relationship exists between certain objects or styles in art and another part of the culture, as between Maori artistic symmetry and socio-political patterns of exchange and vengeance, the socio-political organization reflects the art just as much as the art reflects it. Better, they both instantiate the same cultural principles.

If any relation of priority exists among the institutions of culture, it is doubtless that which Lévi-Strauss called *bricolage*: where some aspect of life serves as a model for the construction of cultural categories or principles which order experience (Lévi-Strauss 1962: 26–33). In Maori culture, for example, the relation between the sexes is probably the source for the form of dualism I have called complementarity, while symmetry may stem, by *bricolage*, from the nature of socio-political relations between human groups. But we should not understand art and other Maori institutions as 'reflecting' or 'expressing' these sources, as if Maori culture were out to get some messages across about sexuality and intergroup relations. These sources serve simply as grounds for the process of analogy by which human experience is ordered and thereby made coherent.

Art does not signify other parts of culture in the way that a road sign signifies falling rock although the sign is neither made of rock, nor falling, and belongs in no other way to that which it represents. One might even say that art does not signify other parts of culture at all. Art is *related* to them, as has been demonstrated here for the Maori case, by homology of form. But what art *signifies* – and the other parts of culture do also – are the cultural principles of which art and other cultural institutions are instantiations. Because those principles give the total culture its form, one might say alternatively that art (or any other institution) signifies not the *rest* of culture but the *entire* culture, including its artistic precincts. The relationship of any institution – artistic or otherwise – to culture is synecdochic: the part recapitulates the whole.

So we arrive at an exception to Korzybski's famous and often true dictum that the map is not the territory (Korzybski 1958: 58, 498, 750–1). As a class of formal instantiations of cultural principles, art may readily be designated as a 'map' of culture. To be sure, it is a map which charts some parts or features of the cultural terrain more precisely than others. Maori art, for example, provides particularly rich and fine representations of the cultural forms of symmetry and near symmetry (as in rafter paintings), but gives poor sketches of the syntagmatics of symmetrical and complementary relationships as they pass through their developmental careers. For that one needs to pore over other maps: mythology, folklore, traditional history. Still, selective depiction characterizes maps of all sorts and is, indeed, immanent to the very concept of mapping. For this reason a full conceptualization of any geographical terrain requires the combination of a variety of maps – some showing rainfall, others land use, others mineral deposits, and so on. Similarly, our understanding of a human culture is built up from studies of its several institutions. It is of course true that the anthropologist makes models of those institutions, and that those models are extrinsic to the culture under investigation. But my argument has been that any cultural institution, by embodying structural principles which also inform other institutions, is a selective microcosm, a map, of the culture. Therefore art, together with other institutions, is simultaneously map and territory. It is intrinsic to the total culture which it synecdochically charts.

Notes

1 I appreciate the assistance of Louise Hanson with the preparation of this essay. Some of the ideas presented here were first developed for our jointly authored, forthcoming book, *Culture in Counterpoint: The New Zealand Maoris.*

2 Some others who have espoused the idea that much of the meaning of Maori art has been lost are Barrow (1972: 9), Menzies (1904), and King (1972; 1975: 438). See also Binney (1968: 135).

3 Some house post carvings do contain symbols which link them with the ancestor they depict. In the house Tama-te-kapua at Ohine-mutu, Rotorua, for example, Tama-te-kapua himself is depicted with stilts, Tutanekai as playing a flute, and Hinemoa as wearing a belt of gourds. These 'props' recall the legendary episodes in which these ancestors are known.

Schwimmer (1959: 48–9) suggests that this sort of representationalism is traditional in Maori carving, but my claim is that it is a modern, probably Enropean-inspired, development. I am not aware of any examples of such graphic allusions to particular mythical figures or episodes in the art of the pre-European or early European period.

4 This view of aesthetics lends itself readily to expression in the vocabulary of information theory. Any art object may be understood as a message: its familiarity is redundancy and its unexpectedness is information (see Weaver 1949).

5 Clearly a close bond exists between this notion of aesthetics and what is often referred to as style or artistic convention.

6 This pattern could also be true of canoe wash strakes if one considers the port and starboard strakes to be the two sides of a single composition with the prow as its centre.

7 A more complete discussion may be found in *Culture in Counterpoint: The New Zealand Maoris*, a forthcoming book by F. Allan Hanson and Louise Hanson.

8 Of course, compositions in which the *manaias* face toward or away from a central *tiki* could also be classed as symmetry.

9 This was by far the dominant style, at least in the nineteenth century. One of Sydney Parkinson's drawings (he accompanied Cook on the first voyage, which visited New Zealand in 1769) depicts a man with a facial design in the *puhoro* style normally found on the thighs, while the frontispiece of Vol. I of White's *Ancient History of the Maori* shows a totally different style, called *kuri*.

10 In an equable spiral the distance between the lines remains constant as one moves out from the centre, while in a logarithmic spiral (such as is observed in a snail shell) the distance between the lines increases.

11 Actually it is even more complicated than that, as comparison of the far right bay of lattice-work with the other bay corresponding to it will reveal.

12 One wonders as to the precise identification of the organ in question. Maoris considered the seat of the emotions to be the *ngakau*, which is better translated as 'viscera' or 'intestines' than as 'heart'.

References

Archey, Gilbert, 1960. *Sculpture and Design: An Outline of Maori Art.* Handbook of the Auckland War Memorial Museum, 2nd edn. Auckland.

1965. *The Art Forms of Polynesia.* Auckland Institute and Museum, Bulletin No. 4.

1977. *Whaowhia: Maori Art and its Artists.* Collins, London and Auckland.

Barrow, Terrence, 1969. *Maori Wood Sculpture of New Zealand.* Reed, Wellington.

1972. *Art and Life in Polynesia.* Reed, Wellington.

Best, Elsdon, 1914. Maori beliefs concerning the human organs of generation. *Man* 14: 132–4.

1921. The Maori genius for personification. *Transactions of the New Zealand Institute* 53: 1–13.

1922. *Some Aspects of Maori Myth and Religion.* Dominion Museum Monograph No. 1, Wellington.

1924. *Maori Religion and Mythology.* Dominion Museum Bulletin No. 10, Wellington.

1925. *Tuhoe: The Children of the Mist.* Polynesian Society, Memoir No. 6 (1).

1929. *The Whare Kohanga (the 'Nest House') and its Lore.* Dominion Museum Bulletin No. 13, Wellington.

Binney, Judith, 1968. *The Legacy of Guilt: a Life of Thomas Kendall.* Published for the University of Auckland by Oxford University Press.

Brougham, Aileen E. and A.W. Reed, 1963. *Maori Proverbs.* Reed, Wellington.

Charbonnier, G., 1969. *Conversations with Claude Lévi-Strauss.* Jonathan Cape, London.

Cheeseman, T.F., 1906. Notes on certain Maori carved burial-chests in the Auckland Museum. *Transactions of the New Zealand Institute* 39: 451–6.

Colenso, William, 1891. Vestiges, reminiscences, memorabilia of works, deeds and sayings of the ancient Maoris. *Transactions of the New Zealand Institute* 24: 445–67.

Cruise, Richard A., 1824. *Journal of a Ten Months Residence in New Zealand*, 2nd edn. Longman, Hurst, Bees, Orme, Brown, and Green, London.

Dieffenbach, Ernest, 1843. *Travels in New Zealand.* 2 vols, John Murray, London.

Earle, Augustus, 1966. *Narrative of a Residence in New Zealand* (edited by E.H. McCormick). Clarendon Press, Oxford (first published 1832).

Elder, J.R., 1932. *The Letters and Journals of Samuel Marsden.* Reed, Wellington.

Firth, Raymond, 1959. *Economics of the New Zealand Maori*, 2nd edn. Government Printer, Wellington.

Fischer, J.L., 1961. Art styles as cognitive cultural maps. *American Anthropologist* 63: 79–93.

Forster, George, 1777. *A Voyage Round the World in His Britannic Majesty's Sloop Resolution . . .* 2 vols, London.

Fry, Roger, 1947. *Vision and Design.* Peter Smith, New York (first published 1924).

Gathercole, Peter, 1974. Reinterpretation of aspects of Maori art. Paper prepared for the Symposium on the Art of Oceania, McMaster University, 1974.

Goldie, W.H., 1904. Maori medical lore. *Transactions of the New Zealand Institute* 37: 1–120.

Grey, Sir George, 1956. *Polynesian Mythology* (English translation of Grey 1971). Whitcombe and Tombs, Christchurch (first published 1855).

1971. *Nga Mahi a Nga Tupuna.* Reed, Wellington (first published 1854).

Hall, H.U., 1920. Maori wood carving and Moko. *University of Pennsylvania Museum Journal* 11: 212–42.

Hamilton, Augustus, 1901. *Maori Art.* New Zealand Institute, Wellington.

Hanson, F. Allan and Louise, 1981. The cybernetics of cultural communication. In *Semiotic Themes* (edited by Richard DeGeorge). University of Kansas Publications, Humanistic Studies, Lawrence.

Forthcoming. *Culture in Counterpoint: The New Zealand Maoris.* Routledge & Kegan Paul, London.

Hiroa, Te Rangi (Peter H. Buck), 1926. *The Evolution of Maori Clothing*. Polynesian Society, Memoir No. 7.

Jackson, Michael, 1972. Aspects of symbolism and composition in Maori art. *Bijdragen tot de Taal-, Land-, en Volkenkunde* 128: 33–80.

King, Michael, 1972. *Moko: Maori Tattooing in the Twentieth Century*. Alister Taylor, Wellington.

1975. Moko and C.F. Goldie. *Journal of the Polynesian Society* 84: 431–40.

Korzybski, Alfred, 1958. *Science and Sanity*, 4th edn. International Non-Aristotelian Library Publishing Co., Lakeville, Con.

Langer, Susanne K., 1953. *Feeling and Form.* Routledge and Kegan Paul, London.

Lévi-Strauss, Claude, 1962. *La pensée sauvage.* Plon, Paris.

1963. *Structural Anthropology.* Basic Books, New York.

McEwan, J.M., 1966. Maori art. *An Encyclopedia of New Zealand* (edited by A.H. McLintock), Vol. 2, pp. 408–29.

McLean, Mervyn and Margaret Orbell, 1975. *Traditional Songs of the Maori*. Reed, Wellington.

Mead, Sidney M., 1968. *The art of Taaniko weaving.* Reed, Wellington.

Menzies, J.H., 1904. *Maori Patterns Painted and Carved.* Smith and Anthony, Christchurch.

Ngata, A.T. and Pei Te Hurinui, 1961. *Nga Moteatea (The Songs), Part II.* Polynesian Society, Maori Texts No. 2.

Phillipps, William J., 1948. Maori spirals. *Journal of the Polynesian Society* 57: 30–40.

1960. *Maori Rafter and Taniko Designs.* Wingfield Press, Wellington (first published 1943 as *Maori Designs*).

Robley, Major-General, 1896. *Moko; or Maori Tattooing.* Chapman and Hall, London.

Rout, Ettie, 1926. *Maori Symbolism.* Kegan Paul, Trench, Trubner & Co., London.

Rowe, W. Page, 1928. *Maori Artistry.* Board of Maori Ethnological Research, Memoirs Vol. 3.

Schwimmer, Eric, 1959. Building art in the Maori tradition: John Taiapa and the carved meeting houses of today. *Te Ao Hou* 28: 31–5, 48–51.

1974. *The World of the Maori.* Reed, Wellington (first published 1966).

Shortland, Edward, 1856. *Traditions and Superstitions of the New Zealanders*, 2nd edn. Longman, London.

Smith, S. Percy, 1913. *The Lore of the Whare-wananga, Part I – Te Kauwai-runga*. Polynesian Society, Memoir No. 3.

Taylor, Richard, 1855. *Te Ika a Maui, or New Zealand and its Inhabitants.* Wertheim and Macintosh, London.

Tregear, Edward, 1904. *The Maori Race.* A.D. Willis, Wanganui.

Turner, Victor, 1967. *The Forest of Symbols.* Cornell University Press, Ithaca.

Weaver, Warren, 1949. The mathematics of communication. *Scientific American* 181: 11–15.

White, John, 1886–90. *The Ancient History of the Maori, His Mythology and Traditions.* 6 vols, Government Printer, Wellington.

Yate, William, 1835. *An Account of New Zealand*, 2nd edn. R.B. Seely and W. Burnside, London.

Chapter 7

From form to content in the structural study of aesthetic systems

James C. Faris

Introduction

Anthropological analysts have generally been cautious in their approach to aesthetic forms from a structural point of view, rarely venturing beyond demonstrative statements.[1] What little attempt there has been to relate structural studies of form to a reading of content and meaning has consisted of vague references to universal classificatory propensities and general patterns of human cognition (cf. Faris 1968; 1972a: 100, 115; Washburn 1977: 6).[2] Beyond revealing something of the complexity of indigenous aesthetic traditions (chiefly, one suspects, in proportion to the ingenuity of the analyst in computing the permutations of form logic; cf. Crowe 1971; Faris 1972a; Friedrich 1970; Watt 1966; Washburn 1977) analysts have so far demonstrated a reluctance to generate anything but the most subjective and speculative theories within which content and meaning can begin to be discussed and understood.

In this paper it will be argued that this study of form divorced from content has diminished appreciation and comprehension of both; indeed that elaborations in form morphology can themselves be read as statements of content. An attempt will be made to link content and form, treating aesthetic traditions as knowledges or ideological practices.

But it must be said that such links between form and content are neither unitary nor necessary; neither are they functional nor determining. They are practices which signify; and are therefore not to be regarded as reproducing, reflecting, revealing or concealing. Again, they are practices which constitute and condition; they neither require nor create.

For each culture's aesthetic productions there is a culturally appropriate 'reading' (or 'seeing' – an established view of the art held by interpolated subjects) founded on values by which aesthetic manifestations are comprehended indigenously. These values or models, which inform and constitute subjects about the particular society, are not designed to inform subjects differentially constituted – for example, those constituted by different social relations – neither can they be required to do so.

Those who observe a particular culture from the outside can marvel at the content of its art, appreciate its style and form, but can rarely be the objects of its practice. We can, however, with care give a reading from our own constituted subjectivity. If we are self-consciously aware of our position and explicit about our methods we can alternatively constitute the link between the element of form and the element of content in another culture's aesthetic manifestations – but this should be recognized as a specific reading from another political view than that of the culture.[3]

Claude Lévi-Strauss, among others, has suggested that cultural models are instrumental and thus 'by definition poor ones, since they are not intended to explain the phenomena, but to perpetuate them' (1963: 281). That such models (here aesthetic systems) should be considered 'poor' reveals an unfortunate empiricism – an appeal to some privileged epistemological standard or value. It is as if Lévi-Strauss regards them as the work of conspirators, designed to conceal or inhibit viewers from comprehending some underlying reality – some 'truth' awaiting explanation.[4]

Indeed cultural models are often well constructed, and because their logic is markedly tautological, aesthetic ideologies do have a sort of inscrutability. This is because they are so often iconographically specific and rule-governed; pleonastic and consistent. They are uniformly discursive, commonly holistic, and exhibit analytical closure about the forms to which they refer.

It will not be argued that the alternative discourses proposed in this paper are from any point of view more 'correct' or 'scientific' – only that they stem from a different set of premises than those which see a hidden, latent, structural function in aesthetic form, to be revealed by clever analysis – or that which proposes the cultural reading or function (as I did for example with the personal art of South-east Nuba – Faris 1972a; 1978). I am simply suggesting a possible significance for aesthetic manifestations based on a political reading – indeed a political critique – of the indigenous social relations.

Such a reading has relevance only with reference to a political theory and is not to be regarded as an epistemological statement. It is not a 'representation in thought' of a reality, for there can be no objective reality or truth in the form and content of aesthetic traditions. There can only be readings whose adequacy and validation stems from the logic of their construction and their political basis. From this view, no theoretical objects exist independently of discourse (see Cutler *et al.* 1977).

By rejecting the privileged position of an epistemology my reading must, therefore, stem from some theoretical basis. This will be shown to be a political scrutiny of, and objection to, the social relations appropriate to each of the aesthetic ideologies studied. But, it may be asked, why adopt *this* political reading and not another? What is objectionable about the culture's social relations and ideological constitution? To answer these questions involves a discussion of the division of labour in human society, and will clarify the perspective of my political focus.

Theoretical background: social production

To be successful social production must involve a projection, a teleology – the created division of labour. This division of labour may be based on technical specialization (such as involved in work organization and serial production); it may be a function of differential natural capacities at particular times of life (strength or infirmity, immaturity or maturity, etc.); it may be a function of differential separation from the means of production or of some type of constituted right (capitalist/worker, lord/serf).

The division of labour – here termed a social relation of production – always involves appropriation. In other words, the products created by division of labour must, at least in part, be distributed to others so as to reproduce the society's total personnel. It will be argued here that social appropriation takes place in all social systems – that it always has and always will so long as any division of labour is maintained – if only in the form of appropriation by the aged, infirm, and very young from healthy producers. A question of rather more interest is 'what knowledges signify and constitute such divisions of labour?'.

What are the conditions of existence of such social relations? If non-producers are to be kept alive by producers; if producers are to surrender part of their product or their labour to others, and if exchange of products or specialization is required, it is possible to look for some knowledge – some ideological form – that signifies these relations. This should be equally true of appropriation by poets, priests and professors. For the structure of any division of labour, whether occasioned by technical considerations or physical condition, can never be regarded as simply given nor can it be assumed. It must be constituted by knowledges – that the youth are to be reared, the aged revered, the infirm kept alive, and that poets, priests and professors are important to moral, spiritual and mental well-being.

The question is, if such a division of labour is, for example, constituted as necessary or desirable, why is it so desired, or how is it necessitated? By what means, knowledges and mechanisms is such a division of labour signified – how are the subjects of such divisions of labour constituted as subjects?[5]

It is suggested here that aesthetic traditions can be read to be significant for such social relations, and divisions of labour. But these significations are thus labelled by my reading, and alternative readings might assign other significances. My reading implies no causality, no essential origin nor functional necessity – and is based only on political critique. The knowledge involved in aesthetic discourse must constitute subjectivity. Art traditions must constitute because they cannot defend or apologize, and their effectivity is not a question of *non sequitur*, force or compulsion. The tautology of the discourse – its own instrumentality – must be ensured; practices have to be believed for reasons other than the absence of alternatives. For the present paper, however, the structure of discursive practices is less important to the discussion than the mechanisms evident in the specific aesthetic traditions under consideration.

Theoretical background: the content of form

As I stated at the beginning, these readings will focus on the content signification and especially the significance of mechanisms of form elaboration. It will be necessary to describe actual examples of stylization and elaboration in detail, and to present these as discursive practices in order to criticize the subjectivity which an art tradition constitutes.[6]

Sociolinguistic and historical linguistic research provide

useful suggestions in relating content and form. Research into speech stratification and differentiation (cf. Labov 1972) and historical and evolutionary change (cf. Kiparsky 1968) has led to the generation of concepts and theories about both the evolutionary characteristics of speech and the inhibitions on such evolutionary change. Diachronically, speech tends towards the progressive elimination of redundancy (phonetically, morphologically, and syntactically) in execution. This tendency is checked on the one hand by the ever-diminishing amount of information such reduced messages transmit linguistically (thus narrowing the size of the linguistic community); and on the other hand by elaboration requirements which we set both by the necessity to communicate to a wider community and by the deliberate maintenance of redundancy as a status marker – a requirement of cultural and linguistic standard.

These tandem processes – reduction and elaboration – are not simply mirror images of one another. Elaboration does not mirror in reverse form the process of reduction – it takes on an autonomous development within certain parameters. This is essentially how dialects, vernaculars, and, eventually, languages arise. It is, literally, a model for the Tower of Babel.

Of particular interest here, of course, is the marking characteristic of elaboration and its maintenance – the preservation and signification of redundancy. When the marking of elaboration is noted in aesthetic traditions – particularly if it is theorized as having potential political effects – it is possible to argue its signification for specific social relations of production.

Consider, for example, Gothic forms of architecture as paradigms of redundancy. This style did considerably more than hold up buildings, as the marked contrast between church and surrounding town demonstrates in sixteenth-century engravings. Gothic elaboration was rigidly rule-governed and compositionally structured and standardized. That is how we can know its form so well. More important for the present analysis is the marked difference of Gothic ecclesiastical architecture from vernacular architecture of the same epoch, and thereby the possible signification for specific social relations, such as between peasants and the landed gentry and clergy. The architecture did not simply represent the social relations, it represented *a way of viewing* that had significance to the social relations. It constituted a subjectivity – logically and coherently – and stemmed from a constituted subjectivity.

This way of viewing aesthetic traditions as discursive practices, which allows us to read a particular relationship between content and form, is what will be attempted here. Meaning and form are not linked in functional unity – as is so frequently implied in anthropological treatises on art. If meaning and form are not potentially independent, then representation is directly reducible to what is represented (cf. Cutler *et al.* 1977). From alternative political positions it is possible to present analyses which posit different, non-functionalist links between form and meaning. If this were not possible, then there would only be one true, correct, accurate, and objective reading of any art tradition.[7]

The art traditions discussed here are all characterized by iconographies that enable meaning to be held – meaning that may be communicated in the most rudimentary of ways or minima of signals. This leaves an entire field open to possible elaboration and redundancy. Icons, indeed, allow identification without compromising such potential for elaboration and redundancy. Thus a reading of the signification of content in form (or, perhaps, the structure in content) is possible.

The Northwest Coast of North America

The art of the Northwest Coast of North America has frequently been described and is universally admired. There are now a few studies of its form, such as the excellent stylistic study by Holm (1965). Later criticisms notwithstanding, the early studies of Boas (1955) remain among the most sophisticated and most sensitive to the interplay of content and form. Indeed, many of the more recent studies not only divorce content from form, but retreat into functionalist symbolic speculation (cf. Vastokas 1978). Consequently, serious and up-to-date theoretical consideration of the relationship between the autonomous elements (content/form) is simply lacking.

Without doubt the most striking feature of Northwest Coast[8] art is its very conspicuousness. In technique, in execution and in every detail, the art displays. It displays the talent, labour and time involved in the acquisition of materials, in construction, and in command over the entire process (or the potential wealth to command such graphic and plastic excellence). Moreover, from the careful studies of analysts such as Boas and Holm, it can now be more clearly seen that part of any display is a statement of the evolution of the form – its history and development – its elaboration of the logic of form permutation.

Elaboration is the most commanding aspect of the display, even when, like the great tradition of nineteenth-century Japanese art, the most exquisite expression of such elaboration is found in its restraint. It is thus possible to witness the powerful contrasts between simplicity and complexity – each leaning on our knowledge of what one could be were it not the other. We can comprehend, particularly with the careful form studies now available, how the most simple and understated design has, in a distinctive sense, totally filled the available space, much like the most complex, expanded expression of the form logic, were it so rendered (Fig. 7.1). As the compositional rules are the same, it is an arrogance of understatement.[9]

We are even required to contemplate the time, talent and labour and its command which goes into an *actual effort of displaying* the aesthetic products. A large totem pole, for example, may be carved from 40 metres of heavy cedar; twenty-metre canoes are hewn from single logs, and carved houses several hundred metres long require, quite apart from their actual execution, considerable organization to acquire and erect (cf. Gunther 1971: 319; Hawthorne 1979: 70). Many of the masks in Northwest Coast art are compound, requiring parts that are moveable or changeable at various points in the dramatic rituals in which they are used (Fig. 7.2). This and other aspects of such rituals required to enhance the display – elaborate staging, trap doors, moving panels, and complex construction – all involved numerous personnel and their command. And provisions for food, shelter and fuel had to be made for those in attendance at the winter rituals at which the aesthetic productions were most manifest.[10]

The theatrical character of such aesthetic production – its display implications – can also be seen in the very many designs which required motion (either of the object or the viewer) for full appreciation (Figs. 7.1–7.4). For appropriate execution this required much more from craftsmen than artistic expression. The theatrical setting was crucial as the dances and dramas were often held at critically important winter ceremonies – considered necessary to the reproduction of the resources and social relations upon which the society depended. Congregations of viewers were bound by kin and clan relations, by supernatural sanction, and by their own productive contribution to the effort in assembling great quantities of food and other items. At some ceremonies accumulated wealth was necessary to enable certain individuals to take titles and to be initiated into various status societies – each of whose definition required elaborate masking traditions, conspicuous display, extensive feasting, formalized oratory and dramatic re-enactment of historical and mythical events.

Much of this was specifically competitive – rivals and competitors were shamed by the display of greater quantities and qualities of goods (exceptionally skilled artisans were even kidnapped by rival chiefs), and more elaborate production. This demonstrated ability to hold substantial celebrations and give away substantial amounts, and, in so doing, to accrue honour and reputation.

Sometimes competitive displays and giving were

Fig. 7.1. Carved and painted Tlingit chest. Note how the end panels complement the elaborate front and back, and elegantly 'fill' the space they occupy, revealing complete and sophisticated control of space – whether saturated or empty. Indeed, as unfolded, the chest loses a dimensional sophistication, and does not so readily reveal the subtle flow and orientation of the end panels. Denver Art Museum, QT 1–117. From Holm 1965.

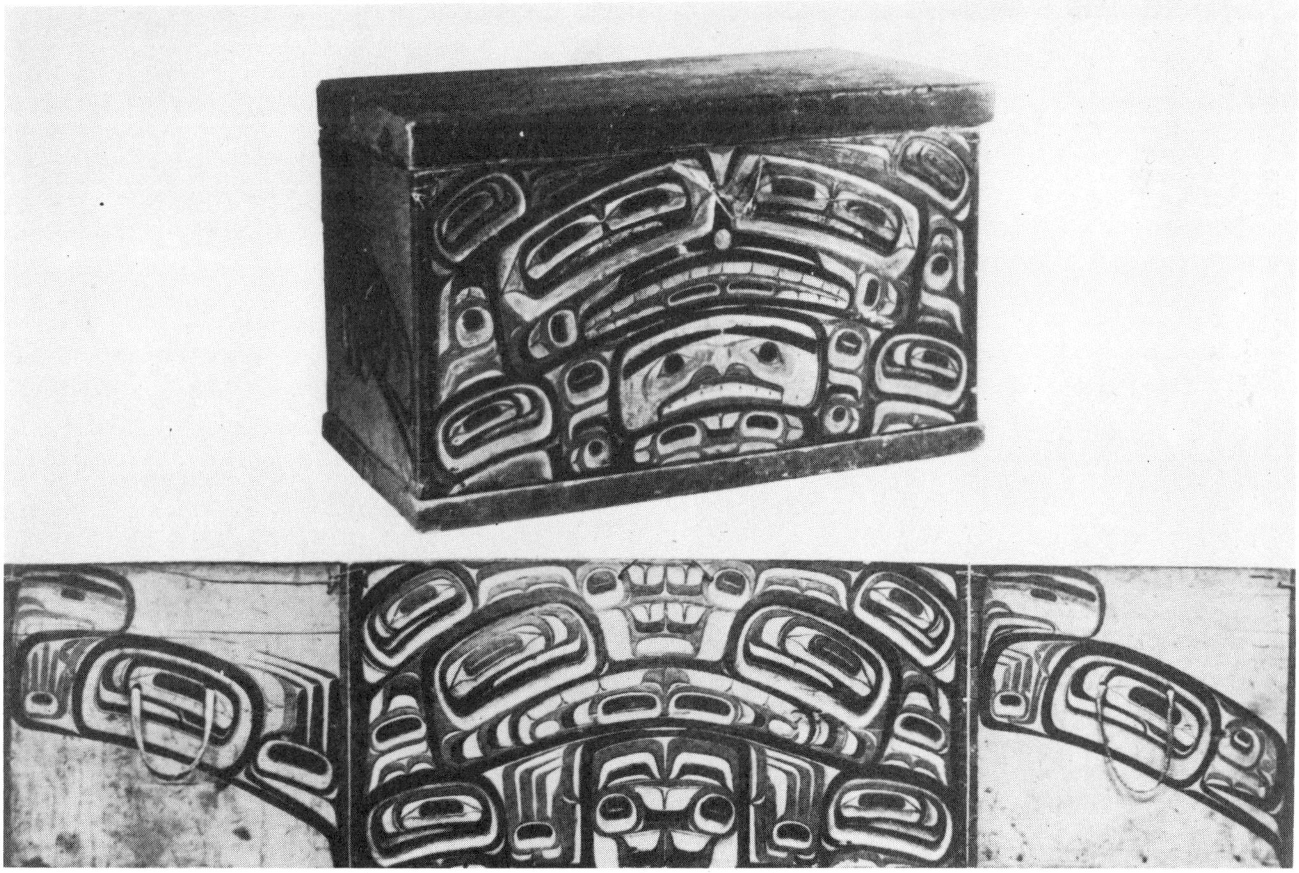

Fig. 7.2. Complex raven-man mask, closed and open. Kwakiutl, from Kingcome Inlet. The elaboration of this mask is extreme – the open form, with all its interior painting, being particularly spectacular. This mask would be dramatically opened at a specific point in the ceremonies, so to reveal the inner crest with its elaborated surroundings. Museum of Anthropology, University of British Columbia, A4497. From Hawthorne 1967.

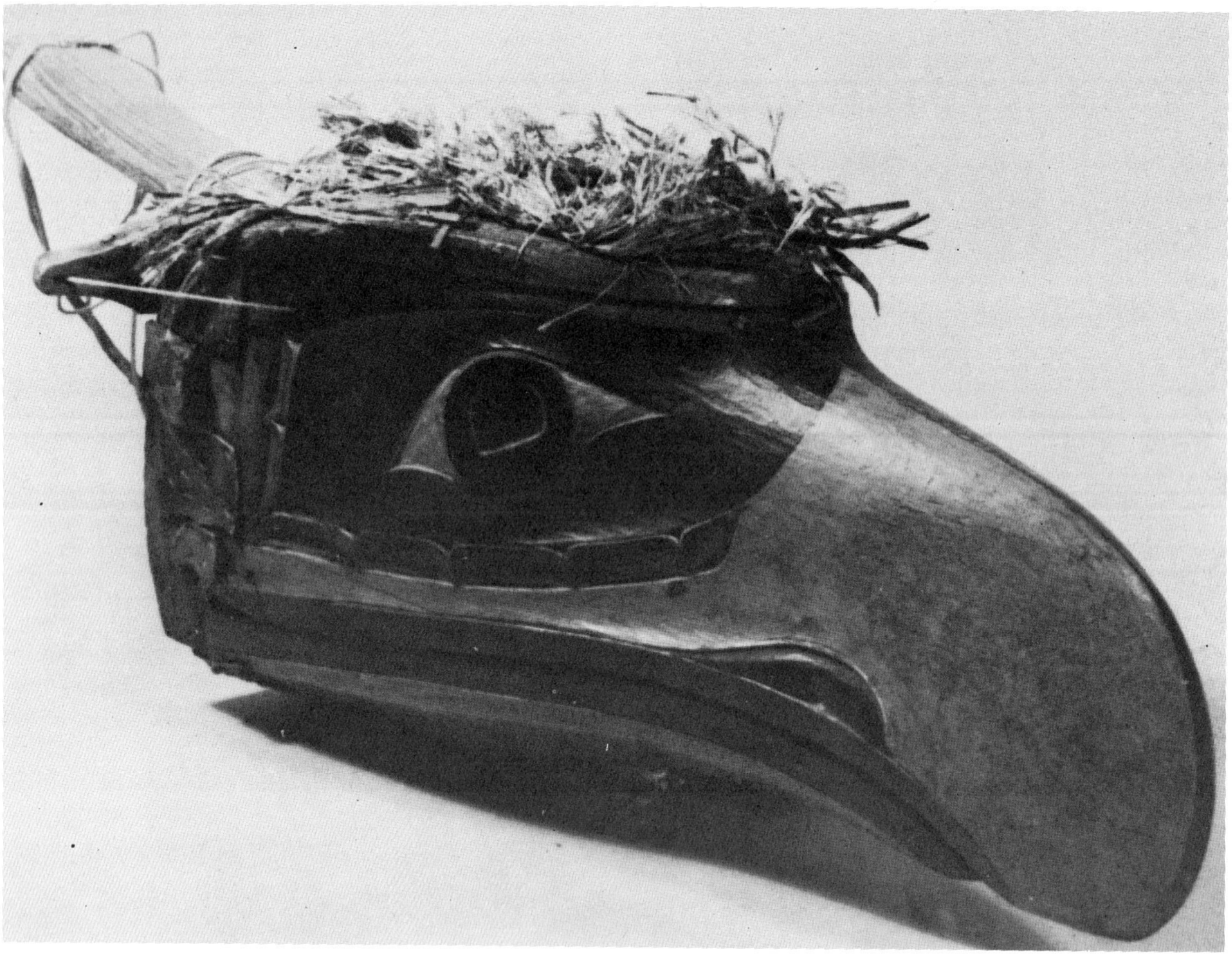

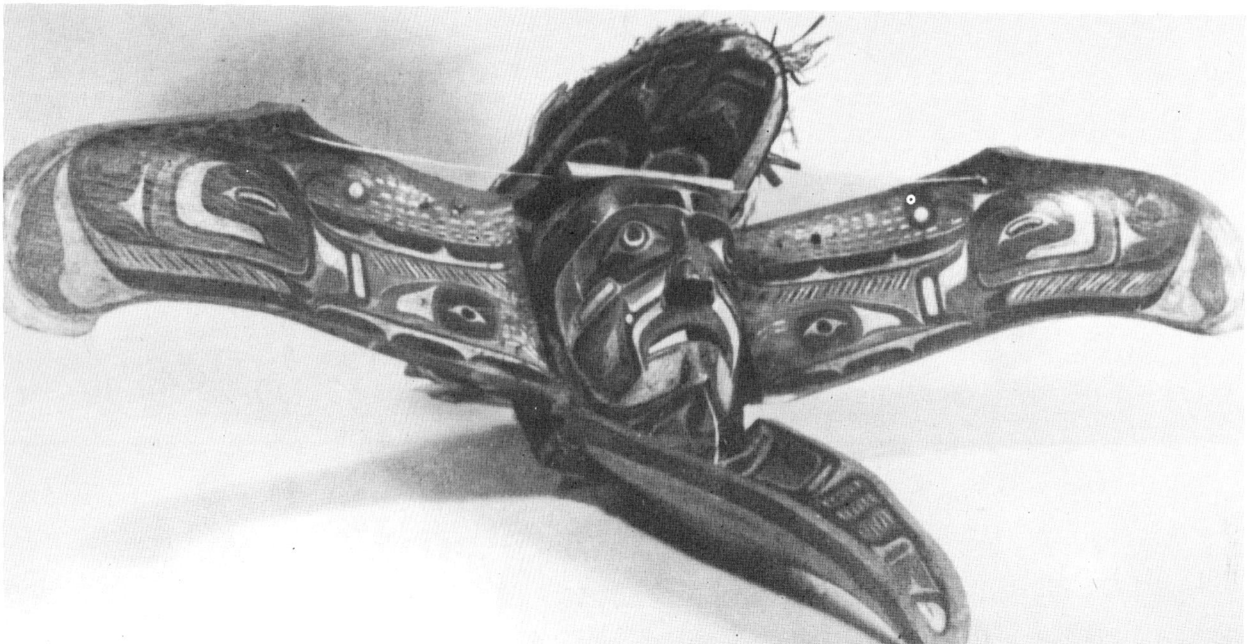

explicitly used by a rival chief or claimant to status. Validation of such status often involved giving in excess of one hundred per cent of the gift received – to demonstrate superiority by giving out interest on gifts received. That rapid inflation should result from such practices is obvious, and this was further fuelled by exploitation of the system by European fur traders. The motives underlying elaboration even took on destructive aspects at certain periods in Northwest Coast history, when riches resulting from the fur trade meant that vast accumulations were possible. The social system could not redistribute the larger amounts accumulated, for this might threaten the structure itself. Thus, display became a matter of immediate consumption in the form of the destruction of accumulated goods and aesthetic productions – even involving human sacrifice at one point (cf. Ruyle 1973: 613; Codere 1950). Great quantities of goods, many of excellent craftsmanship, were destroyed in competitive displays, and values became absurdly inflated (a copper became worth as much as 7,500 blankets – Hawthorne 1979: 35).

At other periods, the continual demand for increasingly elaborate display created problems for the tradition itself. Content came to be so secondary that iconographic sense was lost or compromised (see below, p. 97). Display demanded expansion of dimension which was in some cases handled expertly; in other cases it produced distortion, aesthetic aberrations and 'ungrammatical' expressions, as the form dictates became too rigid to handle other perspectives, dimensions, and styles successfully (Fig. 7.5). This was not the consequence of inexperienced or insufficiently skilled artists; it was the expression of an attempt to elaborate further than the syntax of the design form would, in the circumstances, allow. The form inhibited the possibility of alternative dimensions. At this period the design form and its logic are so well elaborated and so redundant that even an unschooled observer can quickly detect clear failures when they occur, and recognize aesthetic productions which violate the structure of form. This intuitive grasp is possible in part because of the obvious redundancy, repetition and elaboration. Each manifestation reveals saturation of the form structure, such that greater elaboration could only violate the form dictates.

Of course representation was the cardinal foundation of Northwest Coast art: that is to say that it was, at base, illustrative. But it was just as much illustrative of status as it was an icon of what was represented – it had to be oriented for viewing and to viewers. Representation occurred in a variety of perspectives and dimensions as form evolved. Representations occurred in the round, *en face* (Fig. 7.6), and in combinations of two-dimensional perspectives (Figs.

Fig. 7.3. Tlingit food storage box. This kerfed box, the top inlaid with operculum of sea snail, is decorated in typical low relief with the representation of a mythical sea spirit, Kow-e-ko-tate. The artist here has wrapped two facial forms around a single corner. Each side is a duplication of the other, and were the corner pushed flat, two entire, essentially two-dimensional faces would result. Without the box or the viewer in motion, however, the aesthetic effect and sophistication cannot be fully comprehended. Washington State Museum, No. 1396. From Inverarity 1950.

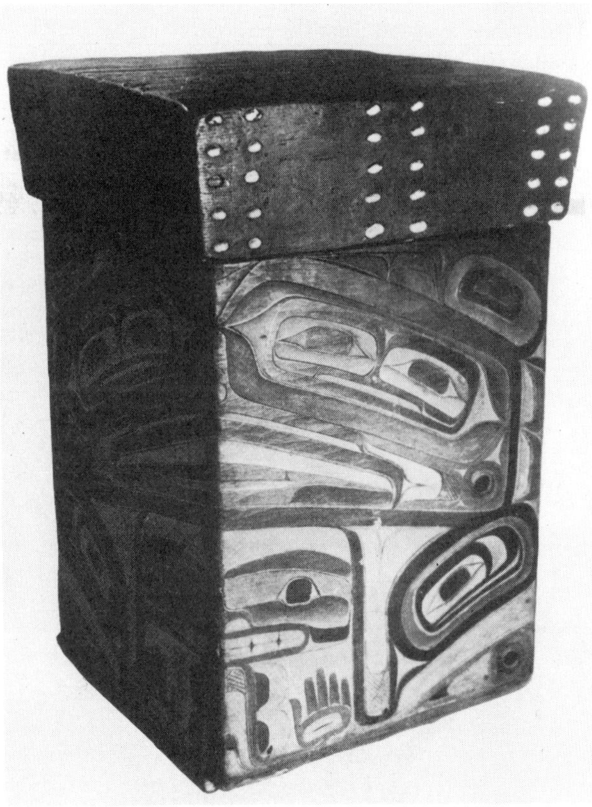

Fig. 7.4. Tlingit fish club, representing a killer whale. This shape, rather like the actual animal represented, has the tail and the dorsal fin of the design folded down so to give a smooth surface. All features are noted, including the vital icon, the dorsal fin spot. This, like so many other Northwest Coast productions, is executed in full round, yet can suffice only in profile. Here the artist both enabled motion and relieved the object (or viewer) of having to move by presenting the design completely in either dimension. American Museum of Natural History, E/242. From Boas 1955.

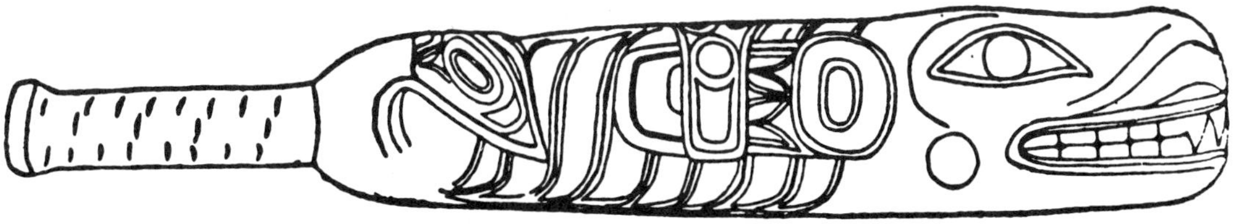

7.3, 7.4). More extraordinary postures, however, came into being as representations (of, for example, an animal) were unfolded, and rearranged (always keeping the viewer in mind), either to conform to an available space or shape, or (more commonly) to express the artist's ability, and ingenuity – and thus that of those who sponsored and possessed the art (Figs. 7.1, 7.3, 7.4, 7.6).

Content, then, the specific meaning of the manifestation, came to be form-dominated in distinct ways. In fact, a final indication of the elaboration, redundancy and elegant display involved in Northwest Coast art may be seen in the manner in which form finally came to compromise content. There is little, if any, aesthetic production in Northwest Coast art which is not specific in content. Every animal or fantasy creature had meaning (Fig. 7.3). This is most magnificently evident in the portrait masks and helmets which include detailed attitudes of emotional expression, age, abnormality, state of being (dead, dying) (Fig. 7.7). More predominant however, were the elaborated crests, masks, and two-dimensional paintings, or carvings, on utilitarian objects or panels, depicting a series of hunted animals – particularly those species whose hunting required considerable resources and organization of labour (such as ocean-going boats and crews to handle them). Perhaps as a consequence of their frequent depiction, an iconography evolved for such animals so that a complex elaboration might proceed and yet the species still be recognizable from some minimal icon – a killer whale might be distinguished from any other whale or fish by a small spot or hole on the dorsal fin (Figs. 7.4, 7.6); a beaver by two large incisors or a hatched tail (even though this might be the only indication in the entire production that it symbolized this animal, or indeed that it symbolized an animal at all). Different bear species were known by the shape of their nostrils; the raven (Fig. 7.2), eagle, hawk, and other meat-eating birds were distinguished by the slightest differences in the angles of their beaks.

This elaboration, however, came to compromise content to the extent that the iconography became lost, obscure or mistaken. Thus, today, a complete informant-responsive iconography is probably no longer possible. It is as if the

Fig. 7.5. Original drawing by Charles Edensaw, representing an eagle carrying away a woman. Here, one of the most experienced and sophisticated Haida craftsmen has utterly failed to transcend the form limitations imposed by the traditional system in attempting to draw an eagle in flight (rather than in crest form – indicating action rather than representation). The crude naturalism collapses into the form the artist commanded at the shoulder and in the profile representation of the bird's head. Perspective is also in error as a body line goes through the near leg. The woman's face and body are totally distorted as the artist confuses profile with *en face* perspective in an effort to indicate the lip ornament. There is uncertainty over whether to treat the nose *en face* or in profile, and both perspectives are evident. Action in the representation defeated the artist, who could certainly have commanded motion required of the viewer of the total representation itself. Display is at base static – its 'story' is in part its very being. From Boas 1955.

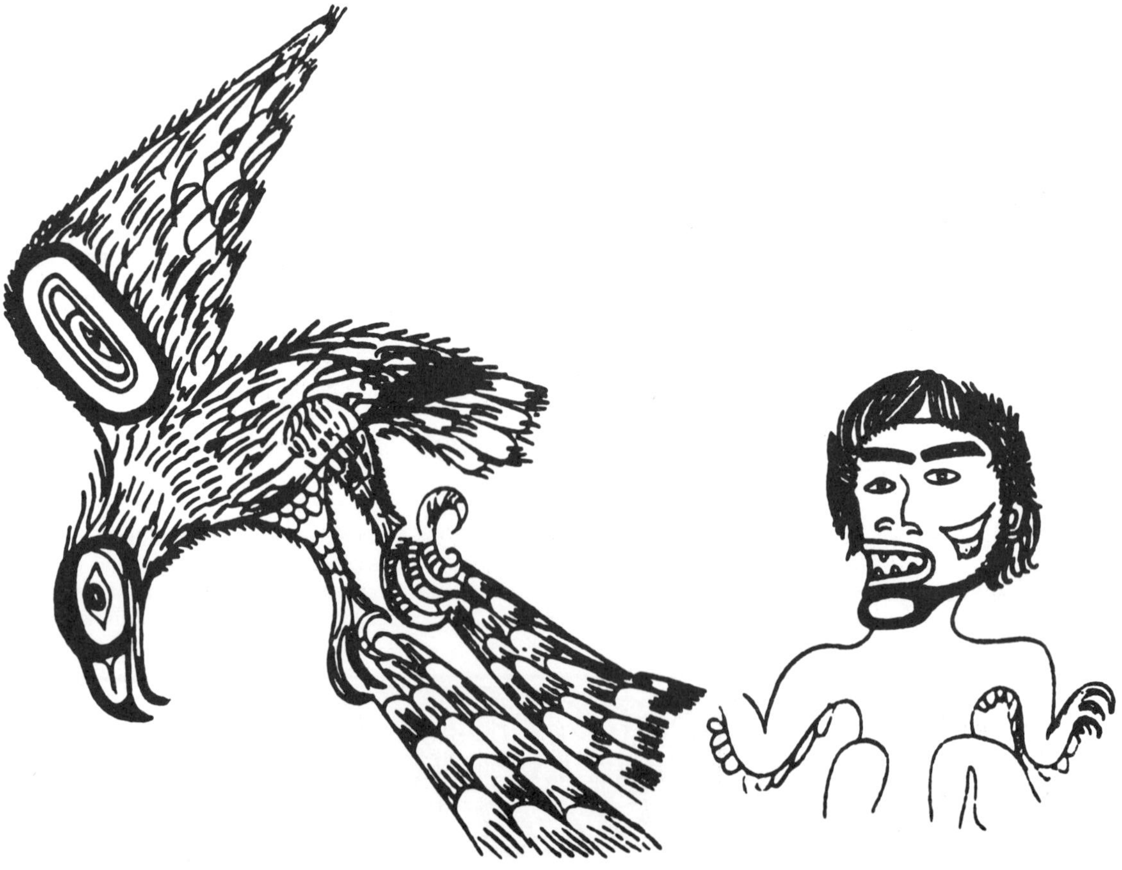

representational features of the art turned in on themselves because they had no other place to turn – space was filled (or grammatically so), dimension saturated, and all possible rearrangements and butchering techniques exhausted. The logical extensions of form *with* meaning had been reached and only meaning could be further compromised. Elaboration was carried to the extreme – it had become a magnificent end in itself. Holm (1965: 9) and others (cf. Boas 1955: 108, 216) have called attention to the difficulties of charting a systematic iconography, as many of the artists themselves and the commentators did not know the identification of certain examples, or offered conflicting identifications, or claimed that knowledge was lost altogether.

Although it was important that crests were accurately copied, it seems as if animal identification was assumed, or had, in some way, come to be absolutely secondary to the display function. The subject of the icon was either swamped, or excluded, or rendered unidentifiable. The representation had been elaborated, whether by its disassembly, unfolding, twisting, expanding, or other form of alteration to fit a given space or shape. The logical permutations of form – ironically, originally based on redundancy in the icon itself – came to obliterate meaning in the representation. It was as if a sentence had been uttered – perfectly grammatical in itself yet involving so much jargon or elaborated vocabulary that any meaning in the vernacular sense was no longer recognizable.

The social relations and divisions of labour which were signified and constituted by such aesthetic production were complex. Though characterized by complicated and impressive forces of production, Northwest Coast social forms were based on a productive foundation of hunting and gathering – and, prior to the fur trade with Europeans, probably little commodity exchange. Nevertheless, surplus was produced sufficient to maintain not only a considerable number of skilled artisans (and thus apprentices) but also a nobility that

Fig. 7.6. Kwakiutl house front painting, killer whale representation. The head of the whale has been split to the tip, folded out and down from the body. The dorsal fin pulled up over the split head and the tail is further split and folded out to support the entire structure. Indeed, the killer whale has thus been anthropomorphized in the rearrangement, and rearranged to be viewed *in toto en face* in such form. From Boas 1955.

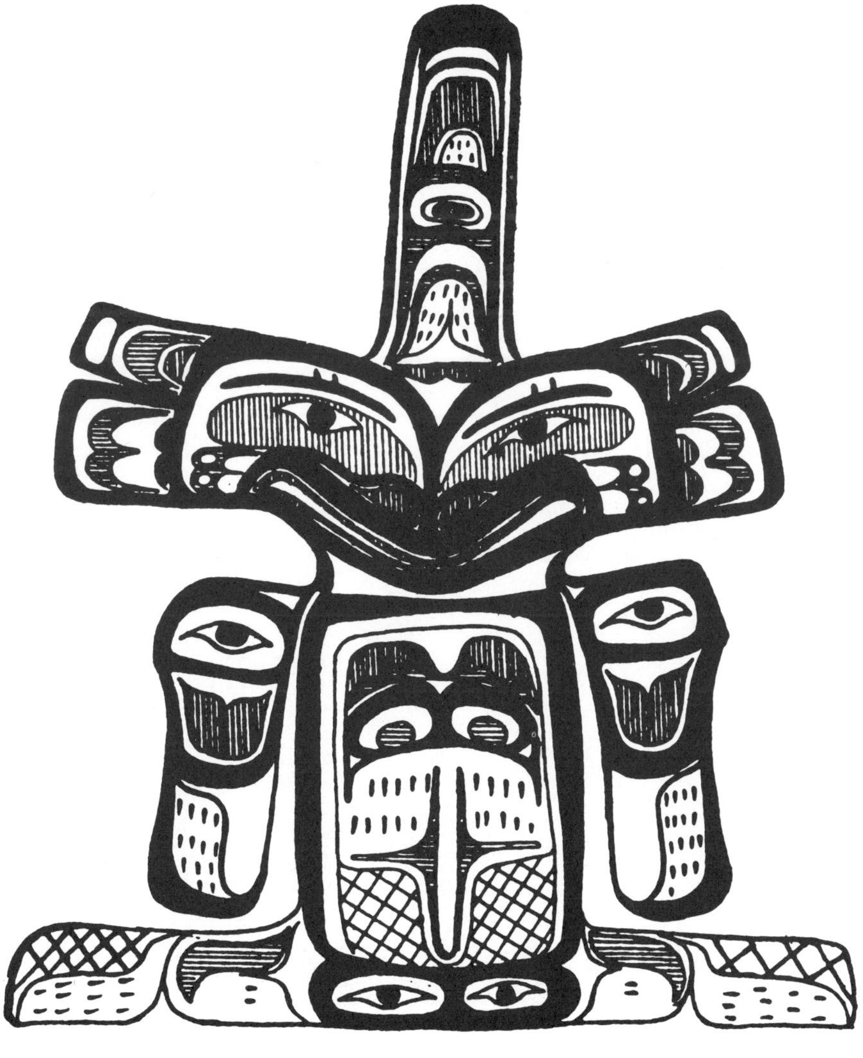

patronized them and for whom their extraordinary talent was one expression.

These complex divisions of labour probably yielded three incipient classes. There were hereditary nobles, some of whom were chiefs (probably only after the period of European destruction and extensive depopulation were noble positions open to commoners – see Ruyle 1973: 605), commoners, and captive slaves. It was on the commoners that the burden of the bulk of production fell, as the role of slaves in all but service capacities (or in later periods as sacrificial victims) does not appear to be great. Commoners, then, were the chief appropriators from nature – in acquisition, processing, rendering and storing. And male nobles (female nobles cultivated 'only mannerisms of speech and movement' (Oberg 1973: 87) but were in other respects active producers) were the principal appropriators from commoners (Drucker 1951: 244).

The surplus commanded by chiefs and nobles came principally by virtue of the mechanisms of extended kin links. All kin of the local group assisted in ritual competitions (potlatches) and winter rituals by providing materials with which the nobles and chiefs competed. This validated the local kin group (and its chief) against others. These competitions were in effect (Codere 1950) fights with property, and great amounts of surplus production were redistributed (or even destroyed in later times), all of which validated the local chief's or nobles' position over rival chiefs and nobles, as well as that of the local kin group. The ideological burden was obvious – since commoners had to be mobilized to provide the materials for these ceremonies, they too were involved in the validation struggles. Everyone appropriated from had to be involved in the celebration of the successful competition, in the most elaborate display, in the satisfaction of group pride and the orgy of local kin sentiment. There was no state system and therefore no fixed set of class relations specific to such a state – there was but an incipient possibility for status, which required constant validation on an ever more grandiose scale. Without the sanction of a state, maintenance of the highly stratified systems required continual competition and validation.

Elaboration is in this respect a concomitant of the requirements of the stratification system – a logical consequence and appropriate mechanism.

Validation was effected most often at potlatches –

Fig. 7.7. Tlingit war helmet. The realism here is striking – possibly a person partially paralysed. The eyes are moveable, perhaps increasing the effect of the abnormality or terror intended. American Museum of Natural History, E/3453.

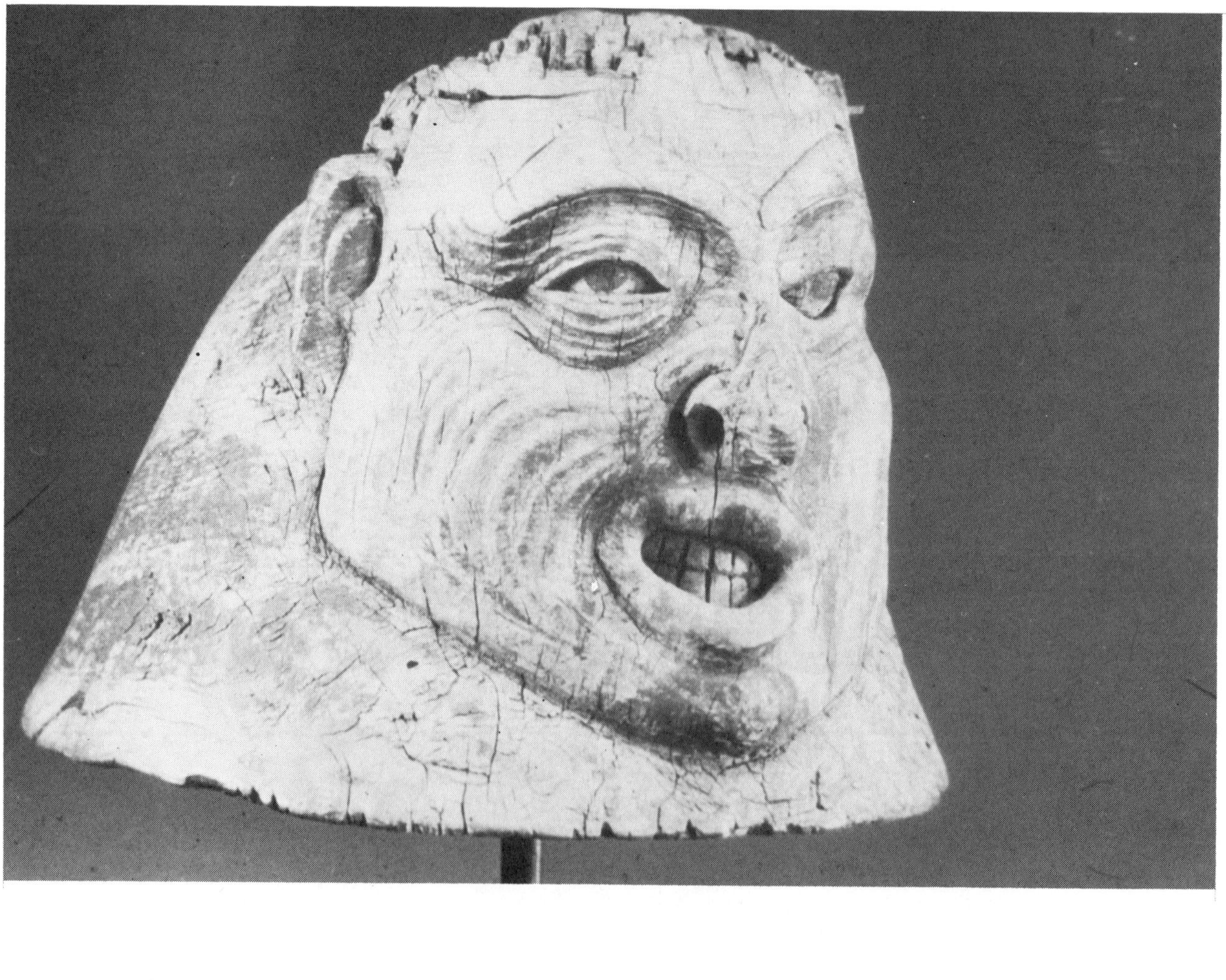

where individual or group entitlement to a position, or relative superiority to the person or group potlatched against was celebrated. The elaborate winter ceremonials may also have had potlatches, but they were principally the time at which titles were taken, where initiations into title societies were effected, and where rituals and dramatizations of the histories of the various societies were presented. Here the display of aesthetic productions was greatest – the chiefs and nobles and title holders wore and displayed their finest masks and robes, ate and entertained from the most exquisite of vessels, filled with abundant foods, stored in elaborately decorated boxes (Figs. 7.1, 7.3), in houses decorated with impressively and elaborately painted and carved panels (Fig. 7.6). The ceremonies were accompanied by great dramatic presentations and the re-enactment of events particular to the myth and history of the group or society. The organization emphasized display – in dance, drama, costume and set. The rituals and dramas required masks and appropriate crests, which could be made for no one but the nobles, for whom the rituals provided the occasion for their display. After these occasions, totem poles were erected to celebrate the memory of the event and its host.

Representation of certain animals or creatures was the sole prerogative of a particular individual or kin group. Commissioning artisans to execute the representation – in the appropriate elaborated form – was an expression of this prerogative. Elaborated design and its elaborated display were the exclusive privilege of elaborated statuses. But as the meanings in crests and representations came to be secondary to the form elaboration, so too did the kin foundation – the *numinas*. The links of kinship and affinity thus became less potent in producing surplus and mobilizing support for the great potlatches and winter ceremonials. Mercantilists and traders came to furnish the goods involved in such competitive displays, and the system degenerated, as did the art, except where now patronized by European collectors and museums.[11]

Northwest Coast art represented and symbolized status and title explicitly in that entitlement to certain crests and their representation was restricted to certain nobles and chiefs. But in addition the very form of the art also constituted and interpolated subjects to the point that the latter came in fact to swamp meaning – resulting in a reversal of the relationship between the elements of form and content. Content was no longer recognizable in form.

It is with such reasoning that we can perhaps make most sense of other traditions where form has come to overwhelm content – as in much Islamic art. Is it not possible that specific representation was once found in this art too, but that, with increasing elaboration – signifying as it did increasing stratification – form came to dominate content (constituted as representation) to the extent that the logic of form came to be totally paramount – indeed, to be the new content? Elaboration had extended to the limits of the morphological system – continuations could arise only at the total sacrifice of meaning. By the time of the emergence of the Islamic state, an actual prohibition on specific representation had come about – a content suppression of pre-Islamic icons, so as to ensure aesthetic conformity to the new supernatural (which, as a state religion, took ritual control of the supernatural out of human hands and rendered causality the privilege of an omnipotent, otiose god). The art was no longer in the hands of elders, chiefs, or kin-group priests whose status had been signified by representational crests. Form became the only possible statement of content, its redundancy and elaboration its own content statement.

The Southeast Nuba of Sudan

The social organization of the small-scale agriculturalists known as the Southeast Nuba has been briefly treated elsewhere (Faris 1969a; 1969b; 1972b), as has their personal art tradition (Faris 1972a; 1978). What follows is an initial attempt to specify the content in form – to indicate an ideological signification for the personal art tradition in the constitution of certain specific social relations and specific divisions of labour.

The age-based art tradition of the Southeast Nuba is principally confined in its most spectacular form to the bodies of young males and young females. Males paint themselves from about twelve years of age until approximately twenty-seven years of age, often daily during the season after harvest and before the next year's planting. Rules confine the colours used for various age categories during this period – for example only the later age groups are eligible to use the greatest elaboration in colour including the deep black and yellow prohibited to younger grades.[12]

Significantly, the elaboration in design and colour for males is restricted to paint, and accompanied not by physiological changes but by changes in productive status and sport. The lower decorating age grade (with most stringent colour regulation and least elaboration) are principally herders for elders of their matri- and patri-clan sections, and involved in extensive brideservice labour for elders of their betrothed's matri- and patri-clan sections. The next or upper decorating age grade, now farmers in their own right, their marriages now consummated, are also active in ritual congregations, and may use the entire repertoire of colours and designs. The elders, no longer decorating, lead and inaugurate rituals which demand sacrifice of the labour and product of juniors; they also pass judgement on the adequacy of design and enforce the rules of colour for those still decorating.

One universe of Southeast Nuba representational designs for males has been formally analysed (Faris 1972a: 93). A series of algorithmic operations were specified, which, operating on phanetic primitives, generated all the productions possible in this universe. These algorithmic operations were each based along axes of semantic significance and no other – thus indicating something of the logical permutation and formal elegance of this elaborated form. The degree to which all possible productions of every possible operation were 'saturated' (that is, actually produced meaningful representations) is another measure of elaboration in the historical evolution and compositional elegance of the finite form morphology (Faris 1972a: 110–11).

In Faris 1972a I viewed this elaboration as a celebration of the productive male body – essentially the reading given to the personal art tradition by Southeast Nuba males themselves. Here, I am attempting to ask what signification such a tradition might have were it to stem from an alternative view – treating the cultural reading as an ideology and positing an alternative discourse, premised in a specific political critique of the cultural reading.[13] It is my view that such an alternative reading helps to comprehend more recent events and changes in the personal art tradition. Thus by adopting a political position and viewing the art tradition in terms of the significance to divisions of labour and social relations of production, I am attempting to specify certain effects that the tradition might potentially have. As will be seen below, changes in the current situation do, in fact, support these theorized effects.

The most technically elaborate male designs can require some time to execute properly, though representational designs do not necessarily require more time than non-representational designs (indeed, as will be argued, actual labour time has become significant only as a result of recent developments). Traditionally, time expended expresses only one, minor aspect of the elaboration. More important here are the expression of the structure of the formal system of representations themselves (Fig. 7.8), and the expression of the style rules of body display (Fig. 7.9) (the former actually executed only in terms of the latter – see Faris 1972a: 82) – even if the expression is morphologically, semantically and stylistically achieved with minimal effort and maximum elegance (Figs. 7.10, 7.11). This expression of elaboration in style and form of the complex evolution of the decorative tradition is argued here to have distinct signification. The degree of formal elaboration does not necessarily reflect the quality of the signification, but the fact that it can do so is indicative.

Fig. 7.8. Representational whole body design form type. This design, of a specific species of leopard, is applied to the body as if the human body is that of the animal. This design, known from the icon expressed in a feature code, is part of a corpus of representational designs whose form morphology is described in Faris 1972a.

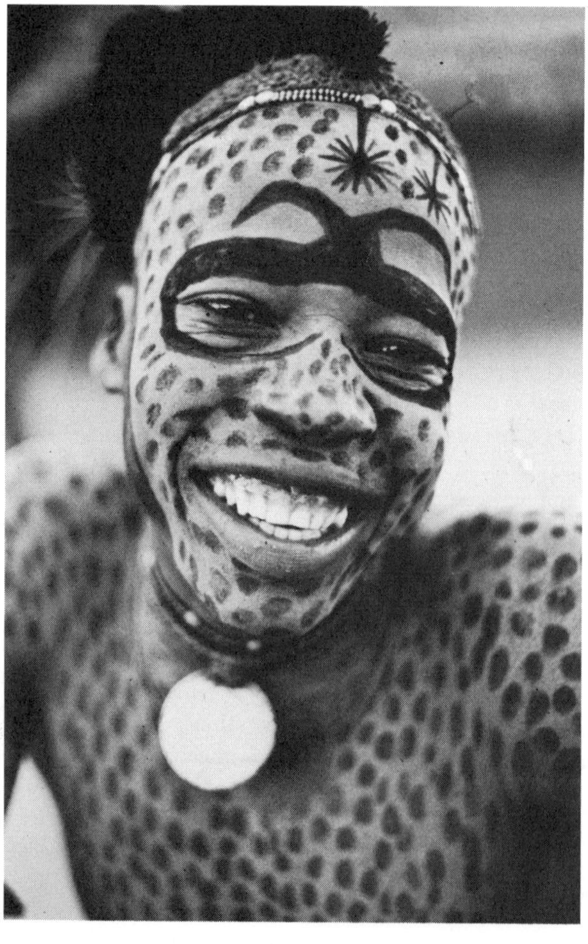

Fig. 7.9. Non-representational design form type. The principal rules of composition for this form type centre about body placement and colour balance.

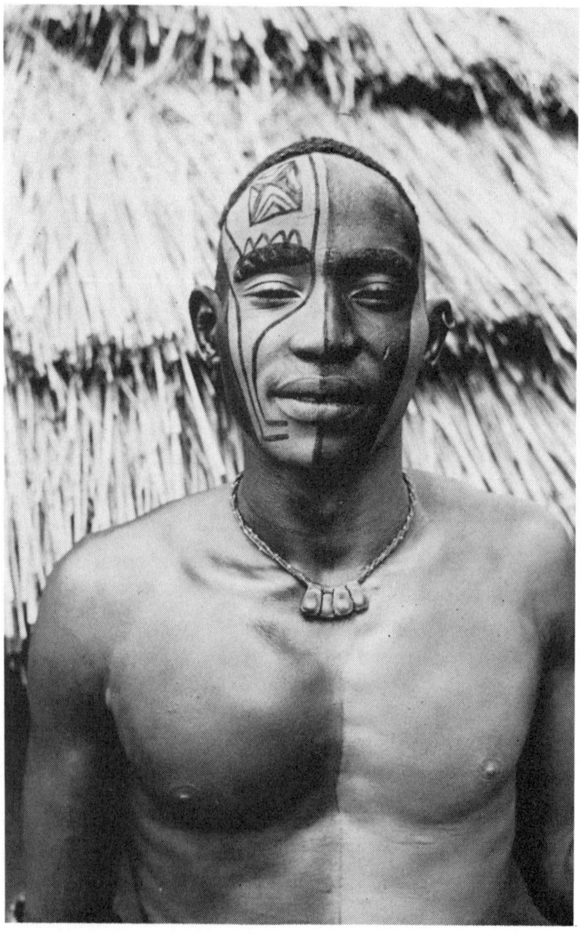

Men's productive socialization, then, is marked and elaborated and makes an effective contrast to the decoration of young females. From the age of about six years (when they are first betrothed) until consummation of marriage, females apply oil and ochre daily (if possible) in colours appropriate to their patri-clan section (see Faris 1972a: 32 for patri-clan specific colours). And, on childbirth and while nursing, they may again wear some oil and ochre on their shoulders – this time the colour appropriate to the infant's patri-clan section.

But a young girl also receives an initial set of body scars on the first sign of approaching maturity when her breasts first start to appear (scars from the navel to the breasts – see Faris 1972a: 34). Other more extensive scars (now covering the entire torso) are cut on initial menses (Fig. 7.12) and a final set covering the back and the back of the legs, arms and neck, are cut after a woman weans her first child. This last set of scars signals sexual availability again after a long post-partum sexual restriction during which time the infant is nursed. The final set is regarded as a beauty necessity, and if a husband refuses to pay for the scarring specialist, a woman may seek a lover who will do so, and her first marriage will end. The scars on a woman's back are regarded as sexually pleasurable to her lovers (Fig. 7.13).

Fig. 7.10. Representational body design form type. This design, of a specific species of wasp, is applied on the whole body, or any part, and so long as it is repeated on any part of the body a minimum of four times, its representation is morphologically adequate (see Faris 1972a: 96, no. 62). The artist has indicated the representation in the most economical (and elegant) way possible.

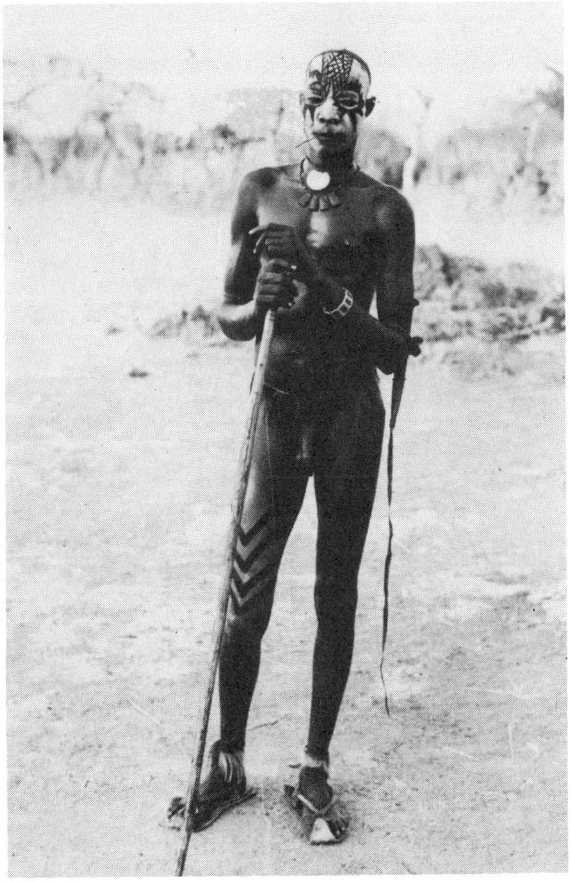

As noted in Table 7.1, the personal art of young women is rigidly structured around physiological changes and reproductive capacities, and rigidly fixed on the body with scarification. Note just what is signified in the female art tradition – physiologically specific diacritica, and patri-clan section diacritica. The significance of the patrilineal–male association has already been indicated (Faris 1969b), and the conceptual associations which assign females, through colouring, a patrilineal (male) address, are clear. The cicatrization marks physiological changes dramatically – extending even to explicit celebration of sexual availability which is important to further reproduction (Fig. 7.13). Production, except for new human beings, is not signified in personal diacritica for females.

For males, on the other hand, physiological changes can be coded lexically (see Faris 1972a: 38), but all visual diacritica emphasize changes in productive status. The most elaborated form is peculiar to the most productively elaborate division – males between about seventeen years of age and twenty-seven to thirty years of age. Here the form is the most visible – the content 'formed' in the most redundant manner.

The social relations of production and the division of labour are clearly signified in the personal art tradition. Although both men and women can and do perform all tasks in cultivation, a division of labour is maintained in most circumstances – not only task-specific, but also within each task. That is, not only technically, but also organizationally.

Men and women rarely work together, although both can and do cultivate on plots to which they have access by virtue of their membership (from birth and irrevocably) in matri- and patri-kin based groups organized as clan sections which hold land and other property communally. The work of women in threshing, for example, is usually carried out individually or in twos without ritual, sacrifice, sociality or ado. It is accomplished with a heavy wooden paddle, much like a cricket bat, used while kneeling to hammer the harvested grain. This is in marked contrast to the threshing activity of men. Men thresh only in groups of up to ten – usually in reciprocal brideservice parties, accompanied by appropriate sacrifices, beer and food. The threshing is carried out standing, using a light paddle with a springy handle, to the chorus of an elder singer who rakes grain from a prepared stack into the paths of the rhythmically pounding threshers. The stack is carefully arranged in attractive and labour-consuming ways designed to show off the productive effort of the grains' male owner (see Faris 1972a: 39), while the stacks of women's grain are simply piled randomly.

The ritual surrounding male threshing activity is significant. A village section priest (or male elder surrogate) will

Fig. 7.11. Non-representational design form type. This form type is the same form type as in Fig. 7.9, only executed in a morphologically acceptable variation. It, like the design of Fig. 7.10, is expressed most economically and in a maximally elegant manner. The greater proportion of black to yellow in this design is a function of the rules of colour weight and balance.

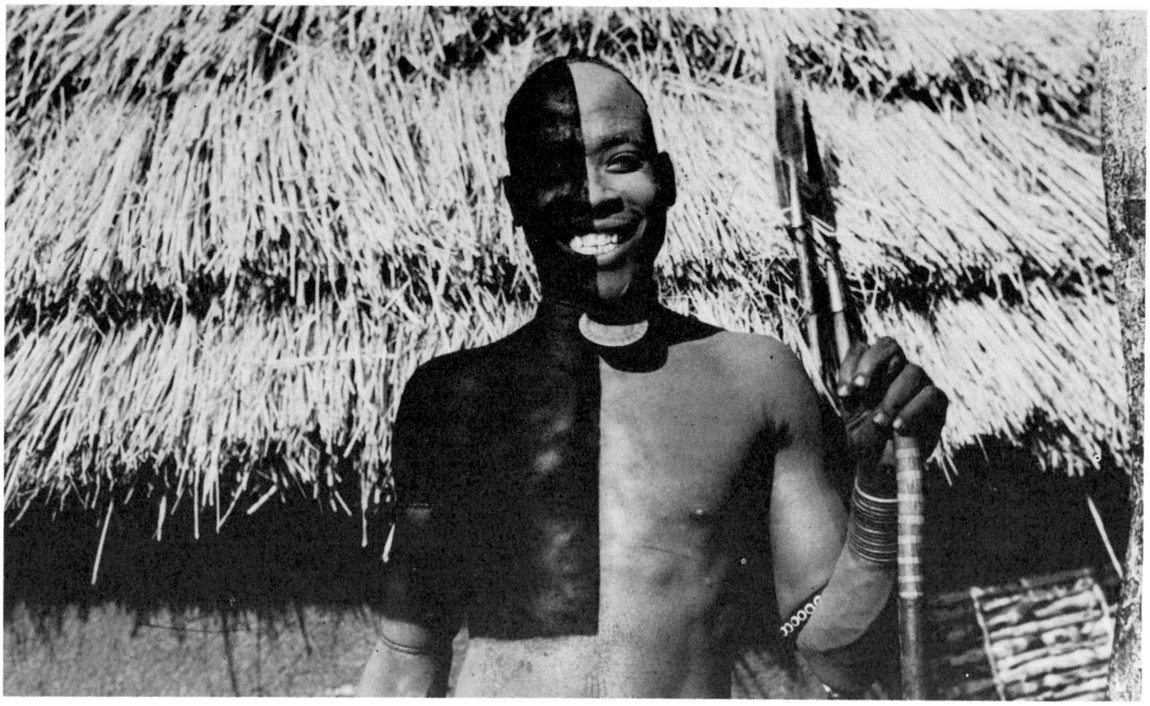

Fig. 7.12. The torso cicatrization indicates this girl has had her first menses, though her marriage has not yet been consummated, as she is still decorating with ochre and oil.

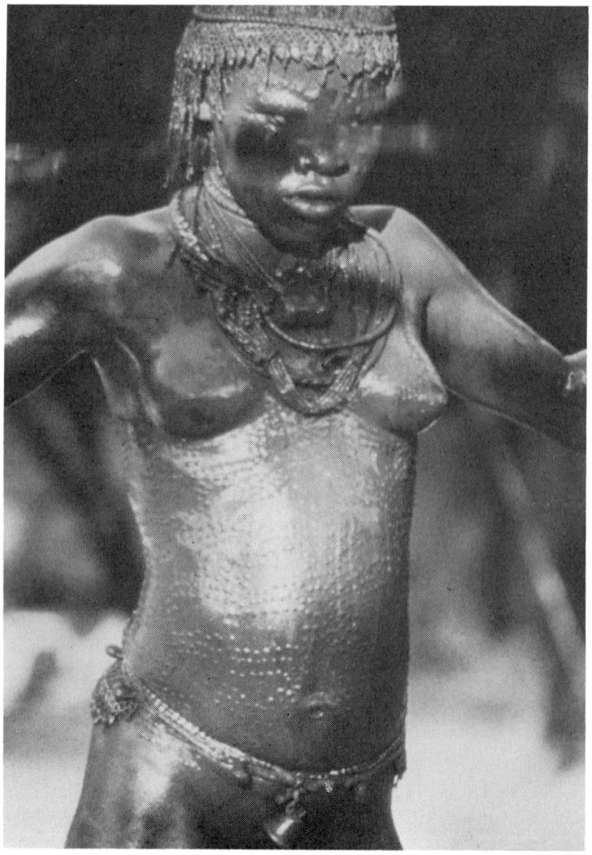

Fig. 7.13. Body scars given after weaning of first child. These also mark sexual availability after a long period of post-partum sexual restriction.

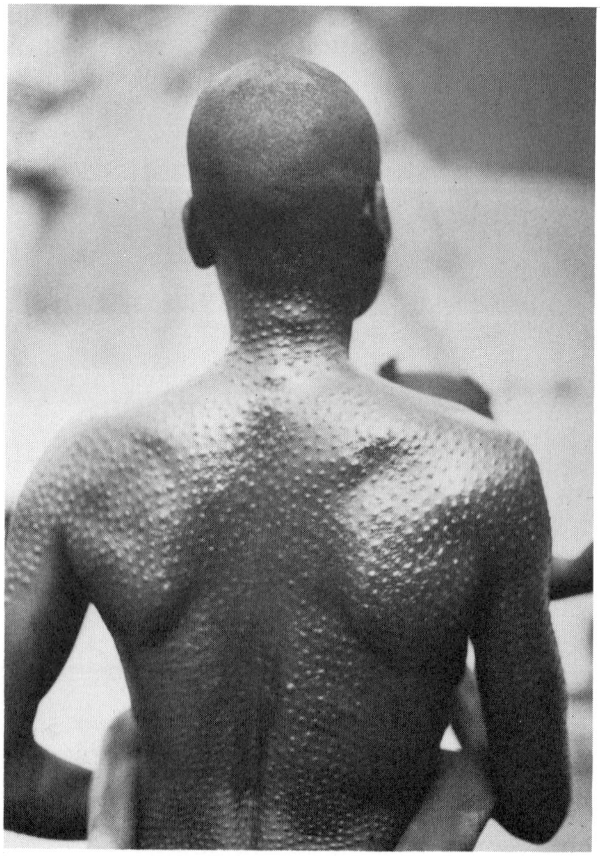

Table 7.1 *Diacritica, Southeast Nuba personal art*

	Quality	*Duration*	*Signification*
Females	simple	fixed	physiology and reproduction, sexual availability, kin-group membership and kin-group membership of offspring
Males	elaborate	changing	production, sport participation

perform a sacrifice, and, tossing some of the blood of the sacrificed animal over the beautifully prepared stack of unthreshed grain, will utter an incantation to ensure that the threshed grain be large in amount, the threshing easy, and the general welfare and an ample food supply be assured. Not to do so would be to run a serious risk, and it is considered that such rituals effectively guarantee that grain failure will not occur. Note, however, the absence of such ritual (or any ritual) in the threshing activities of women. And there is no specific reference in any of the ritual activities to the sexual division of labour.

The grain of women goes into their own granaries and is used to prepare food for the family first. A man's granary will provide grain for beer and sacrifices, and will not be used for food until a women's grain is exhausted. Women, of course, grind the grain, cook and ferment, and make all the other preparations for beer-making (including carrying the water).

The division of labour based on sex is repeated in most productive tasks. Men thus never grind grain; women never herd or hunt with guns. Women primarily carry water and firewood, men primarily thatch roofs and build walls (Fig. 7.14). Elder men spend somewhat more time in ritual activity than elder women. Senior women may appropriate the labour of junior men in brideservice, and there is, in fact, no direct appropriation of a category of men over a woman or over women. Individual men can and do appropriate the labour and product of their wives, mothers and daughters. They do so, however, only in part as men, but more importantly as husbands, sons, or fathers. There is no antagonism between women and men, though not uncommonly structural conflict exists between some men and some women which requires specification in addition to sex for its expression.

Similar social relations of production characterize the

Fig. 7.14. Men in brideservice. These men, a party of age mates, are building a hut for the future father-in-law of one of their group. This many men can finish such walls in two days.

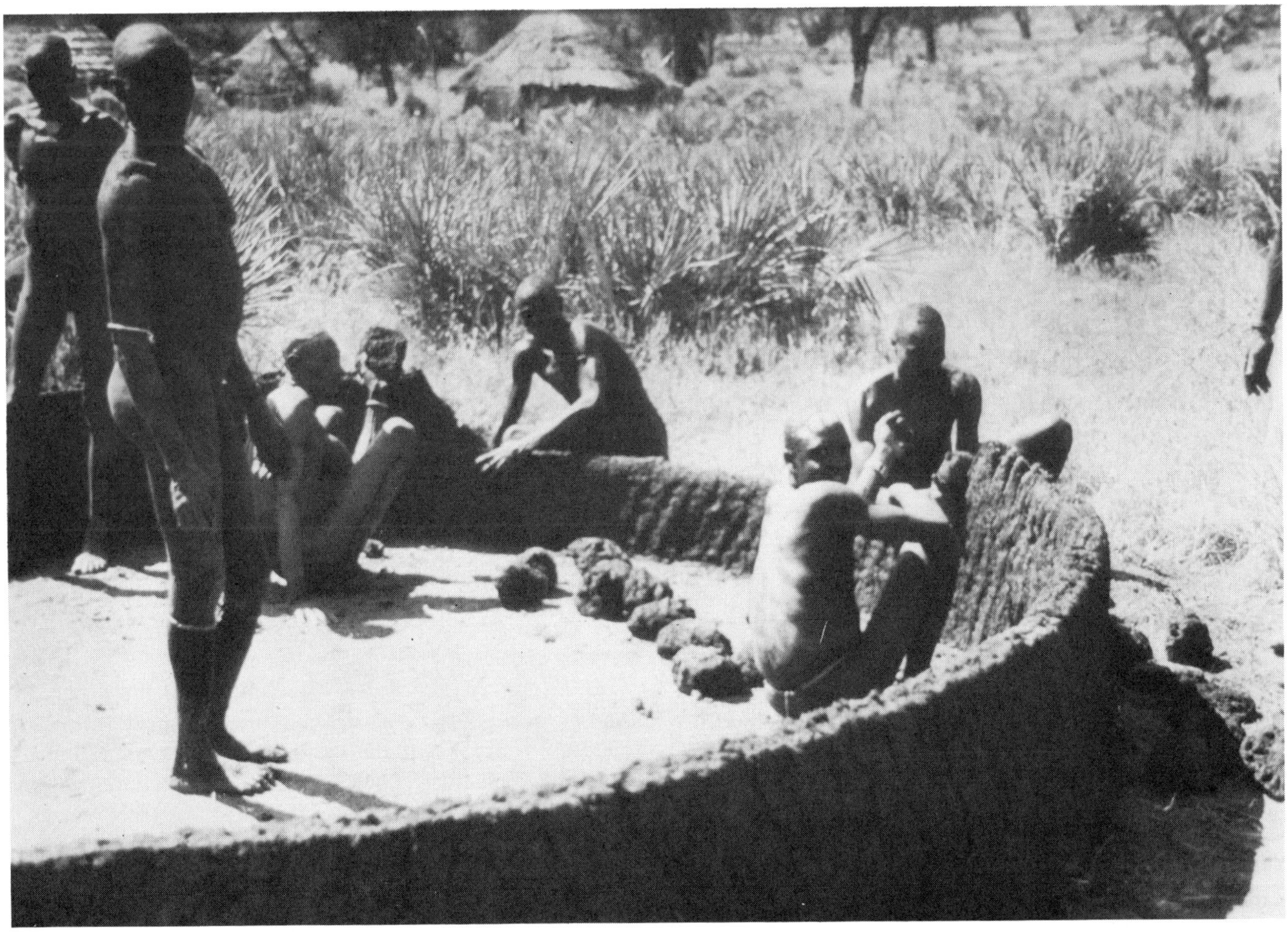

relations between juniors and elders. Elders principally appropriate as individuals through brideservice for their daughters, through parenthood, and through relative age authority within the clan section. Young men work for their betrotheds' parents in weeding, threshing, winnowing, hut-building (Fig. 7.14), and fence construction. Moreover, they must provide them with gifts, such as tobacco, oil and ochre.

Thus, through control over marriage and inheritance, individual elders (both male and female) appropriate from some juniors who structurally, by means of kinship, find themselves in such a position vis-à-vis a given elder. The fundamental enabling mechanism of appropriation of juniors by elders is kinship. But elders are importantly the priests and leaders who direct the age organization activities that form the basis (in addition to sex) for differentiation in the personal art tradition. Thus, the intersection of the age organization and kinship (with its terminological emphasis on generation and sex, as well as provision for elaboration by male speakers over female speakers (see Faris 1969a; 1969b)), are the social mechanisms constituting the foundations of the personal art tradition. We have already outlined the significatory functions of the cultural ideology (cf. Foucault 1972). A different political perspective enables a critique, an alternative reading, another discourse on the same data. Our reading of the significance of the art tradition to the social relations of production is made complete by reference to recent events and contemporary change in the personal art tradition documented during a visit in the spring of 1980.

Since the publication of *The People of Kau* (Riefenstahl 1976), European tourists have repeatedly visited the Southeast Nuba, principally to duplicate Riefenstahl's photographs and capture her experience. 'Africa had never presented me with a finer visual experience [p. 10] . . . the Kau Nuba wild and passionate [p. 6] . . . among the Southeast Nuba, love and sex play a major role which is manifest in their singular cult of body, their erotic dance and knife fights' (1976: 220).[14]

As a consequence of this, the social relations of production are undergoing rapid change – young men are refusing to do brideservice and insisting instead on payment of bridewealth. Kin-group elders no longer have the appropriate grip they once had. Consequently they have less control over the decorating tradition or command over the proper use of colour and design. This is evident in the emergence of a group of young men, principally in the village of Nyaro, who now rarely decorate except for European tourists, in return for payment. Tourists photograph the decorating with still and ciné cameras, and the design forms principally used are those which require more time for their execution, or those whose elaboration is potentially unlimited (thereby enabling the artists to command greater amounts of money for greater time spent in decorating and posing). In the indigenous design system, however, only one design form type is capable of infinite expansion and thus potentially capable of consuming unlimited time in its execution (see Faris 1972a: 74ff.). Predictably, this design form type is now the most common primary form type in use. The invasion of Europeans has also expanded the materials used for decoration – European lip glosses for women are now to be found in the Southeast Nuba male design colour vocabulary. The personal art tradition of young men is now premised in part of the sale of decorating based on the time of its expenditure, just as in the economic relations of capitalism labour is sold in terms of its duration.

It is also significant that the design form type now in vogue has no iconographically coded representations – it is the form type in which elaboration devoid of representational constraint is most possible. Representation is no longer of relevance. Only in bits and pieces are the representational designs of other design form types found on the body, simply because their proper execution as whole body designs is finite, as is the time required for their execution.

European Upper Paleolithic

European Paleolithic art has always presented something of a dilemma, as the aesthetic productions seem excessively sophisticated for the social organizations creating them and the functions they are conceived to have served. In the best of parietal art and in the sculpture, there is a command over subject that is extraordinary. In form, perspective, colour, line, shade and shadow, it solved problems several thousand years ahead of its time. It will be argued here that this very sophistication may be viewed as form elaboration, and thus may be interpreted as significant to content in the art tradition.

However, since the materials are exclusively archaeological,[15] it is difficult to know what might have been an indigenous explanation of the graphic and plastic manifestations. There are extrapolations from existing hunting and gathering social forms, and interpretations of Paleolithic art are myriad. Ucko and Rosenfeld (1967) have provided a useful summary and critique of many of the analyses of parietal art (although curiously eliminating the important analysis of Raphael (1945)). Raymond and Liebowitz (n.d.) have summarized more briefly previous analyses of Upper Paleolithic female figurines, and have put forward an interpretation of their own – essentially, that such figurines reflect and celebrate the critical importance of women to group maintenance. We will suggest an alternative reading – stemming from another discourse.

Descriptively, the most conspicuous features of the cave art are the large Pleistocene mammals (Figs. 7.15, 7.16) – to the marked exclusion of small animals, plants, or men. And of the Gravettian female sculptures, the most conspicuous features are specifically anatomical characteristics and exaggerated breasts and buttocks (Fig. 7.17) to the exclusion of any modelling of heads, arms, hands or feet (even though anatomical accuracy and sophistication are very impressive in animal sculpture). The same distortion may also be found in the few examples of female figures in cave sculpture and parietal petroglyphs (Figs. 7.18, 7.19, 7.20).[16] The forms of all such sculpture are essentially the same: most are quite small (no more than a few centimetres in height) and were probably amulets of some variety (Fig. 7.17). They are worn smooth, but do not appear to have had a specifically practical utilitarian function – they do not appear to be tools or weapons. Thus, the present reading assumes, in common with other interpretations, that they were not explicitly productive. However, the discourse here regards the form itself as significant in that it is female and in that the anatomical distortions and elaborations are what they are.

This reading of the female sculptures, however, is not undertaken in isolation from the cave art – the exquisite presentation of the large mammals of Paleolithic Europe (Figs. 7.15, 7.16). Though there are exceptions, in most cases the animals represented are those whose hunting would normally require time, organization, and talent. Some are herding animals which might require driving; others, such as mammoth and rhinoceros and perhaps the large Pleistocene cattle, would require tracking, and time to overcome them once wounded and cornered. A specialized division of labour and form of hunting is indicated. Animals which could be taken easily by a solitary hunter are simply not represented, though the remains of small animals such as rodents are

Fig. 7.15. Bison from the nave, Lascaux, France. These bison, in rich black and red, are masterfully interlocked by the hind quarters. Dimension and perspective are handled with considerable sophistication. This painting is almost 2.5 metres long. Photograph courtesy of Jean Vertut.

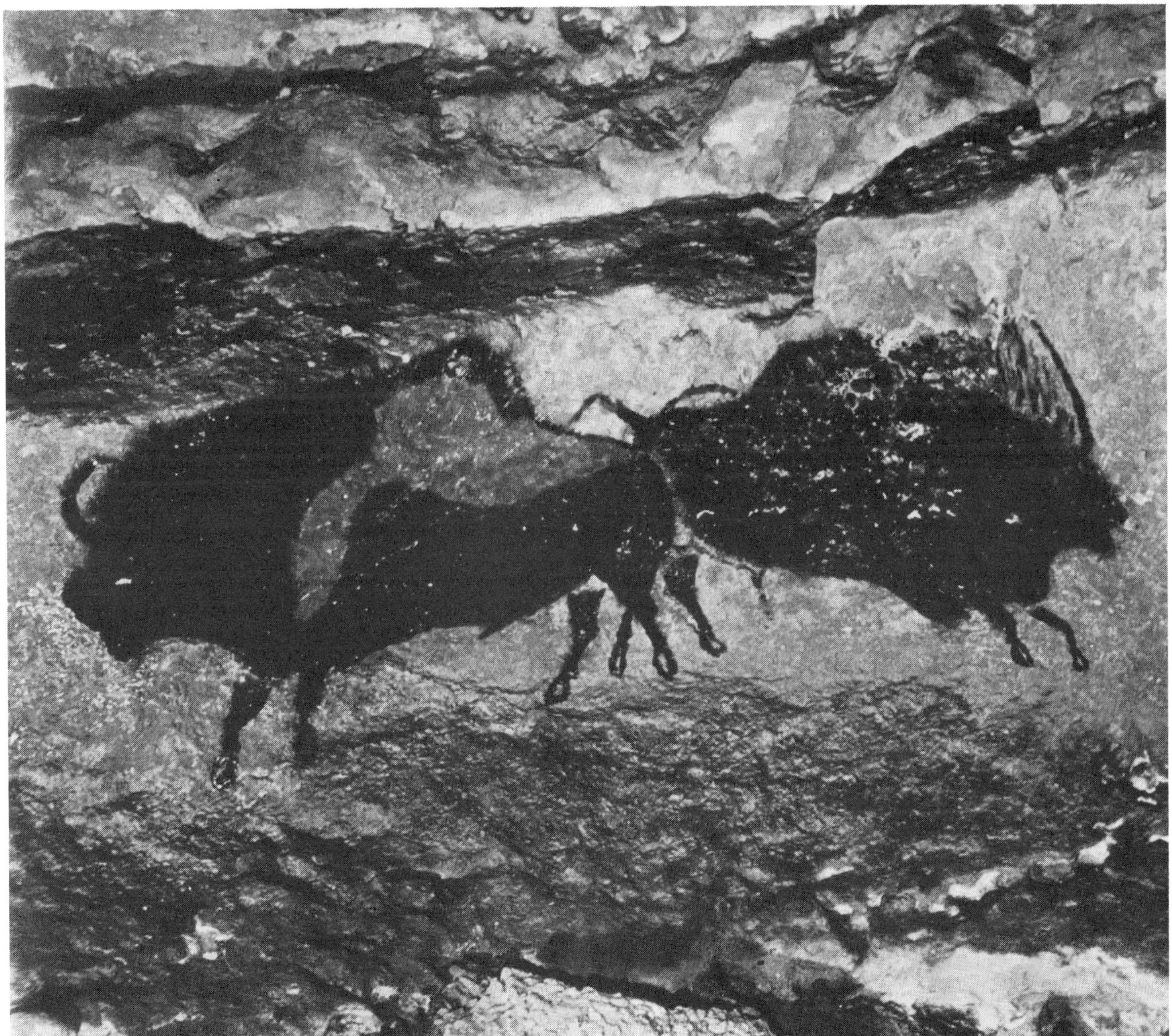

abundantly represented in the camp debris of these Upper Paleolithic social forms. Moreover, though the archaeological record is less clear, if these hunting and gathering forms were in any way similar to most contemporary hunting and gathering peoples, plant foods constituted by far the greatest proportion of their diets.

But as yet we have not discussed the social relations involved in this productive activity, nor any appropriation which might be involved in specific divisions of labour. Certainly both men and women are capable of all activities – even game hunting does not preclude women, as it depends far more on organization than on superordinate strength. Moreover, we have data on the elaborate baby-minding arrangements practised by women in hunting and gathering societies to enable mothers to undertake an extended gathering trip (cf. Lee 1969). There is thus no automatic division of labour apparent from the nature of the productive activity itself.

But, again extrapolating from existing hunting and gathering social forms, and known divisions of labour in such societies, it is very likely that males were organized into parties to pursue the animals illustrated, while females were primarily responsible for carrying water and wood, and gathering the plant foods so critical to the diet. Again comparing with contemporary hunting and gathering forms, women probably also hunted small animals such as rodents, either deliberately with snares or casually when encountered on gathering trips. It is likely that men spent most of their time in organizing hunting parties, in actual hunts, in minor hunting (which sharpened skills and probably provided the major source of meat, albeit from smaller, less celebrated animals that could be easily killed by a single hunter) and in discussions, tales, art, and ritual endeavour surrounding the hunt.

This is not, of course, the only possible division of labour, but it is consistent with the constellation of social relations of production with which we are familiar from existing hunting and gathering groups, and which we intuitively associate with the Paleolithic as well. It is in such a context that, I would argue, we can read the significance, in its elaborated form, of Upper Paleolithic art traditions. We can see the aesthetic manifestations as constituting social relations in which one half of the productive population (all men) engages in activity which produces a minority of the subsistence of the group, while another half of the productive population (all women) produces a majority of the subsistence for the group.[17] Here is the content which is signified by the observed form – this is the means by which the elaboration may be read.

The form of the female figures is thus relevant. There is a deliberate avoidance of individuation of heads or faces. (Figs. 7.18, 7.19.) Emphasis and elaboration is evident in ponderous breasts and in mid-body obesity (or pregnancy?) (Figs. 7.17, 7.18). If females actually had these shapes, they could not have engaged comfortably in hunting pursuits – nor, indeed, perhaps in anything else that required much physical exertion except the minimum required specifically for child-rearing, nursing, and camp-bound activity. They are

Fig. 7.16. Frieze of rhinoceros and frieze of mammoth, the Breuil gallery, Rouffignac, France. The mammoth and rhinoceros appear in outline only, though dimension and perspective are illustrated in the animal legs. Each rhinoceros is approximately 101 cm high, and each mammoth about half that size. From Leroi-Gourhan 1967. Photograph courtesy of Jean Vertut.

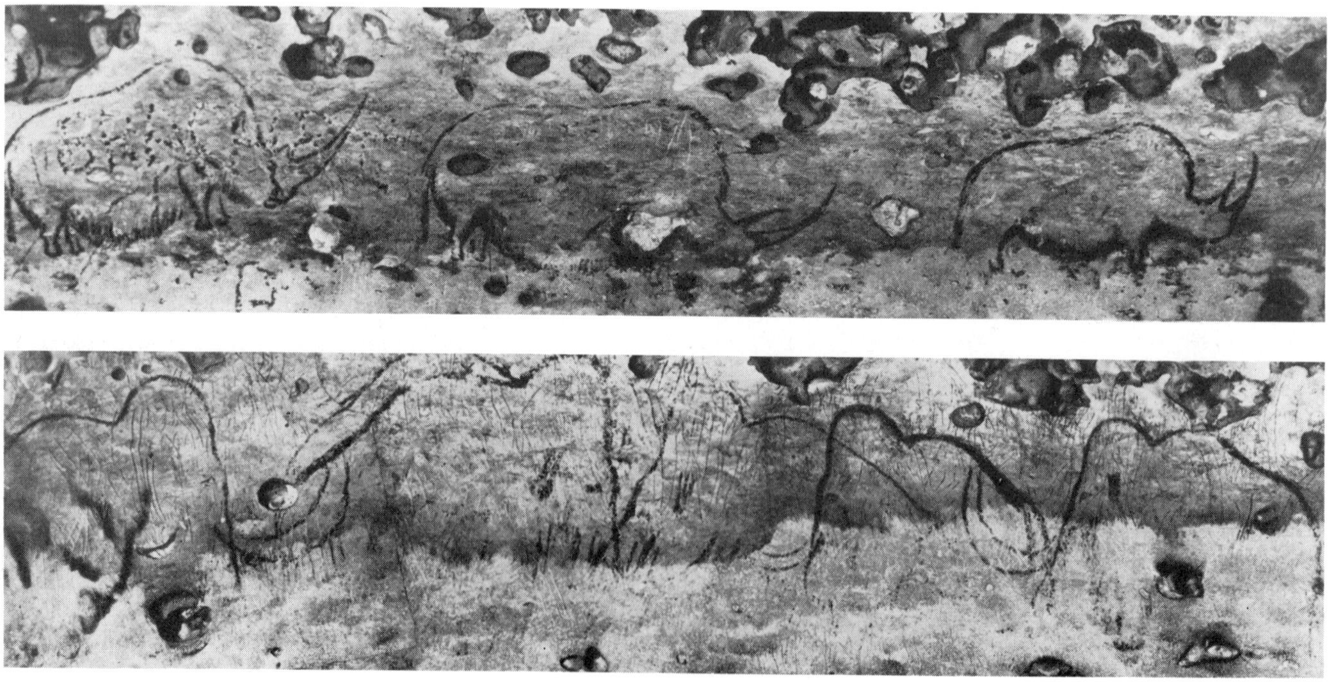

presented in a nomenclature of storage and reproduction – of milk and fat – in the steatopygic buttocks and bulbous breasts, or they are presented in sexual or reproductive postures (Figs. 7.19, 7.20). Certainly in every case there is signified some aspect of female physiology, usually in the form of some attribute of reproduction. Production, indeed, is denigrated. Elaboration is in the direction of significance to reproduction.

In contrast, the anatomical accuracy and particular presentation of animal forms in the parietal art or in sculpture is striking. Even where the art forms become haptic (Fig. 7.15), control and sophistication are evident, and such distortion gives the impression of command, not error. Moreover, an impressive array of colours is used, and not infrequently the paintings are at the tops of chambers, so that elaborate scaffolding was undoubtedly required. The overall impression, then, is one of considerable time consumed in such endeavour – in actual execution, as well as perhaps in training to master the nuances of shade, perspective and line so impressive in Upper Paleolithic art.[18]

Fig. 7.17. This chart, from Leroi-Gourhan (1967: 520), indicates the modelling of the female figures. These small sculptures, from a wide geographic area, with their deliberately avoided heads, arms and feet, and their deliberate attention to mid-body obesity and ponderous breasts, are shown in full round. The sophisticated mid-body musculature and obesity is striking. a, b: Kostienki (Soviet Union); c: Lespugue (France); d: Willendorf (Germany). c and d are from Musée de l'Homme, Paris, and Museum of Natural History, Vienna, respectively.

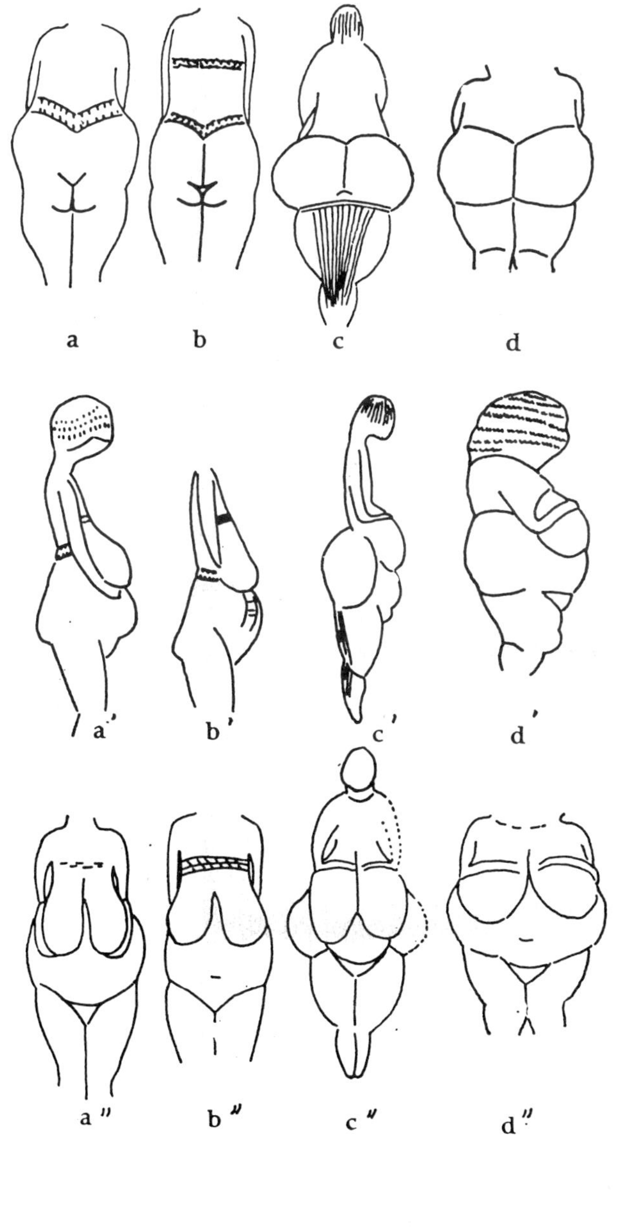

The totality of the art, then, can be read as significant to the social relations of production – assuming such relations are as noted for contemporary hunting and gathering groups. The aesthetic manifestations vividly constitute such social relations – such divisions of labour. Both male and female activities are represented in their most extreme characters – men as pursuers of game they did not always pursue, but which required an organization and knowledge not perhaps so necessary for less flamboyant beasts (which probably furnished the bulk of meat consumed). Women are represented in a caricature of physiology and reproductive dimensions, when in all likelihood women did not appear anything like this, and could not have done so and been active in most ways. But it is the significance of the art form that is of interest to the reading here, and this, particularly when seen alongside the manifestations that do not occur – plants, small animals, and men in any posture – enables such a reading.

The subjects of the division of labour so signified were constituted thus: men as pursuers of great Pleistocene animals, and women as nurses and reproducers. That men and women, of course, actually sometimes did these things is important, but it is equally important, extrapolating from contemporary hunting and gathering forms, and considering the Upper Paleolithic aesthetic tradition, that men appropriated from the gathering and hunting activities of women, and that small animals and plants so acquired probably formed the majority of subsistence. The elaboration in form, indeed, gives meaning to the content, and significance to the aesthetic tradition for the social relations of Upper Paleolithic social forms of Europe.

Conclusions

The focus on elaboration is generally part of the structuralist tradition in art history and anthropology. Many analyses have spelled out the concatenation of form dictates, and we now have many examples of rigorous descriptions which elucidate structural morphology and the permutations of compositional logic. But a political reading of such elaboration – the content *in* form – has received less attention. What, in other words, could be the significance of elaboration in form?

I have indicated here a reading of the content of form, the structure of content – the elaboration – involving a relationship of the elements existing as an effect of the process of signification for the social relations of production. Our focus on elaboration stems from an explicit political theorization of the social relations and what significance might be appropriate to them. This gives us the readings of the specific traditions presented. In other words, could the Upper Paleolithic Venuses or the Rubensesque poses of Figure 7.19 have significance for non-sexist (and non-appropriative) social relations? I have argued to the contrary, and thus read them as constituting a division of labour based about gender. And, if our extrapolation from contemporary hunting and gathering forms is adequate, they may be read as sexist and relevant to appropriative social relations of production.

These readings can perhaps best be understood by contrast with alternative readings of social relations of production such as those that would read social forms in Upper Paleolithic Europe or the Southeast Nuba as basically egali-

Fig. 7.18. Female parietal sculpture, Laussel, France. These sculptures are very much in the genre of the small amulets of Fig. 7.17. The significance of the bison horn is unclear (though it may contain something), but the obesity of the mid-body is again evident, in sophisticated representation. Arms, heads, feet, and hands are again unregarded. The line drawing illustrates the identical outline of three sculptures, establishing the less-defined petroglyph as part of the same group and the same genre. All from Leroi-Gourhan 1967. Photographs courtesy Jean Vertut.

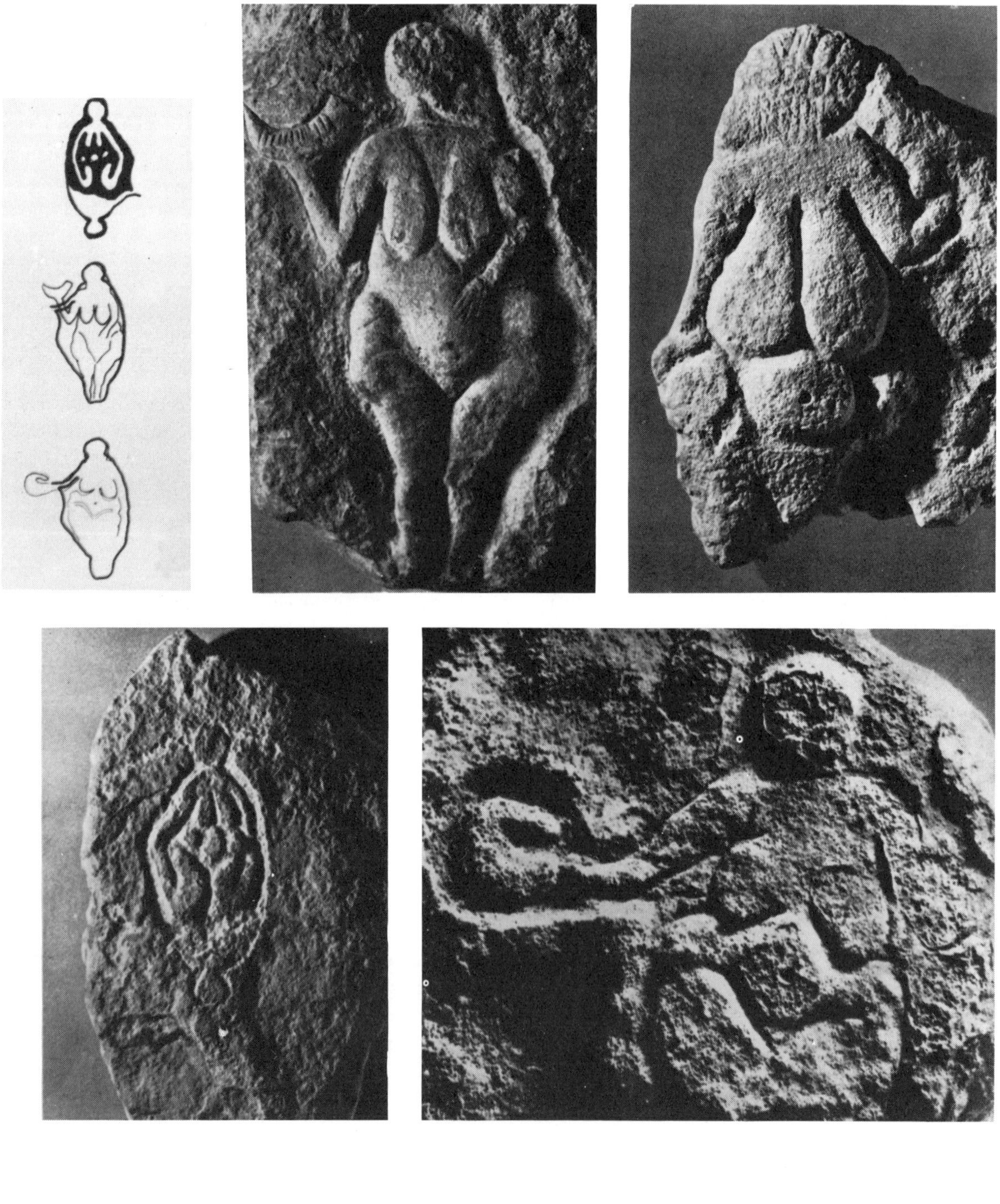

Fig. 7.19. These two delicately sculpted females from La Magdelaine, France, are unique in Paleolithic art and curiously modern in posture. But the Rubensesque pose can also perhaps be read as significant. There is no conceivable productive activity that could be represented here. Both photographs from Leroi-Gourhan 1967. Courtesy Jean Vertut.

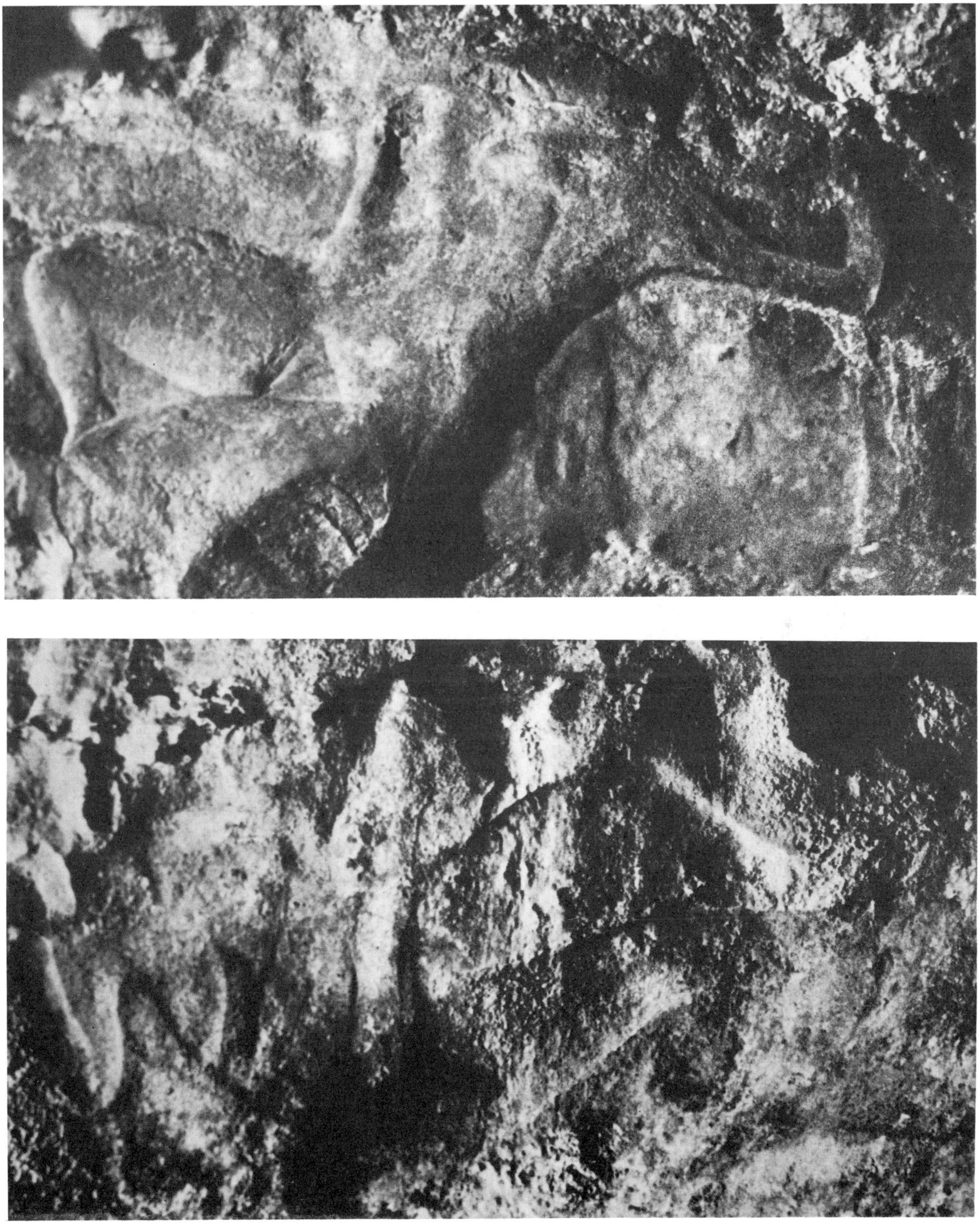

tarian, and thus not consistent with the significance we have assigned to the art traditions (this view is found, for example, in the work of Eleanor Leacock (cf. Leacock 1978)), or those views of Northwest Coast social forms which argue that the social relations of production are basically redistributive or ecologically maintaining (Suttles 1960; Vayda 1961). In such alternative readings the signification of the art traditions would necessarily be something else.

However, in the readings suggested here, essentially around the elaboration in form – in the content *of* form – we can perhaps also emancipate the art traditions from the authority in which they are held by the indigenous cultural discourse (cf. Benjamin 1969: 220) and thus appreciate them for ourselves. For with the advantage of history, the Bastille and the Cheops pyramid are no longer massive symbols of repressive systems, but free to the aesthetics of our own ideological system.[19]

Fig. 7.20. Frieze of women from Angles sur l'Anglin, France. This line drawing is of a low-relief and engraved petroglyph, and the women are shown from the waist down only. Whatever the reading, the representation here is clear and the physiological foci unmistakable. From Ucko and Rosenfeld 1967.

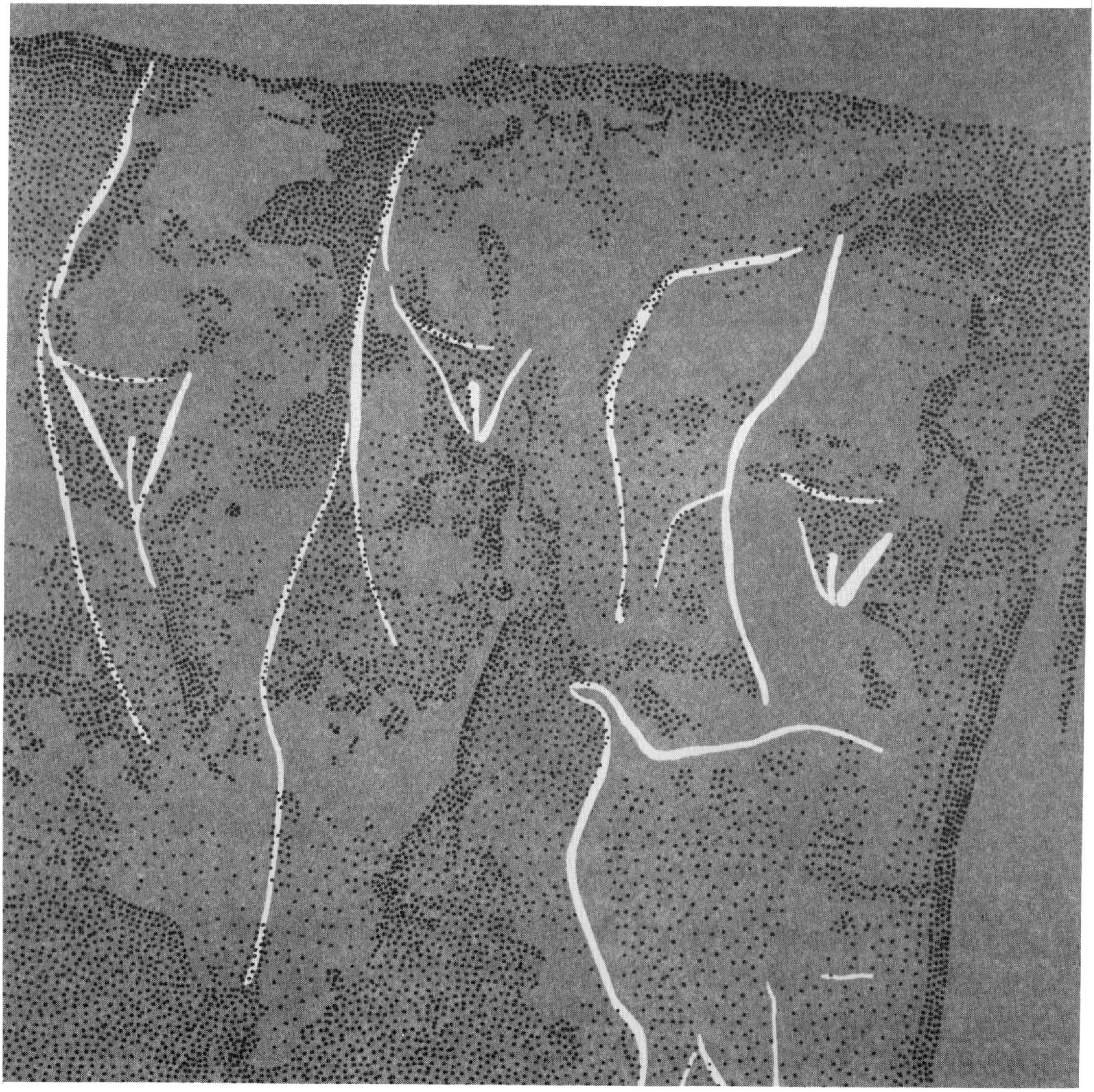

Notes

1 Washburn (1977) for example, modestly suggests little more of her impressive work than improved systematic comparison in ceramic classification.

2 Quite apart from their essentialism, such references are analytically superficial and of no significance from a formal point of view.

3 For development of the notion of such 'reading', and of the development of epistemologically free discursive practices, see Foucault 1973; Hindess 1977; Ennew 1976; Rose 1977; Fish 1980.

4 However instrumental he may consider cultural models, Lévi-Strauss is more interested in elucidating a structural 'operator' common to all ideologies, resting in human reason, and expressed in all cultural manifestations: 'I believe there is always a mediator between *praxis* and practices, namely the conceptual scheme by the operation of which matter and form, neither with any independent existence, are realized as structures, that is as entities which are both empirical and intelligible' (1966: 130) (emphasis and syntax in original). In the present analysis, such a 'conceptual scheme' reveals but another empiricist appeal – to yet another 'reality'.

5 The focus on production and the consequent division of labour is not to be understood as some type of economic determinism or an essentialist reduction of human social activity to labour. It is simply the basis of a political reading which criticizes other readings (argued here also to be implicitly political) in an attempt to solve certain theoretical problems as to how to approach aesthetic traditions and other ideologies. These problems involve a specification (or indicate or eliminate what they could not specify) of the effects of egalitarian social relations – in particular effects in and of aesthetic traditions. In attempting to establish such discourse, we read potential significance of existing traditions for these theorized alternative social relations. In other words, we examine the structure – the content and form – of constituted aesthetic systems, and ask if these could be significant to egalitarian social relations. If not, then our political critique suggests their significance to the actual social relations under scrutiny, social relations which we argue are not egalitarian. Then we are in a position to suggest how form in the aesthetic tradition can be read to signify content. The term 'political' retains its classical meaning, but its use here is theoretical, and not rhetorical.

6 This is by no means to suggest any generality or universality. It is only meant to suggest that in these circumstances, in these conditions, elaboration may be viewed to have these effects by reference to the political reading of the analysis.

7 Indeed, if a fundamental functional unity is theorized (and thus a 'correct' reading established), political struggles become battles over different conceptions of reality instead of struggles over better ways to arrange social relations.

8 'Northwest Coast' is here meant to include all those social forms (and their art products) from the Kwakiutl of Vancouver Island and adjacent mainland to the south, to – and including – the Tlingit of southeastern Alaska to the north. It includes the offshore Haida as well.

9 Indeed, while abstraction may be viewed as a reverse of redundancy, the two cannot be confused. Mondrian and Kandinsky eliminated redundancy in their abstraction, whereas De Kooning and Pollock, for example, expressed their abstraction in redundancy and elaboration. In all cases, meaning was the expression of the abstraction itself.

10 Indeed, early ciné films of dances and other display events are interesting, for the choreography itself was executed to display the robes, masks, crests, helmets, etc. of the dancers, and not their footwork as such. The dance and drama served the plastic and graphic art, and not vice versa.

11 This brief presentation is inadequate to consider exhaustively the detailed division of labour, particularly as it involved sexual divisions. Women of commoner status are seldom mentioned, except as providers of services and production. Drucker, in fact, classes them, with only one exception, with commoners who laboured (Drucker 1951: 253). Even though females were probably the actual artisans in some woven productions such as capes and baskets, the crests and masks and representations in the art traditions are almost never of natural phenomena which were probably the subject of women's productive activities (i.e., they were principally of hunted animals and never of gathered foods and only rarely of smaller animals which women predominantly secured).

12 Indeed, as certain representations require specific colours (and not others), elaboration is also possible in the species represented with increasing age – until 'retirement' to non-decorating elderhood (see Faris 1972b).

13 Though earlier accounts were adequate descriptions of the logic of form permutation and elaboration, such treatments remained politically impotent in that the signification of such traditions was not theorized beyond the local ideology (Faris 1972a; 1978).

14 There are, of course, no 'knife' fights. Riefenstahl's grotesque treatment of the Southeast Nuba (for critique, see Faris 1980; Iten 1977), celebrated in the popular press and elsewhere, has had very unfortunate consequences in a wide area of Southern Kordofan, and indeed, for serious research elsewhere in Sudan.

15 In time, the period covered includes the Gravettian, Solutrean, and Magdalenian – from approximately 23,000 to approximately 12,000 years ago; and the area involved covers northern Spain, southern France, and central and eastern Europe.

16 Raymond and Liebowitz (n.d.) suggest that the 'Venuses', as they are known, survive and are presented to us in excess of their importance, and the scholarly emphasis on the female forms is a function of more contemporary sexism. However true the latter may be, men are very rarely represented in any clear form whatsoever in Paleolithic art. And however true the sexism in their presentation to date, an alternative political reading of the sculptural forms is still required.

17 Even if big game meat is considered sufficiently important to require expending one half the productive population in its acquisition, this still begs the question as to why the half so engaged is all male. If such a division of labour were indeed biologically necessitated, its aesthetic constitution would be irrelevant, unnecessary, and probably impossible.

18 The female sculpture is the product, of course, of equal time and expended skill – indeed, a point in this reading is the exaggerated direction of elaboration in both parietal and in sculptural form. The female representations are quite sophisticated and deliberate in their execution.

19 I want to thank Robin Brown and Dorothy Washburn for their help in clarifying the discussion herein. Of course this acknowledgement does not commit them to the unclarity remaining, nor to agreement with the thesis.

References

Anderson, R., 1979. *Art in Primitive Societies.* Prentice Hall, Englewood Cliffs, N.J.

Benjamin, W., 1969. *Illuminations.* Schocken Books, New York.

Boas, F., 1955. *Primitive Art.* Dover, New York.

Codere, H., 1950. *Fighting with Property: A Study of Kwakiutl Potlatching and Warfare, 1792–1950.* Monographs of the American Ethnological Society, No. 18.

Crowe, D., 1971. The geometry of African art I. Bakuba art. *Journal of Geometry* 1 (2): 169–82.

Cutler, T., B. Hindess, P. Hirst, A. Hussain, 1977. *Marx's Capital and Capitalism Today*, I. Routledge and Kegan Paul, London.

Drucker, P., 1951. *The Northern and Central Nootkan Tribes.* Bureau of American Ethnology Bulletin No. 44. Washington, D.C.

Ennew, J., 1976. Examining the facts of fieldwork: considerations on method and data. *Critique of Anthropology* 7: 43–66.

Faris, J., 1968. The lexicon of occasions in Cat Harbour: validation in ethnographical description. *Man* 3 (1): 112–24.

1969a. Sibling terminology and cross-sex behavior: data from the Southeastern Nuba mountains. *American Anthropologist* 71 (3): 482–8.

1969b. Some cultural considerations of duolineal descent organization. *Ethnology* 8 (3): 243–54.

1972a. *Nuba Personal Art.* Duckworth, London.

1972b. Southeastern Nuba age organization. In *Essays in Sudan Ethnography Presented to Sir Edward Evans-Pritchard*, edited by I. Cunnison and W. James. C. Hurst, London.

1978. The productive basis of aesthetic traditions: some African examples. In *Art in Society*, edited by M. Greenhalgh and J. Megaw. Duckworth, London.

1980. Polluted vision. *Sudanow* 5 (5): 38.

Fish, S., 1980. *Is There a Text in This Class?*. Harvard University Press, Cambridge, Mass.

Foucault, M., 1972. *The Archaeology of Knowledge.* Tavistock Publications, London.

1973. *The Birth of the Clinic.* Tavistock Publications, London.

Friedrich, M., 1970. Design structure and social interaction: archaeological implications of an ethnographic analysis. *American Antiquity* 35 (3): 332–43.

Gunther, E., 1971. Northwest Coast Indian art. In *Anthropology and Art*, edited by C. Otten. Natural History Press, Garden City.

Hawthorne, A., 1967. *Art of the Kwakiutl Indians.* University of Washington Press, Seattle.

1979. *Kwakiutl Art.* University of Washington Press, Seattle.

Hindess, B., 1977. *Philosophy and Methodology in the Social Sciences.* Harvester Press, Hassocks, Sussex.

Holm, B., 1965. *Northwest Coast Indian Art.* University of Washington Press, Seattle.

Inverarity, R., 1950. *Art of the Northwest Coast Indians.* University of California Press, Berkeley.

Iten, O., 1977. Bilder und Zarrbilder der Nuba. *Tages Anzeiger Magazin.* Inhalt Nr. 50 (17): 6.

Kiparsky, P., 1968. Language universals and linguistic change. In *Universals in Linguistic Theory*, edited by E. Bach and R. Harms. Holt, Rinehart and Winston, New York.

Labov, W., 1972. *Sociolinguistic Patterns.* University of Pennsylvania Press, Philadelphia.

Leacock, E. 1978. Women's status in egalitarian societies: implications for social evolution. *Current Anthropology* 19 (2): 247–75.

Lee, R. 1969. !Kung Bushman subsistence: an input–output analysis. In *Environment and Cultural Behavior: Ecological Studies in Cultural Anthropology*, edited by A. Vayda. Natural History Press, Garden City.

Leroi-Gourhan, A., 1967. *Treasures of Prehistoric Art.* H. Abrams, New York.

Lévi-Strauss, C., 1963. *Structural Anthropology.* Basic Books, New York.

1966. *The Savage Mind.* Weidenfeld and Nicolson, London.

Oberg, K., 1973. *The Social Economy of the Tlingit Indians.* University of Washington Press, Seattle.

Raphael, M., 1945. *Prehistorical Cave Paintings.* Bollingen Series, Pantheon Press, Washington, D.C.

Raymond, N., and L. Liebowitz, n.d. Venuses and penises: anthropomorphic figurines of the Upper Paleolithic.

Riefenstahl, L., 1976. *The People of Kau.* Harper and Row, New York.

Rose, N., 1977. Fetishism and ideology: a review of theoretical problems. *Ideology and Consciousness* 2: 27–54.

Ruyle, E., 1973. Slavery, surplus, and stratification on the Northwest Coast: the ethnoenergetics of an incipient stratification system. *Current Anthropology* 14 (5): 603–31.

Suttles, W., 1960. Affinal ties, subsistence, and prestige among the Coast Salish. *American Anthropologist* 62: 296–305.

Ucko, P., and A. Rosenfeld, 1967. *Paleolithic Cave Art.* McGraw-Hill, New York.

Vastokas, J., 1978. Cognitive aspects of Northwest Coast art. In *Art in Society*, edited by M. Greenhalgh and J. Megaw. Duckworth, London.

Vayda, A., 1961. A re-examination of Northwest Coast economic systems. *Transactions of the New York Academy of Sciences* (series 2) 23: 618–24.

Washburn, D., 1977. A symmetry analysis of Upper Gila area ceramic design. *Papers of the Peabody Museum of Archaeology and Ethnology*, No. 68. Harvard University, Cambridge, Mass.

Watt, W., 1966. Morphology of the Nevada cattlebrands and their blazons, Part 1. *National Bureau of Standards Report* 9050. Government Printing Office, Washington, D.C.

Chapter 8

Temporal shifts in the structure of traditional Southwestern textile design

Kate P. Kent

The textile arts have been an essential component of prehistoric Southwestern cultures from the earliest known horizons to the coming of the Spanish in the mid-sixteenth century, and survive today in the context of ceremonial costumes among the Pueblo peoples.[1] The earliest fabrics were made by a number of non-loom processes of yarn spun or twisted from wild plant fibres, human hair, and the hair and wool of a number of wild animals and of the domestic dog. They took the form of carrying bands, cradle bands, weft-twined and looped bags, braided sashes, apron fronts, warp-faced belting, some footgear, fur blankets, and possibly plain weave fibre yarn blankets. Cotton, introduced among the Hohokam of southern Arizona and the Mogollon of southwestern New Mexico, perhaps as early as A.D. 1, made its appearance in the Four Corners area among the Anasazi by A.D. 600. Some four hundred years after that time, the cotton plant was being grown all over the Southwest wherever conditions permitted. Cotton yarn quickly displaced indigenous fibres for virtually all clothing needs, although plant fibres and animal and human hair were used where durable or warm yarns were desired. Most cotton fabrics were woven on a loom equipped with heddles. The list of products is long, and includes blankets, shirts, kilts, breechcloths, sashes, belts, and bags. Certain non-loom processes survived from earlier times.

In spite of their undoubted artistic, economic, social, and religious importance, only about 3,000 examples of prehistoric fabrics, mostly fragmentary, have survived in archaeological sites. Of this number less than 150 bear the kind of complex geometric patterning on which this analysis of design styles is based. Tables 8.1 and 8.2 list 77 of these which were large enough to yield usable information.

There are many problems inherent in the study of archaeological textiles. They are not only limited in number, but their distribution in time and space, regulated by the physical conditions to which they have been subjected through the centuries, may not reflect cultural realities. Vegetal material generally survives only if protected from moisture. This means that a village constructed in a cave or under a cliff overhang, as for example White House in Canyon de Chelly, will yield a considerable quantity of textiles, whereas very little survives in an open site of comparable cultural sophistication such as Pueblo Bonito in Chaco Canyon. This does not mean that woven clothing was not fully as important at Pueblo Bonito as in other Southwestern communities of the time; it simply indicates the inevitable deficiencies in our records. While our data base is thus severely limited, it is not apt to be expanded at any time in the future. It seems important to offer some interpretation of the little we have, nevertheless, in the hope of adding to our knowledge of the evolution and interrelationships of Southwestern art forms.

Source or Figure no.	Provenience	Article	Symmetry processes
Fig. 8.4B	Prayer Rock Caves, BM III	Under surface of sandal sole	Mirror reflection across a central vertical axis
Tanner 1976: Fig. 3.13a, 2nd from left	"	Under surface of sandal sole	Mirror reflection across a central vertical axis
Fig. 8.5D	"	Woman's apron front	Field divided horizontally into two panels. Within each panel motifs move by reflection.
E.A. Morris 1980: Fig. 66c	"	Woman's apron front	Field divided horizontally into two panels. Motif moves by reflection in top panel; reflection across the central vertical axis in bottom panel.
E.A. Morris 1980: Fig. 66d	"	Woman's apron front	Field divided horizontally into 4 panels. Motifs, different in each panel, move by reflection. Total design shows reflection across the central vertical axis.
Fig. 8.3B	"	Under surface of sandal sole	Field divided into vertical panels. Motifs in mirror reflection with textural counter-change across vertical axis.
Tanner 1976: Fig. 3.13a, far right	"	Under surface of sandal sole	Same
Fig. 8.5B	"	Woman's apron front	Motif reflects across central vertical axis with colour counterchange.
Fig. 8.4A	"	Upper surface of sandal sole	Two design units. Bifold rotation of motifs in each unit. One unit moves into other by bifold rotation around a point on the central axis.
Kent 1957: Fig. 47A1	Vandal Cave BM III	Carrying band	Motifs paired along vertical axis. Move by bifold rotation. Many design irregularities.
Fig. 8.6	Duggagei Canyon BM III	Woman's apron front	Two design units. Bifold rotation of motifs in each unit. One unit moves into other by bifold rotation with colour counterchange around a point on the central vertical axis.
Fig. 8.5C	Prayer Rock Caves, BM III	Woman's apron front	Field divided into 8 vertical panels. Each motif worked over 3 panels by bifold rotation. One motif rotates into the next with colour change. 3 colours.
Fig. 8.3F	Prayer Rock Caves, BM III	Narrow band	Field divided into oblique bands. Two motifs alternate with colour counterchange. Motifs move by bifold rotation.
Tanner 1976: Fig. 3.13b, centre	Prayer Rock Caves, BM III	Upper surface of sandal sole	Design motifs move by bifold rotation along oblique line axes.
Fig. 8.5A	Prayer Rock Caves, BM III	Woman's apron front	Field divided by oblique lines. Motifs move by bifold rotation with colour counterchange along each line.

Source or Figure no.	Provenience	Article	Symmetry processes
Fig. 8.3E	Ruin near Nitsie Canyon BM III-P I?	Cradle band	Field divided into 3 blocks. Two motifs alternate. Bifold rotation of motifs within each block.
Tanner 1976: Fig. 3.13a, centre	Prayer Rock Caves, BM III	Under surface of sandal sole	Central vertical line cuts field in half. Halves relate by translation. Within each half symmetry movements are vertical reflection and bifold rotation.
Tanner 1976: Fig. 3.13b, left	Prayer Rock Caves, BM III	Upper surface of sandal sole	Field divided in half vertically. Motifs move by vertical reflection and bifold rotation.
Fig. 8.3D	Northern Arizona, BM III?	Carrying band	Same
Kent, in press: Fig. 129F	Tsegi, P I	Carrying band	Same
Kent, in press: Fig. 129D	Tsegi, P I	Carrying band	Two vertical zigzag line motifs move by reflection and bifold rotation.
Tanner 1976: Fig. 3.15c	Site? BM III-P I	Carrying band	Field divided into oblique panels. Triangles move along obliques by translation.
Tanner 1976: Fig. 3.15d	Site? BM III	Carrying band	Same
Fig. 8.3A	Prayer Rock Caves, BM III	Under surface of sandal sole	Field divided into 5 vertical panels. Motifs move by translation with textural counter-change.
Kent, in press: Plate 5	Canyon del Muerto, BM III	Upper surfaces of a pair of sandals	Design probably asymmetric. Repeats in soles with colour counterchange.
Kent, in press: Fig. 129A	Tsegi, BM III	Carrying band	Field divided into 5 rectangular blocks. Two motifs alternate.
Tanner 1976: Fig. 3.13b, right	Prayer Rock Caves, BM III	Upper surface of sandal sole	Finite design on toe section. Bilaterally symmetrical.
Keleman 1944: Fig. 170c	Northern Arizona ?BM III-P I	Carrying band	Design 'extracted' from 2-dimensional pattern based on slide reflection and bifold rotation.
Tanner 1976: Fig. 3.15b	Prayer Rock Caves, BM III	Carrying band	Field divided into rectangular blocks by horizontal lines. Designs within blocks too dim for analysis.
Tanner 1976: Fig. 3.15b	Site? BM III	Carrying band	Same
Tanner 1976: Fig. 3.15b	Site? BM III	Carrying band	Same
Fig. 8.3C	Northern Arizona BM III	Carrying band	Field divided into 7 rectangular blocks by horizontal lines. Remaining motifs show bifold rotation.

Explanatory notes: Thirty-two narrow band designs have been analysed. These appear on the upper and under surfaces of sandal soles, carrying bands, cradle bands, and women's apron fronts. Designs on the upper surfaces of sandal soles, women's aprons and narrow bands are generally created by coloured wefts, although a very few are painted. The under surfaces of sandal soles are patterned by designs worked in a knotting technique, so that one finds textual variation, rather than colour contrasts.

Source or Figure no.	Provenience	Article	Symmetry processes	Other design characteristics
Anasazi				
Fig. 8.9	Nitsie Canyon	Weft-wrap openwork rectangular cloth, 39 cm x 31.7 cm	Bifold rotation & slide reflection. Centre motif & four arms.	Large scale. Terraced triangle. Anasazi style.
Fig. 8.11B	Northern Arizona	Slit tapestry band fragment	Centre motif from design based on bifold rotation & slide reflection	Large scale. Br/w negative design. Terraced triangles.
Fig. 8.10	Grand Gulch	Diamond twill tapestry blanket	Bifold rotation & slide reflection	Red/br/w small scale elements, terraced triangles.
Kent 1957: Fig. 66	Northern Arizona	Diamond twill tapestry fragment	?	Large scale. Br/w negative design. Terraced triangles.
Kent 1957: Fig. 67A	White House	Irregular twill tapestry fragment	?	Large scale. Bl/w negative design. Terraced triangles.
Fig. 8.12	Mesa Verde	Probably irregular twill tapestry border on plain weave cloth	Design extracted from two-dimensional pattern. Bifold rotation.	Br/w. Terraced triangles.
Kent 1957: Fig. 97A1	Grand Gulch	Twill weave cloth, white, 33.6 cm square. Black centre motif.	Finite	Smooth-edged triangles, Sinagua–Salado style.
Fig. 8.11A	White House	Tapestry weave breech cloth front. Extra-weft float pattern.	Centre motif from design based on bifold rotation & slide reflection	Large scale. Bl/w negative design. Terraced triangles.
Kent 1957: Fig. 85	White House	Plain weave fragment, painted	Bifold rotation of motifs within design bands	Red/white negative painting.
Fig. 8.13	Painted Cave	Plain weave blanket, painted	Bifold rotation & slide reflection. Centre motif & 4 arms. Bifold rotation of small motifs within arms.	Large scale. Bl/w negative painting in arms of design.
Haury 1945: Plate 12a	Painted Cave	Plain weave painted blanket	Same	Bl/w negative painting in some arms of design. Large scale.
Haury 1945: Plate 12b	Painted Cave	Plain weave shirt, painted	Asymmetric linear border design.	
Kent 1957: Fig. 32F	White House	Twined-stitch embroidery on plain weave fragment	Bifold rotation. Meander pattern.	
Kent 1957: Fig. 117A	Kiet Siel	Tapestry weave apron band	Alternate translation of two motifs. Oblique axes.	Br/w, terraced triangles.

Source or Figure no.	Provenience	Article	Symmetry processes	Other design characteristics
Kent 1957: Fig. 119	Northern Arizona	Tapestry weave apron band	Motifs move by bifold rotation	Br/w, terraced triangles.
Kent 1957: Fig. 22E	Canyon de Chelly? (Design indicates a trade piece)	Weft-wrap openwork fragment	Design structure not evident	Triangle-hooks, Sinagua–Salado style plus sharp triangle, Hohokam style. Plain white.
Kent 1957: Fig. 27	Kayenta area? (Design indicates a trade piece)	Weft-wrap openwork fragment	Design structure not evident	Triangle-hook, Sinagua–Salado style. Plain white.
Sinagua–Salado				
Kent 1957: Fig. 31	Clear Creek, Verde Valley, Sinagua	Extra-weft float pattern weave bag, 13.9 cm × 7.6 cm	Bifold rotation & slide reflection	Br/w. Small bars replace triangles.
Kent 1957: Fig. 36	Walnut Canyon, Sinagua	Embroidered fragment	Probably bifold rotation & slide reflection	Br/blue/w, colour counterchange. Triangle hook motif, Sinagua–Salado style.
Kent 1957: Fig. 37A	Tonto Monument, Salado	Embroidered border on plain weave cloth, fragment	Probably bifold rotation & slide reflection	White on white. Triangle-hook motif.
Kent 1957: Fig. 37B	Tonto National Monument, Salado	Embroidery on plain weave cloth, fragment	Same	Dark blue-green embroidery on white. Triangle-hook motif.
Kent 1957: Fig. 39	Hidden House, Sinagua	Plain weave tapestry, quiver body	Bifold rotation & slide reflection	Br/blue/w, colour counterchange. Triangle-hook motif.
Kent 1957: Fig. 41	Hidden House, Sinagua	Plain weave tapestry, quiver tab	Elements placed along oblique axes	Br/blue/w colour counterchange. Triangles, triangle-hook, rectangle. Sinagua–Salado style.
Kent 1957: Fig. 43	Hidden House, Sinagua	Plain weave kilt with tapestry insets	Triangles move along oblique axes by reflection	Bl/blue/w colour counterchange. Triangles. Sinagua–Salado style.
Kent 1957: Fig. 70	Wupatki, Sinagua	Irregular twill tapestry weave border on plain weave cloth, fragment	Slide reflection & bifold rotation	Br/blue/w colour counterchange. Triangles, Sinagua–Salado style.
Fig. 8.8	Clear Creek near Camp Verde, Sinagua	Extra-weft float pattern weave cloth. 18.7 cm wide.	Bifold rotation & slide reflection	Br/w. Sharp triangles, Hohokam style.
Kent 1957: Fig. 72B	Hidden House, Sinagua	Irregular twill tapestry weave, quiver	Probably bifold rotation & slide reflection	Br/bl/w colour counterchange. Triangle-hook motifs.

Source or Figure no.	Provenience	Article	Symmetry processes	Other design characteristics
Fig. 8.14	Tonto Monument, Salado	Irregular twill tapestry weave breech cloth front	Bifold rotation & slide reflection	Br/blue/w colour counterchange. Triangle, rectangles, Sinagua–Salado style.
Kent 1957: Fig. 78	Montezuma Castle, Sinagua	Weft-float pattern weave bag made from cloth 63.5 cm x 14.6 cm	Symmetry not evident. Possibly mirror reflection.	Black wefts, white warps. A-typical design, may be imported from Mexico.
Kent 1957: p. 560	Montezuma Castle, Sinagua	Same	Same	Same
Kent 1957: Fig. 87	Hidden House, Sinagua	Plain weave painted blanket	Off-set quartering of field, but structural lines parallel warps & wefts	Black/white design, resembles Kayenta pottery.
Kent 1957: Fig. 111	Tonto Monument, Salado	Interlinked white shirt	Bifold rotation & slide reflection. Motif centred on shirt front.	Hooks & triangles used separately, Hohokam style, as is white openwork.
Kent, in press: Plate 15	Site near Montezuma Castle, Sinagua	Embroidery on white gauze weave, fragment	Hooks move along oblique axes by bifold rotation with colour counterchange	4 colours of weft. Gauze and hooks used without triangles, Hohokam style.
Kent 1957: Fig. 30B	Canyon Creek, Salado	Extra-weft float pattern weave fragment	Probably bifold rotation & slide reflection	Br/w. Sharp triangles, Hohokam style.
Kent 1957: Fig. 47C	Palatki, Salado	Plain weave tapestry band, 11.4 cm wide	Design possibly extracted from pattern based on bifold rotation & slide reflection	Three colours, colour counterchange. Triangles, Sinagua–Salado style.
Kent 1957: Fig. 24A	Cottonwood, Verde Valley, Sinagua	Plain weave cloth fragment, 39.3 cm long. Weft-wrap openwork finite designs.	Finite, bilateral symmetry	Triangles, Sinagua–Salado style. Plain white.
Fig. 8.17B	Canyon Creek, Salado	Weft-wrap openwork design on white cotton bag	Finite, bifold rotation	Triangles, Sinagua–Salado style. Plain white.
Hohokam and Mogollon				
Fig. 8.18	Mule Creek Cave, Southwest New Mexico, Mogollon	Weft-wrap openwork fragment, 22.8 cm x 20.7 cm	Two-dimensional, hooks in bifold rotation	Hooks used without triangles, and white openwork, Hohokam style.
Kent 1957: Fig. 21	Ventana Cave, Hohokam	Weft-wrap openwork fragment ca. 5 cm square	Design symmetry not evident. Bifold rotation of triangle elements.	Triangles, Hohokam style. Plain white.

Source or Figure no.	Provenience	Article	Symmetry processes	Other design characteristics
Kent 1957: Fig. 23	Ventana Cave, Hohokam	Weft-wrap openwork fragment, 44.4 cm x 44.7 cm	Design structure not evident. Bifold rotation of hooks in one band.	Hooks and sharp triangles, Hohokam style. Plain white.
Fig. 8.17E	Ventana Cave, Hohokam	Weft-wrap openwork & gauze weave child's poncho. Finite design on chest.	Finite, bilateral symmetry	Triangle-hook motif, Sinagua–Salado style. Plain white.
Fig. 8.17D	Bear Creek Cave, Southwestern New Mexico, Mogollon	Weft-wrap openwork fragment	Finite, bilateral symmetry	Plain white. Triangles, Sinagua–Salado style.
Fig. 8.17C	Casa Grande, Hohokam	Weft-wrap openwork fragment	Finite, asymmetric	Triangles, Sinagua–Salado style. Plain white.
Fig. 8.17A	Graham County, southeastern Arizona, Hohokam	Plain weave cloth 17.1 cm square, centre design in weft-wrap openwork	Finite, bilateral symmetry	Triangle-hook, Sinagua–Salado style. Plain white.
Fig. 8.17F	Tularosa Cave, Southwestern New Mexico, Mogollon	Diamond twill tapestry motif on plain weave white cloth	Finite, bifold rotation	Br/blue motifs, colour counterchange. Triangles, Sinagua–Salado style.

Explanatory note: Table 8.2 lists the forty-five late prehistoric textiles which furnished evidence of design styles. Seventeen come from Anasazi sites, although weft-wrap openwork fragments from Canyon de Chelly and the Kayenta area are certainly trade pieces from central or southern Arizona. Thirteen examples come from Sinagua sites in the Verde Valley and Wupatki, and seven from Salado sites. Sinagua–Salado pieces are listed together in the second part of the table. The third part includes five examples from southern Arizona, listed as Hohokam, and three Mogollon pieces from southwestern New Mexico. Diagnostic features of style other than design symmetry are listed in the right-hand column.

Kiva murals illustrating textile forms and designs have been found in the old Hopi towns of Awatovi and Kawaika-a, and at Pottery Mound and Kuaua in the middle Rio Grande Valley near the modern city of Albuquerque. These extend the record from about A.D. 1450 to the time of Spanish arrival in the Southwest in 1540. Our knowledge of historic textiles is drawn from museum collections dating from about 1850 to the present, as well as a handful of eighteenth-century fragments.

Textile designs may be grouped into two classes. The first, self-patterns, automatically derive from the construction process. This includes simple stripes, plaids, checks, and the various diagonal, herringbone, or diamond rib patterns created by twill weaves. The second class consists of complex designs built from small geometric elements, units or motifs. Prehistorically these were produced through the processes of plain and twill weave tapestry, brocade, weft-float pattern weave, warp-float pattern weave, weft-wrap openwork, and interlinking (or twine-plaiting). They were also applied to woven cloth by painting, tie-and-dye, and embroidery. Historically they are to be found only on textiles patterned by Hopi 'brocade' or embroidery. Such designs do not emerge automatically from the construction process. They are conceived by the artisan and imposed on his fabric in accordance with a kind of mental blueprint. An example may make the distinction clear. Suppose that the loom is strung for diamond twill. The weaver can then produce a self-pattern of all-over concentric diamonds simply by carrying each weft pick from selvage to selvage and maintaining a regular heddle order. The growth of the pattern is a mechanical process. The choice of weft materials and colours will affect the character of the finished product, but the structure will be identical no matter where or by whom the piece is woven. Using the same heddle rig, but a tapestry technique, the weaver can make each diamond or sets of diamonds a different colour, and thus build a complex pattern from small colour blocks (Fig. 8.10). The process is by no means automatic. The pattern results from conscious choice. Geometric patterns from different parts of the world may be quite varied in style even if woven in the same technique, because different choices have been made.

Geometric textile design styles may be defined in terms of two interrelated but conceptually distinguishable characteristics. The first is the overall *structure* – that is, the way in which the field has been subdivided for decoration, and the type of symmetry this creates. The second is the *composition* of the pattern, which encompasses the nature of the elements, units or motifs employed to fill subdivisions of the field – their shape, relative colour values, spacing, and the symmetry processes by which they have been combined. There are several excellent analyses of prehistoric and historic Pueblo pottery design utilizing these approaches (Shepard 1948, 1956; Smith 1952; Washburn 1977; Greenberg 1975). It is apparent from these studies, and from observation of contemporary Pueblo potters, that the total field was first sectioned off by the main structural lines of the design, and the areas thus defined further divided and filled in with motifs composed of small elements. It was not the elements themselves that primarily concerned the painter, but the symmetry of the total pattern and the larger motifs which it contained (Bunzel 1929: 13–51; Guthe 1925: 78).

This was unquestionably the way design was applied to painted fabrics prehistorically, but in the case of woven fabrics the pattern had to be built line by line, element by element. Technique controlled design to a degree not found in a medium like painting. The total composition and the structure on which it was based existed only in the abstract in the weaver's mind. He could not produce the main structural lines in physical form as a first step in creating his pattern. Instead he had to choose a construction technique which would allow him to weave elements of such a shape and size that, when combined in certain ways, they would create the desired structure.

There is a close correlation between weave technique and the shape and positioning of elements. For example, if the weaver wishes to produce a pattern of triangles along an oblique line, and uses a plain weave tapestry technique, the line will have a terraced or stepped appearance (Fig. 8.1A). If he weaves his triangles in diamond or irregular twill, his line will be smooth (Figs. 8.1B, C). If he chooses to weave a terraced triangle in diamond twill, the element will be placed obliquely to the warp–weft axis (Fig. 8.1D). Even the relative number and spacing of warps and wefts will affect the proportions of elements and motifs, thus influencing the appearance of the whole pattern (Figs. 8.1E, F). Differences in technical processes may thus furnish a partial explanation for differences in regional styles and for temporal changes in style. Technique, however, does not determine the symmetry processes by which a design is structured.

An analysis of the structure and composition of traditional Southwestern textile design allows identification of six regional and temporal styles: Early Anasazi (A.D. 300–900); three Late Prehistoric styles (A.D. 1100–1450) – Pueblo III Anasazi, Sinagua–Salado, and Hohokam; Protohistoric (A.D. 1450–1550); and Historic Pueblo (A.D. 1700–present). Late prehistoric period textiles from Mogollon sites in Southwestern New Mexico are very limited in number. Stylistically most of them fit the description I give for Hohokam material. Certain of them, however, relate more closely to Sinagua–Salado.

Early Anasazi, or Basketmaker–Pueblo I (A.D. 300–900) sites are localized in the San Juan drainage of northeastern Arizona, southeastern Utah, and southwestern Colorado. Baskets and textiles from these sites are described and illustrated in Morris and Burgh (1941), Elizabeth A. Morris (1980), and Tanner (1976). Table 8.1 (pp. 114–15) lists the thirty-two examples of narrow bands, apron fronts, and woven sandals on which my design analysis is based. Figures 8.2A and 8.2B illustrate (for comparative purposes) a Basketmaker II twined-woven bag and a Basketmaker III coiled carrying basket, although these classes of material have not been analysed by me.

Pueblo III Anasazi (A.D. 1100–1300) sites are centred in the Four Corners area, with extensions south to include Canyon de Chelly and Chaco Canyon, and east to the Rio Grande and Chama Valleys from the city of Albuquerque north to Abiquiu. Material from Pueblo III sites was described in my earlier publication (Kent 1957). Table 8.2 lists textiles of the region which have been analysed in terms of design style.

I see the locus of Sinagua and Salado peoples between about A.D. 1000–1400 in central and east central Arizona, from the Verde Valley east to the New Mexico line south of the Mogollon Rim and including the Tonto Basin. Others use the term 'Western Pueblo' for cultures in this region, or incorporate them with Mogollon. Although it is a culturally mixed region, drawing from the Mogollon, Hohokam and Anasazi, textiles from the area show a distinctive style (Kent 1957). Table 8.2 lists 20 examples from the area analysed for this study. Certain of the pieces from the Upper Verde Valley and Tonto Monument, because of design characteristics relating them to the Ventana Cave material, I consider Hohokam.

Hohokam material, other than that from Ventana Cave (c. A.D. 1100–1400) is strictly limited because of the open nature of desert sites and the Hohokam custom of cremating their dead. Table 8.2 (pp. 116–19) lists the pieces which have been used in this study.

Protohistoric textile information is drawn from mural paintings at the old Hopi towns of Awatovi and Kawaika-a, and at Pottery Mound and Kuaua near Albuquerque (Smith 1952; Hibben 1975; Dutton 1963). The murals date to just before the entry of the Spanish into the Southwest in 1540.

Geometric designs found on nineteenth- and twentieth-century embroideries, Hopi brocade, and warp-float pattern weave belts indicate that a sixth regional style evolved from the Protohistoric to become stabilized probably by the early 1700s as the Historic style (Mera 1975).

Early Anasazi design style: Basketmaker–Pueblo I, A.D. 300–900

The fundamental parts (that is, the basic asymmetric parts) of a design motif relate to each other by mirror reflection (i.e. the appearance of a mirror image of the part across a horizontal or vertical line axis), translation (i.e. simple repeats of the part along a line axis), bifold rotation (in which the part rotates about a central point to reproduce itself), or slide reflection (which involves reflection of the fundamental part across a line and its translation along that line into the succeeding position, a process which has been compared to the left–right movement in walking). All these processes are fully described in Washburn 1977: 1–45. Called symmetry operations, they are the structure on which a design is based.

The symmetry operations selected by the Early Anasazi to move a design motif from one position to the next are, in order of importance: (1) reflection (Fig. 8.4B); (2) bifold rotation (Fig. 8.4A); (3) translation, including alternate translation, by which I mean the alternating of two different motifs along a line axis (Fig. 8.3A); and (4) a combination of bifold rotation and mirror reflection (Fig. 8.3D).

In most cases there is no visual continuity between the design motifs. All but seven of the 32 narrow band patterns analysed show the design field sectioned off by vertical and/ or horizontal lines, real or imaginary, into rectangular blocks.

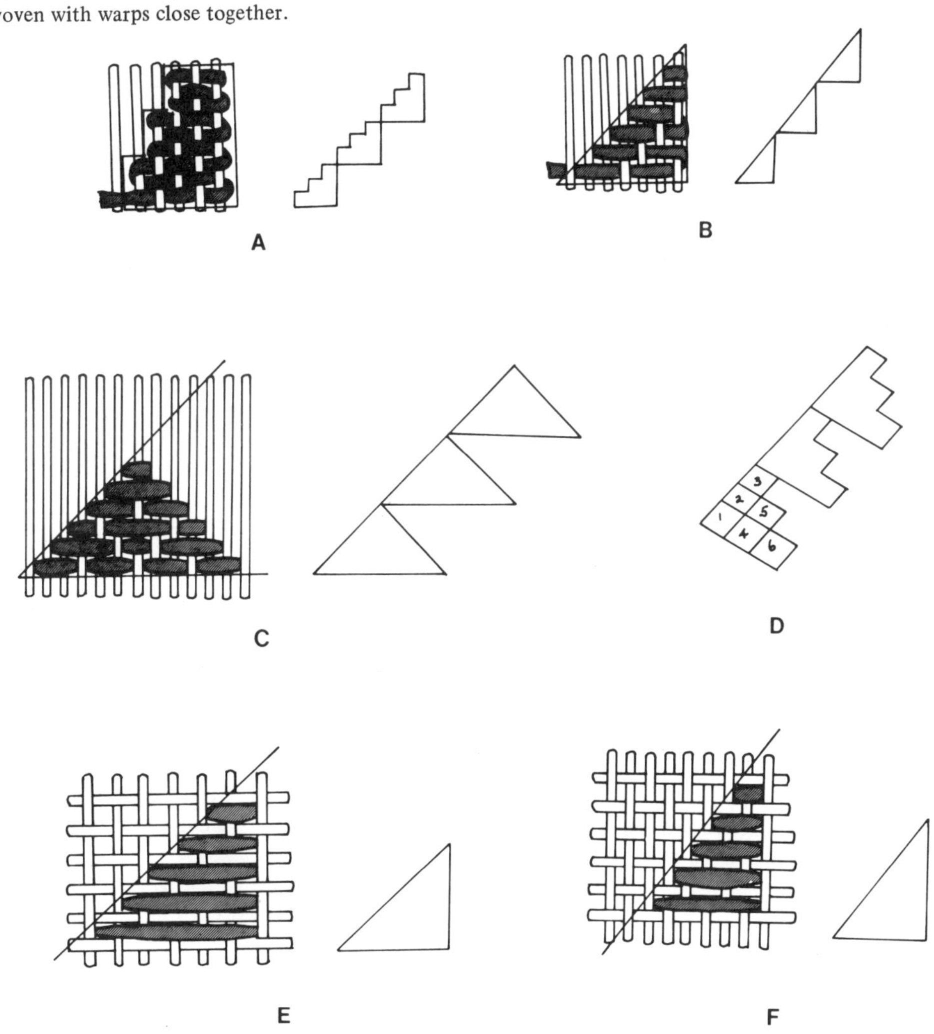

Fig. 8.1. Variations in the triangle element resulting from differences in weave technique.
A. Terraced triangle woven in plain weave tapestry. In this technique the lines of the figure will parallel the warp and weft axes.
B. Triangle woven in irregular twill weave.
C. Triangle woven in irregular twill or diamond twill weave.
D. Terraced triangle woven in diamond twill. Each triangle is composed of six small diamonds.
E. Triangle woven with widely spaced warps.
F. Triangle woven with warps close together.

Each block contains a design motif which is repeated in its neighbour, or in alternating blocks, sometimes with colour or textural counterchange (Washburn 1977: 13). With few exceptions, even bifold rotation, a movement often employed to generate a dynamic design in which motifs seem to flow along the axis without a break, has not been used so as to contribute a dynamic feel to Basketmaker band patterns. The movement of motifs is interrupted by the vertical or horizontal lines dividing the field (Fig. 8.3E). (For an example of this manner of handling bifold rotation in coiled basketry design see Fig. 8.2B.)

Another device which can lend a dynamic feel to design is the presence of oblique lines. These are employed to structure the design field in only five of the bands (Figs. 8.3F and 8.5A). In some instances, to be sure, elements are strung along oblique lines *within* a design block, but such motifs are terminated when they meet a vertical or horizontal structural design line (Fig. 8.3C). For the most part the main lines of the pattern and of individual elements as well are parallel to the warp–weft axes.

Most Basketmaker–Pueblo I designs are one-dimensional, growing along a single axis. Lacking a stress on both oblique and continuous lines, most are not dynamic – they do not flow. There is a static, balanced quality to the designs.

Design elements and units include bars, triangle-and-bars, hooks, keys, terraced triangles and terraced diagonal lines. These right-angled elements probably developed originally in the techniques of coiled basketry and finger-weave tapestry. They continued to be produced in many weave techniques, and in painted and in tie-and-dye designs by the Anasazi throughout prehistoric times, and are dominant motifs on contemporary Pueblo embroidery (Figs. 8.20, 8.21). It is characteristic of Early Anasazi design that the individual elements tend to be 'absorbed' into large colour blocks (Figs. 8.2, 8.6).

Interest and lightness are added to Early Anasazi designs through the counterchange of colours or by framing a solid-coloured element with a line of contrasting colour. Red and black or brown are the usual colours used, in combination with the natural yellowish tone of the undyed yarns.

A shift to the dynamic, flowing two-dimensional design style which is described below as characteristic of Late Prehistoric textiles manifests itself on only one Early Anasazi band (Keleman 1944: fig. 170C). The piece is documented as Basketmaker, but is so out of character for those early people as to put the documentation in question. It is true, however, that at some time between late Basketmaker and Pueblo III times (i.e., between about A.D. 600 and 1100) a major change in the structure of textile design did occur. The change may have accompanied the introduction of loom-woven textiles and of weaving on a wide loom from southern Arizona or southwestern New Mexico. The assumption is that early Hohokam and Mogollon loom-woven textiles were

Fig. 8.2.

A. Basketmaker II twined-woven bag from White Dog Cave, the design showing similarities to Basketmaker narrow band patterns. Similarities include: the zoning of the design field into horizontal bands, the use of contrasting colours in opposed bands of triangles, and the outlining of a figure with a line (of small triangles, in this case) of another colour. The elements move by mirror reflection along the horizontal axes. (After Guernsey and Kidder 1921: pl. 28)

B. Basketmaker III coiled basket, Canyon del Muerto. The rim area is clearly divided into rectangular design blocks, or zones, by vertical lines. Within each block the motif shows bifold rotation with colour counterchange. The motif moves from block to block by rotation, but the motion is interrupted visually by the vertical dividing lines. (After Morris and Burgh 1941: fig. 15b)

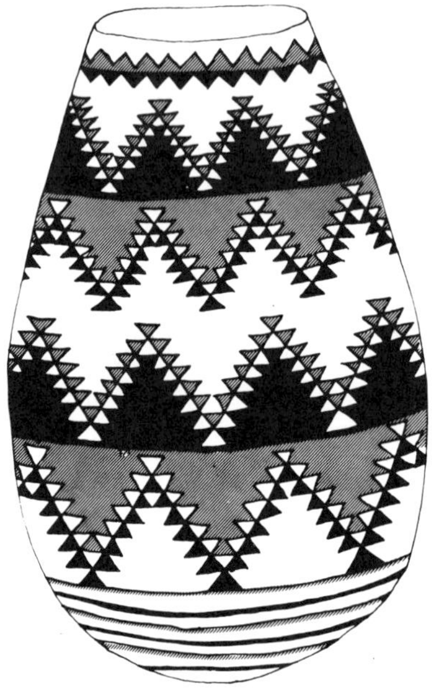

A

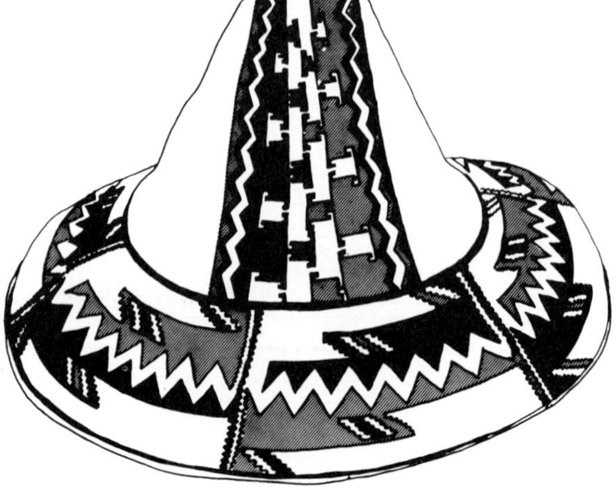

B

Fig. 8.3. Early Anasazi narrow band patterns.

A. Basketmaker III sandal sole with raised pattern, Prayer Rock Caves. The design field is divided into vertical panels. Motifs are repeated by alternate translation, a–b–a–b–a. (After Tanner 1972: fig. 3.13a, far left)

B. Basketmaker III sandal sole with raised pattern, Prayer Rock Caves. The field is divided into vertical panels. Triangle motifs are in mirror reflection with textural counterchange across the vertical axes. (After Morris 1980: fig. 76c)

C. Basketmaker tumpline, San Juan Valley. The field has been divided into rectangular blocks by horizontal lines. The motifs are missing from all but two blocks. (After Kent in press: fig. 130B)

D. Basketmaker III or Pueblo I tumpline, Northern Arizona. The design structure is based on mirror reflection, a–a′, across the axis marked with a dotted line, and bifold rotation of the fundamental part around the point marked *x*. (After Kent 1957: fig. 47 A2)

E. Basketmaker III or Pueblo I tapestry weave cradle band, Nitsie Canyon. The field is divided into three rectangular design blocks by horizontal lines. Motifs within each block show bifold rotation. Two motifs alternate, a–b–a. (After Kent 1957: fig. 46)

F. Basketmaker III narrow band, probably the front of a woman's fringed apron, Prayer Rock Caves. The design field is divided into oblique panels. Panel motifs alternate with colour counterchange, a–b–a′–b′. (After E.A. Morris 1980: fig. 65b)

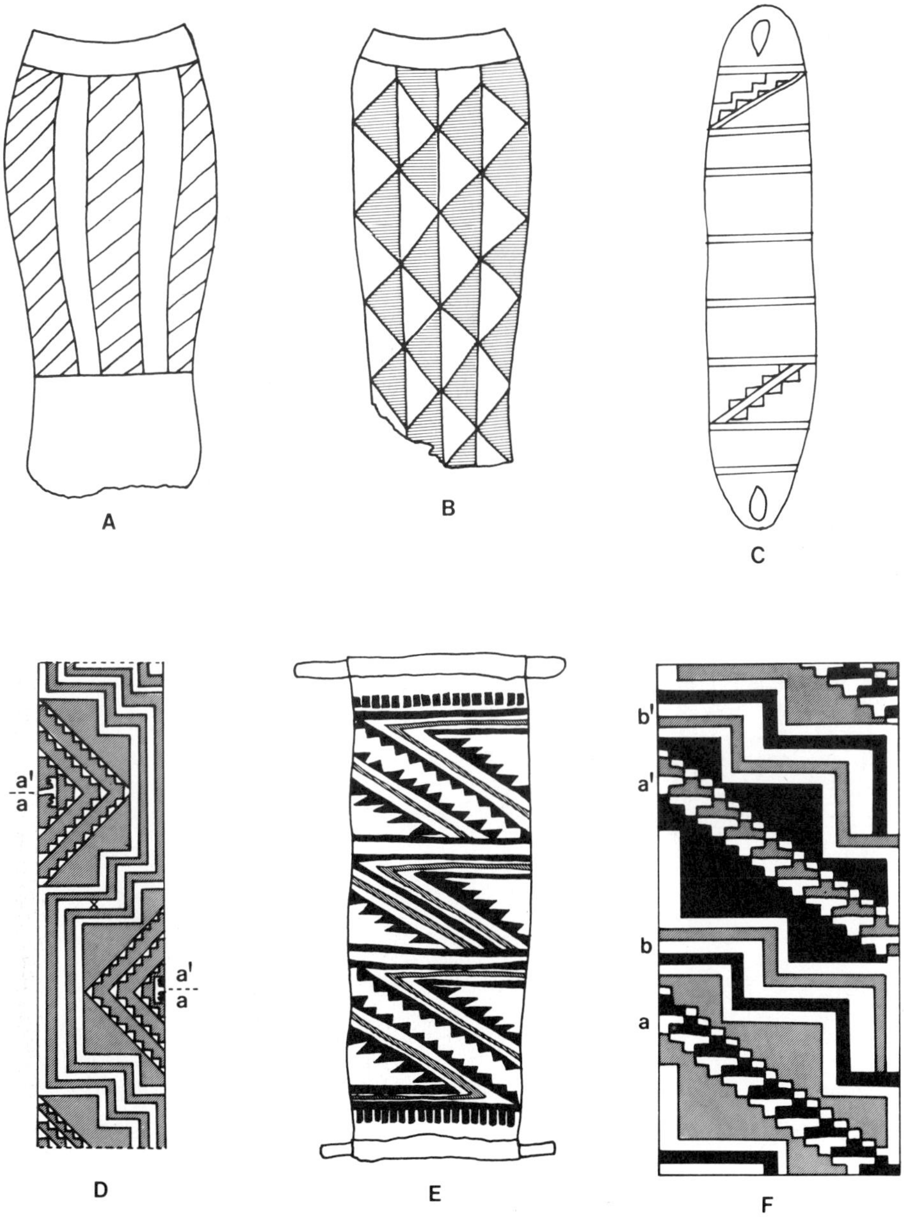

patterned by two-dimensional designs, and that these designs were taken over by the Anasazi along with loom weaving technology.

Late Prehistoric textile design styles: Pueblo III Anasazi, Sinagua–Salado, Hohokam, A.D. 1000–1400

Designs on Late Prehistoric loom-woven cotton cloth are, then, quite different in character from those on most Basketmaker–Pueblo I textiles. The difference is due not so much to the nature of the geometric elements, which are generally similar to those on the earlier pieces, as to the overall structure and composition. Elements are not absorbed by heavy colour masses, but are distinct entities. The design field is not segmented into rectangular blocks by vertical and horizontal lines – indeed the main structural lines are oblique to the warp–weft axes. The predominant symmetry processes used for both motifs and the total design are bifold rotation and slide reflection, which impart a feeling of motion.

One common way of structuring Late Prehistoric design is to move the motifs along the weft axis by rotation, so that they are, or appear to be, joined into a continuous band, like a scroll. Adjacent scrolls are juxtaposed by slide reflection (see Fig. 8.7). The overall pattern created by a series of these bands is seen as consisting of oblique lines offset around central motifs of interlocking hooks or triangles (Fig. 8.8). Designs are two-dimensional, growing along both horizontal and vertical axes.

Stylistic differences between the three Late Prehistoric regional styles – Pueblo III Anasazi, Sinagua–Salado, and Hohokam – are not to be defined in terms of symmetry processes, which are common to all three, but in terms of other differences in composition – that is, in the various ways of expressing and placing elements (which, as pointed out on p. 120, relate to differences in weave techniques), in the scale of the design motifs, and in colour preferences. Each of the three styles is described separately below.

Pueblo III Anasazi textile design, A.D. 1100–1300

The Anasazi customarily handled the two-dimensional patterning described above by enlarging the scale of a central motif and placing it at midpoint in the field of decoration. In large fabrics the oblique arms of the motif, and those of its neighbours, cut the field into offset quarters (Figs. 8.7F, 8.9). There is an extraordinary diamond twill blanket from Grand Gulch in southeastern Utah in which the pattern is not centred on a single motif (Fig. 8.10). It is atypical for the Pueblo III Anasazi, at least as we know their textiles on the basis of other finds. The terraced triangle elements in the design are, however, distinctively Anasazi.

Several small Anasazi fabrics are patterned by what amounts to a centre motif alone, filling the entire design

Fig. 8.4. The two surfaces of a Basketmaker III sandal sole from Prayer Rock Caves.
A. The inner surface with tapestry weave weft pattern. Each design motif shows bifold rotation about the points marked *x*. One motif rotates about point *y* into the next: however, the motifs are visually clearly separated by the vertical unpatterned space between them.
B. Under surface of the same sandal sole, patterned by raised knots. Motifs are in mirror reflection across the central line axis. (After E.H. Morris, n.d.)

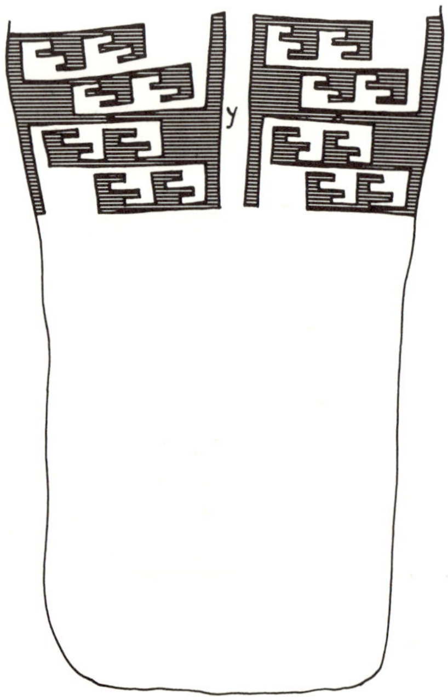

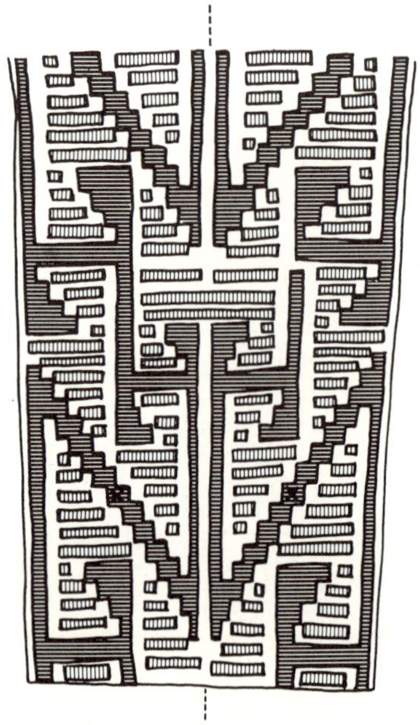

field (Fig. 8.11). The border design of a fragment from Mesa Verde is composed of a series of such motifs set in a horizontal band (Fig. 8.12). While the designs on these pieces may be classified as one-dimensional, they actually derive from a two-dimensional pattern held in the weaver's mind.

Fitting the two-dimensional design to the field by enlarging and centring a single motif is not characteristic of surviving Late Prehistoric textiles from other parts of the Southwest, with the exception of a white interlinked shirt from Tonto National Monument (Tanner 1976: fig. 3.34a).

Fig. 8.5. Basketmaker III women's apron fronts, Prayer Rock Caves.

A. Field divided by two oblique axes. Pairs of motifs in bifold rotation with colour counterchange are placed along each axis.
B. The entire field is divided by a central vertical line. The two halves of the design are in mirror reflection with colour counterchange.
C. The field is divided into vertical panels. Each design motif is worked out across three panels and shows bifold rotation. Each motif rotates into the next with a colour change.
D. The field is divided into two zones, *a* and *b*. Motifs are repeated by mirror reflection within each zone.

(After E.A. Morris 1980: figs. 65a, b, c; fig. 66a.)

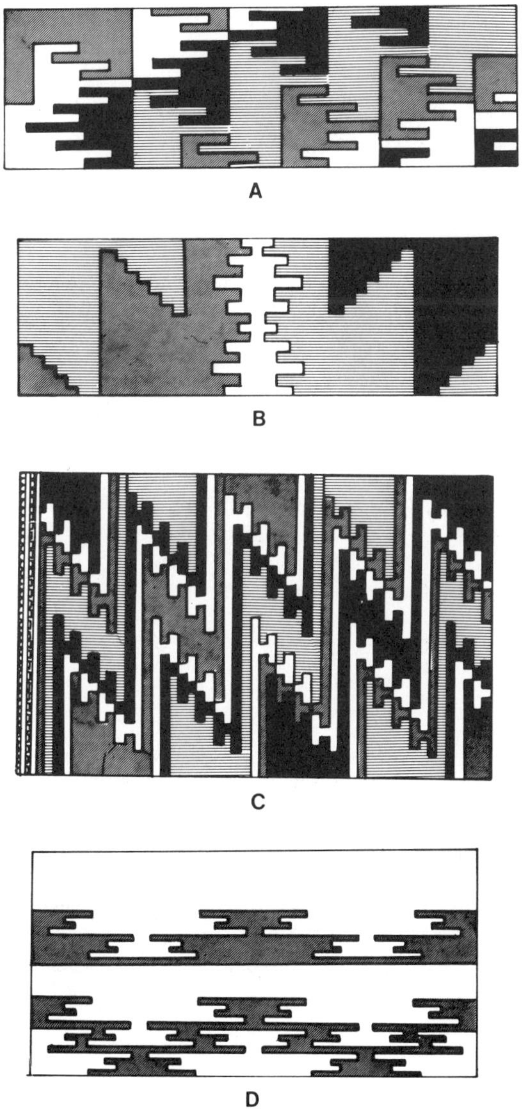

Most Pueblo III designs are carried out in black-or-brown and white, with the two tones evenly balanced, or the dark used as a background on which white motifs and lines create a negative pattern (Fig. 8.11). This treatment probably originated in the process of tie-and-dye, wherein small design elements are tied off to resist dye, and only the background receives the colour. It is expressed by the Pueblo III Anasazi in both woven and painted textiles, as well as in tie-and-dye.

Unlike the oblique structural lines of the design, vertical and horizontal lines are used in elements and motifs. The terraced lines and triangles of Basketmaker–Pueblo I textiles continue to dominate Anasazi design in Late Prehistoric times.

Painting is a freer technique than weaving, and when using it to decorate their fabrics, the Anasazi included in the designs many of the complex elements and motifs found on their painted pottery but not on woven textiles. As seen on blankets from Painted Cave, such motifs are arranged as one-dimensional bands within the oblique arms of the overall two-dimensional pattern (Fig. 8.13).

Sinagua–Salado textile design, A.D. 1000–1400

Most Sinagua–Salado textiles are patterned with the kind of two-dimensional design structure based on bifold rotation and slide reflection described above as common to Late Prehistoric textiles from all parts of the Southwest. Motifs are repeated all over the field of decoration rather than being centred on it in any way (Fig. 8.14). The impression is that the weaver envisioned a pattern and wove as much of it as he needed, breaking it off arbitrarily at the edges of the piece or of the design field. Even when used on borders, the patterns are 'limitless'. There seems to have been no feeling that the size or shape of the decorative field should modify the pattern.

Sinagua–Salado design often employs two or more colours plus the white of the background, as opposed to the standard black and white of most Pueblo III woven patterns. A dominant motif is the triangle-and-hook, composed of a right triangle set with legs parallel to warp and weft, with a hook extending from the vertical leg (Fig. 8.15A, B). A favourite practice was to arrange a series of these figures of a given colour along an oblique arm of the design. A second series of a different colour was set along a parallel oblique, with the hooks interlocked or addorsed to those of the first set (Tanner 1976: figs. 3.40c and d). Black-or-brown and blue were the most frequently paired colours. Colours are balanced with the plain white ground so that, in a sense, negative patterning is present in Sinagua–Salado textile design. The white motifs, however, scarcely show on the polychrome fabrics. Negative patterning is also found on their white openwork textiles, in which solid plain weave areas form a design between and within the motifs worked in lace-like holes. On these as well as on the polychrome cloths the effect is lost because there is no sharp contrast of dark and light.

Colour counterchange was noted as a prominent feature of Early Anasazi design, but not of Anasazi Pueblo III fabrics. It seems curious that it should, instead, be found in Late Prehistoric times outside of the Anasazi area.

The triangle-and-hook motif, so common in Sinagua–Salado design, does not appear on Anasazi Pueblo III woven textiles with the exception of a few weft-wrap openwork fragments. Weft-wrap openwork is without question a decorative weave characteristic of Sinagua, Salado, Mogollon, and Hohokam, and I consider the fragments to be trade items. The motif does appear on Hohokam textiles, but only in finite figures or in the centre motifs of two-dimensional patterns (Figs. 8.8, 8.17A, B). It may be a combination of the triangle set in plain weave tapestry and derived from Anasazi textiles and a popular southern (probably Hohokam) element, the simple hook.

A second common element in Sinagua–Salado design is the smooth-edged triangle, woven in irregular twill tapestry and set with hypotenuse parallel to the weft axis. Triangles are often arranged in opposing rows, like the triangle-and-hook, with colour counterchange (Figs. 8.14, 8.15C). Smooth-edged triangles, but of a somewhat different nature, are also characteristic of Hohokam design (see below).

It may well be that the smooth-edged triangles of Sinagua–Salado and Hohokam weavers were conceptually the same as the terraced triangle of the Anasazi – the differences in shape having evolved from different weave techniques. Whatever the origin of its several forms, it is the variation in shape and orientation of the triangle that furnishes one guide in distinguishing textiles from the three Late Prehistoric regions.

Hohokam textile design, A.D. 1000–1400

What evidence we have suggests that Hohokam textiles were in some ways distinct from either Sinagua–Salado or Anasazi fabrics in design, and that the textiles of the Mogollon of southwestern New Mexico may have resembled those of the Hohokam. The structure and symmetry movements of two-dimensional patterns are like those of other Late Prehistoric textile design styles, and patterns are placed on the field without regard to any central motif. In this, Hohokam material is like that of the Sinagua and Salado.

Principal motifs are based on a smooth-edged triangle and a hook used as separate elements (except, as remarked above, in the case of finite designs and of the central interlocking hook motifs in two-dimensional patterns) (Figs. 8.8, 8.17A, E, 8.18). The elements are set along very steeply pitched obliques. The triangle is often placed with its longest leg parallel to the warps, or vertically on the cloth. When warps markedly outnumber wefts per unit of measurement,

Fig. 8.6. Basketmaker III woman's apron front, Duggagei Canyon. The motif is repeated by bifold rotation with colour counterchange. (ASM 3128. Photograph by E.B. Sayles, courtesy Arizona State Museum, and University of Arizona.)

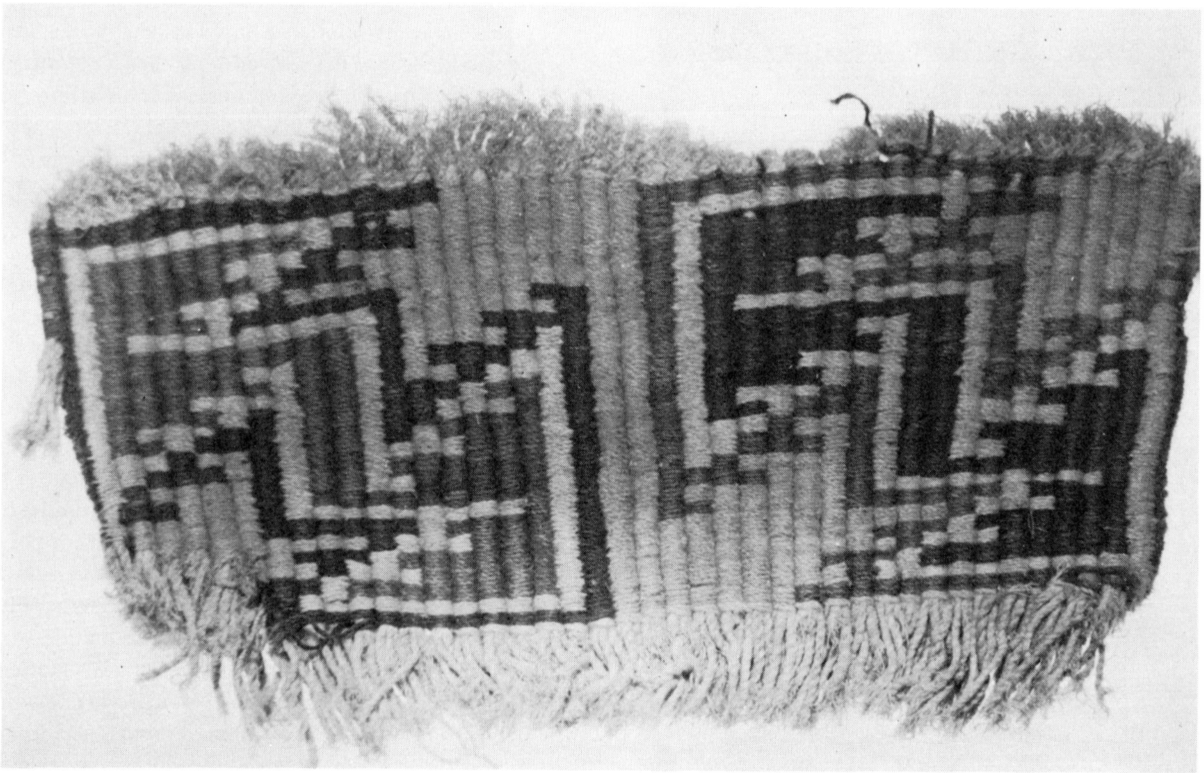

Fig. 8.7. Construction of a Late Prehistoric two-dimensional design through the symmetry processes of bifold rotation and slide reflection.
A. The fundamental part
B. Fundamental parts joined into a scroll by bifold rotation
C. Mirror reflection of two fundamental parts
D. Two fundamental parts in slide reflection
E. A centre motif extracted from the larger pattern, enlarged in scale, and used as the complete design on a fabric
F. Centring a motif on the field, with the oblique arms cutting the field into off-set quarters
G. Multiple scrolls in slide reflection, forming the two-dimensional 'limitless' pattern
(After Kent in press: fig. 134)

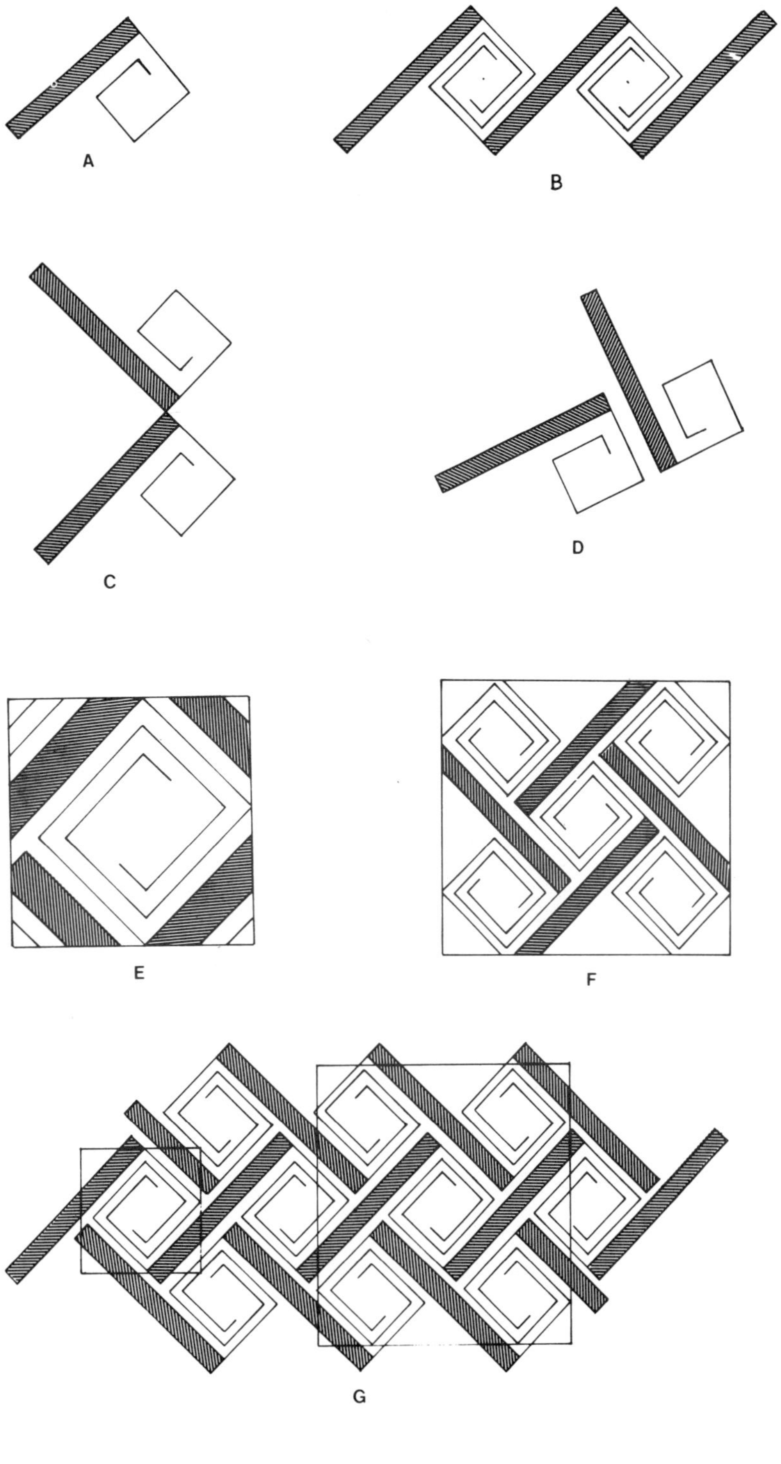

as they do in most Hohokam textiles, the short legs of such a triangle are at obtuse angles to the weft axis. The triangle is elongated vertically. This gives a steep pitch to the main structural design lines, which are formed by rows of triangles (Fig. 8.15D). The designs resemble those on brocaded fabrics (possibly prehistoric) from Chihuahua (Fig. 8.16).

In addition to two-dimensional designs, finite designs are quite common on Hohokam fabrics (Fig. 8.17). One of these appears as a small medallion on the chest area of a child's gauze weave poncho from Ventana Cave (Tanner 1976: fig. 3.31a). A series of small finite figures were arranged to form a border design on a cloth from Casa Grande. A small rectangular cloth from Graham County in southern Arizona is patterned by one large finite design, and four small finite figures appear on another cloth rectangle (which I believe to be of Hohokam manufacture) from the Verde Valley.

We have so few textile fragments from the Hohokam that a clear sense of their colour preferences does not emerge. In the Ventana Cave material, however, plain white openwork fabrics predominate. This is true, also, of Mogollon textile remains from southwestern New Mexico.

Protohistoric textile design, A.D. 1450–1540

Textile representations are plentiful in the fifteenth-century murals of Pottery Mound, Kuaua, and the Hopi towns of Kawaika-a and Awatovi. One can identify with

Fig. 8.8. A brocaded cotton fragment from the Clear Creek group of cavate lodges near Camp Verde. The steep pitch and position of the triangles are reminiscent of Hohokam design, although the piece comes from Sinagua territory. The hook and triangle elements are joined in the centre motifs, as shown by the heavy shading of one such motif. Triangles are used without hooks along the oblique lines of the pattern. (After Kent 1957: fig. 29A)

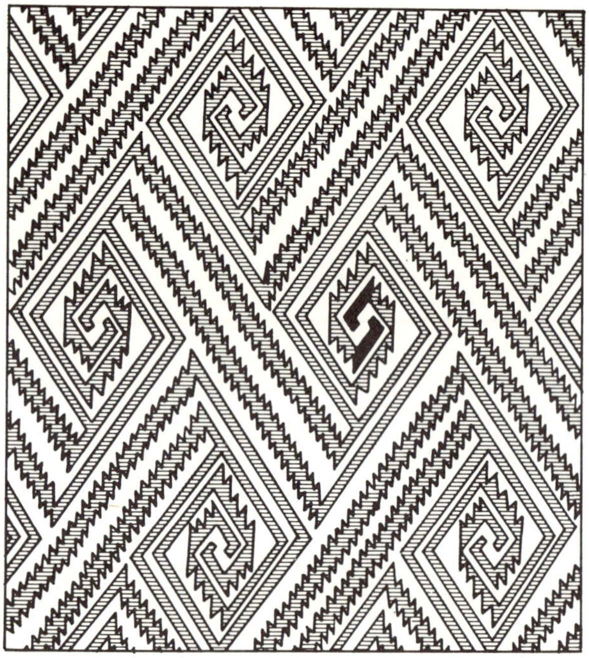

Fig. 8.9. Pueblo III Anasazi weft-wrap openwork cotton cloth rectangle, 38 cm by 31 cm complete, Nitsie Canyon. Openwork portions are shaded. Centring of a design motif, the increase in scale of the motif, and the effect of offset quartering of the field, as well as the terraced triangle element, mark the cloth as Anasazi even though weft-wrap openwork was not one of their weave techniques. (After Kent 1957: fig. 22A)

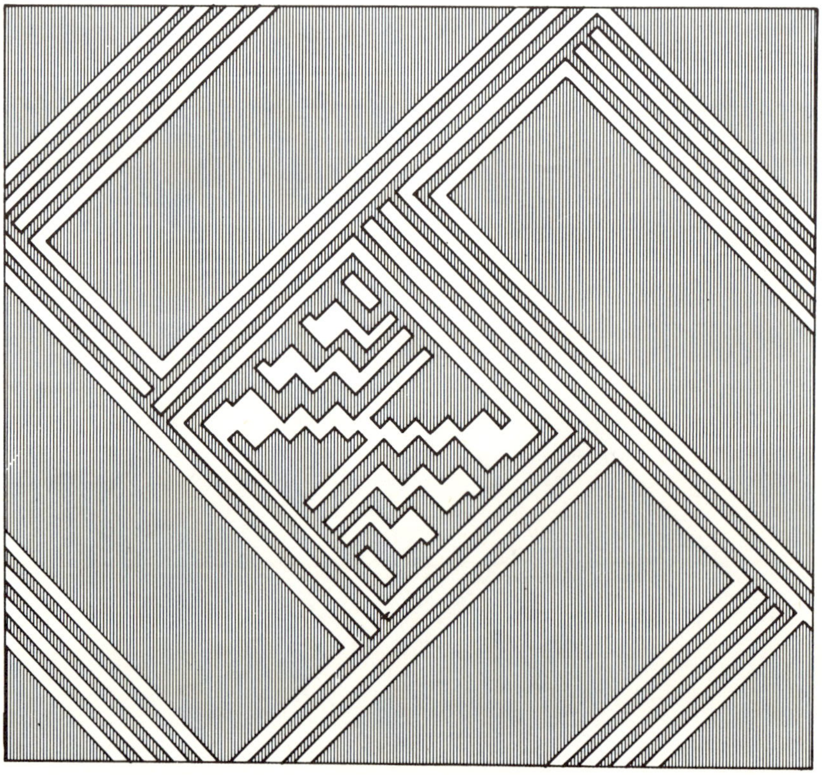

Fig. 8.10. The design on a Pueblo III Anasazi diamond twill weave cotton blanket from Grand Gulch, southeastern Utah. (Drawing by Kenneth Chapman. Photograph courtesy Laboratory of Anthropology, Museum of New Mexico.)

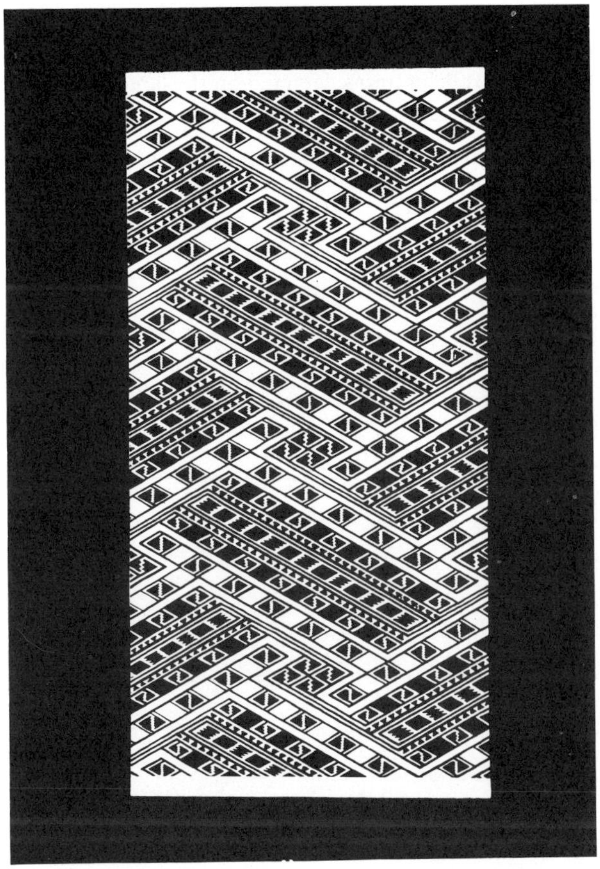

Fig. 8.11. Pueblo III Anasazi textile design showing negative patterning and the use of large scale motifs.

A. The design on a breech cloth front (14 cm wide) from White House, Canyon de Chelly. Compare the way in which a single diamond motif has been enlarged to fill the whole field with the 'limitless' pattern of small elements on the breech cloth front of about the same size (16.75 cm) from the Salado site of Tonto Monument (Fig. 8.14). (After Kent 1957: fig. 76 B1)

B. Design in black and white on a tapestry weave band fragment (14.5 cm wide) from Northern Arizona. (After Kent 1957: fig. 47B)

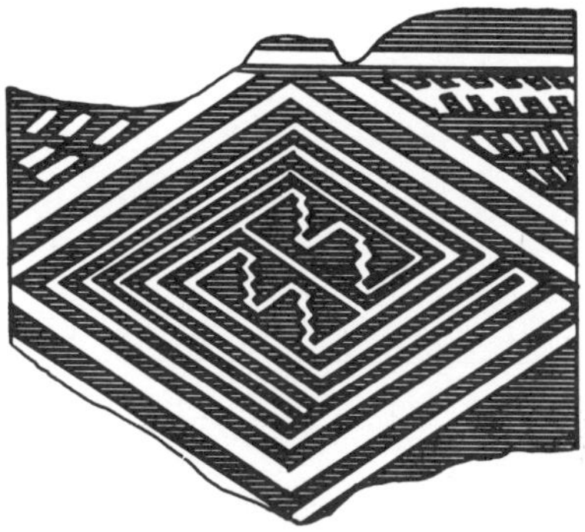

A

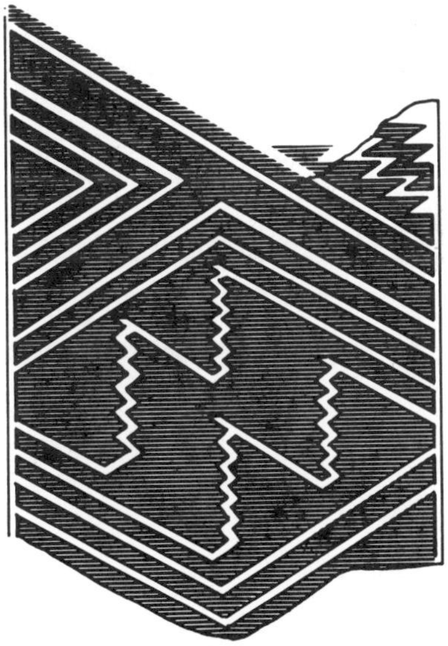

B

Fig. 8.12. The border design on a Pueblo III Anasazi cotton cloth from Mesa Verde is shown between the dotted lines on the drawing. The design has been extended above and below the lines to show the two-dimensional nature of the pattern from which the border was mentally extracted. (After Kent 1957: fig. 69)

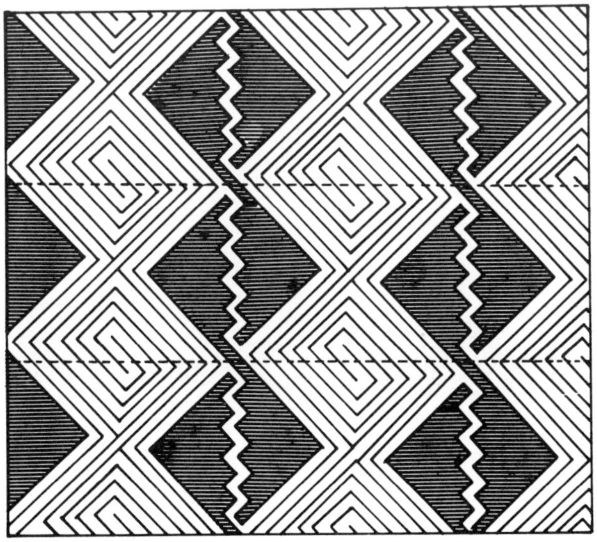

some assurance techniques and design ideas found in Late Prehistoric fabrics from all parts of the Southwest. Many of the dresses and kilts are patterned by what appears to be tie-and-dye or negative painting in the kind of two-dimensional design so typical of Late Prehistoric times. White rectangles with centre dots are placed along oblique lines so as to form large-scale hook motifs on a black surface (Fig. 8.19D). Blankets patterned by offset quartering of the field are illustrated at Pottery Mound, and geometric elements of the kind we have been discussing appear in kilt and manta borders in the Hopi murals (Fig. 8.19).

There is no question that the artists were picturing textiles like those we find in earlier archaeological horizons. However, while patterns depicted on the large design fields

Fig. 8.13. Anasazi Pueblo III painted blanket, width 133 cm, Painted Cave. One-dimensional band patterns are oriented within the oblique arms of the two-dimensional design. (Photograph courtesy Amerind Foundation)

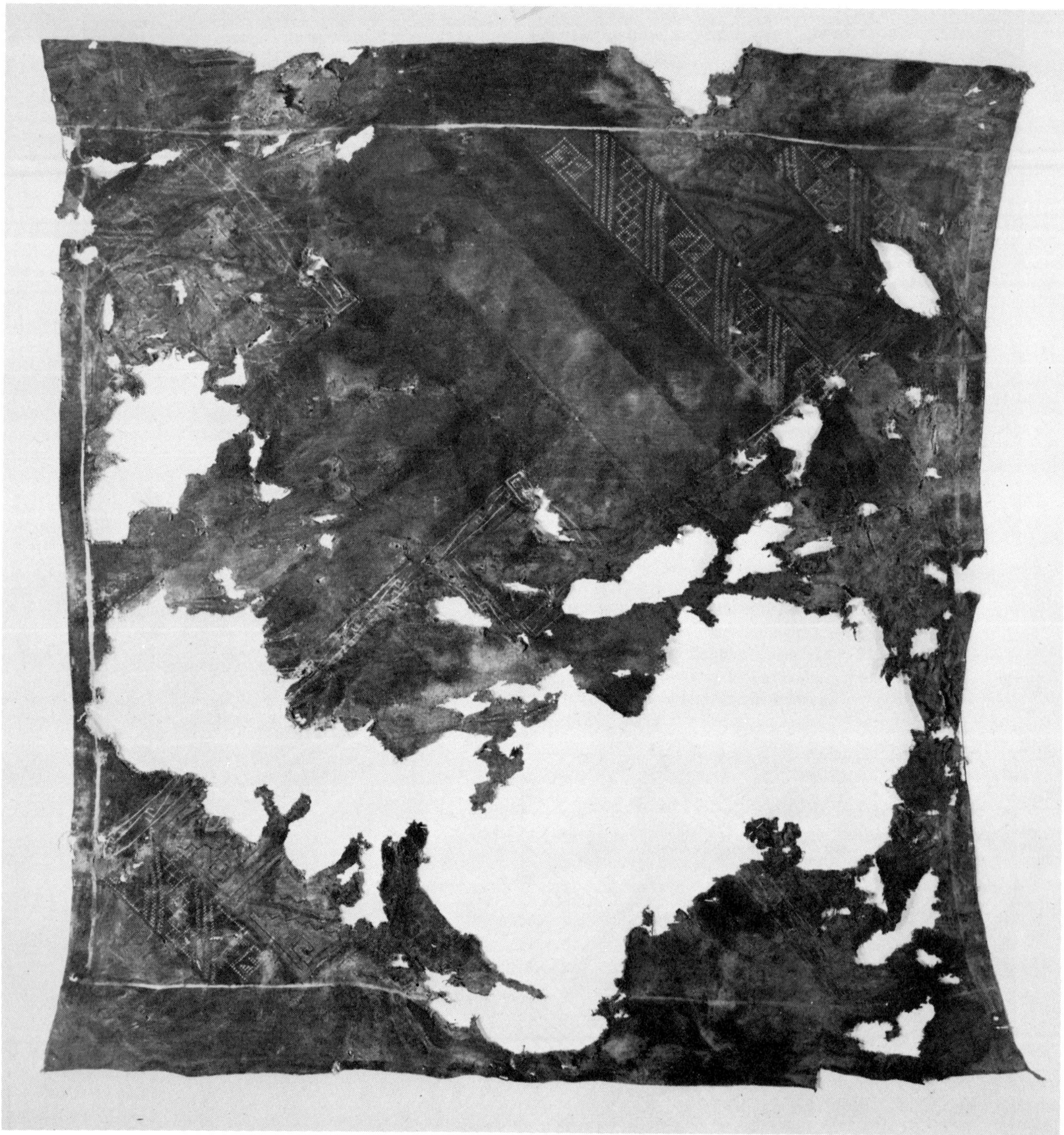

of most of the pieces are two-dimensional, border designs are definitely one-dimensional, and not of the type derived from a two-dimensional mental blueprint. They show simple patterns in which elements are ordered by the processes of translation or mirror reflection, sometimes with a colour change. The border area is carefully ruled off horizontally into zones, each of which contains a set of element repeats or simple horizontal lines. Only one kilt border shows a pattern of oblique lines within a border zone (Fig. 8.19E).

Negative designs are present, sometimes in black and white, and sometimes in two colours and white. Colour counterchange is suggested but, perhaps as a result of artistic licence on the part of the painter, is not carried out with precision. It is more a matter of alternating a dark and a light shade to add interest to the design.

In short, protohistoric border designs lack the dynamic character of Late Prehistoric design. In terms of symmetry processes they are more like Early Anasazi narrow band patterns, and like the one-dimensional patterns found within the oblique arms of the two-dimensional Pueblo III Anasazi blanket designs (Fig. 8.13).

Fig. 8.14. The two-dimensional design in blue, brown, and white on a breech cloth front (16.75 cm wide) from Tonto National Monument. (After Kent 1957: fig. 76 A1)

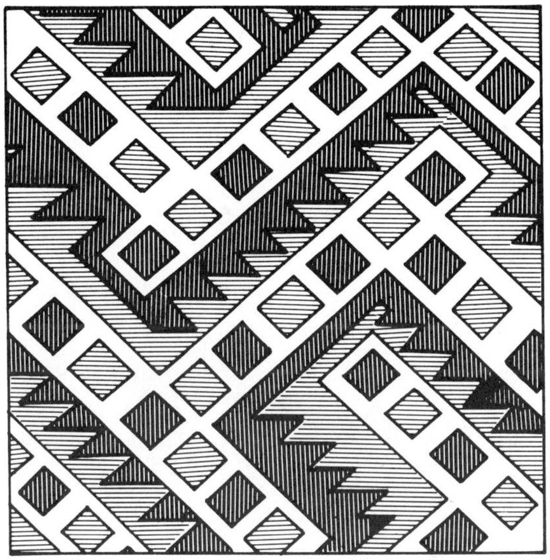

Fig. 8.15. A, B, C. Sinagua–Salado design elements. D. The position and proportions of Hohokam triangle elements.

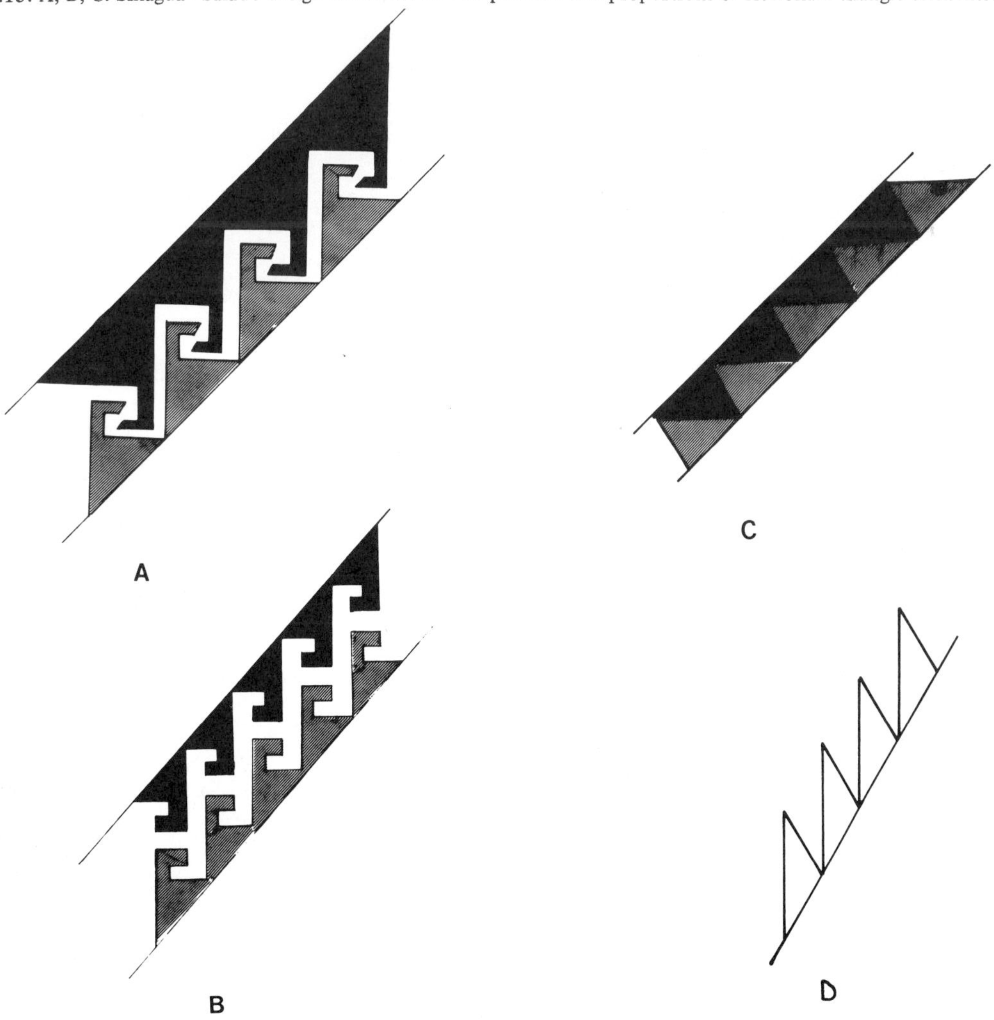

Fig. 8.16. A prehistoric fragment of white cotton cloth brocaded in blue from Chihuahua, Mexico. Compare the position and shape of the triangle elements with those on the brocaded cloth from the Verde Valley (Fig. 8.8). (SAR/MNM 9452/11. School of American Research collections in the Museum of New Mexico. Photograph courtesy Museum of New Mexico.)

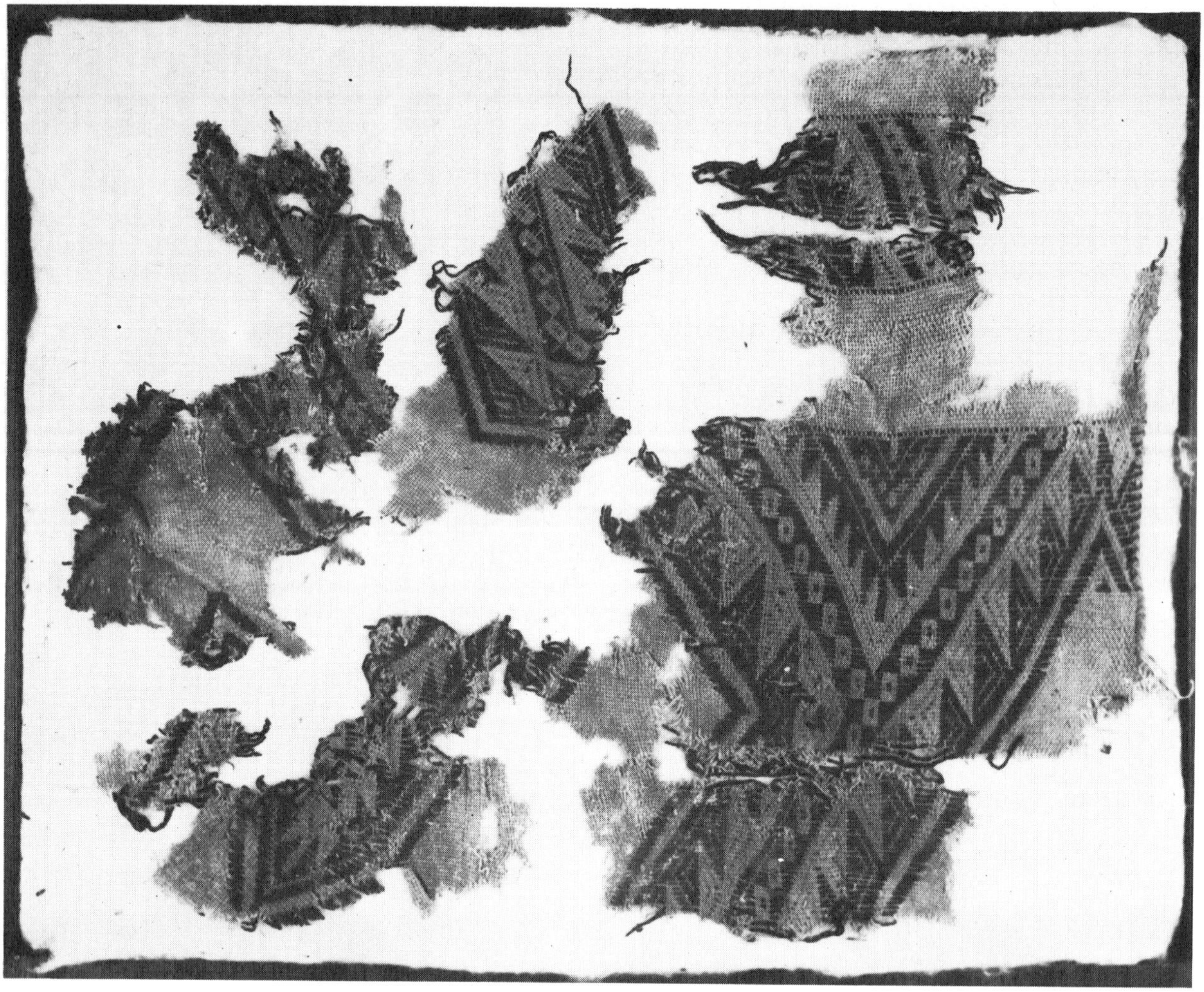

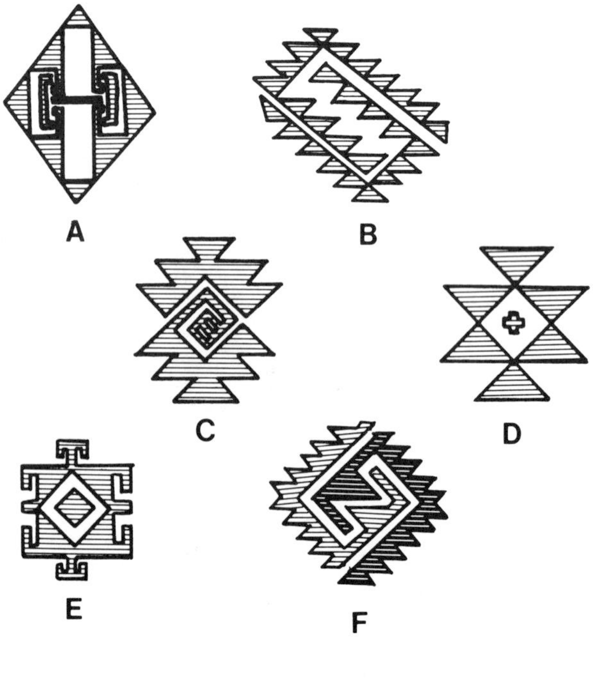

Fig. 8.17. Late Prehistoric finite designs.
A. Weft-wrap openwork design on a 16 cm square cloth from Graham County, Arizona. Hohokam.
B. Weft-wrap openwork design on a cotton bag from Canyon Creek. Salado.
C. Weft-wrap openwork design used in a series as the border pattern on a cloth from Casa Grande. Hohokam.
D. Weft-wrap openwork design on a cloth from Bear Creek Cave, southwestern New Mexico. Mogollon.
E. Weft-wrap openwork design on a child's poncho from Ventana Cave. Hohokam. (The same motif appears on a cloth from the Verde Valley.)
F. A finite design with colour counterchange worked in diamond twill tapestry on a fragment from Tularosa Cave, southwestern New Mexico. Mogollon. (Colours are blue and brown.)
(After Kent 1957: figs. 139 and 62 A2)

Historic textile design, A.D. 1700–present

The one-dimensional design style of the Awatovi and Kawaika-a kilt borders, established prior to the arrival of the Spanish, has survived into historic times in the embroidered borders of kilts, mantas, breechcloths and shirts (Figs. 8.20, 8.21). Individual elements are drawn from all three late prehistoric areas, so that we find the hook, triangle, triangle-and-hook, rectangle with centre dot, terraced line, terraced triangle, and so forth. Finite figures reminiscent of Hohokam design are also worked into the borders or placed on the centre field between borders. Elements have become more involved so that the designs look complex, almost ornate in some cases, but structurally they remain simple one-dimensional repeats, rigidly confined within horizontal zones. Solid areas of dark colour are relieved by negative design lines and in certain instances by vertical bars of a lighter colour which cut through them and are seemingly unrelated to the design of the border as a whole. Meanwhile, the body of the garment is woven in simple plain weave or self-patterned twill. The dynamic two-dimensional patterning of prehistoric textiles is totally lacking. It apparently disappeared completely in early historic times along with the complex weave techniques, tie-and-dye, and painting in which it had been carried out.

Concluding remarks

We have evidence for two major shifts in the structure of traditional Southwestern textile design in the Anasazi area. The first, commencing sometime toward the end of the Early Anasazi period, was accomplished by A.D. 1100. It involved a shift from one-dimensional band patterns to dynamic two-dimensional 'limitless' patterns based most frequently on a combination of slide reflection and bifold rotation. This shift seems to correlate with the introduction of the wide loom and weaving of large articles of clothing in cotton. The technological innovations were apparently accompanied by new ideas of design structure from central and southern Arizona and southwestern New Mexico.

Two-dimensional patterns are certainly more appropriate for large textiles than for narrow articles, but the presence of large decorative fields does not automatically lead to the weaving of such patterns. Simple stripes serve in many parts of the world. Basketmaker band patterns could have been adapted in this form to the new fabrics. Indeed, stripes were used on Anasazi self-patterned textiles. One wonders why the symmetry of geometric textile designs changed so radically after Pueblo I. A possible explanation is that loom weaving was developed by Pueblo men, whereas Pueblo women might well have been the designers of the earlier non-loom articles. Learning a new skill may simply have included for the men learning the design structure of their instructors (or of the pieces they copied).

The second major change involved a shift in protohistoric times from two-dimensional patterns and border patterns derived from two-dimensional systems to one-dimensional patterns. This change occurred during a period when many different cultural traditions and probably different groups of people from several parts of the Southwest were converging in the Hopi country. The one-dimensional patterns may derive from those depicted in the oblique 'arms' of Anasazi Pueblo III painted blankets.

Fig. 8.18. Late Prehistoric design on a weft-wrap openwork cloth from Mule Creek Cave, southwestern New Mexico. Mogollon. Hooks are used as independent elements, without triangles. The design structure is two-dimensional with hooks in bifold rotation along the oblique axes. (After Kent 1957: fig. 20)

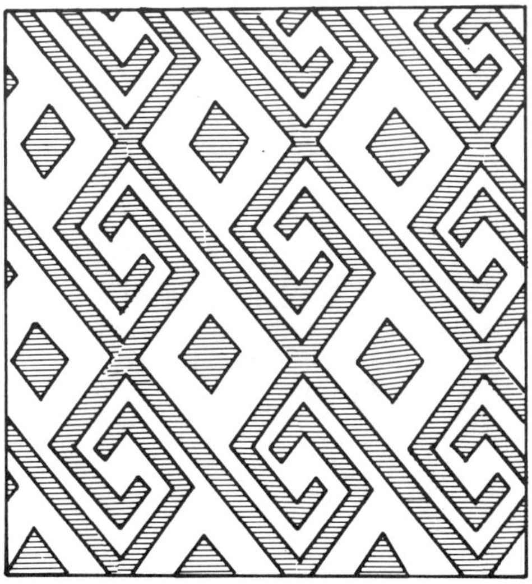

Fig. 8.19. Designs on kilts from the protohistoric Hopi murals. (After Kent 1957: fig. 140)
A, B, C, and E are border designs probably depicting embroidery. The motifs in A and B move by translation. C shows mirror reflection with colour counterchange. E is unusual in that the elements are placed along oblique lines. D represents an entire kilt, with a border design showing alternate translation, and the body of the kilt patterned by a large scale tie-and-dye motif.

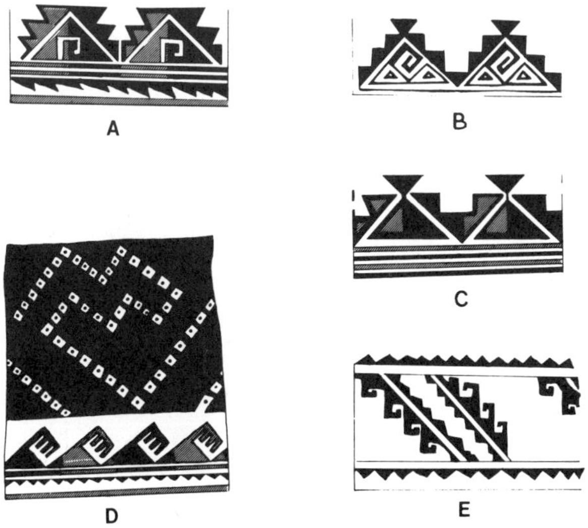

Fig. 8.20. Contemporary Pueblo embroidery designs showing relationship to prehistoric and protohistoric Southwestern textile patterns.

A. Hohokam type finite figure from an embroidered Jemez cotton shirt.

B. Hohokam and Mogollon type finite figure from the border of a woollen manta, Acoma.

C. Portion of the border design on a woollen manta, Acoma. *a* and *c* may be seen as the upper and lower portions of finite figures such as B. *b* should be compared with the Hohokam finite design illustrated in Fig. 8.17E.

D. Designs from an embroidered cotton manta, Acoma.

1. One of two finite figures centred on the manta just below the upper border.
   a. A motif resembling that on a kilt border in the Hopi murals (Smith 1952: fig. 25i)
   b. Breaking the solid dark field of embroidery with a vertical band of a lighter colour, a device noted in kilt designs in the Hopi murals.
2. The upper border design
   a. Terraced triangles, an Anasazi motif.
   b. A vertical band of light colour breaking the dark field.
   c. Triangle-hooks, a Sinagua–Salado motif.
3. The lower border design
   a. The upper part of a Hohokam type finite figure like B.
   b. Negative line design, an Anasazi design device.
   c, d. Terraced triangles, an Anasazi motif.

E. Design from an embroidered cotton kilt, Acoma.

a. The Salado–Sinagua triangle-hook element, somewhat elaborated and set along a horizontal line. See Fig. 8.19D for use of this motif in the Hopi murals.
b. Triangles set along an oblique line, a Salado–Sinagua motif.
c. Small squares in an oblique line, reminiscent of Anasazi tie-and-dye and negative painted patterns. (Compare Fig. 8.19D)
d. Triangle-hooks set along an oblique line, a Salado–Sinagua motif, although the elements are here placed horizontally rather than vertically.
e. Negative line design.

F. Design from a cotton kilt, contemporary Pueblo.

a. Paired terraced triangles.

(After Kent 1957: fig. 141)

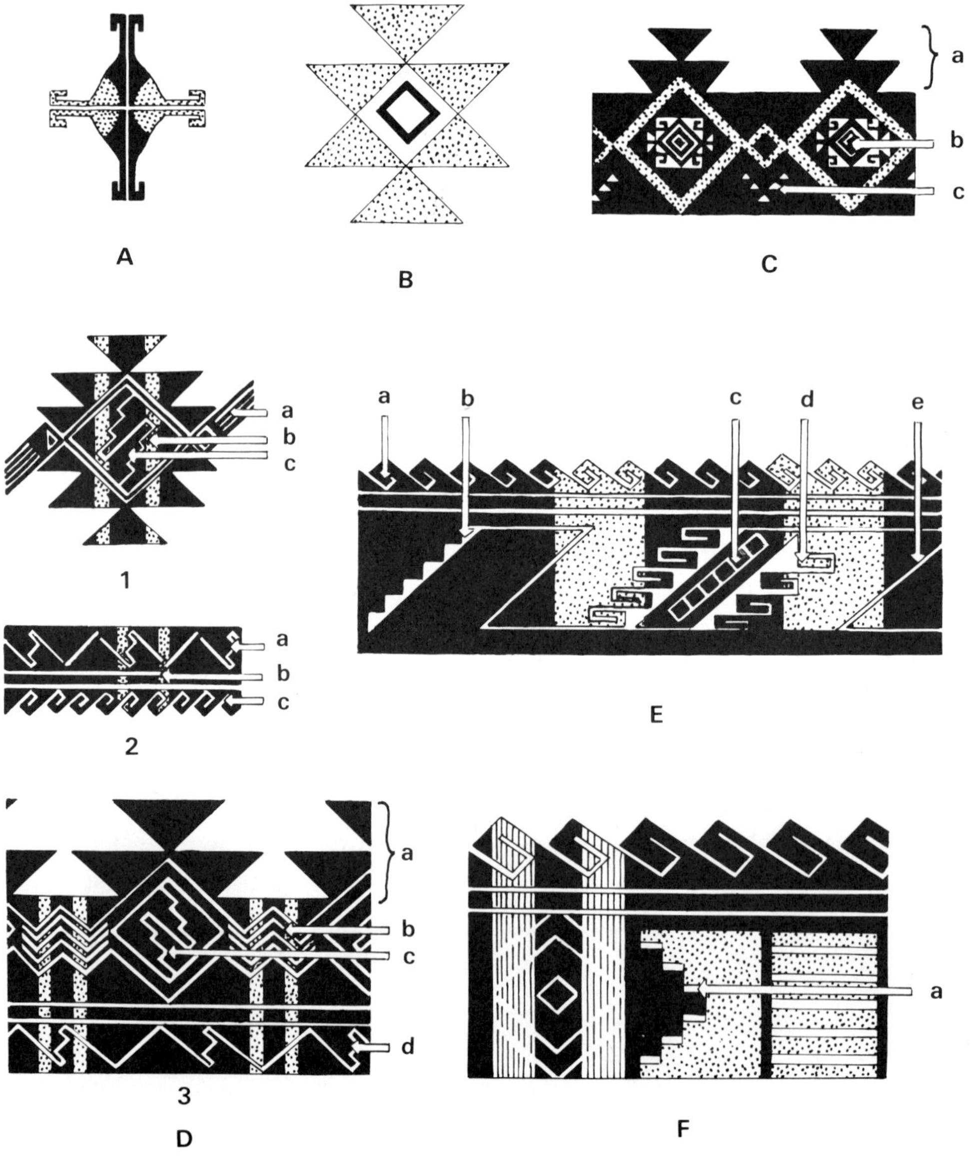

It is not difficult to define changes in the structure of a design style through history, but questions remain as to the significance of the changes. Greenberg (1975: 45) has suggested 'that the structure of designs should be logically related to the structure or structuring of other . . . systems'. She demonstrates such a theoretical relationship between one type of contemporary Hopi pottery design and world view. The pottery analysed is of the Sikyatki style, a protohistoric and early historic (1400–c. 1600) type which was revived towards the end of the nineteenth-century and popularized by the Hopi–Tewa potter, Nampeyo. Her characterization of the style correlates in many ways with our description of Late Prehistoric Anasazi textile design. For example, she finds her patterns and motifs generated around central points, a balance between dark and light tones, a preference for rotational rather than bilateral symmetry (or reflection), and a dynamic quality due in part to the emphasis on oblique structural lines. Her quotation from Ortiz (1972: 142) seems to give symbolic content to the centred patterns illustrated here (Figs. 8.9, 8.13) as well as the preference for bifold rotation in which motifs move around a central point:

> All the Pueblos also have a well-elaborated conception and symbolization of the middle or center of the cosmos, represented by a *sipapu*, an earth navel, or the entire village . . . If only four directions are given symbolic elaboration, the center will be the fifth direction.

Similarly, remarks drawn from Thompson and Joseph (1944: 44) concerning the nature of Hopi duality seem to fit the phenomenon of negative patterning, wherein black and white are of equal importance to the design, and of bifold rotation, in which a motif repeats itself exactly so that the two parts of a figure complement one another:

> Duality in the Hopi world view exists only insofar as it represents two correlates in a reciprocally balanced universal scheme, and each correlate is conceived as an indispensable part of the whole, neither one being essentially subordinate to the other.

There are other parallels between Pueblo world view, Sikyatki-type pottery design and Late Prehistoric Anasazi textile design, and it is tempting to assume that the world

Fig. 8.21. Black wool manta embroidered in indigo blue and green handspun yarns, and ravelled red, 105 cm × 148 cm. Acoma Pueblo (?) 1850–60. With the exception of the floral motifs along the inner edges of the borders, all design elements are drawn from prehistoric textiles, as is the use of negative line patterning. (Catalogue number T-44. Photograph courtesy School of American Research.)

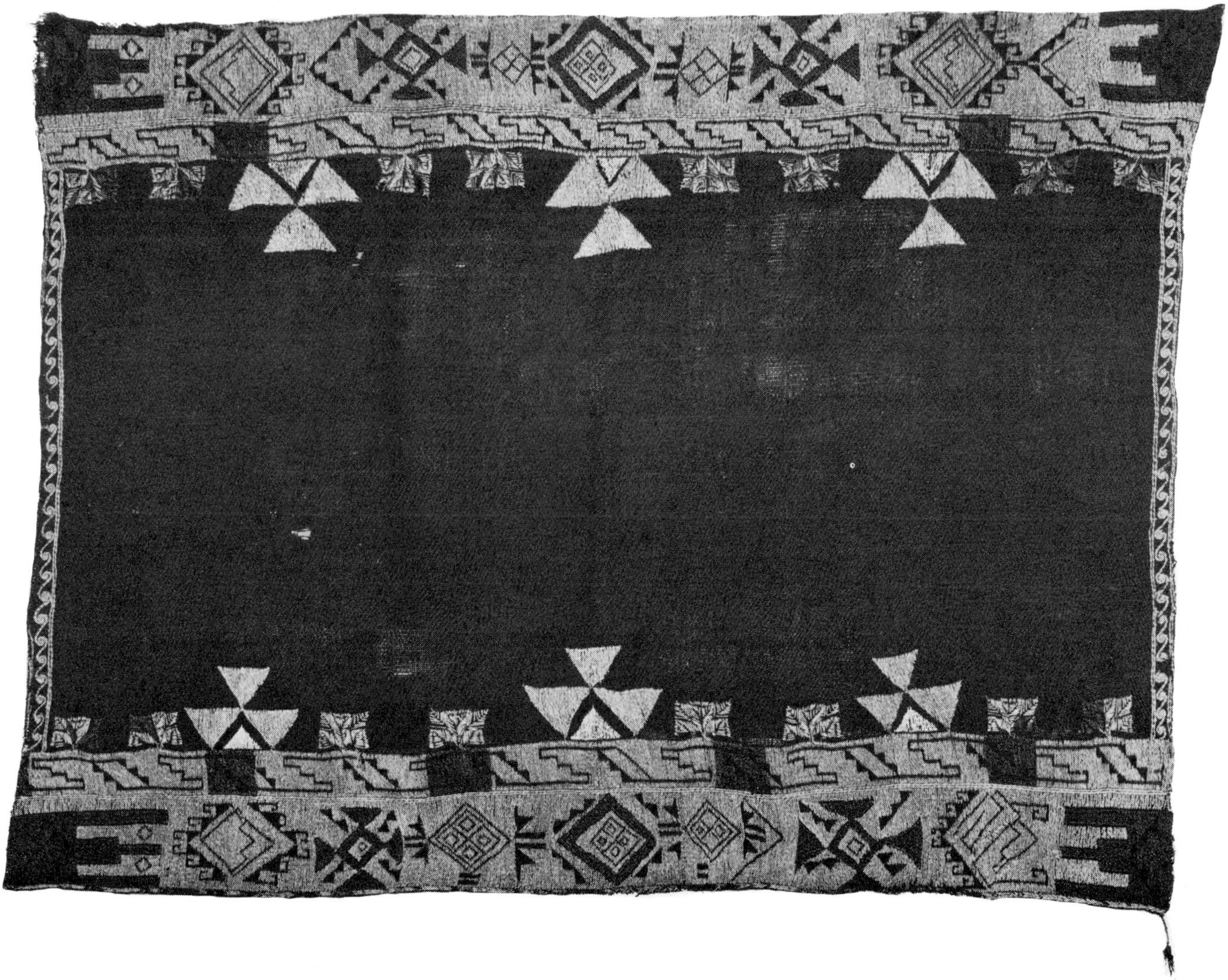

view of the prehistoric people was the same as that of contemporary Pueblos, and that it was given visual expression in their textiles. If this is so, however, how do we explain the change in textile design style that occurred in early historic times? Are we to infer that such a change reflects a change in other cultural systems? Or does world view remain constant and art style, perhaps marginally linked to group assumptions, change readily through simple copying of a foreign style, or loss of technical skills? Is the complete loss of dynamic design structure in early historic times to be explained solely by loss of the weave techniques associated with it? This hardly seems the final answer. Embroidery survived as an alternative decorative technique, and it is easily adaptable to any design system, since it is a free decorative process, similar to painting, and not bound by technique in the way that weaving is. It would certainly be adequate for perpetuating the two-dimensional limitless patterns of prehistoric times, but was simply not utilized in such a way.

The survival of the protohistoric border design style through some four hundred years of drastic culture change under Euro-American domination is more easily explained. It identifies the article quite clearly as Pueblo. As long as this is an important statement to Pueblo people, the art style will not change significantly.[2]

Postscript

After this paper was submitted for publication I received a copy of Zaslow's 'Pattern Dissemination in the Prehistoric Southwest and Mesoamerica', in which the author outlines the evolution of Hohokam decorative patterns and compares them to patterns from the Upper Gila and the Valley of Oaxaca. His evidence for the Hohokam is taken from ceramics and, for the Sacaton Phase (A.D. 1000–1100), from an etched shell and one weft-wrap openwork cotton cloth, as well. Upper Gila designs are from ceramics dated between A.D. 1200–1300, as analysed by Washburn (1977), and the Oaxacan patterns come from stone mosaics on the walls of the Temple of Columns at Mitla (Late Monte Alban V, or from A.D. 1000 to the Spanish conquest).

Zaslow finds correlations in the mathematical structures of patterns from the three geographical areas, although design styles (compositions) differ. In his words (p. 30) 'the correlations are too specialized to have resulted from isolated parallel developments'. He suggests that pattern properties were disseminated through visual communication resulting from the spread of a variety of decorated trade items, of which light-weight articles such as baskets, mats, and textiles were probably most important.

The pattern structure Zaslow illustrates (his figs. 12, 13) for Sacaton Phase Hohokam (A.D. 1000–1100), on Oaxacan architecture (figs. 19, 22), and Upper Gila ceramics (figs. 16, 17) is the same two-dimensional structure, based on slide reflection and bifold rotation which is so basic to Southwest textile design between A.D. 1000 and 1400. From his findings, it would appear that this and other Late Prehistoric textile pattern structures were part of an artistic convention once widely disseminated among pre-Spanish populations from southern Mexico to southern Utah, and expressed on a variety of media.

Notes

1 While basketry and mats are often classed as textile arts, we will not be concerned with them except where appropriate for purposes of design comparison. Our emphasis is on flexible fabrics constructed from twisted or spun fibres. We are not including Navajo textiles, which followed a separate evolution in historic times.

2 Some of the photographs and drawings in this article are taken from my 1957 monograph and my forthcoming book on prehistoric textiles. They are reprinted with permission of the American Philosophical Society and the School of American Research. Julie Wagner drew Figures 8.1, 8.2, 8.3 (in part), 8.4, 8.12, 8.15, 8.18, and redrew Figures 8.7, 8.8, 8.17. The analysis of design in the more recent publication and in this article has benefited from the application of symmetry analysis, a tool not used in the earlier study. This has given me an understanding of the logical system on which a pattern is built so that complete designs could be reconstructed from the very small scraps usually found in archaeological sites. Symmetry analysis has also helped in identifying certain fabrics traded into one area from a textile centre in which design structure was quite different in nature.

References

Bunzel, Ruth L., 1929. *The Pueblo Potter: a study of creative imagination in primitive art.* Columbia University Press, New York.
Cosgrove, C.B., 1947. Caves of the Upper Gila and Hueco areas in New Mexico and Texas. *Papers of the Peabody Museum* 24 (2). Harvard University, Cambridge, Mass.
Dutton, Bertha P., 1963. *Sun Father's Way: the Kiva murals of Kuaua.* University of New Mexico Press, Albuquerque.
Greenberg, Laura J., 1975. Art as a structural system: a study of Hopi pottery designs. *Studies in the Anthropology of Visual Communications* 2 (1): 33–50.
Guernsey, Samuel James and Alfred Vincent Kidder, 1921. Basket-maker caves of Northeastern Arizona. *Papers of the Peabody Museum* 8 (2). Harvard University, Cambridge, Mass.
Guthe, Carl E., 1925. *Pueblo Pottery Making.* Yale University Press, New Haven.
Hibben, Frank C., 1975. *Kiva art of the Anasazi at Pottery Mound.* KC Publications, Las Vegas.
Keleman, Pál, 1944. *Medieval American Art 2.* Macmillan, New York.
Kent, Kate P., 1957. The cultivation and weaving of cotton in the Prehistoric Southwestern United States. *American Philosophical Society Transactions* 47 (3).
In press. Textiles of the Prehistoric Southwest. *Southwest Indian Art Series.* School of American Research, Santa Fe.
Mera, H.P., 1975. *Pueblo Indian Embroidery.* William Gannon, Santa Fe.
Morris, Earl H., n.d. Unpublished research notes. Arizona State Museum, Tucson.
Morris, Earl H. and Robert F. Burgh, 1941. Anasazi basketry, Basket-maker II through Pueblo III. *Carnegie Institution of Washington Publication* 533.
Morris, Elizabeth Ann, 1980. Basketmaker caves in the Prayer Rock district, Northeastern Arizona. *University of Arizona Anthropological Papers* 35. Tucson.
Ortiz, Alfonso, 1972. Ritual drama and the Pueblo world view. In

New Perspectives on the Pueblos, edited by A. Ortiz. University of New Mexico Press, Albuquerque.

Shepard, Anna O., 1948. The symmetry of abstract design with special reference to ceramic decoration. *Carnegie Institution of Washington Publication* 574.

1956. Ceramics for the archeologist. *Carnegie Institution of Washington Publication* 609.

Smith, Watson, 1952. Kiva mural decorations at Awatovi and Kawaika-a. *Papers of the Peabody Museum* 37. Harvard University, Cambridge, Mass.

Tanner, Clara Lee, 1976. *Prehistoric Southwestern Craft Arts.* University of Arizona, Tucson.

Thompson, Laura, and Alice Joseph, 1944. *The Hopi Way.* University of Chicago Press, Chicago.

Washburn, Dorothy K., 1977. A symmetry analysis of Upper Gila area ceramic design. *Papers of the Peabody Museum* 68. Harvard University, Cambridge, Mass.

Zaslow, Bert, 1981. Pattern dissemination in the Prehistoric Southwest and Mesoamerica. *Arizona State University Anthropological Research Papers* 25. Tempe.

Chapter 9

Symmetry analysis of ceramic design: two tests of the method on Neolithic material from Greece and the Aegean

Dorothy K. Washburn

Introduction

Determining the temporal and spatial sensitivity of variations in artifact attributes has been a problem in archaeological methodology. While it is clear that attributes vary through time and space, it has been difficult to find attributes whose variation can be measured and compared systematically and objectively through time and across broad areas. This paper presents two test cases where symmetry analysis is used to demonstrate how the attribute – pattern structure – is a sensitive temporal and spatial cultural marker.

The method involves use of the principles of symmetry to describe the motions which generate a repeated design (Washburn 1977a). The resulting symmetry class assignments define the structural arrangements of the design elements within the design fields. This structure has been found to be culturally specific and temporally and spatially restricted (Washburn 1977b), and thus should be useful analytically for the reconstruction of certain aspects of past lifeways.

The first test case shows how structural changes can highlight shifts in cultural activities throughout long temporal periods. Changes over a period of 3,000 years in the structure of incised designs on sherds from seven stratified levels at Knossos are examined and shown to correlate with other interaction shifts in the Aegean cultural sphere.

The second test case suggests how similarities and differences in ceramic design structure from a number of Early and Late Neolithic sites on mainland Greece may be related to geographical and cultural factors.

The method: symmetry analysis

Although the principles of symmetry were established largely by Russian crystallographers at the turn of the century (Shubnikov and Koptsik 1974), and the procedure of symmetry analysis for archaeologists has been detailed in Washburn (1977a), a brief summary is presented here for the convenience of readers of this chapter. Symmetry describes the superposition of parts of a design of equivalent size and shape as these parts move along a line axis and/or about a point axis during the generation of a given pattern. A pattern is defined as any design with regularly repeated parts, called fundamental parts. These fundamental parts move along the axis by one or a combination of several geometric motions, and it is these motion classes which are used to describe a particular repeated pattern.

The number of motion classes is not necessarily infinite, but it is restricted by the character of the axial configuration. Thus, patterns whose parts move about a point axis are called finite, because eventually the parts will move full circle to superimpose upon the original starting point (Fig. 9.1A). Patterns whose parts move along a line axis are called one-dimensional infinite, since their generation in one direction can theoretically be repeated an infinite number of times without superimposition on the original part (Fig. 9.1B). Likewise, patterns whose parts move along two line axes are called two-dimensional infinite, since their generation in two directions can be repeated an infinite number of times (Fig. 9.1C).

Finite, one-dimensional and two-dimensional patterns are the three plane pattern categories which can describe all repeated designs on baskets, pottery, textiles, paintings, carvings, or any other flat surface or media which can be conceptually flattened. Three-dimensional forms and their symmetries are not considered in this study.

There are four motions basic to the above three plane pattern categories: translation, rotation, mirror reflection, and slide reflection. If a design is subdivided into the smallest equivalent fundamental parts which can be superimposed, and these parts are conceptualized as asymmetric commas, then the simplest symmetry motion, translation, can be represented as a series of commas moving along a single line axis (Fig. 9.2A). Thus, the generation of a pattern by translation is accomplished by successively superimposing commas along a linear axis. Given the linear orientation, translated patterns can only be present in one- and two-dimensional categories. Although all other symmetrical designs which are generated by more complex motions also can be said to be translated designs, the symmetry of any given design is always described by the most complex motion or motions which generate that design.

The motion of rotation (Fig. 9.2B), whereby fundamental design parts are moved around a point axis, can describe designs generated in all three plane pattern categories considered here. In finite designs the parts can rotate around the central point axis any number of fold rotations. In one-dimensional designs only bifold (two-fold) rotation is admitted, since any other number of rotations would move the parts off the line axis. In two-dimensional designs only two, three, four or six-fold rotations are possible.

The motion of mirror reflection (Fig. 9.2C) described the mirror reflection position of two symmetrical fundamental parts across a mirror plane. This motion is present in all three plane pattern categories. Another type of reflection, slide or glide reflection (Fig. 9.2D) refers to the mirror reflection of design parts across a mirror plane and then the translation of the parts along the line axis. Because line axes are involved, the motion of slide reflection is present in only one- and two-dimensional patterns.

The above discussion provides a classification for repeated designs in three plane pattern categories which have parts of identical size, shape and colour. Patterns also exist whose parts are of identical size and shape, but whose

Fig. 9.1.
A. Finite structure, Class 211.
B. One-dimensional structure, Class 1–211.
C. Two-dimensional structure, Class 2–211.

A

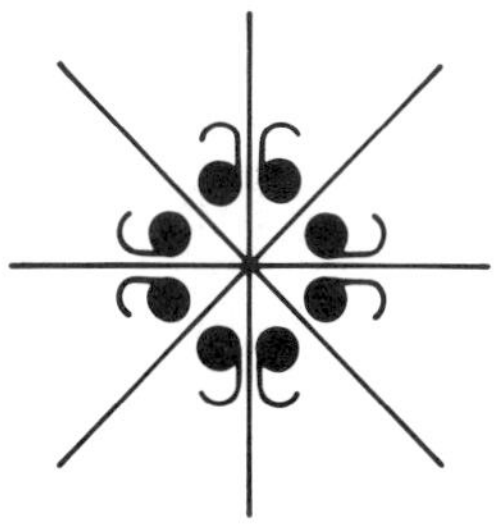

B

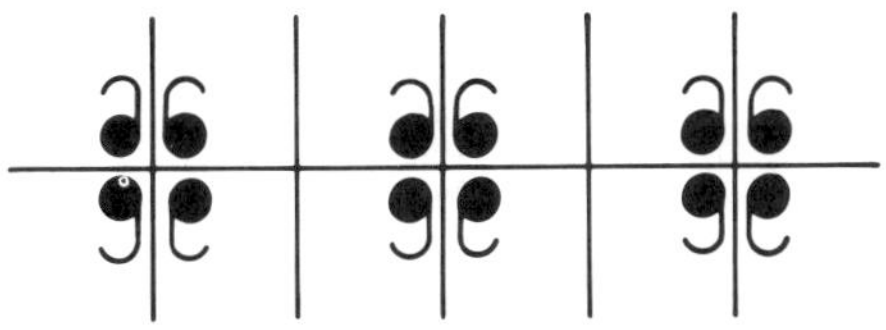

C

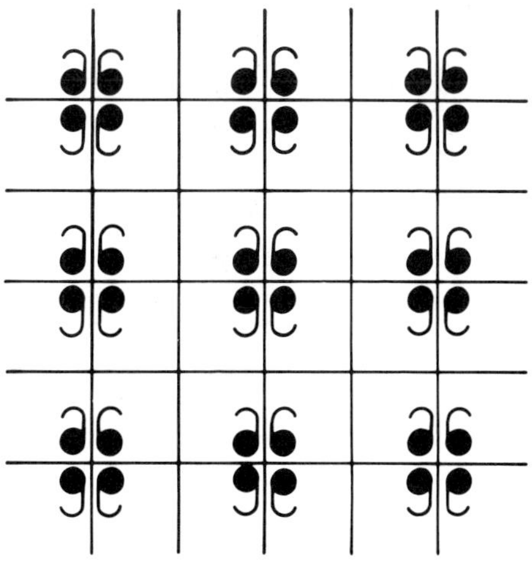

Fig. 9.2.
A. Translation, Class 1–100.
B. Bifold rotation, Class 1–200.
C. Horizontal mirror reflection, Class 1–110.
D. Slide reflection, Class 1–100x^1.

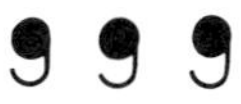

A

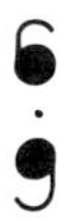

B

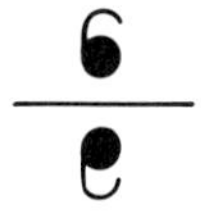

C

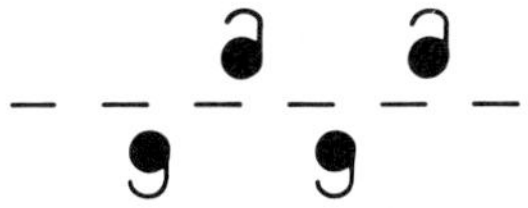

D

colours alternate, most frequently in an A–B–A–B fashion, although any number of colour alternations theoretically may be admitted. Such patterns are said to have colour reversal or counterchange. The classification of these patterns involves determination of the specific type of colour reversal class within the general one-colour motion class.

The nomenclature for each motion class is detailed in Washburn 1977a. Briefly, the prefix indicates the category; the first digit, the number of translations or rotations; the second digit, the presence/absence of horizontal reflections; and the third digit, the presence/absence of vertical reflections.

Cultural basis of structural analysis

Given the systematic nature of symmetry analysis and the comparable results obtainable, it is appropriate to compare this system to the other typological and descriptive classifications of ceramics now in use (see also Washburn 1978).

One of the major thrusts of current archaeological theory is the isolation and study of individual factors responsible for variation and change. Inherent in this approach is the assumption that there are a number of different factors operating to produce any given event or object and that the study of variation or change in an event or object requires analysis only of the relevant factor or factors.

Typologies were developed to describe and differentiate quantities of cultural material in order to arrange sites in general spatial and temporal chronological sequence. No effort was made to address specific questions, since the emphasis was on the establishment of areal culture histories. Because types are only general indices of cultural similarity, they include many factors ranging from those relating to the environmental availability of clays, temper and paint to those relating to cultural choices of design elements or colour. In practice, typological studies are subjective processes, since not every sherd possesses all of the different factors attributed to a given type. Thus, a sherd may be assigned to a particular type even if not all attributes characteristic of that type are present on that sherd. Furthermore, each investigator may have a bias toward the importance of different factors when determining inclusion or exclusion within a type. As a result, a false indication of the occurrence of a particular factor may be obtained. This lumping of attributes clearly will not enable study of individual factors. The shortcomings of standard typological classifications of ceramics for the investigation of current archaeological problems are legion.

This paper presents an alternative method of artifact analysis – classification by the symmetry of the repeated patterns – which focuses on one attribute – design structure – which seems to relate directly to an identifiable, specific aspect of culture.

Analysis of designs from well-documented baskets of a number of California Indian tribes (Washburn 1977b) has shown that a given cultural group or groups which interact and have the same lifeway produces designs based on the same set of symmetry structures. Although the designs may appear quite variable due to the variety of elements and motifs used in their construction, the important point is that the basic structural arrangement of the elements is consistent for a given cultural group. Indeed, the same design elements may be used in common by tribes which do not interact as well as by those which do. The critical factor, again, is the specific way that the elements are structured into the whole design. It is this structure which appears to be unique for each cultural group.

Thus groups which may be neighbours and thus interact frequently and have culturally similar lifeways tend to use similar design structures. Conversely, groups which are enemies, have little contact, or which pursue different organizational and life patterns use markedly different symmetries to structure their designs. Thus, identity in design structure seems to be indicative of homogeneous cultural composition and intensity of cultural interaction. Differences in design structure suggest the absence of interaction, whether it be due, for example, to linguistic incompatibility, environmental barriers, migrations, wars or sudden cultural replacement.

Two ways to understand a given interaction pattern defined on the basis of artifactual distributions involve (1) querying ethnographic studies for similar interaction pathways and the patterning in artifactual evidence that results, and (2) defining a series of models of interactions that could exist at different organizational thresholds and examining their feasibility vis-à-vis the data.

Although not vast, the body of ethnographic literature relating to group interaction patterns is growing with the awareness of both ethnographers and archaeologists of the need to collect such data. Since this paper is concerned with types of interaction networks that would be produced by potters, the following discussion is limited to (1) observations on the relation of design styles of family or tribal units, and (2) observations on the kinds of exchange networks fostered by particular ceramic production situations.

The conservative nature of the potter, both in technological and decorative aspects, leads to village or tribal styles (Stanislawski and Stanislawski 1974). Balfet comments that Maghreb area pottery has decorations which

> follow fairly strict rules of application especially the cutting of surfaces and the filling in of these areas according to a fairly strict symmetry . . . each region has its personal style which differs markedly from others . . . there may be minute variations from village to village, but they are clearly recognizable.
>
> (Balfet 1965: 161–2)

In societies where pottery is produced solely for home use, with little attention given to elaborate decoration, potters from different groups still manage to produce discrete forms and styles of decoration.[1] Even potters who produce for markets are conservative artisans who only reluctantly vary from their village style to accept innovations in order to improve their sales. Foster has observed that the 'reason lies in the nature of the production process . . . which places a premium on strict adherence to tried and proven ways . . . ' (Foster 1965: 49).

Balfet illustrates the implications these practices have for archaeologists investigating changes in design styles by correlating the sequence of change in design with changes in other organizational aspects of prehistoric Maghreb society. During the Neolithic, the 'rich variety of procedures and decorative effects' on the sherds suggested that 'pottery was a local, even a family production, each decorative formula having its area of expansion within the frontiers of still limited social groups'. Suddenly, during the Chalcolithic, decorations and finish deteriorated, and vessel shapes and decoration became monotonously similar. This 'seem[s] to bear witness to products wrought by only a few hands, implying a certain degree of, as yet, very elemental artisonal specialization'. However, by the Early Bronze Age, 'clearly defined types . . . are found . . . in many sites'. The 'homogeneity, both technical and stylistic . . . [suggests] specialists-artisans produced them for a fairly large clientele' (Balfet 1965: 175–6).

Remarkably, at least for many parts of north Africa, pottery produced for household use is far more varied in design detail than the 'mass produced' wares artisans produce for market sale. Furthermore, although both occasional and professional potters adhere to certain community-wide rules, market oriented workshops produce widely distributed quantities of homogeneous wares, whereas families producing for their own consumption make wares which can be recognized by individual family styles.

Among the Fulani, pottery is produced for local household consumption (David and Hennig 1972: 21). 'Most pottery remains in the same quarter of the village in which it is made, and rarely travels more than 200 metres between producer and consumer.' However, because Fulani marriages are never long-lived, women, in effect, circulate among husbands in different households and villages. This introduces a counter effect whereby at some period a village has more than enough women potters to supply household needs, and thus 'exports' pots. At other times a village may have too few potters and will need to 'import' pottery. In the village of Bé, for example, forty-five per cent of the pots had been brought in (over a period of twenty years) by visitors from neighbouring hamlets. Twenty-five per cent were purchased in three markets, all within a 22 kilometre radius from Bé; less than five per cent were imported from villages more than 23 kilometres from Bé.

In contrast, Mexican artisans who produce for market sale may transport their pots to a number of different local markets, 16–24 kilometres from the home village. Even longer trips may be made to towns where a seller's market is assured (Foster 1965: 45).

These differences in the styles and in the nature of distribution of pottery produced for local use versus that produced for market sale are remarkable. The magnitude of these differences suggests that they should be visible in the archaeological record. Indeed, in her now classic study of potters in San José, Michoacan, Mexico, Friedrich suggested three 'indicators of intensity of communication': organization of spatial divisions, classification of design configurations, and functions of design elements in a configuration that can be recorded on archaeological ceramics (Friedrich 1970: 338–9).

This paper focuses on the organization of parts of designs and shows how symmetry analysis can describe this organization in a systematic fashion. Further, the comparable nature of symmetry analysis which allows relation of vast areas is thus uniquely suitable for discovery and description of areas of pottery production and networks of pottery trade. The results of the following two tests suggest types of interaction information that structural analysis of repeated designs can reveal.

Test I: Delineation of temporal aspects of cultural change by symmetry analysis: an example from the Neolithic levels of Knossos and Saliagos

Introduction

The beginnings of civilization in the Aegean have long posed an intriguing problem for archaeologists. This test examines in some detail the lengthy Neolithic record in order to focus upon certain types of shifts in ceramic production which appear to be sensitive to externally induced cultural change. Specifically, marked increase in variety of design structures on decorated ceramic vessels seems to coincide with the period of inception of the inter-island trading network at the end of the Early Neolithic that was to become so important for the development of Mediterranean civilizations. Examination of design structural changes on sherds from seven stratified levels at Knossos representing 3,000 years of prehistory reveals that such local exchange networks between neighbouring islands were operative as early as the Middle to Late Neolithic. One such localized link revealed by structural analysis is that between the sites of Knossos on Crete and Saliagos in the Cyclades.

The method of symmetry analysis assists in defining the character of the design system of a cultural group as well as in comparing the systems of several groups. Optimum conditions for achieving the first objective necessitate examination of single component sites with deep continuous stratigraphic profiles, suggestive of continuous occupancy by the same population group. The choice of a situation unencumbered by major stratigraphic hiatuses or disconformities in occupation caused by group abandonment or replacement should minimize the effects of externally induced changes. This would thus allow maximum opportunity to define the design system and the type of internal changes it slowly undergoes. Furthermore, a continuous stratigraphic profile containing many different artifactual forms which show patterns of gradual change through time comparable to those observed in the designs would give the investigator maximal evidence to reconstruct the events that promoted these changes. Two sites, Knossos and Saliagos, meet the criteria of stratigraphic continuity and contemporaneity necessary for the proposed study.

Data

The site of Knossos on the island of Crete has had a lengthy history of excavation. Sir Arthur Evans undertook the first major investigation in 1900 and excavated again in 1923 (A.J. Evans 1900). The pottery recovered during the first series of excavations was analysed by MacKenzie (MacKenzie 1903) and later was reanalysed in depth by Furness (Furness 1953). In 1957 Hood reopened sections of the central court in order to obtain more information on the character of Neolithic houses. This work was continued by J. Evans until 1960. Both the test pits of A. Evans in the west court and those of J. Evans in the central court yielded uninterrupted sequences of cultural materials from the surface to virgin soil or bedrock.

The Neolithic is a lengthy period at Knossos. Test pits located near the centre of the settlement, i.e. the area of the central court, contained from 8 to 10 metres of cultural deposits. The deepest deposits are from the Early Neolithic and indicate a lengthy occupation of almost 1,500 years. MacKenzie's subdivision of the Early Neolithic into two phases has been maintained by Furness and J. Evans. According to Evans' excavations in the central court, the Early Neolithic I (EN I) is represented by levels VII, VI, and V; while the Early Neolithic II (EN II) is represented by level IV. The Middle Neolithic (MN) is represented by level III and the Late Neolithic (LN) by levels II and I (J.D. Evans 1964).

J. Evans estimates that although the Early Neolithic settlement initially may have covered only half an acre, it continually grew in size, covering 5 acres during the Middle Neolithic and finally 11 acres by the Late Neolithic (J.D. Evans 1971). Carbon 14 dates (half life 5570 years) from the lowest level X range from 6100 ± 180 B.C. to 5790 ± 130 B.C. Dates from level V, the latest level in the EN I, range from 5050 ± 180 to 4190 ± 150 B.C. (J.D. Evans 1968: 272).

The data base for this study was limited to that available in J. Evans's detailed and well-illustrated site report (J.D. Evans 1964). Although MacKenzie observed the same general changes in types through time (MacKenzie 1903), the sherds from his excavations were not illustrated, and information on the different types was discussed only in terms of levels no smaller than one metre deep. Furness examined material from eight of A. Evans's test pits, but the large proportion of burnished wares masked differences in relative amounts of the other types of decorated wares. These later wares, designated as 'ornament' by Furness, had rippled, incised, plastic and pointillé types of surface treatment, and usually comprised less than one per cent of the collection from any level. With two exceptions, Furness notes the same distribution of patterns in the EN I, EN II, MN and LN periods as did J. Evans. The exceptions are a two-dimensional zigzag, oriented vertically (pattern G) which Furness noted as an EN I pattern (Furness 1953: fig. 9, no. 15) but which J. Evans did not find until EN II, level IV; and a pattern which Furness found in the MN strata but which J. Evans found slightly earlier in the EN II, level IV strata. For the purposes of consistency and because Furness was limited by the somewhat dubious sorting and labelling of the sherds into boxes by MacKenzie,[2] I have chosen to limit my analysis of the data to those recovered by J. Evans since they were carefully provenienced and well illustrated.

Although J. Evans recovered sherds with a variety of surface treatments, only the pointillé and incised designs have been examined in this paper since the other forms of decoration (appliqué and rippled) are not amenable to symmetry analysis. However, since J. Evans expressed the quantity of sherds recovered in kilograms (J. Evans 1964: fig. 46), rather than in raw counts of each decorated type, only a presence/absence accounting of the different structural subgroupings of the two types of surface treatment per level could be employed. A total of eighty sherds from the Early Neolithic level VII to the Late Neolithic level I in Areas AC–BC of the central court were analysed. The selection was limited to those illustrated with a sufficient amount of design observable for symmetry classification.

J. Evans noted changes in frequencies of four types of surface treatment (plastic, pointillé, incised, and rippled) of these wares from level I to level VII (J. Evans 1964: fig. 46). Although each technique overlaps in the strata with its predecessor and successor technique, there is, nevertheless, a definite change in preference for type of surface decoration from plastic to rippled through time. Although ten cultural levels were observed in the test areas, only levels VII to I contained pointillé and incised sherds that can be analysed by symmetry analysis. Pointillé wares were found in levels VII, VI, and V while the incised wares were found in levels V, IV, III, II, and I. It is notable that J. Evans found some sherds decorated with both pointillé and incised techniques. This is in accord with the other indications of a situation of continual, undisturbed growth and change. While some innovations were gradually being developed to replace other innovations, there was a period of overlap in use of different techniques.

The beginning of pointillé wares in level VII is associated with a shift in house construction techniques from mud brick to packed mud walls on a stone foundation. This event occurred during the first phase of the Early Neolithic (EN I). Only small quantities of incised wares were found by Furness and J. Evans in the EN I levels. The second phase of the Early Neolithic (EN II) is represented in level IV (C 14 date of 3730 ± 150), and is characterized by three periods of house construction. House walls are of stones and clay; some floors are paved with pebbles. Pointillé decoration continues to be produced, but in smaller amounts, since it is largely being replaced by the use of incised decoration. Level III represents the Middle Neolithic at Knossos. J. Evans believes that it represents a relatively short period that is characterized by one building phase and a predominance of ripple burnished ware. Incised ware continues to be produced but the elements are now more frequently filled with hatching. The Late Neolithic begins in level II and culminates in level I, which is overlain by Bronze Age Minoan materials.

The above discussion is a brief summary of the Neolithic levels, their ceramic contents and the interpretations that J. Evans was able to glean from this material. In a review of the Neolithic at Knossos, J. Evans (1971: 109) observed that the most notable change occurred in level III during the Middle Neolithic: 'it is at this point that there is the first evidence of significant acceleration in the rate of change, which I believe is almost certainly to be correlated with a gradual increase in contact with other parts of the Aegean'.

Indeed, such an event should represent a marked shift in orientation of a cultural group previously relatively isolated, and should be observable in many types of changes in the artifactual remains. Evans, for example, cites the appearance at Knossos of several new vessel forms (chalices, fruitstands, carinated bowls, and spouted vessels) (J. Evans 1971: 109, footnote 2). The following discussion adds the dimension of coincident structural change and increased variation in ceramic designs.

An examination of the ceramic evidence from level III (Fig. 9.3) shows only a slight increase in pointillé ware from EN II, layer IV and only a slight decrease in incised wares from EN II, layer IV. Plastic decoration becomes nonexistent. From Evans' analysis of surface treatment and design, only the marked increase in ripple decorated wares suggests the arrival of new influences at Knossos.

However, it would seem inconsistent that the new vessel forms that he documents which appear in level III would be unaccompanied by other changes. Indeed, if one analyses the structure of the designs on the pointillé and incised wares produced before and after the period of contact, it is clear that, although the percentage of each technique changes little, the patterns and structures of those patterns produced are markedly different. In short, the results of a symmetry analysis support the suggestion of the initiation of outside contact as indicated by the appearance of new vessel forms.

Eighty sherds with nineteen patterns (Fig. 9.4) were analysed by their structure classes and arranged in the proper stratigraphic sequence from Early Neolithic to Late Neolithic, levels VII to level I (Fig. 9.5). J.D. Evans observed a shift from pointillé to incised decoration techniques, and this is documented in Figure 9.5, where the four pointillé patterns all occur in the EN I, levels VII, VI, and V, while incised sherds predominate in levels IV, III, II, and I (J.D. Evans 1964). These four patterns are generated by two structures: Class 1–201 for patterns A, B, and C; and Class 1–101 for pattern D. No pattern is counterchanged and no pattern has its symmetry of structure reduced by the addition of pointillé dots (here considered as a form of embellishment) within each element shape. Thus, four patterns generated by two one-dimensional symmetry classes characterize the design output from the first phase of the Early Neolithic.

Strikingly notable is the dramatic increase in number of patterns and symmetry classes used in the late phases of the Early Neolithic in level IV. Pointillé decoration is replaced by a predominant use of incised patterns. More importantly, there are now thirteen different patterns in use, only one of which (pattern E) is a hold-over from level V. This particular pattern, however, is not composed by the pointillé technique.

The structures of the thirteen patterns of EN II are generated by ten different symmetry motions. Class 1–101 generates patterns D, E, and O; Class 1–110 generates patterns K and L; Class 1–211 generates pattern N; Class 1–200 generates pattern M, and Class 1–201 generates patterns P and Q. These nine patterns are all one-dimensional designs. The other four patterns are two-dimensional designs. Class $2\text{–}201x_1^1$ generates pattern G; Class $2\text{–}210y_1^1$ generates pattern H; Class 2–211 generates pattern R; and Class 2–411 generates pattern F.

In short, sixty-two per cent of the structures of level IV designs are structures which were not in use in the previous periods. Only thirty-eight per cent structural overlap and only eight per cent design overlap exists between the Early Neolithic I and the Early Neolithic II. Furthermore, in contrast to the patterns produced during EN I times, the structures of the EN II designs are frequently reduced due to element embellishments (patterns N, M, O, P, Q), and some designs are counterchanged (patterns F and R).

J. Evans was able to observe from the varying weight frequencies in his histograms that the pointillé decoration in level IV was characterized by 'fewer rows of triangles' and more 'other patterns' (J.D. Evans 1964: 216). Alternatively, because symmetry analysis is a more objective and systematic analytical procedure, a more specific characterization of the changes in design can be obtained. Thus, the earlier 'rows of triangles' can be reclassified as various motion classes of one-dimensional patterns and the later 'other patterns' as two-dimensional patterns. This shift from designs arranged along a single axis to complex all-over two-dimensional patterns marks a major shift in design construction. The fact that this change can be quantified by simply counting the relative frequencies of the various design structures, and that these same trends can be compared among a number of sites, improves the accuracy and thus the usefulness of the inferences regarding the cultural meaning of the structural shifts.

Furthermore, symmetry analysis can eliminate the need to use subjective design labels such as 'herringbone', 'tree-pattern', 'chevrons', and 'ladders'. For example, 'herringbone' patterns are Class $1\text{–}100x^1$, i.e., one-dimensional designs generated by slide reflection. 'Chevrons' are Class 1–110 designs; i.e., one-dimensional designs generated by horizontal mirror reflection.

During the Middle Neolithic, five of the seven patterns (O, P, Q, R, and E) are carried over from the EN II period. The two new patterns (S and T) use symmetry structures (1–201 and 1–211 respectively) that were used during the previous periods. The more predominant new characteristic of Middle Neolithic designs is the use of hatching to embellish the structure (patterns O, P, Q). In doing so, the symmetry of the structure is reduced. One pattern (R) is counterchanged. Thus, level III designs show one hundred per cent overlap in structural continuity and seventy-one per cent overlap in design patterns with level IV patterns. This continuity is in marked contrast to the discontinuity observed between the previous EN I–II periods.

During the Late Neolithic no new patterns were introduced and only three patterns continue to be produced (Q, R, and T). Patterns Q and T have their structures reduced due to added embellishments, and pattern R is counterchanged. Again, the continuity observed for the Middle Neolithic continues into the Late Neolithic.

Symmetry analysis has clearly indicated that the point of greatest change in ceramic design was in the EN II, level IV. Let us now reexamine the evidence to account for the discrepancy between Evans' suggestion that the change occurred during the Middle Neolithic, level III, and the evidence presented here which suggests that the critical change

Fig. 9.3. Frequency of major types of surface treatment of Neolithic pottery from Knossos (after J. Evans 1968: fig. 46).

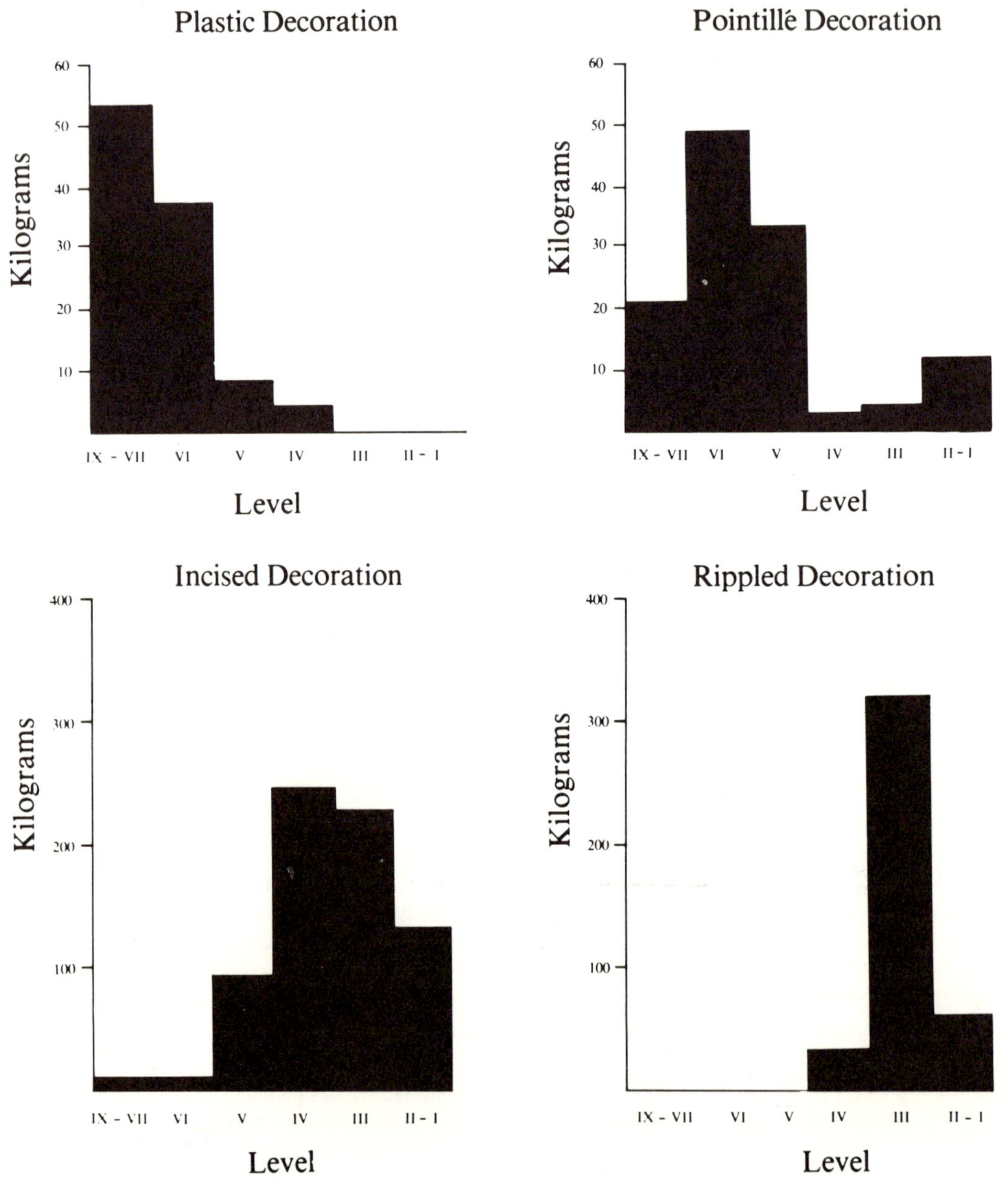

Fig. 9.4. Nineteen idealized patterns from Knossos, levels I–VII. Dotted patterns are pointillé; line drawings are incised.*

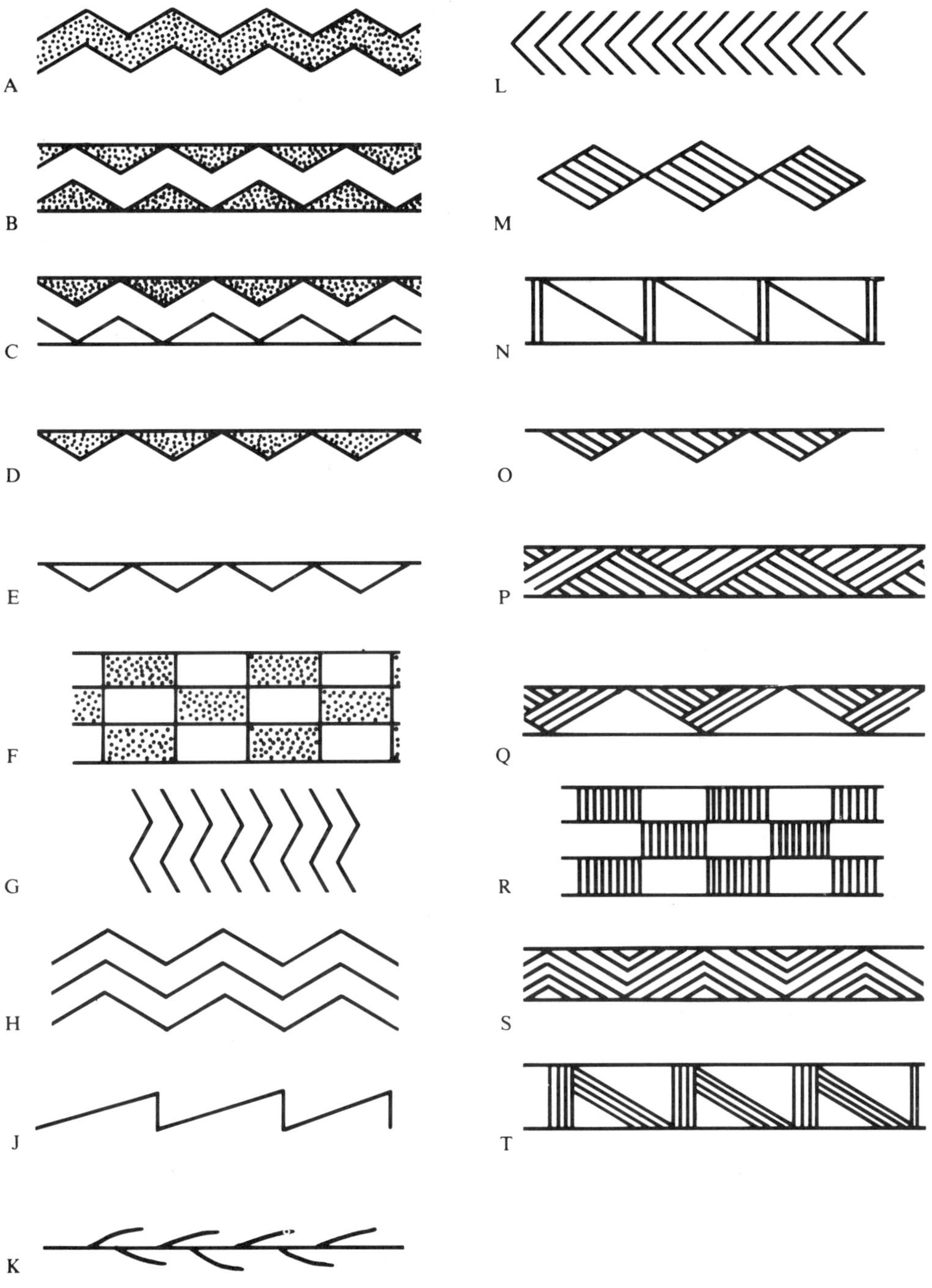

*Pattern	Reference in Evans 1964
A	Fig. 27, #4
B	Fig. 27, #7
C	Fig. 27, #8
D	Fig. 27, #24
E	Fig. 28, #6
F	Fig. 32, #12
G	Fig. 32, #21
H	Fig. 32, #23
J	Plate 47, 3 #2
K	Fig. 32, #26

Pattern	Reference in Evans 1964
L	Plate 43, #3
M	Fig. 32, #31
N	Plate 47, 4 #1
O	Fig. 35, #25
P	Fig. 32, #22
Q	Fig. 38, #6 & 7
R	Fig. 38, #11
S	Plate 49, 1 #4
T	Plate 50, 1 #1

occurred slightly earlier, during the EN II, level IV. The above analysis has clearly indicated a marked increase in the number of different design patterns and structures through time as well as a shift from simple patterns to ones which are reduced by additional embellishments or which are counterchanged. In short, there has been, through time, a definite increase in the number and complexity of the patterns. J. Evans claimed that this marked 'acceleration in the rate of change' occurred during the Middle Neolithic, level III. However, if one assumes that the greatest cultural change occurs during the period of the greatest increase in structural complexity of designs, then one would suggest that the change occurred slightly earlier during the Early Neolithic II (level IV) period.

One way to investigate this problem would be to search for evidence of similar designs and structures from contemporaneous sites in the Aegean to confirm that the contact that Knossos had with other groups was the source for all the new designs in level IV. Although the task of discovering design similarities between sites in the Aegean would seem to be straightforward, it has been hampered by the paucity of sites with sherds or whole vessels of sufficient size to enable characterization of the design structures, and a sufficient number of sites with C 14 dates which will attest to their contemporaneity.

Furness conducted an extensive search for ceramic parallels among early sites in the Aegean islands and neighbouring coastal areas (Furness 1956). However, despite the fact that incised and pointillé decorated sherds were recovered at all the sites mentioned, the use of this superficial coincidence in technique to indicate cultural contact must be questioned. Symmetry analysis and specific pattern identification have shown these similarities to be specious.

For example, a common incised pattern from Tigani on Samos (Furness 1956: fig. 2, F5–F15) is a 1–201 zigzag composed of multiple parallel lines which are not continuous (Fig. 9.6A). This specific pattern does not occur at Knossos. The designs on incised sherds from Kalimnos have an entirely different layout from those from Knossos (Furness 1956: plate XX, no. 6) (Fig. 9.6B). Conversely, while Knossos patterns H and L are found on sherds from Thermi (Lamb 1936: fig. 35, nos. 10, 14) (Fig. 9.6C), the assignment of an Early Bronze Age date for the material from this site obviates its contemporaneity with the late Early Neolithic incised patterns from Knossos. Thus, the presence of pointillé or incised techniques at several sites, even those which may be contemporaneous, does not necessarily indicate that these similarities are the result of contact.

However, similarities in both structure and pattern were discovered at the site of Saliagos in the Cyclades. The range of C 14 dates from Saliagos, from 4300 to 3700 B.C., from the three strata, overlap with those from strata VI to IV at Knossos. During this period, a more than twofold increase in number of patterns and design structures appeared at Knossos. Six designs (Fig. 9.7) from Saliagos illustrated by Evans and Renfrew (1968), although executed in a white paint rather than in the incising technique, are distinctly similar to those from Knossos. Notably, five of the six Knossos patterns (G, H, M, R, L) first appeared in the Early Neolithic, level IV at Knossos; pattern T appears in the Middle Neolithic level III at Knossos.

It is important to consider the geography of the

Fig. 9.5. Correlation of design structures from 19 pointillé and incised patterns from Knossos with temporal periods. X indicates presence of pattern.

Structural Reductions							$2-4_3 1_2 1_2$							1–200	1–100	$1-100x^1$	1–100	$2-2_3 1_2 1_2$		1–200
Structure Classes		1–201	1–201	1–201	1–101	1–101	2–411	$2-201x_1^1$	$2-210y_1^1$	1–200	1–110	1–110	1–200	1–211	1–101	1–201	1–201	2–211	1–201	1–211
Periods	Levels																			
LN	I																X	X		X
LN	II																X	X		X
MN	III					X									X	X	X	X	X	X
EN II	IV					X	X	X	X	X	X	X	X	X	X	X	X	X		
EN I	V		X	X	X	X														
EN I	VI	X	X	X	X															
EN I	VII	X	X	X	X															
Patterns		A	B	C	D	E	F	G	H	J	K	L	M	N	O	P	Q	R	S	T

Aegean islands as well as of mainland Greece when evaluating these structural design similarities. The mountain chain which forms the backbone of mainland Greece continues into the Aegean; the higher peaks surface as the Cyclades. Only small valleys or coastal plains are found sandwiched among the rough terrain. The mountainous countryside of Crete, the largest island in the Aegean, is dominated by four mountain peaks. Although its southern perimeter offers an inhospitably steep coastline, the northern shores are broken by fertile valleys and terraced hillslopes.

Thus, the islands, although predominantly composed of largely unusable high mountainous regions, contain a number of viable and culturally important micro-environments: alluvial plains for small vegetable and grain farms; hillslopes for grapes and olives; lower mountain slopes for grazing; as well as the many resources of the earth – obsidian, marble, emery, andesite, silver and kaolin – and the resources of the sea.

Faunal and botanical evidence from Knossos indicates that there was a shift in the subsistence base from a predominant use of sheep and goat in the earliest levels to an increasing dependence on cattle and pig, as well as cereal grains (J. Evans 1968). The inhabitants of Saliagos were primarily dependent on tunny and shellfish (Evans and Renfrew 1968: 80), although evidence of sheep and barley was recovered.

Despite the apparent self-sufficiency of these early farmers and herders, several lines of evidence, here outlined in design similarities, point to the early development of an 'outward orientation' of these island peoples for the exchange of different products. The following reconstruction briefly outlines one possible developmental route for such a situation.

It might be expected that archaeological evidence of sporadic contact would consist of relatively infrequent finds of non-locally made pottery. The designs on these vessels would be easily distinguishable from those of the local site. Conversely, the establishment of more formalized exchange relationships would lead not only to an increase in people and goods moving between the loci involved, but also to an increase in the frequency of exchanges. More vessels, either traded for their own value or containing goods to be traded, would pass before the eyes of the local potters more frequently in both areas, and local copies of non-local ideas would be produced and incorporated into the local design system.

Gradually, the artifacts from the many formerly isolated, self-sufficient areas of the Aegean would assume similar characteristics. Each group would still retain its own particular cultural character (manifested by a distinctive style in each centre: i.e., the incised pottery of Knossos versus the white painted ware of Saliagos), but their participation in an exchange network would encourage some exposure to and adoption of new decorative ideas.

More extensive contacts, such as those produced by a conquering or immigrant group, would have introduced a different type of change in the local culture from that which is apparent either at Neolithic Knossos or at Saliagos.

Fig. 9.6. Idealized designs from sites in the Aegean not similar or contemporaneous with Knossos.

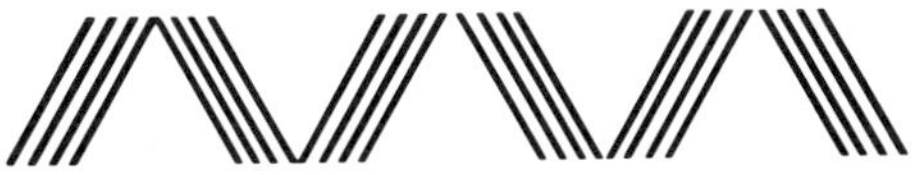
A

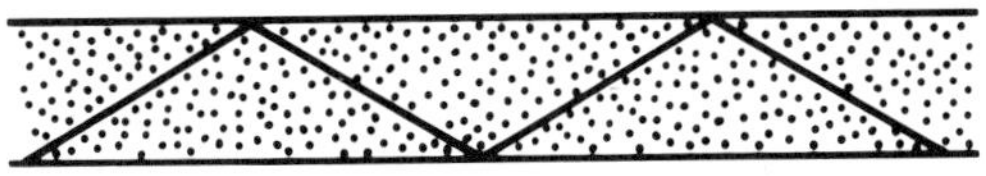
B

C

Fig. 9.7. Idealized designs from Saliagos.*

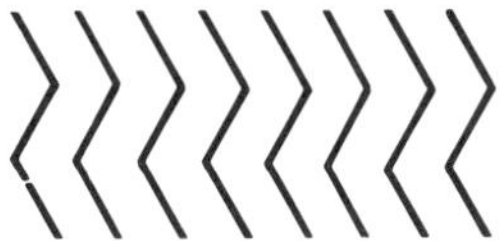
A

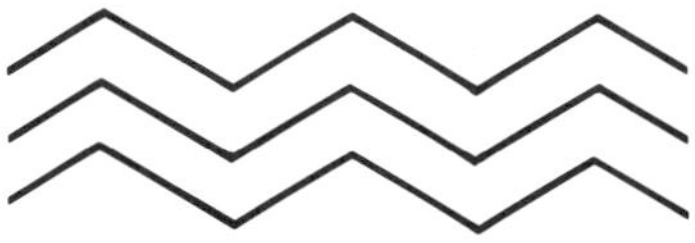
B

C

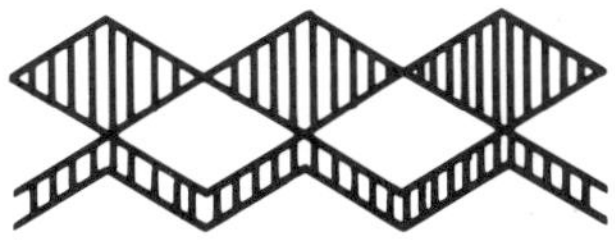
D

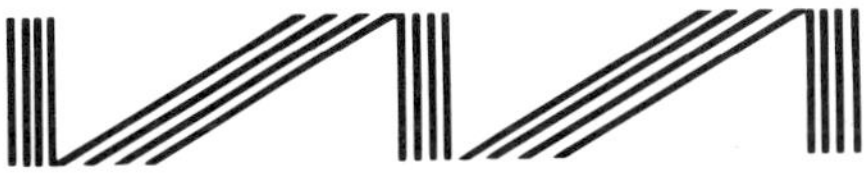
E

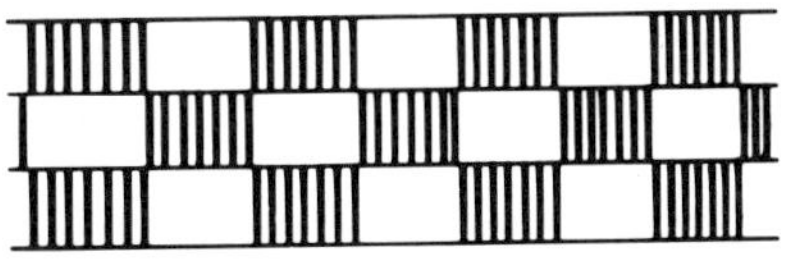
F

**Pattern*	*Reference in Evans and Renfrew 1968*
A	Fig. 50, #17
B	Fig. 54, #16
C	Fig. 55, #6
D	Fig. 55, #17
E	Fig. 48, #8
F	Fig. 31, #2

Although there is a dramatic influx of new ideas in Knossos level IV, the stratigraphic profile remains continuous and undisturbed. There is no wholesale replacement of one pottery type by another. The artisans, influenced by ideas from outside, began to copy new designs, yet continued to execute them in their local technology.

Thus structural analysis of design changes at Knossos has been able to document the gradual, indigenous development of a local culture followed by the beginning of outward expansion for the purposes of interaction with neighbouring island groups for their mutual benefit. The use of a symmetry classification was able to highlight the marked changes in design structure which appeared with the beginnings of inter-island contact in the Aegean. The fact that symmetry analysis was able to confirm both the Early Neolithic I uniformity and continuity and the point of Early Neolithic II to Middle Neolithic change suggests that it should be given consideration as a particularly useful analytical means to document temporal parameters of cultural change.

Test II: Delineation of spatial aspects of cultural change by symmetry analysis: an example from Neolithic sites on mainland Greece

Introduction

Despite many efforts to elucidate the Neolithic prehistory of mainland Greece, many questions remain unresolved. To date there are very few sites with long, continuous stratigraphic profiles and a correlated series of C 14 dates. Much of the evidence for the Neolithic comes from isolated surface finds of a few sherds or material which has been incidentally encountered in the bottom of test pits probing later cultures.

Ceramic styles were defined largely on the basis of the type of decorative treatment – polychrome, incised, or matte painted – as well as on the basis of differences in painted motifs, such as nets, flames, zigzags, and steps (Tsountas 1908; Wace and Thompson 1912).

Archaeologists generally consider sites with constellations of such stylistically similar sherds to be roughly contemporaneous within each of the general divisions of the Neolithic: Early, Middle, and Late (Weinberg 1962; Theocharis 1973). However, since these descriptors are so general and, when applied to material from sites throughout mainland Greece, result in very broad distribution patterns, it is not possible to infer specific temporal and spatial information about inter-site relationships.

This test seeks to demonstrate how similarities and differences among the ceramic structure style systems of various population groups may be systematically described and compared by symmetry analysis. Given the more precise definition of similarities and differences among styles that can be attained from symmetry analysis, and given the premise that similar structural styles result from population interaction, it should be possible to use this method to determine more accurately interrelationships among sites.

This test of the sensitivity of structural analysis for delimiting spatial aspects of site interrelationships was conducted using published reports of decorated ceramics. Although tighter temporal control beyond the general Early and Late Neolithic divisions was not available, it is hoped that the marked differences in design structure distribution between these periods, which seem to correlate with topographical constraints and the development of external routes of interaction, will stimulate further studies in this direction.

If one predicts a relationship between terrain and the type and degree of human interaction, the marked variations and constraints in the topography of Greece would seem to be an important limiting factor relative to the development of cultures and their interaction patterns. The many precipitous mountain ranges which are separated by deep gorges cut Greece into many valley isolates. The only flat, open floodplains with extensive arable land are in Thessaly and Macedonia; further south in Boeotia and the Peloponnese the area is dominated by limestone highlands. The few coastal plains are small, isolated, and afford comparatively little fertile soil.

If we assume that increased cultural interaction leads to artifactual similarities (other cultural factors remaining relatively stable), the expansive nature of the valley systems in Thessaly and Macedonia would facilitate interchange between village groups and thus lead to the development of similar artifactual styles over large areas. Conversely, the restrictive nature of the precipitous mountain ranges and river gorges further south would confine information and product exchange within fairly circumscribed areas.

Given this terrain and the model of interaction, one could posit that during the Early Neolithic, under conditions of low population density, isolated, self-sufficient subsistence farming groups predominated in topographically divided southern Greece. In contrast, the broad floodplains of northern Greece would encourage more widely ranging networks of interaction.

Indeed, although it may be an accident of archaeological discovery, most of the known early Neolithic settlements hug the coastline and are especially prevalent along broad fertile floodplains which occur where several river systems discharge into the sea. The largest such area is the Thessalian plain, a square 96 kilometres on a side, divided into a northern and southern sector by a low range of hills extending southeastward from the Chasia mountains. The northern sector, the plain of Trikkala, is drained by the Peneios River; the southern sector, the plain of Larissa, occupies the lowlands south of the Peneios River.

The primary barrier to east–west population movement and interchange is the mountain range which extends in a northwest to southeast direction down the central 'spine' of Greece. Only one river, the Megdhova, crosses this chain;

the others drain either eastward or westward. Very few Neolithic sites are known on the western side. Most of the Early Neolithic sites are clustered along the east coast, especially in the fertile floodplain of the Peneios River in Thessaly and along the Axios and Aliakmon Rivers in Macedonia.

During this period the site density is much lower in central and southern Greece. Most of this area is comprised of limestone-based highlands. The few coastal plains are small, isolated, and afford comparatively little arable land. Thus, it is clear how these topographic differences promoted the development of an economy based on cereals and cattle in Thessaly but was compatible only with an economy based on grapes and olives on the hill slope environment of southern Greece.

By the Late Neolithic, an increase in number of sites (Renfrew 1972) suggests an increase in population, even in the inhospitable areas of southern Greece. Renfrew (1972) has suggested that the variety of micro-environments in southern Greece gave rise to new types of food production and craft specialization which in turn led to the development of networks of communication for product exchange. In this situation, he predicted the rise of market centres surrounded by ancillary dependent villages.

The results of a symmetry analysis of the ceramic designs from Early and Late Neolithic ceramics seem to reinforce such a model in which a series of Early Neolithic interaction areas, the extent of which seems directly dependent upon topographical constraints, shifts by the Late Neolithic to a situation of hierarchically ranked towns.

Methodology

The data for this study were selected from an extensive literature search for illustrated sherds and whole vessels from Neolithic sites on mainland Greece. All patterned designs were sorted first according to site. This procedure facilitated reconstructing whole patterns from several sherds, since many of the larger, well-known sites had been studied by a number of archaeologists over the years and large collections had been amassed for some sites. The design fragments which were insufficient in size or extent or pattern were discarded. Thus, the sample was limited to illustrated sherds or whole vessels with designs amenable to symmetry classification.

In order to demonstrate the increase in spatial specificity obtainable from symmetry classification, both the current stylistic and symmetry classifications have been applied to the same selected data base. No frequency counts were used. The study was based simply on a presence/absence accounting of classifiable designs from each site. Given the tradition of careful reporting of the whole range of excavated material, it was assumed that a representative range of surface treatments and decorative styles were published.

Most of the sherds analysed were dated by the investigators within the general Early Neolithic (EN), Middle Neolithic (MN), and Late Neolithic (LN) scheme established by Tsountas (1908) and Wace and Thompson (1912). However, there was substantial material from the very early phases of the EN that could not be included in the framework established at the turn of the century. Consequently the chronological divisions of the Early Neolithic into two phases EN I and EN II will be used here (Rodden 1968).

If not definitive because of the above limitations, it is hoped this study may suggest one potential avenue of research that should be retested with more rigorous sampling techniques.

Early Neolithic I

It is regrettable that so little has been recovered from sites considered to have been occupied during the earliest phases of the Early Neolithic. Of the eight published sites examined having sherds with identifiable patterns from that period (Rodden, personal communication), six are in Thessaly (Otzaki, Argissa, Pyrasos, Achilleion, Sesklo, Prodromos), one in Macedonia (Nea Nikomedeia), and one in Boeotia (Elateia) (Table 9.1). Only two (H, J) of the ten patterns (A–K) found at these sites actually represent whole patterns (Fig. 9.8); the others come from such fragmentary sherds that they can only be considered to be motifs (i.e., parts of a design).

All sites with pattern H are in Thessaly; pattern J is represented by one site in Macedonia and one in Thessaly. Although undoubtedly more patterns are known than the sample discussed here, the tendency toward site location on the Thessalian plain is clear.

Only two patterns (A and H) reappear at a number of sites. Patterns A, B, and C are all variations on the basic form of a series of pendant isosceles triangles (Class 1–101). Pattern H is a simple repetition of a zigzag line in two dimensions (Class $2-201x_1^1$). Both are fairly simple patterns, and for this reason it is not surprising to find them recurring in several areas.

Some element combinations, such as patterns D and F from Nea Nikomedeia and pattern E from Argissa, are unique occurrences. These may represent situations where lines of inter-site communication were weakly developed and as a result each community developed its own distinctive ceramic decorative styles. This possibility is certainly reinforced by a detailed study of the Early Neolithic pottery from Nea Nikomedeia (Washburn 1977c). Although the extensive excavations at Nea Nikomedeia have yielded perhaps one of the largest collections of Early Neolithic pottery, comparison of Nea Nikomedeia ceramic designs and design structures with those from other contemporaneous sites reveals that the ceramic assemblage at Nea Nikomedeia is unique in this area at this time.

Because the patterns are so basic and unelaborated, i.e., single rows of triangles or zigzags, and because the sample is

Fig. 9.8. Ten patterns from the Early Neolithic I.*

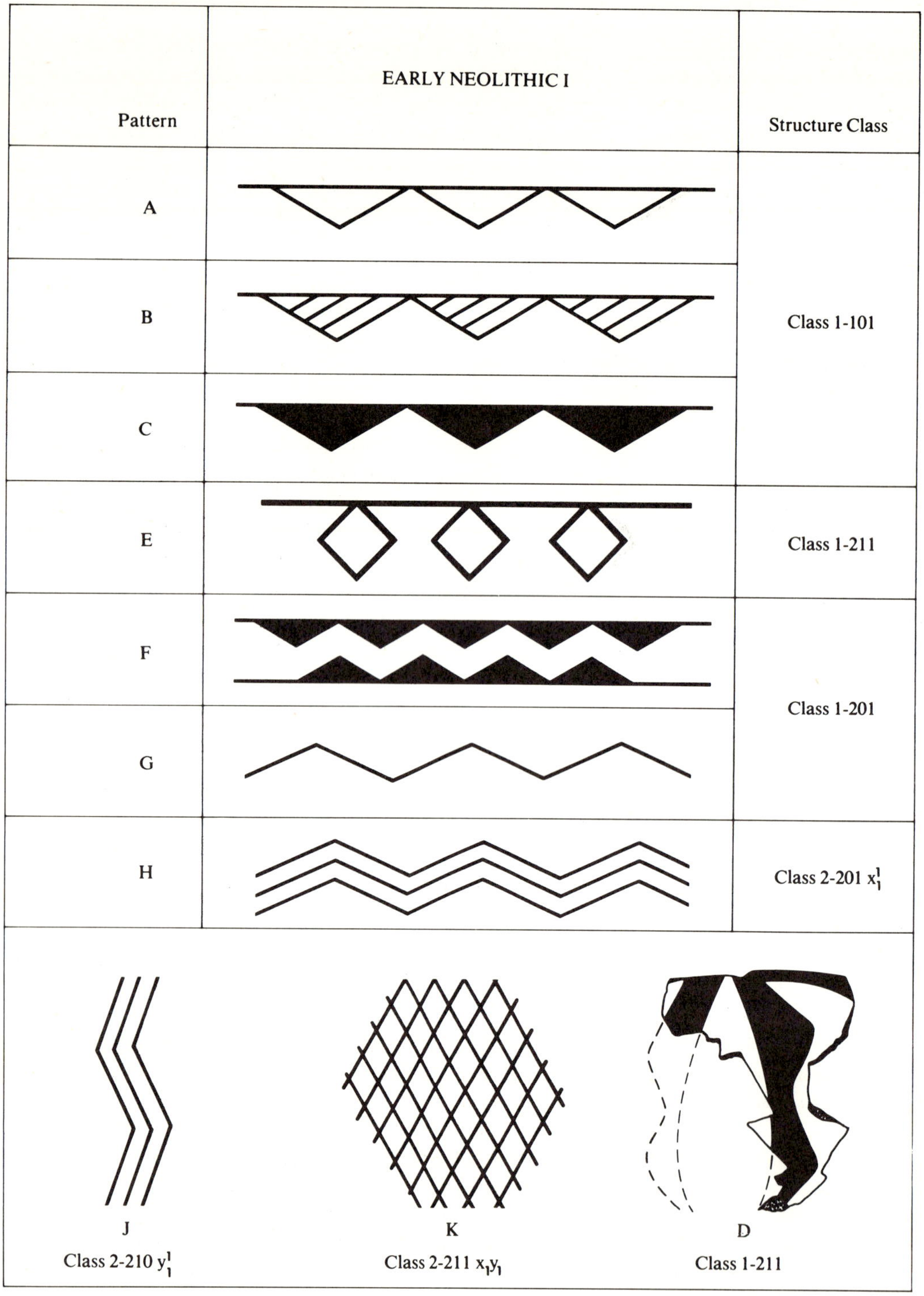

**Patterns A, B, C*
- Nea Nikomedeia — D3/2 (2); D3/1 (5) field drawings of sherds
- Argissa — Milojcic 1959: fig. 6, #8
- Otzaki — Milojcic 1971: plate III
- Pyrasos — Theocharis 1959: fig. 9, p. 42
- Elateia — Weinberg 1962: plate 55d

Pattern D
- Nea Nikomedeia — H7/1a (6); H8/1a (9); H8/1aA(2) field drawings of sherds

Pattern E
- Argissa — Milojcic 1959: fig. 6, #9

Pattern F
- Nea Nikomedeia — L5/1 (5) plough zone, field drawings of sherds

Pattern G
- Achilleion — Gimbutas 1974: fig. 17, p. 294; fig. 19, p. 294

Pattern H
- Otzaki — Milojcic 1959: fig. 9, #10
- Pyrasos — Theocharis 1959: fig. 15, p. 48
- Achilleion — Gimbutas 1974: fig. 19, p. 294
- Sesklo — Theocharis 1967: fig. 26, #5
- Prodromos — Daux 1972: fig. 254, p. 695

Pattern J
- Nea Nikomedeia — B6/2 field drawings of sherds
- Sesklo — Theocharis 1963: plate 171a

Pattern K
- Achilleion — Gimbutas 1974: fig. 19, p. 294
- Elateia — Weinberg 1962: plate 56b

Table 9.1 *Classification of Early Neolithic I designs by symmetry class*

Symmetry: *Class*	1–101	1–211	1–201	$2–201x_1^1$	$2–210y_1^1$	$2–211x_1y_1$
Pattern	A B C	D E	F G	H	J	K
Site						
Nea Nikomedeia	x	x(D)	x(F)		x	
Argissa	x	x(E)				
Otzaki	x			x		
Pyrasos	x			x		
Achilleion			x(G)	x		x
Sesklo				x	x	
Prodromos				x		
Elateia	x					x

largely limited to northern Greece where broad floodplains facilitate widespread contact, several possible interpretations may be considered. The simplified aspect of the patterns may be indicative of a nascent design system which has not yet developed distinctive elaborations, or a very widespread design system which became generalized because of the great distances and perhaps infrequent contact among the participating groups who bought, sold, or adopted the ideas.

Early Neolithic II

This undifferentiated situation is not characteristic of the design systems from sites on mainland Greece, particularly from areas to the south of the Thessalian Plain, by the later phases of the Early Neolithic, EN II. By this period, although it would appear from the Wace and Thompson (1912) solid style variants that design systems are still widespread generalized phenomena (net, flame, stepped, zigzag), a structural analysis clearly shows divisions according to geographical constraints, which can be interpreted as indicative of some changes in cultural interaction patterns. The following discussion compares inferences possible from the established stylistic assignments with those from a structural study in order to clarify how a structural analysis can pinpoint more sensitively shifts in cultural contact zones.

The A3β style, also referred to as the 'solid style', has a widespread distribution in Thessaly and central Greece (Fig. 9.9). It has many variations, such as the 'flame' style at Tsani, Pyrasos, Servia, Zerelia, Tsangli, Sesklo and Otzaki; or the 'stepped' style at Tsani, Achilleion, Zerelia and Pyrasos. In this paper these will be referred to as element styles, since the variant names – flame, net, etc. – are names for the elements which characterize the style variant.

Nets and zigzags appear to be coincident with the greatest range of the A3β style, being present at sites on the entire eastern shore of Greece. The flame and step styles are centred on the Thessalian Plain, but do appear as far north as Nea Nikomedeia in Macedonia and as far south as Lianokladhi in the Spercheios River valley in Phthiotis. If the standard archaeological assumption that stylistic similarity indicates cultural contact is used to interpret the above widespread distribution of these ceramic styles, then it might be inferred that there existed a very extensive communication network encompassing almost all of northern and central Greece during the fifth millennium B.C.

However, from ethnographic research among the Tarascans in Mexico, Friedrich (1970) has noted that design elements are easily copied. Thus, their widespread use through space and time does not necessarily indicate situations of close contact, but rather could represent fleeting exposure to an idea or item. Heeding this 'cautionary tale' of the dangers of design element distributions, analysis of the same situation was carried out using another approach.

Alternatively, if the structural organization of the elements in the designs is examined, it is clear that, although each style is based on a certain element, such as a series of right triangles resembling 'flames' or a series of attached squares resembling 'steps', the arrangement of these elements into repeated designs varies greatly. In this paper I will first demonstrate that these differing design structures have very different – in some cases discrete – spatial distributions, and second, suggest several models which may explain the activity patterns which produced these distributions.

It is clear from Tables 9.3, 9.4, and 9.5 that a variety of structures was used to arrange each of the four elements (nets, zigzags, flames, and steps). Each of the patterns are illustrated in Figure 9.10 and their structures and the sites where they were found are listed in Table 9.6.[3] In the case of these four decorative element styles, the fact that so many different motion classes have been used to structure these elements into patterns argues for the presence of these generalized elements in all design systems all over Greece. Conversely, more intensive exchange within a localized population, stimulated, for example, by the sharing of design ideas among a group of potters who live in the same village, as in

Table 9.2 *Distribution of styles in A3β ware*

	Styles			
Sites	Flame	Solid step	Net	Zigzag
Achilleion	x	x	x	x
Sesklo	x		x	x
Zerelia	x		x	x
Tsangli	x		x	x
Servia	x			x
Tsani		x	x	x
Otzaki	x			x
Persoufli	x			
Pyrasos	x	x	x	x
Chaeronea			x	x
Corinth			x	x
Elateia			x	x
Nemea			x	x
Sarakinov Cave			x	x
Ghediki	x	x	x	
Orchomenos			x	
Polyjira			x	
Pyrgos			x	
Lianokladhi	x		x	x
Lerna				x
Franchthi Cave				x
Prodromos				x
Nea Makri				x
Nea Nikomedeia		x		x
Soufli	x			
Ayios Vissarion		x		
Eutresis			x	

Table 9.3 *Distribution of 'flame' style by symmetry class*

	Symmetry class			
Site	1–200	1–101	1–211	1–201
Achilleion			x	
Otzaki	x	x	x	
Persoufli			x	
Pyrasos			x	
Servia		x	x	x
Sesklo		x	x	x
Tsangli	x	x	x	x
Zerelia			x	

Table 9.4 *Distribution of 'net' style by symmetry class*

	Symmetry class				
Site	2–411	$2–4_3 1_2 1_2$	$2–211x_1y_1$	$2–211x_2y_2$	2–200
Achilleion	x	x	x		
Chaeronea		x	x	x	
Corinth			x		
Elateia	x	x	x	x	
Franchthi Cave			x		
Ghediki			x		
Lerna			x		
Lianokladhi	x	x		x	
Nemea			x		
Orchomenos			x	x	
Nea Makri			x		
Polyjira				x	
Pyrasos			x	x	
Pyrgos		x	x		
Sarakinov Cave		x	x		
Eutresis			x		
Sesklo				x	
Tsangli			x		
Tsani	x		x		x
Zerelia			x		

Table 9.5 *Distribution of 'zigzag' style by symmetry class for A3β ware*

	Symmetry class		
Site	1–201	$2–210x_1^1$	$2–210y_1^1$
Achilleion	x	x	
Chaeronea		x	
Corinth		x	
Elateia		x	
Franchthi Cave		x	
Lerna		x	x
Lianokladhi		x	
Nemea		x	
Otzaki		x	x
Pyrasos		x	
Servia			x
Sesklo		x	x
Tsangli		x	
Tsani		x	
Zerelia		x	
Nea Makri	x		
Nea Nikomedeia			x

Fig. 9.9. Distribution of A3β wares in the Early Neolithic II.

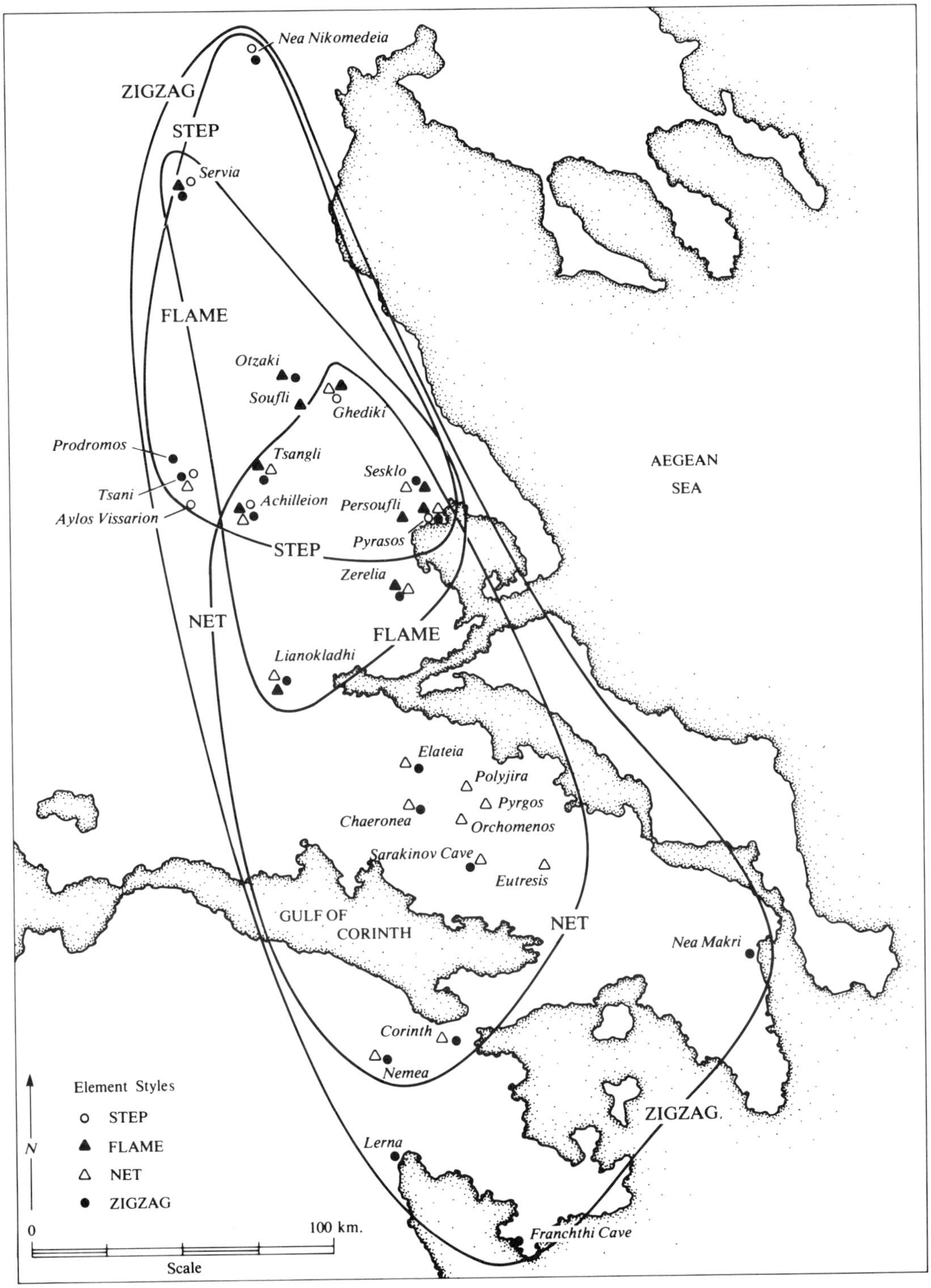

Fig. 9.10. Nine structure classes of the four element styles from the Early Neolithic II.*

Pattern	EARLY NEOLITHIC II	Structure Class
I	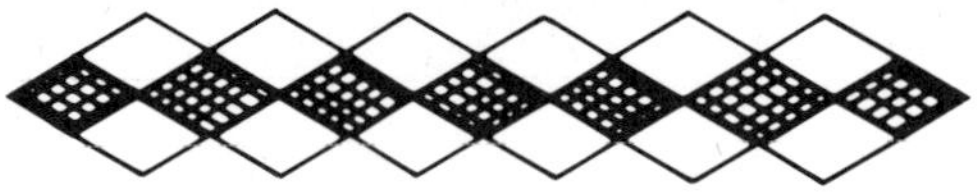	Class 2-211 x_1y_1
II	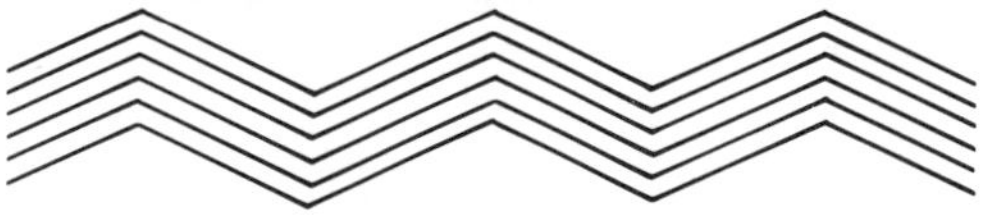	Class 2-201 x_1^1
III	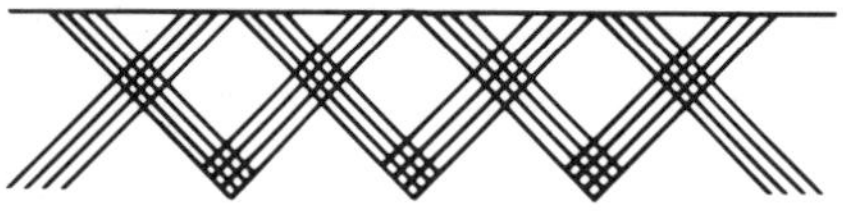	Class 1-211
IV		
V		Class 1-200
VI		Class 1-101
VII		Class 1-201
VIII	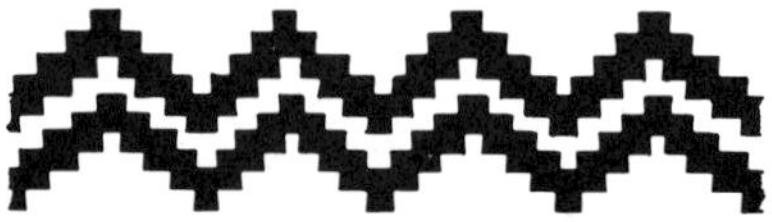	Class 2-201 x_1^1
IX	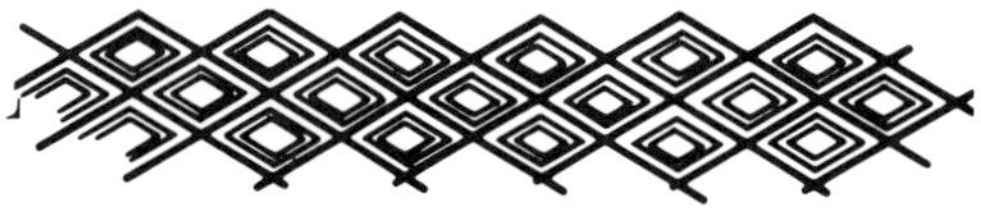	Class 2-211 x_1y_1

**Pattern I*
- Franchthi Cave — Jacobsen 1969
- Lerna — Caskey 1957: plate 48; Caskey 1958: plate 36
- Asea — Holmberg 1944: plate IIIa, b

Pattern II
- Franchthi Cave — Jacobsen 1969: plate 96b
- Hageorgitika — Blegen 1931: fig. 1, p. 56
- Corinth — Kosmopoulos 1948: plate Ib

Pattern III
- Chaeronea — Zervos 1962: plate 248, p. 232
- Orchomenos — Kunze 1931: plate 15, #2
- Pyrgos — Kunze 1931: plate 19, #5f, 5g
- Elateia — Weinberg 1962: plate 56C
- Eutresis — Caskey, J.L. and E.G. 1960: plate 43

Pattern IV
- Otzaki — Zervos 1962: plate 263, p. 240
- Persoufli — Daux 1965: fig. 1
- Zerelia — Wace and Thompson 1912: fig. 97, p. 154
- Servia — Heurtley 1939: fig. 1, p. 135
- Tsangli — Wace and Thompson 1912: fig. 48, p. 94
- Sesklo — Tsountas 1908: plate 7

Pattern V
- Otzaki — Zervos 1962: plate 267, p. 242
- Tsangli — Zervos 1962: plate 266, p. 242

Pattern VI
- Otzaki — Zervos 1962: plate 280, p. 248
- Sesklo — Zervos 1962: plate 240, p. 228
- Tsangli — Wace and Thompson 1912: fig. 45, p. 93
- Servia — Zervos 1962: p. 255
- Achilleion — Gimbutas 1974: fig. 22, p. 297

Pattern VII
- Servia — Zervos 1962: plate 292, p. 254
- Zerelia — Wace and Thompson 1912: fig. 98, p. 155
- Otzaki — Milojcic 1959: fig. 12

Pattern VIII
- Tsani — Zervos 1962: plate 232, p. 223
- Achilleion — Gimbutas 1974: fig. 22, p. 297

Pattern IX
- Tsani — Zervos 1962: plate 230, p. 221
- Tsangli — Wace and Thompson 1912: fig. 46, p. 94
- Lianokladhi — Wace and Thompson 1912: fig. 118, p. 174

Table 9.6 *Symmetry classes of nine Early Neolithic II patterns*

Symmetry: *Class*	$2-211x_1y_1$	$1-211$	$2-201x_1^1$	$1-211$	$1-200$	$1-101$	$1-201$	$2-201x_1^1$	$2-211x_1y_1$
Pattern	I	II	III	IV	V	VI	VII	VIII	IX
Site									
Asea	x								
Franchthi Cave	x	x							
Lerna	x								
Pyrgos			x						
Elateia			x						
Orchomenos			x						
Chaeronea			x						
Hageorgitika		x							
Zerelia				x			x		
Eutresis			x						
Corinth		x							
Servia				x		x	x		
Tsangli				x	x	x			x
Pyrasos				x					
Persoufli				x					
Otzaki				x	x	x	x		
Sesklo				x		x			
Achilleion						x		x	
Tsani								x	x
Lianokladhi									x

the Mahgreb example, would presumably have resulted in a group of highly similar designs coincident in both structure and pattern. Thus, an examination of the distribution of pattern structures should lead to isolation of specific areas of information exchange. In this paper I shall call these areas 'interaction spheres'.

Figure 9.11 and Table 9.6 show the distribution of nine specific patterns (I–IX) (Fig. 9.10).[4] Each pattern is structured by a different symmetry class, although only four element styles are represented: patterns I, III and IX are net designs; II is a zigzag design; IV, V, VI, VII are flame designs; and VIII is a step design. If these nine designs from twenty mainland sites are grouped according to similar structure, rather than element style, it is evident that the distributions of these patterns have been significantly localized, particularly in central and southern Greece.

The four flame patterns (IV, V, VI, VII) each occupy a more restricted area (Fig. 9.11) than that indicated for all flame patterns together (Fig. 9.9). Patterns V, VI and VII are found in both the northern and southern sectors of the Thessalian Plain. Apparently the low range of hills and the Peneios River did not act as impenetrable barriers to intercommunication between these two areas. The sites in the centre of the area – Otzaki, Tsangli and Achilleion – appear to have all or most of the four flame patterns. This may be reflecting their 'central place' location: i.e., they may have acted as centres for exchange of produce from the valley farms and thus be the termini for ceramic containers from a number of surrounding sites.

Net designs occur on three patterns (I, II and IX). Only two sites, Tsangli and Tsani, are linked with the site of Lianokladhi in the Spercheios valley by the common presence of pattern IX. Since no other Thessalian area patterns are found on vessels at Lianokladhi, it may be that this sphere represents a one-way contact route. Pots were being manufactured in Lianokladhi and moved by trade or gift exchange to Tsani and Tsangli.

The five sites in Boeotia with pattern III are all found in a closely knit group. The mountains to the north and south probably played an important role in isolating this group of sites and encouraging the development of a unique design system based on structure Class $1-211$. No patterns of any other group were found here, nor was pattern III, which was apparently manufactured here, traded to the outside, since it has not been found at any of the other sites examined.

Two small but overlapping interaction spheres in the Peloponnese share distinctive forms of the zigzag and net element styles. Pattern I is a diamond, Class $2-211x_1y_1$ form of the net, and pattern II is a series of two-dimensional horizontal zigzags, Class $2{-}201x^1_1$. Again, the severely rugged terrain has apparently restricted the distribution of these specific structural arrangements of very common design elements.

In brief, then, during the later phases of the Early Neolithic, the period of manufacture of A3β wares, mainland Greece appears to have been intensively populated in the Thessalian Plain. The extensive contacts which such a topographic situation would allow are confirmed by the equally widespread distribution of common design structures.

The more localized nature of the contact groups in central and southern Greece is probably largely due to the topographic limitations. The more isolated site clusters in the smaller valleys in Boeotia and on the limestone hills in the

Fig. 9.11. Distribution of the nine structure classes in the Early Neolithic II.

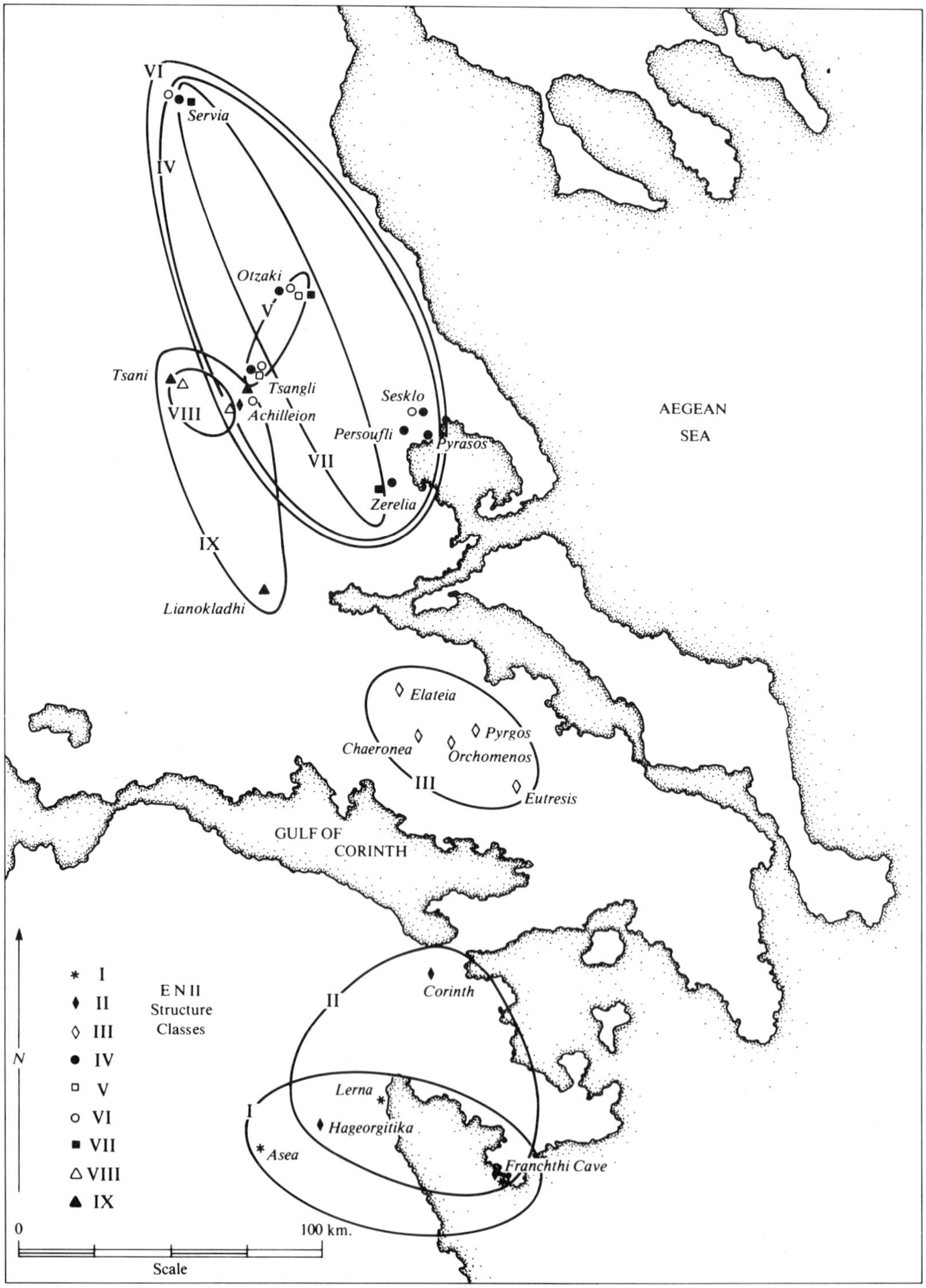

Peloponnese suggest that population contact networks as large as those in the Thessalian Plain were not possible given topographic restrictions.

Nevertheless, it was this environmentally impoverished southern area that was later to replace Thessaly in political and economic dominance. This shift is clearly documented in a study of the design structures on incised wares from the Late Neolithic. The small isolated contact areas characteristic of the Early Neolithic have been replaced by the unequal growth of a few population centres which are surrounded by subsidiary villages. These centres may be developing as bulking and redistribution marketing places.

Late Neolithic

Of all the different surface treatments on the Late Neolithic ceramics only the B2 (incised) and B3α (Dimini ware) varieties were present in sufficient quantity and size for symmetry analysis. Six specific patterns of B2 ware (Fig. 9.12), each with a different design structure (Table 9.7), have been isolated from the sample studied.[5] It will immediately be noted from a plot of their distribution (Fig. 9.13) that all but one of the patterns occurs at Orchomenos.

The exception, pattern II, may actually belong to pattern VI, since the orientation of pattern II sherds is not certain. Convention usually dictates that rim sherds be illustrated with the rim edge along the upper edge. However, perusal of the literature (cf. Zervos 1962), reveals that many authors do not follow this convention. Orientation of many of these sherds is a particularly difficult task since they are body sherds. If, however, the pattern II sherds are misoriented as published (Zervos 1962: II, 294, fig. 374; Weinberg 1962, plate 62d), they would belong to pattern VI. In this case, all of the five structure classes are represented at Orchomenos.

Furthermore, if only five patterns are present, each pattern, except pattern II, is present at only two sites, Orchomenos and one other site. Such a distribution suggests the appearance of a new form of site integration vastly different from that discussed above for the Early Neolithic II. The site of Orchomenos, with all five patterns, appears to have become more important than the other surrounding sites (Lerna, Sarakinov Cave, Corinth, Elateia). One possible explanation might be that potters in each of the surrounding sites were producing pottery and taking it to Orchomenos for exchange for other types of products. In such a situation, people in the surrounding sites were specialists – potters, farmers, and craftsmen of other types – producing specific items in excess of their families' needs to take to a marketing centre for exchange for items they needed but did not produce.

The other Late Neolithic B series style with sufficient sherds for symmetry analysis is B3α, or Dimini ware. The unusual nature of this black-on-white ware has suggested to some researchers that it is an import (Benton 1947; Hammond 1972). Others believe that, despite its apparent differences, it is a natural outgrowth of the Early Neolithic II Sesklo series (French 1966: 104).

A symmetry analysis revealed that patterns from nine sites with classifiable Dimini ware sherds were structured by nineteen different motion classes (Table 9.8). The site of Dimini had sherds with thirteen different structures, and the neighbouring site of Sesklo had sherds with eight different structures. The other sites had fewer different structures, but then the sherd sample from these sites was far smaller than that from Dimini or Sesklo.

One possible interpretation for the situation where the sites in the Dimini area have most of the design structures and the outlying sites in the Larissa area have less variety in design structure is that it is analogous to the situation with Orchomenos and the surrounding sites in the Late Neolithic incised case just described. However, a closer examination of the designs themselves suggests that the distribution pattern of Dimini ware may have been caused by a different set of activities. Evidence for this is enumerated below.

Although there was an insufficient sample of B series decorated wares (excepting B3α) to compare with the B2 incised wares, it was clear that the patterns used on non-Dimini incised and non-Dimini painted wares were not identical. Most evident was the predominant use of the one-dimensional axial arrangement on B2 incised (non-Dimini) wares. In contrast there is a predominant use of the two-dimensional axial arrangement on B3α *painted* Dimini wares *and* B2 *incised* Dimini wares. In short, the B3α painted wares and the B2 incised wares from the Dimini sites use the same range of structures for the designs, although they are executed in two different techniques. Although most of the B2 incised Dimini ware sherds are very fragmentary, the use of structure Classes 2–200, $2\text{–}201y_1^1$, $2\text{–}210x_1^1$ and $2\text{–}211x_1y_1$ to structure certain patterns is clear (Fig. 9.14). Thus, the structure and pattern of the painted and incised Dimini designs contrasts greatly with the non-Dimini B2 and B3 series of incised and painted wares from sites in southern Greece.

These differences may suggest that there may have been many active centres of ceramic production in the Dimini–Sesklo area. One might envision workshops of potters all producing decorated wares – some incised, others painted – but all having the characteristic Dimini–Larissa area two-dimensional structure. Specific patterns may vary, but the underlying axial arrangement rarely does. In contrast, the situation in southern Greece appears to be one of small family specialists, producing different designs based on different structures for exchange in a larger market. These two situations are similar to the workshop versus family types of pottery design and distribution described earlier for the Mahgreb.

Two other aspects of Dimini ware support this hypothetical reconstruction. One is the wide variety of patterns and structures used; the other is the consistent use of a panelled layout.

Table 9.7 *Symmetry classes of six Late Neolithic patterns*

Symmetry: *Class*	1–101	$2–210y_1^1$	1–201	1–201	$2–211x_1y_1$	$2–201x_1^1$
Pattern	I	II	III	IV	V	VI
Site						
Orchomenos	x		x	x	x	x
Sarakinov Cave			x			
Elateia		x			x	
Corinth		x		x		x
Lerna	x					

Table 9.8 *Nineteen symmetry classes of Dimini ware*

Symmetry class	1–100	1–200	1–101	1–201	1–110	$2–201x_1^1$	$2–210y_1^1$	2–211	$2–211x_1y_1$	$2–211x_2y_2$	2–411	$2–4_31_21_2$	$2–2_31_21_2$	2–200	$2–200x_1y_1$	$2–2_101x_2^1$	$2–2_300$	2–101	200
Sites																			
Dimini	x	x		x		x	x	x	x	x	x	x		x	x	x			
Sesklo						x			x	x	x	x		x				x	x
Argissa		x		x		x								x					
Otzaki									x										
Neleia			x	x					x		x		x						
Rakhmani				x	x	x	x			x	x			x			x		
Valtokhori												x							
Tsani														x					
Koufovouno									x										

The EN II situation, where each of the nine contact areas was defined by the coincident occurrence of designs with the same structure and pattern, is not characteristic of the Late Neolithic Dimini ware sites. Here, although all the patterns are based on a two-dimensional axis, *no* patterns are identical. Furthermore, nineteen *different* two-dimensional motion classes have been used to structure the B3α wares in the sample studied here. One explanation for this difference may be that small family groups of potters in the EN II might have used the same patterns,[6] whereas non-related artisans in a large workshop situation in the LN were free to develop their own unique and different two-dimensional patterns.

Secondly, it is important to investigate the peculiar spatial divisions of the surface to be decorated in which the two-dimensional patterns were placed. On sherds from thirteen of the eighteen sites where Dimini ware was found, the designs are placed in two broad panels on opposite sides of the exterior of bowls and jars. The two panels are separated by two blank vertical spaces which often contain a pair of pierced lug handles. On the interior of bowls the two-dimensional pattern covers the entire surface, except where it is interrupted with inset patterns which have no symmetrical relationship with the overall pattern.

Furthermore, regardless of their interior or exterior location, the two-dimensional patterns are truncated by the banding lines. The truncation does not occur at a natural point between axes in the design, but cuts through the pattern, as if the artist had not planned the exact placement of the pattern and had to end it when he reached the banding line. This 'abnormal' truncation is accentuated by the frequent slanting of the pattern relative to the rim.

In contrast the non-Dimini B2 incised patterns from Boeotia and the Peloponnese do not have banding lines, abnormal truncation of the pattern or panelled layouts. The consistent use of these layout features in the Dimini area, in conjunction with the variety of structures and patterns, reinforces the idea that these designs were produced by a group of artisans in a workshop situation where certain decorative conventions were the rule, but within which each artisan was free to invent his own specific pattern. Furthermore, the fact that these characteristics are not found on

Fig. 9.12. Seven structure classes of incised patterns from the Late Neolithic.*

Pattern	LATE NEOLITHIC	Structure Class
I	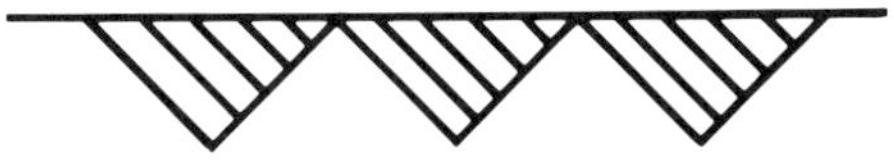	Class 1-101
II	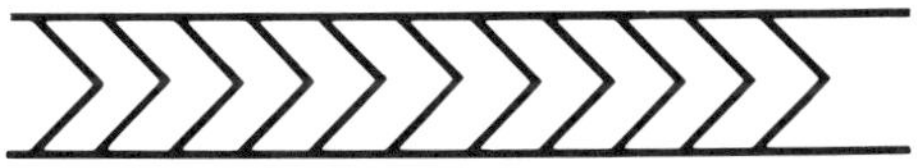	Class 1-110
III	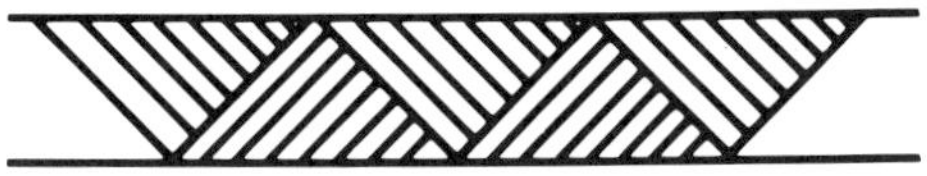	Class 1-201
IV	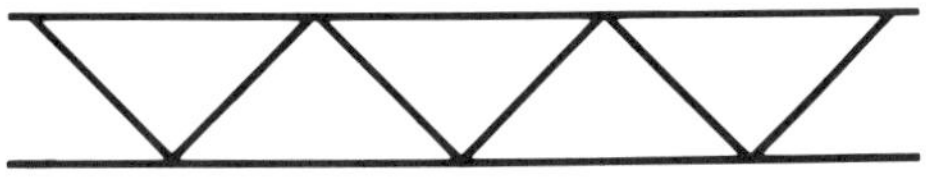	
V	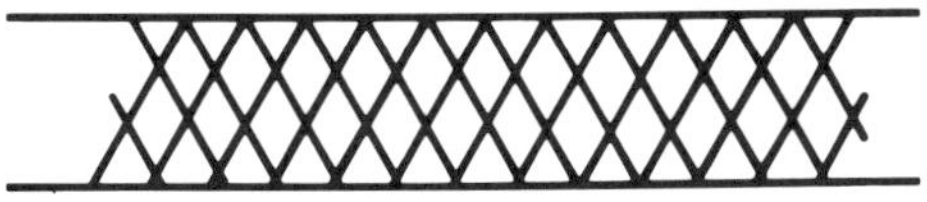	Class 2-211 x_1y_1
VI		Class 2-201 x_1^1
VII	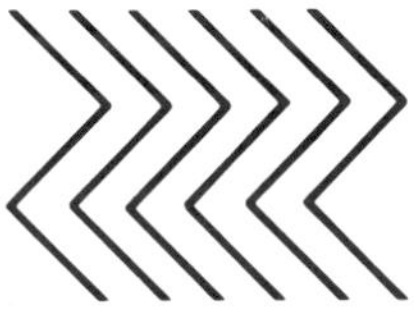	Class 2-210 y_1^1

**Pattern I*

Orchomenos	Kunze 1931: plate I
Lerna	Caskey 1958: plate 36c

Pattern II

Corinth	Zervos 1962: plate 374, p. 294
Elateia	Weinberg 1962: plate 62D

Pattern III

Orchomenos	Kunze 1931: plate IX
Sarakinov Cave	Spyropoulos 1973: fig. 2, p. 204

Pattern IV

Orchomenos	Kunze 1931: plate XIII
Corinth	Zervos 1962: fig. 376, p. 294

Pattern V

Orchomenos	Kunze 1931: plate X
Elateia	Weinberg 1962: plate 62D

Pattern VI

Orchomenos	Kunze 1931: plate XIII
Corinth	Zervos 1962: plate 375, p. 294

ceramic designs earlier in time and/or adjacent in area argues that this style may indeed be an import.

This unique Dimini style did, however, exert influence on local artisans producing B3δ 'solid style' designs. A 'stepped' pattern from Sesklo (Zervos 1962: 319, fig. 419) and a more Dimini-like hatched pattern from Otzaki (Zervos 1962: 319, fig. 418) both show the two-panel layout with two handles in the opposite empty spaces dividing the two panels.

Two-dimensional layouts from the site of Lianokladhi can be viewed as products of a relatively isolated group: occasional contacts with peoples of the north produced

Fig. 9.13. Distribution of six structure classes in southern Greece during the Late Neolithic and distribution of Dimini ware sites in northern Greece during the Late Neolithic.

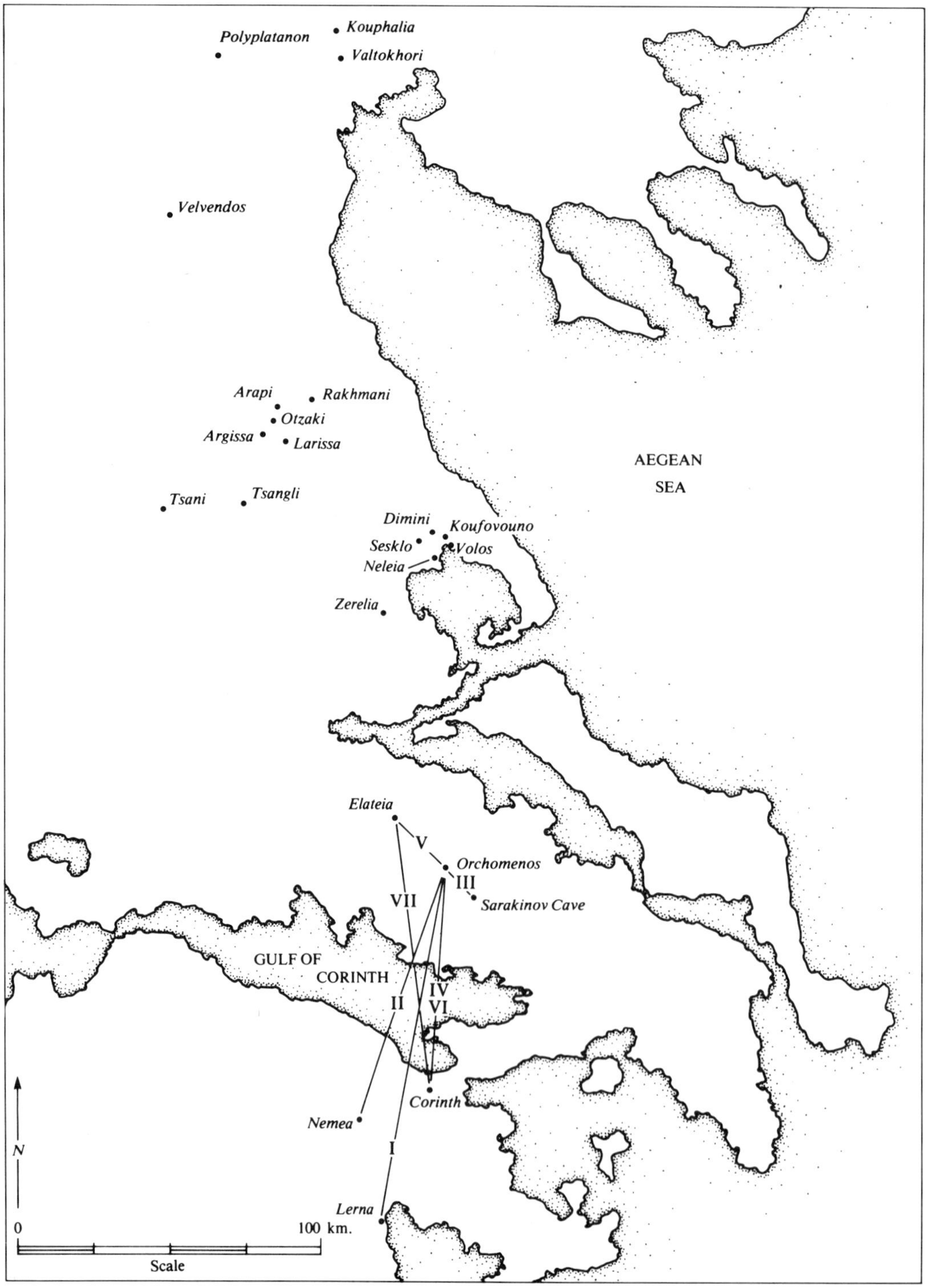

designs similar in general layout (i.e., based on a two-dimensional axis) but unique in detail (no two-panel layouts, no identical patterns). The one-way contacts that Lianokladhi had with Tsangli and Tsani during the Early Neolithic II appear to have persisted into the Late Neolithic. In this case, however, the direction of idea/item exchange seems to have been reversed. Whereas during the Early Neolithic II it appeared that most of pattern IX was produced at Lianokladhi and the ideas or items traded north to Tsangli and Tsani, it seems that the two-dimensional axial arrangement idea flowed south to artisans at Lianokladhi, who took this idea and elaborated it in a style distinctive to Lianokladhi.

During a period slightly later in time, which some investigators even place as transitional to the Early Bronze Age, designs similar to B3α were produced at Rakhmani. These are unmistakably Dimini in character, with axial and layout arrangements identical to those of the classic Dimini period.[7]

Interpretation

The following is a preliminary attempt to examine the type and degree of interaction between Neolithic village groups in Greece by suggesting the most likely activities which resulted in these Early and Late Neolithic interaction

Fig. 9.14. Two-dimensional B2 incised Dimini designs from Orchomenos and Dimini, Late Neolithic.*

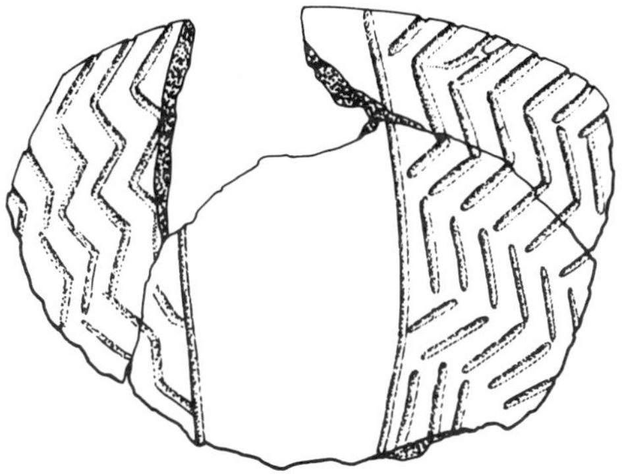

A

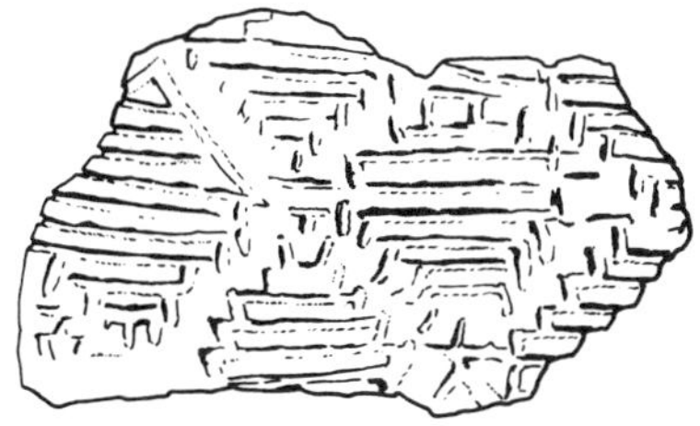

B

*Orchomenos Kunze 1931: plate 5
Dimini Tsountas 1908: plate 17

spheres. An interaction sphere is defined as an information/item exchange system through which aspects of culture are transferred and which ultimately produces regional similarities. The concept of 'interaction sphere' has been used, for example, by Michaels (1968) to describe trade goods found at Sheep Rock Shelter, Pennsylvania.

There are a number of different classifications of exchange systems, each concerned with a different aspect of the exchange process. At the most basic level one should define what is being exchanged. In the case of pottery, it could be the potters themselves, ideas about pot manufacture and/or designs, or actual pots. Naturally we have as yet little information relevant to Neolithic social organization in Greece and cannot entertain the extent or frequency of movement of the potters. Since spread of ideas about an item inevitably accompanies spread of the item itself, the physical evidence we have in Greece of the distribution of the nine design patterns during the Early Neolithic II and the six patterns during the Late Neolithic suggests that we must envision an exchange mechanism involving the spread of both material and non-material goods.

Fundamental to the postulation of an interaction sphere is an interrelated subsystems perspective of culture. Thus, changes and/or continuities in one subsystem should be reflected in all other subsystems. Under normal conditions, cultures persist in a situation of negative feedback, which essentially is a mechanism that reinforces conservatism. In the decorative subsystem this would be manifested in the maintenance of extant traditional design styles and technological procedures. Conversely, cultures are involved in a positive feedback situation during periods of change. For example, this might be reflected by the appearance of new design configurations. Renfrew has labelled these 'fundamental and irreversible changes in structure' (1975: 36), that set in motion a whole series of changes in the culture, the 'multiplier effect'. One way to examine interaction, then, is to find evidence for shifts in the *organization* of interaction within and between cultural systems.

Interactions 'imply information flow' (Renfrew 1975: 53). Moreover they are two-way flows. 'The more cohesive a group is . . . the greater the frequency of interaction among its members' (Renfrew 1975: 5). And from this it follows that the greater the frequency of interaction, the greater the amount of information that is passed among the interacting members. The archaeologist has access to this communication system through observation of repetitions in artifactual properties.

A number of geographical models offer ways to explain the repetition the archaeologist sees in the data – in this case, the continuities in symmetry structure. For example, Bunge's six models of 'minimum distance' routes (Haggett 1966: 65) focus upon the problem of minimizing travel to loci given a variety of environmental and social constraints. Other models are concerned with changes in the network structure over time. Taaffe, Morrill and Gould, for example, have presented a four-stage diachronic model for network development in an underdeveloped country (Haggett 1966: 80). Such attention to the temporal parameters of network development is particularly appropriate for archaeological data.

Anthropological exchange models for the transfer of goods are frequently evolutionary in nature. At the lowest level is *reciprocity*, or exchange of goods and services based on kin obligations. The sharing of the parts of a large animal kill among a group of hunters and gatherers is one such example. *Redistribution* involves the existence of a central place where goods will be brought from surrounding areas for redistribution/exchange for goods from other areas. *Market* exchange necessitates central authorities who control the flow of goods which are transferred via a currency.

Renfrew (1975: 41) has listed nine different exchange arrangements, and Beale (1973: 141) offers another sequence of four types. Both imply an evolutionary developmental sequence and reflect the kinds of data archaeologists can recover – spatial arrangements of trading partners and material evidence of items exchanged.

Despite the limited data base for the Greek Neolithic, the evidence in the form of the interaction spheres defined by symmetry analysis can allow elimination of some forms of exchange so that further attention can be focused on testing those models which appear most likely. Since Renfrew's list is the most exhaustive, I shall discuss the interaction spheres defined by the ceramic design structure for Neolithic Greece in terms of his categories.

Undoubtedly 'home-base reciprocity' was practised during both the Early and Late Neolithic. Locally available clays within a restricted area may have fostered the growth of a pottery-making tradition in one village within a valley system. Likewise certain potters may have been particularly skilled at producing certain vessel shapes or executing certain designs for special occasions. Other homemakers would have to travel to that village to obtain pots and perhaps exchange other goods they produced. These potters were probably all part-time specialists.

During the Early Neolithic II times (Fig. 9.11) the small scale interaction spheres in Boeotia (pattern III) and the Peloponnese (patterns I and III) may be reflecting 'home-base reciprocity' exchange systems. Even the larger spheres in the Thessalian Plain may be involved in this type of exchange, since more distant transport across a flat plain was largely unimpeded.

There is no specific evidence, in the form of similar goods exchanged at loci midway between living centres, for 'boundary reciprocity'. Nor is there evidence for 'down-the-line' or trickle trade. This type is manifested in the archaeological record by an inverse relationship between quantity of goods present and an increase in distance from the source. No quantitative data exist which would reveal decreasing quantities of pots, nor are the interaction spheres arranged in a linear or dendritic fashion typical of such exchange routes. Furthermore, there is little evidence for the largely prestige and/or luxury nature of the material normally moved along in this fashion. The effort to move pottery, unless perhaps of a special nature or only at certain times of the year, by this means is prohibitive due to the bulk and weight and low value of the items.

'Central place redistribution' or possibly 'central place market exchange' may well describe the type of exchange taking place in Boeotia and the Peloponnese during the Late Neolithic. In these exchange systems people from different villages bring their goods to a central market area. There is no information as to whether the obvious candidate for a Late Neolithic central place as indicated by the design data, the site of Orchomenos, was somehow larger and had the facilities for operating such a market. Furthermore, from the evidence shown on Figure 9.10, it is not known whether Orchomenos was in a central position. The distribution of sites in Figure 9.10 suggests that either (1) centrality is not necessarily a prerequisite, since other factors relative to the suitability of the site vis-à-vis non-movable resources available only in the Orchomenos area may have been more important in determining its location; or (2) there are sites as yet unknown to the northeast and southeast of Orchomenos which also participated in this interaction sphere. In this case, Orchomenos would indeed lie in a central position.

Renfrew emphasizes that regional diversity will favour the appearance of 'central place redistribution'. The rugged topography and isolated micro-environments of southern Greece most certainly meet this criterion. Because, as Renfrew points out, 'central place market exchange' (1) usually involves money exchange, for which there is no evidence from Late Neolithic Greece, and (2) usually involves less information exchange (as opposed to exchange of specific types of design information, which would result in specific similarities in design structure and pattern as outlined above), this exchange form was probably not yet operative. However, the pre-conditions for it, in the form of a *centre* for exchange and the *need* to exchange products from varied resource zones, were certainly being developed in the Late Neolithic.

It may be that during the Late Neolithic two types of distribution were operative: (1) some sort of vertical market network between outlying villages and a central market place; and (2) a horizontal market ring system among the villages (Smith 1974). In the latter case, the exchange was primarily horizontal among peasants who were exchanging different subsistence-oriented goods. Renfrew's 'home-based reciprocity' may be equivalent to this ring model. Vertical markets, on the other hand, involve not only peasants who bring in goods to sell and buy other goods, but also, more importantly, the process of bulking these goods into larger and larger quantities which then move vertically via middlemen to still larger population centres for distribution.

Thus, archaeologically, at a central market one would expect to see larger quantities of a wider variety of goods from different environmental zones in the surrounding area. The existence of six different design patterns at Late Neolithic Orchomenos correlates well with this model. In this respect, Orchomenos would represent one level in the hierarchy of a vertical trade system so organized as to qualify for the spatial, functional and resource criteria of Central Place Theory. At one level, the outlying villages would be exchanging subsistence items in a horizontal fashion. On the next level, at more central loci, the villagers would gather to exchange more valued items along vertical connections to larger urban centres or even to groups outside the country.[8]

In sum, there are a number of viable forms of exchange that may describe the Early Neolithic II and Late Neolithic activities which produced the interaction spheres illustrated in Figures 9.11 and 9.13. During the Early Neolithic the equality among sites, in terms of numbers of different patterns, suggests some type of horizontal subsistence-based reciprocal exchange. This type of exchange, however, does not preclude the existence of pottery specialists, even if they are operative only seasonally.

By the Late Neolithic the exchange system was apparently based on some type of hierarchical network with one town functioning as a central depository. Since each outlying village had only one pattern, it does not seem likely that they were recirculating the pottery among the villages. Rather, the potters were going to a central market place in order to exchange their pots for other necessary produce. The vessels, once gathered, could then be moved to a larger centre, or be shipped outside the country.

Summary

In both test cases evidence of similarities and differences in design structures has been offered as indicative of information exchange and population contact and interaction. Test I investigated the sensitivity of the design structure output from one site to externally induced political change, and found that a dramatic increase in structures used was coincident with the beginnings of contact of Knossos with other sites in the Aegean. Test II investigated the sensitivity of design structure from a number of sites to site distribution, geographical barriers and economic change. During the later part of the Early Neolithic small geographically isolated interaction spheres were defined by one pattern organized by one structure. By the Late Neolithic unequal distribution of design structures suggests that villages in southern Greece were apparently hierarchically organized in some type of centralized market system, while villages further north displayed characteristics of specialized workshop centres of ceramic production.

Above all, the purpose of this article has been the presentation of an alternative method of analysing ceramic design – one which may lead to new insights about site interaction patterns and cultural change.[9]

Notes

1 E.g. David and Hennig 1972:6 for a discussion of the differences among Fulani, Gisiga, and Lamé pottery.

2 See for example footnote 7, p. 95, and footnotes 12 and 13, p. 98 in Furness 1953.

3 There are methodological limitations which can reduce the sample usable for structural analysis, since the fragmentary nature of the sherds often allowed assignment to one of the four element styles, but precluded assignment to a structural class. Thus, for example, although step patterns have been found at six sites, only three sites had sherds displaying a sufficient amount of the step pattern to allow assignment to a structure class.

4 Since all patterns analysed except pattern VI were either on jar or bowl exteriors, the vessel form apparently did not proscribe the patterns depicted. Pattern VI was located on bowl interiors as well as bowl exteriors. Furthermore, and more importantly, *within* any element style, such as flame or net, there are no differences in the choice of design field locations on the vessel surface. It was never the case that flame pattern IV, Class 1–211, was on bowl interiors, while flame pattern V, Class 1–200 was on jar exteriors, and flame pattern VI, Class 1–101, was on bowl exteriors, or some other mutually exclusive association of design structure and vessel form.

5 Controversy exists concerning the Late Neolithic date of some of these ceramics. The original published dates have been used in this test.

6 See Friedrich 1970 for a Tarascan case.

7 Cf. Wace and Thompson 1912, plate I for an example.

8 Cf. Scott 1972 and McKim 1972 for discussions of such market systems in west Africa.

9 This research was completed while the author was a Fellow of the Miller Institute for Basic Research in Science at the University of California, Berkeley, 1976–8. Many thanks are due to the Institute for their generous support and to Professor Robert Rodden whose work at Nea Nikomedia was the springboard for this research. Thanks are also due to Professor Karen Vitelli whose comments have greatly improved the presentation of this material.

References

Balfet, Helene, 1965. Ethnographical observations in North Africa and archaeological interpretation: the pottery of the Maghreb. In *Ceramics and Man*, edited by Frederick R. Matson, pp. 161–77. Aldine, Chicago.

Beale, Thomas W., 1973. Early trade in highland Iran: a view from a source area. *World Archaeology* 5 (2): 133–48.

Benton, S., 1947. Hagios Nikolaos near Astakos in Akarnania. *British School at Athens Annual* 42: 156–83.

Blegen, Carl W., 1931. Gonia. *Metropolitan Museum Studies* 3 (1930–1): 55–80.

1975. Neolithic remains at Nemea: excavations of 1925–1926. *Hesperia* 44 (3): 251–79.

Caskey, John L., 1957. Excavations at Lerna, 1956. *Hesperia* 26 (2): 142–62.

1958. Excavations at Lerna, 1957. *Hesperia* 27 (2): 125–44.

Caskey, John L. and Elizabeth G., 1960. The earliest settlements at Eutresis: supplementary excavations, 1958. *Hesperia* 29 (2): 126–67.

Daux, Georges, 1965. Chronique des fouilles et découvertes archéologiques en Grèce en 1964. *Bulletin de Correspondance Hellénique* 89 (2).

1972. Chronique des fouilles et découvertes archéologiques en Grèce en 1971. *Bulletin de Correspondance Hellénique* 96 (2).

David, Nicolas and Hilke Hennig, 1972. The ethnography of pottery: a Fulani case seen in archaeological perspective. *McCaleb Module in Anthropology* 21: 1–29. Addison–Wesley Modular Publications.

Evans, Arthur J., 1900. Knossos: summary report of the excavations in 1900. *British School at Athens Annual* 6: 3–93.

Evans, J.D., 1964. Excavations in the Neolithic settlement of Knossos, 1959–1960, Part I. *British School at Athens Annual* 59: 132–240.

1968. Excavations in the Neolithic mound of Knossos, 1958–60. *Bulletin of the Institute of Archaeology* 4: 34–60.

1971. Neolithic Knossos: the growth of a settlement. *Proceedings of the Prehistoric Society* 37 (1): 95–117.

Evans, J.D. and Colin Renfrew, 1968. *Excavations at Saliagos near Antiparos.* The British School of Archaeology at Athens, Supplementary Volume.

Foster, George M., 1965. The sociology of pottery: questions and hypotheses arising from contemporary Mexican work. In *Ceramics and Man*, edited by Frederick R. Matson, pp. 43–61. Aldine, Chicago.

French, D.H., 1966. Some problems in Macedonian prehistory. *Balkan Studies* 7 (1): 103–10.

Friedrich, Margaret Hardin, 1970. Design structure and social interaction: archaeological implications of an ethnographic analysis. *American Antiquity* 35 (3): 332–43.

Furness, Audrey, 1953. The Neolithic pottery of Knossos. *British School at Athens Annual* 48: 94–134.

1956. Some early pottery of Samos, Kalimos and Chios. *Proceedings of the Prehistoric Society* 22: 173–212.

Gimbutas, Marija, 1974. Achilleion: a Neolithic mound in Thessaly: preliminary report on 1973 and 1974 excavations. *Journal of Field Archaeology* 1: 277–302.

Haggett, Peter, 1966. *Locational Analysis in Human Geography.* St Martin's Press, New York.

Hammond, N.G.L., 1972. *A History of Macedonia* I. Clarendon Press, Oxford.

Heurtley, W.A., 1939. *Prehistoric Macedonia.* Cambridge University Press, Cambridge.

Holmberg, Erik J., 1944. *The Swedish Excavations at Asea in Arcadia.* Skrifter Utgivna av Svenska Institutet i Rom, No. 11, C.W.K. Gleerup, Lund, Sweden.

Jacobsen, Thomas W., 1969. Excavations at Porto Cheli and vicinity, preliminary report 2: the Franchthi Cave, 1967–1968. *Hesperia* 38 (3): 343–81.

Kosmopoulos, Leslie Walker, 1948. *The Prehistoric Inhabitation of Corinth* I. Müchner Verlag Bisher F. Bruchmann, Munich.

Kunze, Emil, 1931. *Orchomenos II Die Neolithische Keramik.* Academie der Wissenschaften, München, Philosophisch-historische Abteilung, Neue Folge, 5.

Lamb, Winifred, 1936. *Excavations at Thermi in Lesbos.* Cambridge University Press, Cambridge.

MacKenzie, Duncan, 1903. The pottery of Knossos. *Journal of Hellenic Studies* 23: 157–205.

McKim, Wayne, 1972. The periodic market system in northeastern Ghana. *Economic Geography* 48 (3): 333–44.

Michaels, Joseph W., 1968. Settlement pattern and demography at Sheep Rock Shelter: their role in culture contact. *Southwestern Journal of Anthropology* 24 (1): 66–82.

Milojcic, Vladimir, 1959. Hauptergebnisse der Deutschen Ausgrabungen in Thessalien 1953–1958. *Jahrbuch des Romisch-Germanischen, Zentral-museums* 6: 1–56. Mainz.

Milojcic, Vladimir and Johanna Zumbusch, 1971. *Das Frühe Neolithikum*, Teil II (Katalöge, Abbildungen, Tafeln, Beilagen und Plane), Die Deutschen Ausgrabungen Auf der Otzaki-Magula in Thessalien I, Beitrage Zur Ur- Und Frühgeschichtlichen Archäologie des Mittelmeer-Kulturraumes für das Institut for Ur- und Frühgeschichte der Universität Heidelberg, Bonn.

Renfrew, Colin, 1972. *The Emergence of Civilization.* Methuen, London.

1975. Trade as action at a distance: questions of integration and communication. In *Ancient Civilization and Trade*, edited by J.A. Sabloff and C.C. Lamberg-Karlovsky, pp. 3–59. University of New Mexico Press, Albuquerque.

Rodden, Robert James, 1968. Pottery and flint-working traditions in the Early Neolithic of southeastern Europe: and the spread of farming economy. Unpublished Ph.D. dissertation, University of Cambridge.

Scott, E.P., 1972. The spatial structure of rural northern Nigeria: farmers, periodic markets, and villages. *Economic Geography* 48: 316–32.

Shubnikov, A.V. and V.A. Koptsik, 1974. *Symmetry in Science and Art.* Plenum Press, New York.

Smith, Carol A., 1974. Economics of marketing systems: models from economic geography. *Annual Review of Anthropology* 3.

Spyropoulos, Theodore G., 1973. Introduction to the study of the Copaic area. *Archaiologika Analekta ex Athenon* 6 (2): 201–14.

Stanislawski, M.B. and B.S. Stanislawski, 1974. *Hopi and Hopi-Tewa Ceramic Tradition Networks.* Paper presented at the 73rd Annual Meeting of the American Anthropological Association, Mexico City.

Theocharis, D.R., 1959. Pyrasos. *Thessalika* 2: 29–68.

1963. Thessalia Sesklon. *To Ergon Tis Archaiologikis Etaireias Kata to 1962*, pp. 39–48.

1967. *I Avgi Tis Thessalikis Proistorias*: Archi Kai Primi Exelixi Tis Neolithikis Thessalika Meletimata No. 1. Volos, Greece.

1973. *Neolithic Greece*. National Bank of Greece.

Tsountas, C., 1908. *Ai Proistorikai Akropoleis Diminiou kai Sesklou.* Bibliothiki Tis en Athinais Archaiologikis Etaireias, Athens, Greece.

Wace, A.J.B. and M.S. Thompson, 1912. *Prehistoric Thessaly.* Cambridge University Press, Cambridge.

Washburn, Dorothy K., 1977a. A symmetry analysis of Upper Gila area ceramic design. *Papers of the Peabody Museum* 68 Harvard University, Cambridge, Mass.

1977b. An ethnographic test of structure analysis as an indicator of group interaction: designs on Northwest Coast California baskets. Paper presented at the Kroeber Anthropological Society Meetings, Berkeley.

1977c. A study of the red/cream and cream/red designs on Early Neolithic I ceramics from Nea Nikomedeia. Manuscript on file at the California Academy of Sciences, San Francisco.

1978. A comparative examination of design structure analysis and ceramic typology. Paper presented at the Cibola Ceramic Conference, Museum of Northern Arizona, Flagstaff.

Weinberg, Saul S., 1962. Excavations at Prehistoric Elateia, 1959. *Hesperia* 31 (2); 158–209.

Zervos, Christian, 1962. *Naissance de la Civilisation en Grèce I, II.* Editions 'Cahiers D'Art', Paris.

INDEX